THE INTEGRATION OF THE EUROPEAN ECONOMY, 1850–1913

Also by Lee A. Craig

TO SOW ONE ACRE MORE: Childbearing and Farm Productivity in the Antebellum North

Also by Douglas Fisher

MACROECONOMIC THEORY

MONETARY AND FISCAL POLICY

MONETARY POLICY

MONETARY THEORY AND THE DEMAND FOR MONEY

MONEY AND BANKING

MONEY, BANKING AND MONETARY POLICY

MONEY DEMAND AND MONETARY POLICY

THE INDUSTRIAL REVOLUTION: A Macroeconomic Interpretation

THE ROLE OF SMALL INDUSTRY IN THE PROCESS OF ECONOMIC GROWTH (*with M. Shinohara*)

The Integration of the European Economy, 1850–1913

Lee A. Craig
Associate Professor of Economics
North Carolina State University, and
Faculty Research Fellow
National Bureau of Economic Research

and

Douglas Fisher
Professor of Economics
North Carolina State University

First published in Great Britain 1997 by
MACMILLAN PRESS LTD
Houndmills, Basingstoke, Hampshire RG21 6XS and London
Companies and representatives throughout the world

A catalogue record for this book is available from the British Library.

ISBN 0-333-58036-2

First published in the United States of America 1997 by
ST. MARTIN'S PRESS, INC.,
Scholarly and Reference Division,
175 Fifth Avenue, New York, N.Y. 10010

ISBN 0-312-12963-7

Library of Congress Cataloging-in-Publication Data
Craig, Lee A. (Lee Allan), 1960–
The integration of the European economy, 1850–1913 / Lee A. Craig
and Douglas Fisher.
p. cm.
Includes bibliographical references and index.
ISBN 0-312-12963-7
1. Europe—Economic integration—History.   2. European Economic
Community countries—Economic policy.   I. Fisher, Douglas. 1934–
. II. Title.
HC241.C73   1996
337.4—dc20   96–1268
                                                                            CIP

© Lee A. Craig and Douglas Fisher 1997

All rights reserved. No reproduction, copy or transmission of this publication may be made without written permission.

No paragraph of this publication may be reproduced, copied or transmitted save with written permission or in accordance with the provisions of the Copyright, Designs and Patents Act 1988, or under the terms of any licence permitting limited copying issued by the Copyright Licensing Agency, 90 Tottenham Court Road, London W1P 9HE.

Any person who does any unauthorised act in relation to this publication may be liable to criminal prosecution and civil claims for damages.

The authors has asserted their rights to be identified as the authors of this work in accordance with the Copyright, Designs and Patents Act 1988.

This book is printed on paper suitable for recycling and made from fully managed and sustained forest sources.

10 9 8 7 6 5 4 3 2 1
06 05 04 03 02 01 00 99 98 97

Printed in Great Britain by
The Ipswich Book Company Ltd
Ipswich, Suffolk

To Jackie and Josi

Contents

List of Tables and Figures   xi
Preface   xv

PART I   EUROPEAN ECONOMIC GROWTH BEFORE 1914

1 Economic Integration in Theory and Practice   3
   1.1   Introduction   3
   1.2   Defining economic integration   3
   1.3   The concept of integration in this study   12
   1.4   Concluding comments   15

2 The Political Integration of the European States   17
   2.1   Introduction   17
   2.2   Country studies   19
   2.3   Conclusions   38

3 The Nature and Causes of Economic Growth, 1850–1913   39
   3.1   Introduction   39
   3.2   The growth of real per capita output   43
   3.3   Population growth and migration   47
   3.4   Important indicators of modern industrial expansion   53
   3.5   Catching up: a new interpretation of an old debate   60

PART II   THE FINANCIAL SYSTEM

4 Money, Banking and Financial Sophistication   65
   4.1   Introduction   65
   4.2   Money, prices and national income   67
   4.3   The evolution of banking   74

4.4	Monetary neutrality	93
4.5	Conclusions	97

5 Central Banking before 1914 — 99
5.1	Introduction	99
5.2	Central banking, 1850–1913	100
5.3	Maintenance of the gold standard	118
5.4	Integration among monetary bases	121
5.5	Conclusions	128

6 Money and Prices, 1850–1913 — 130
6.1	Introduction	130
6.2	European monetary growth and inflation: an overview	132
6.3	The stationarity of the data	138
6.4	Cointegration tests for money and prices	142
6.5	Granger-causality tests	149
6.6	The law of one price and mean reversion	154
6.7	Conclusions	158

7 The Demand for Money — 160
7.1	Introduction	160
7.2	Econometric specification of money demand	161
7.3	Tests of money demand in nine countries: summary	165
7.4	Discussion of individual countries	173
7.5	The income elasticity of money demand	182
7.6	Conclusions	185

PART III GROWTH AND CYCLES: TOWARDS AN INTEGRATED ECONOMY

8 The Integration of Product and Capital Markets — 189
8.1	Introduction	189

8.2	European integration: some general issues	190
8.3	The foreign sector: exports and imports	193
8.4	The interaction of capital markets	202
8.5	Interest rates	208
8.6	Conclusions	219

9 The European Trade Cycle, 1850–1913 — **222**

9.1	Introduction	222
9.2	Previous work on the pan-European cycle	223
9.3	Interaction among real national products	226
9.4	The behaviour of the pro-cyclical variables	229
9.5	Country studies: five major economies	234
9.6	International dimensions of cycles: further results	267
9.7	Conclusions	270

10 The Integration of the European Economy by 1913 — **272**

10.1	Introduction	272
10.2	Growth and trade: twin engines of integration	273
10.3	Financial integration	281
10.4	Final observations	286

Notes and References	287
Technical Appendix	296
Data Appendix	303
Bibliography	307
Index	318

List of Tables and Figures

Tables

3.1	Output per capita: levels and growth rates, 1820–1913	44
3.2	Annual growth rates of real per capita output in domestic currency for selected European countries and the United States, 1850–1913	46
3.3	Population size and growth rates for selected European countries and the United States, 1850–1913	49
3.4	Net emigrants from Europe per 1000 population, 1850–1913	52
3.5	Percentage of the population residing in urban areas for selected European countries and the United States, 1850–1910	53
3.6	Annual compounded growth rates of indices of industrial production (per cent) for selected European countries and the United States, 1850–1913	54
3.7	Measures of industrial activity for selected European countries and the United States, 1850 and 1913	56
3.8	Average growth rates of per capita industrial activity, selected European countries and the United States, 1850–1913	58
3.9	Output per capita and annual growth rates of steel, sulphuric acid and electric power, for selected European countries before 1913	59
4.1	Growth rates of money (M), prices (P) and real income (y), various dates to 1913	67
4.2	Financial sophistication indices, 1851–1913	71
4.3	Average growth rates of assets held by financial institutions in Europe, 1854–1913, and ratio of assets held by financial institutions to national product in Europe, 1880–1913	73
4.4	The Granger-causal influence of real income on financial sophistication	96
5.1	Summary of European central banks before 1914	117
5.2	Correlations among monetary bases and gold	123
5.3	Unit root tests, monetary bases, 1871–1913	124
5.4	Granger-causal tests of gold and the monetary base, 1871–1913	126

xii List of Tables and Figures

6.1	Money growth and inflation, 1850–1913	135
6.2	Correlations among inflation rates and money growth, 1851–1913 compared to 1873–1913	136
6.3	Standard deviations of money growth and inflation, 1850–1913	139
6.4	Unit root tests for money and prices, 1850–1913	141
6.5	Cointegration of money stocks and price levels, 1851–1913 compared to 1873–1913	144
6.6	Tabulation of cointegration results for Table 6.5	146
6.7	Granger-causality tests for inflation and money growth, 1851–1913 compared to 1873–1913	150
6.8	Summary results: Granger-causality test	152
6.9	Estimates of autoregressive coefficient relative wholesale prices, 1873–1913	155
6.10	Model specification for mean reversion test	157
7.1	Demand for money, 1850–1913, basic model, one interest rate	166
7.2	Demand for money, 1850–1913, basic model with structural variables	169
7.3	Demand for money for nine countries, 1873–1913	172
7.4	Income elasticities of money demand, 1850–1913	183
8.1	Compound growth rates of real exports and imports, 1850–1913	194
8.2	Unit root tests, exports and imports, 1850–1913	195
8.3	Correlations of log-level exports and imports, 1850–1913	196
8.4	Cointegration results: frequency	199
8.5	Granger-causality of exports and imports, 1850–1913	200
8.6	Growth rates and investment in Europe, 1850–1913	204
8.7	Investment and investment ratios, unit root tests	205
8.8	Correlations among interest rates, 1850–1913	210
8.9	Unit root tests for interest rates, 1870–1913	215
9.1	Unit root tests and data description measures of real national product or income	226
9.2	Integration of business cycles: frequencies	228
9.3	Industrial production: phase coincidence	231
9.4	Investment: phase coincidence results	232
9.5	Real imports: phase coincidence	233
9.6	Growth rates of various indicators in the United Kingdom, 1855–1913	235
9.7	Reference cycle turning points in the United Kingdom, 1854–1913	237

9.8	Business cycle indicators for France – growth rates	246
9.9	The role of agriculture and industrial production in the major declines in French real GDP	248
9.10	Business cycle indicators for Germany, growth rates of the data, 1851–1913	251
9.11	NNP, unemployment and employment cycles in Germany, 1880–1913	255
9.12	Business cycle indicators for Italy, growth rates of the data, 1851–1913	258
9.13	Business cycle indicators for Sweden, growth rates of the data, 1851–1913	263
9.14	The international business cycle among five major European economies, 1851–1913	268
9.15	The international business cycle among six other countries, 1851–1913	269
10.1	Per capita bank deposits in Europe, growth rates, 1870–1913	283

Figures

3.1	Population and output growth rates compared, c. 1850–1913	50
3.2	Ratio of industrial to agricultural production, 1850–1913	55
4.1	Financial sophistication indices, 1850–1913	70
5.1	Monetary bases and world gold, 1871–1913, normalized	122
6.1(a)	Wholesale price inflation, 1873–1913	133
6.1(b)	Money growth rates, 1873–1913	133
7.1	Residuals tests for Table 7.1	168
7.2	Residuals tests for Table 7.2	170
7.3	Recursive short-run income elasticities	184
8.1(a)	Investment levels, normalized, 1850–1913	206
8.1(b)	Ratio of investment to national product, 1850–1913	206
8.2(a)	Long-term nominal rates, 1850–1913	212
8.2(b)	Long-term real rates, 1850–1913	212
8.3(a)	Short-term nominal rates, 1850–1913	214
8.3(b)	Short-term real rates, 1850–1913	214
9.1	United Kingdom unemployment and changes in GNP, 1851–1913	241
9.2	Changes in real product in France and Germany, 1851–1913	245
9.3	Italian and Swedish national product growth rates, 1861–1913	260
10.1	Per capita national products – normalized, 1850–1913	274
10.2	Industrial production indices – normalized, 1850–1913	275

10.3 Real exports – normalized, 1850–1913   277
10.4 European business cycles, number of countries in recession each year, 1851–1913   279
10.5 Fluctuations in national product, industrial economies, 1850–1913   280
10.6 Per capita bank deposits normalized, 1850–1913   282

Preface

This study documents the integration of the European economy over the critical period 1850 to 1913. We argue that by 1913 the national economies of western and central Europe were sufficiently integrated in most important aspects of economic life that one could refer to them for all practical purposes, as composing a 'European economy'. This economy was in turn part of a global economy that included several past and present members of European empires at that time. We realize that the term 'global economy' is in vogue now, and refers to a much broader concept, but it is our belief that, with respect to integration, the modern European economy was largely in place by 1913, and that many of its important interactions were well established long before that date; furthermore, later arrivals to the global fraternity essentially attached themselves in one way or another to the existing economic structure. In any case, we think that readers interested in the further extension of the present version of the global economy might find some material to interest them in our study of a series of events that seem very similar to those of today.

This study concentrates on the macroeconomic aspects of this integration, although from time to time we digress into microeconomic topics, as the situation requires. By 'macroeconomic aspects' we refer both to the nature of the data that we consider and to the econometric tests we apply to these data. The data, in the first instance, are primarily those that appear in the national income and product accounts, but for various reasons we consider it to be within our purview to analyze manufacturing and agricultural production figures (or indices) and, occasionally, subcategories of the production figures. We do this because we are interested in the interaction between structure and growth, and find it impossible to probe the nature of general economic integration without such disaggregation. We also pursue monetary data that, after all, refer to just one sector (banking) for the most part. Money and banking is a traditional macroeconomic topic area, to be sure, but we are also interested in the issues that arise in this area because there do exist both broad policy concerns (such as the those surrounding the implementation of the gold standard) as well as the possible interaction of nominal (money) and real factors in both growth and cycles.

Our methods of research will be discussed more fully in Chapter 1, but for now the reader should know that we shall be calculating and comparing growth rates of various economic variables; computing correlation coefficients, generally for the same variables across countries; engaging in the astructural 'cointegration' and Granger-causality tests; and even calculating the coefficients of a structural relation (the demand for money), and comparing such estimated coefficients across countries. The purpose of these analytical tests is to demonstrate the relative power of the integration hypothesis, wherever the data permit such investigations.

We tackle the problem in three stages. In Part I, we begin by discussing what we mean by 'integration' in this study. Our definition focuses on the increasing similarity of economic structures in this period and discusses the roles of transfers of goods, factors of production, and technology in producing this result. We note that a substantial amount of goods, factors, and knowledge had already been transferred by 1850, although we are not in a position to document this behaviour in view of the limited availability of appropriate data for that earlier period.

Our second topic in Part I is a consideration of the political integration of the countries we are studying, because many issues affecting economic integration are the result of political decisions. Tariff policies affect international trade; banking regulations affect monetary policy; and direct government investment – in railways, for example – affects economic growth. Since we are analyzing the economic integration of a set of nation states, we must first consider the formation of those states. Furthermore, because we are interested in the role their initial level of development played in the rate and nature of their subsequent economic growth, we also focus on the effect their path to nationhood had on their early economic development; this is sometimes considerable.

We conclude this first part of the volume with a survey of real growth rates, both overall and in key sectors, for each country. We find that growth rates differ markedly among these nations, but that the differences can often be explained in terms of resources and opportunities. In any case, what is most noticeable in this review is that the countries studied appear to have been developing similar industrial structures as the period progressed. A key factor in this development is the interaction between the timing of a country's industrialization, the leading industries at that time and the state of the country's financial sector.

What we do in the remainder of the book is conduct a series of empirical tests, including correlation, cointegration and Granger-causality tests, in order to reveal the existence of integrating mechanisms. These tests suggest the presence and perhaps the extent of economic integration, but we must rely on economic theory and the historical record to explain the presence or absence of various forms of integration. We also employ these other forms of testimony to explain our empirical results.

Preface

In Part II we consider financial topics. We document, in Chapter 4, the increasing similarity of the financial structures of these nations. This similarity is not surprising, of course, in view of the existence of the gold standard for much of this period – from the mid-1870s to 1914. The latter is discussed in Chapter 5. In Chapter 6, we show that the traditional monetary interaction hypothesis is difficult to support because money stocks do not appear to be closely related across countries. It turns out, however, that price levels are integrated in this period, and increasingly so as the end of the period approaches. It is conceivable that financial integration under the gold standard occurred through what is called the 'monetary approach to the balance of payments'. While the operation of this mechanism has been claimed for this period by others before us, what we contribute is a full-scale documentation of the sort of evidence that might support this proposition, including (in Part III of the study) real interactions. Finally, in this financial section (Chapter 7), we show that the demand for money functions of these countries could be claimed to be stable functions of a few key variables – as the monetarists often claim – so that this particular source of potential difficulty for the payments system is probably not present in this period. This result, in fact, is somewhat qualified here, but it does introduce some structure into what is mainly an astructural statistical discussion.

In Part III of the study we consider in the main real interactions among these countries. This section includes a discussion of the strong integration of exports and imports across these countries (Chapter 8). In this discussion we also find that industrial production indices show increasing integration over the period, as do various measures of national output, providing very strong evidence in favour of the basic hypothesis of the study. Finally, in Chapter 9, we look at the business cycles of these countries. In an earlier study, Craig and Fisher (1992) document the similarity of cycles in the national product data for five countries, but here we extend the analysis to the full set of countries for which data are available and bring in further variables (as coincident or lagging indicators of the cycle) in a more general exercise in macroeconomic cycle dating. While this exercise is performed on annual data, and further series could be exploited in this search, we go on record with a dating of the 'European' cycle that, we believe, shows closer coincidence across nations as the period wears on. Our summary and conclusions, then, are in Chapter 10.

Some individuals have helped us in the preparation of the manuscript and we now wish to acknowledge their kind assistance. Some of our material was read to the Triangle Universities' Economic History Seminar, generally in earlier versions, and we thank the members of that group for their comments. Michael Bordo, John Komlos, Philip Meguire and Jan Klovland provided us with data, and we are pleased to acknowledge their assistance. Tom Grennes read Part I and Doug Pearce Part II, and both helped to strengthen the product. We obtained secretarial assistance from Gloria Thacker and research assistance from Kelly Hunter-Markson. In the final analysis, though, the responsibility for the usefulness and accuracy of the final product is the authors'.

LEE A. CRAIG
DOUGLAS FISHER

Part I

European Economic Growth before 1914

1 Economic Integration in Theory and Practice

1.1 INTRODUCTION

Before looking at our detailed study of economic integration in the European economy prior to 1914, we need to engage in a methodological discussion. We are not approaching the topic of integration in exactly the way others would, and so in this chapter we have set ourselves the task of explaining just where our work fits into the literature on integration. In order to be entirely clear on the many questions that arise, we feel that a straightforward way to proceed is to review the various definitions, including ours, in Section 1.2; to look at the general implementation of these notions in the relevant literature (again, in Section 1.2); and then to point out in Section 1.3 exactly what we propose to add to the literature. Section 1.4 provides a summary and some important qualifications.

1.2 DEFINING ECONOMIC INTEGRATION

A dictionary definition of 'integration' would generally emphasize something like 'the bringing together or incorporation of parts into an appropriate whole'. This definition implies a dynamic *process* but takes the overall entity – the thing being integrated – as given. Clearly, in the context we are considering – which is European growth and integration before 1914 – both the process and the overall entity are growing and, without a doubt, are interacting in various ways. Along these lines, in *A History of Thought on Economic Integration*, Machlup (1977, p. 13) argues that integration can be thought of as a process as well as a state of affairs. We shall adopt this dichotomy in general, continuing in this section to explore the difference between the two concepts – a changing condition on the one hand, and a process on the other.

At this juncture, it is important to recognize that there is more to the problem of integration than can be subsumed under the heading of 'economics'. There is, in fact, a plethora of economic, social and political aspects to consider, at least if one wants to cover all the uses of integration in the social sciences, and there is no simple way to reconcile all the different perspectives and interests one finds. Nevertheless, it is necessary to concentrate on the economic literature, and we have set ourselves the general objective in this chapter of reviewing a number of interpretations of the historical process of economic integration and of offering a version of our own, that, though different in some respects, complements the other interpretations.

The literature that has emerged from studies of integration in the social sciences recognizes two broad components of national integration, each of which contains a number of more specific aspects. The first of these broad components is territorial integration, and the second is social integration. *Territorial integration* can be thought of as the physical linking or consolidation of a region or regions. It includes subcomponents such as geographical, economic and political integration. We can speak of an area as being intergrated geographically when transportation and communication systems connect its regions. Here topography – that is, physical geography – figures importantly. Although they are by no means separable from the geographic aspects, economic factors exist in territorial integration when exchanges of goods, populations, capital and technology occur across regions. Finally, and also inseparably, political integration would involve the recognition of and submission to a common political heirarchy.

Territorial integration, then, relies importantly on political and economic integration. Scholars interested in the evolution of economic and political units have long been conscious of some underlying cohesiveness which could be found across geographical regions and among various populations. One such factor, important both politically and economically, is the formation of a coherent and stable tax base. Both North (1981) and Friedman (1977) argue that the source of tax revenues will determine the size of the political unit. Friedman further predicts that political units that derive their revenue primarily from trade will be larger than those that rely on rent or labour. The costs of integration, however, are often not trivial. As we shall illustrate in Chapter 2, much of the political integration of Europe occurred through wars of conquest, generally at considerable cost to both winners and losers. As a result, Europeans have a long history of seeking less contentious means of achieving at least some of the returns to political and economic integration.

One of the most common forms of economic and political integration has been the 'customs union'. The theory of customs unions has been formed over a long period of time, partly because customs unions themselves go back a long way. More recently, comprehensive statements exist in the writings of Meade (1955) and Viner (1950). The latter offers the following description of the relationship between political and economic integration (pp. 91–2):

Of the more serious movements which involved a great power and a small country or a number of small countries, it appears to have been the case without exception for the great power that political objectives were the important ones, while the economic consequences of customs unions were accepted without enthusiasm ...

For small countries considering custom unions with great powers ... only the economic consequences as a rule were regarded as attractive ...

Only where the prospective partners have not been greatly disparate in size, or where neither has been a great power ... has the question of customs union been dealt with as wholly or predominantly an economic question.

In recent decades, the formal economic union of the European Economic Community (EEC) reflects the mutually agreed objective of its member countries of curbing the incentive to integrate by force in order to achieve political and economic objectives. Recent attempts to characterize the European Community in purely economic terms recognize explicitly that the efforts to integrate the economy further are causally linked to the costs of previous political conflicts. As Overturf writes (1986, p. 8):

Many were committed after World War II to establishing an integrated Europe in order to avoid the mistakes of the interwar years. After the war there seemed to be a general and serious spirit of cooperation regarding breaking down the old Nationalistic barriers.

In this scenario it is important to recognize the interactions between political and economic integration. For example, a common monetary unit declared and supported politically by the member states would probably stimulate trade by lowering transaction costs. For another, legally permitted mobility of resources (capital and labour) would facilitate the development of infrastructure, and vice versa – even common infrastructure; this might be partly financed by state treasuries to the extent that they are perceived as public goods, even across existing borders. The railway system of Europe is a case in point. Indeed, while meant only in the *ceteris paribus* sense, the greater the extent of trade, investment and migration among people in different geographic regions, the more likely the regions are to converge towards a common political and economic structure.

International trade theory predicts that countries would specialize in the production of products for which they have a comparative advantage. If there is one leader in each product line, this could produce political and social polarization as well. In fact, as we shall show in Chapter 3, the experience of Western economies since the eighteenth century is for the development of *diversified* economies, with specialization in more narrow product lines, if at all. Similar economies with (potentially) dissimilar product lines would, further, fit well into the model of a successful customs union. For example, in his *Theory of Customs Union*, Meade argues that 'the formation of a customs union is more likely to lead to a net increase in economic welfare if the economies of the two partner countries are actually very competitive or similar but potentially very complementary or dissimilar' (Meade, 1995, p. 107). By this standard, Europe in 1913 looked like a good fit for a successful customs union, as we shall demonstrate in later chapters of this study.

Turning to financial integration for a moment, let us consider another topic much discussed in connection with modern Europe: the development of what is referred to as an 'optimum currency area'. Mundell (1961, p. 663), for example, argues that the free flow of economic resources – capital and labour – defines an optimum currency area:

> If the world can be divided into regions within each of which there is factor mobility and between which there is factor immobility, then each of these regions should have a separate currency which fluctuates relative to other currencies.

Of course, government policies may impede the free flow of goods and factors of production. Tariffs, quotas and taxes on labour and capital, for example, might inhibit the flow of resources between two regions, thus creating the opportunity to achieve maximum welfare gains by establishing separate monetary regimes. In addition, even though the free flow of factors may be present between two regions, it still might be optimal for one region to have a different inflation rate from the other. Canzoneri and Rogers (1990), for example, show that since inflation taxes are distortionary, the optimal spreading of tax distortion may require different rates of inflation and thus different rates of money growth in various (European) regions. In the late nineteenth century, when a currency union was not on the European political agenda (but many countries adhered to the rules of the gold standard), money growth rates were very similar across these countries; ironically, in the late twentieth century, as Europe strives to achieve a monetary union, they are not.

We could cite numerous other examples of movements towards integration, but the point should be clear: before a region can be considered to be integrated territorially some appropriate level of integration in the geographic, economic and political spheres must be observed. At this point we must enter a strong *caveat*: the history of nation building contains no universal quantifiable criteria by which one could accept or reject the hypothesis that a specific region was integrated territorially at a specific point in time. Even so, while territorial integration remains a somewhat elusive concept, some of its subcomponents do lend themselves to quantification. As we illustrate below, political and economic integration, in particular, have been specified and tested in a number of ways. Of course, we propose to add to the material on the latter with respect to modern European nations.

The second component of national integration is *social integration*. Generally an even less precise concept than territorial integration, social integration is often defined by the presence of such characteristics as a common culture, loyalty to the ruling hierarchy, and even spiritual cohesiveness among the people of a region. For example, a common religion (Catholicism), a ritualized public art form (grand opera) and a ruling hierarchy (the Dukes of Milan) contributed towards making the Piedmont region of northern Italy socially integrated in the eighteenth century. Clearly, as with territorial integration, it is easier to recognize integration when one sees it in particular cases than to define explicit criteria by which cases can be judged. Unlike many economic variables, however, cultural variables are not easily calibrated, making social integration a less tractable concept than either economic or political integration.

In this volume we shall focus our attention necessarily on territorial integration in general and economic integration in particular, although we shall from time to time refer to the presence (or absence) of cultural integration when doing so best suits our purposes. We will, though, put some time into a discussion of political integration (in Chapter 2) because of our belief – shared, we feel, by many who have worked on these problems – that the political and economic aspects of cohesion are themselves too integrated to be left entirely apart.

Let us consider *economic integration*. Machlup (1977) notes that while the term 'integration' is a fairly recent addition to the economic lexicon, the concept has been around for some time. Indeed, in a chapter entitled 'Historians of Customs Unions and Integration Projects', he cites several works dating from the seventeenth century (Machlup, 1997, pp. 115–137). Those citations refer primarily to dynastic unions or to the elimination of internal tariffs. The modern use of the term by mainstream economists, however, occurs more recently in a number of works published during the 1930s.[1] For our purposes, the seminal work on economic integration can be found in Heckscher's *Mercantilism* (1935). Heckscher argues that the mercantilistic practices of early modern European monarchs played an important role in ending the economic and political disintegration that marked the earlier feudal and manorial systems. In this, Heckscher views integration primarily as a process, and specifically as a process that is promoted through the elimination of internal barriers to trade.

For our purposes, Heckscher's perspective is clear, though limited. His contribution lies in the identification of specific acts, in this case the elimination of internal tolls, which he predicts will lead to specific outcomes, in this case an increase in trade and thus overall economic integration. This contribution is important, but it is limited, as noted, because it focuses almost exclusively on one aspect of integration, the physical exchange of goods, and it involves a single dimension, that more trade is associated with less disintegration. Where this idea runs into trouble, aside from ignoring technology transfer, factor markets, and social and political aspects of integration, is in being unable to comprehend an increasing integration that produces a slowing down of the trade flows because of the exhaustion of the benefits of both absolute and comparative advantage. In fact, as we document in Chapter 7, a noticeable slowing of both export and import growth occured in the 1850–1913 period. A possible explanation, as already pointed out, is that the major European countries became structurally and financially more similar as they geared up their iron and steel, coal, railway, chemical and textile industries along similar lines, at least in a technological sense. To be sure, growing tariff protection and more slowly growing economies are also evident in this period, so we certainly should not be interpreted as having produced conclusive evidence against the measurement of integration by trade figures in this period. We do wish to point out, though, that 'growing alike', in the sense just described, is an example of yet another meaning of economic integration and it results from technology, capital and goods flows across co-operating and competing nations.

Recent scholarship on the international convergence of per capita output or incomes across nations extends Heckscher's concept of trade as the means by which integration is increased. 'Convergence', as the term is used by Barro and Sala-i-Martin (1992) and Hutchinson (1992), refers to the more rapid economic growth of poorer countries or regions relative to richer ones, where growth is defined typically as an increase in per capita income or output. The prediction of convergence derives from growth models of a competitive economy; the keys to the convergence prediction are the similarity of preferences across areas and sufficient access to the dominant technology. Even so, the possibility exists that technological innovation is location specific (Mokyr, 1990). If so, then it might not be movable in the short run; in the long run, though, one could reasonably argue that a world in which producers utilize similar technologies (that require certain conditions to be used) must already be integrated in some meaningful sense. In Chapter 3, we pursue the narrower notion of convergence by looking at the national incomes of a number of European countries. These statistics suggest that, indeed, the leading country (the United Kingdom) loses ground relative to quite a few other European countries. There is also increasing cointegration of national incomes and, as studied in Chapter 9, business cycles – partly measured by the behaviour of national income – appear to be more closely in phase in Europe at the end of the period (1900–13) than they are at the beginning (in 1850).

Convergence, at least in the sense that the term is used by Barro and Sala-i-Martin and Hutchinson, tells us little about either the state or process of economic integration; however, convergence is often associated with a related intellectual notion that in fact has much to say about economic integration. From time to time convergence has been used synonymously with 'catching up', an older and, quite probably, a broader concept.[2] The two concepts are clearly related, since convergence of per capita incomes is a measure by which one country can be said to catch up with another, but the literature on catching up distinguishes it from convergence as just defined in at least two important ways.

First, the catching-up literature addresses the issue of why some countries *initially* lag behind others, and incorporates changes in the initial conditions as part of the process of catching up. The convergence literature generally takes the initial ranking of countries as being exogenously determined. If preferences are identical and similar technology is available to all, then why do some countries begin at lower levels than others? Clearly, conditions must have existed that created the initial gap between richer and poorer countries, and changes in these conditions may well contribute to the pace of catching up.

As an example of the importance of initial conditions and the role of the diffusion of new technologies, Abramovitz (1986) quotes Thorstein Veblen on German industrialization. Veblen observes that while the conditions in the German states in the eighteenth century were not conducive to the savings behaviour that financed early industrialization in Britain, changes in industrial technology taking place in the late nineteenth century – in particular, new and larger scale industries – led to social and institutional changes – social democracy and mixed banking being especially important – that contributed to Germany's emergence as an industrial power. Recognizing that economic, political and social forces were present and that they favoured the growth of one nation (Britain) in Europe at one time and then, after changes in the initial conditions, favoured much of the rest of Europe at a later date, indicates that one cannot compare the growth rates of income or output without regard to where one is in time. What we think – and this is an important theme of this study – is that the transmission of technology from other countries, combined with evolving local conditions, contributed to the integration of Germany (and other countries) into what became a European economy. This exchange of information and technology, as well as the movement of goods and factors of production, facilitated that integration but was itself the result of an earlier integration, the nature of which involved a considerably less rich diet of industrial activities, but which, in its own place, involved important economic (and political) ties. We believe these comments apply to all the countries we discuss in this study, so this is an example of the importance of considering both state and process when one considers the topic of integration.

In addition to addressing the initial conditions, the concept of catching up can be a more valuable metaphor for integration because countries can catch up in many ways, whereas convergence, at least in much of the literature, involves only (per capita) income or output. Perhaps the best known proposition about how poorer countries actually catch up is due to Gerschenkron (1962, 1970). Gerschenkron, argues that the pace of growth coincides with the degree of economic 'backwardness', but unlike the growth theorists referred to here, he appears to have a broader concept of backwardness than they do of growth.[3] In fact, Gerschenkron emphasizes differences in preferences and technologies across national boundaries. For example, international differences in important industries, the concept of 'dominant technologies', the degree of financial sophistication and differences in entrepreneurial 'spirit', can all be found in Gerschenkron's comparative economic histories. Because our focus is macroeconomic, we shall not pursue most of these topics; we do, however, investigate the role of the financial sector in integration and catching up, especially in Chapter 4.

Gerschenkron focuses on the differences in the banking sectors of various countries, and he attempts to explain the nature of those differences by reference to the countries' degrees of backwardness. For example, the least backward country, the United Kingdom, did not rely on a sophisticated financial sector to finance industrialization, employing instead what Karl Marx called 'original accumulation'; in Gerschenkron's words (1970, p. 101) this is the 'storing up of wealth from previous national incomes'. In his view, the more backward countries could not rely on wealth that they had stored up, because it was inadequate; indeed, when their time came, the stakes had increased and so relatively more sophisticated financial regimes – and often foreign capital – were called upon to finance their industrialization. Germany was Gerschenkron's ideal 'moderately backward country', and the German joint-stock or mixed bank, which provided both investment capital and managerial support, served as a substitute for Britain's original accumulation. There is significant evidence of this process in France, Italy and Sweden as well, in this period. This scheme implies that latecomers into the European matrix should have experienced an acceleration in the growth and development of their financial sectors in the late nineteenth century, and, as we shall see in Chapter 4, this is generally the case.

It should be apparent at this point that both 'convergence' and 'catching up' describe processes by which economies evolve over time, and that an important element of the path of their evolution is their economic position relative to that of other economies. The problem we have is that neither of these ideas addresses explicitly the issue of economic integration – that is, the state of or process by which individual economies became part of a larger whole. Yet integration lies at the heart of both concepts. For example, a world in which technologies are available equally to all is certainly 'technologically integrated', whether or not the nations employ the technologies in similar ways (if at all!). Similarly, a world in which poorer countries seek to attain the economic success of richer ones through varying degrees of imitation and substitution – as in the relative backwardness model – must also be integrated to some extent, whether or not they succeed in closing the gap. It is our intention in this volume to provide some tests of changes in the extent or degree of integration over time – thus to a limited extent testing both convergence and catching up, as these terms are typically used – but our major interests lie elsewhere. We propose to test whether changes in the aggregate economic activity in one country affected aggregate economic activity in others during the late nineteenth and early twentieth centuries, and we seek the sources of these effects. For example, we examine whether the growth rates of the German and French economies were related in such a way that growth in one was correlated with growth in the other; we also look to see if a shock to the real output of one led to a shock in the real output of the other.

Note that asking if and how the economy of one country was related to that of another's logically should precede any discussion of the relationship among their growth rates. As we have seen, however, this course is not chosen by either the neoclassical growth theorists or those writing in the tradition of Gerschenkron, though clearly such relationships form the foundations of Heckscher's views on integration. Our objective is to test the extent of the world's 'globalness' (or at least that among the European countries and the United States) a century ago. Without getting too far ahead of our story, we note at this point that we believe that Europe, at least, has been quite 'global' for some time, and much of what follows in the subsequent chapters develops evidence for this view. Furthermore, the developed world at this time appears to have been highly and increasingly 'integrated' in the various ways that we will measure this concept; this is also what we think the modern literature is referring to when it speaks of 'the global economy' of our own time.

1.3 THE CONCEPT OF INTEGRATION IN THIS STUDY

As we noted above, our interests lie in historical processes, but our approach is that of the economist. Much of the discussion concerning integration in modern economics derives from the statistical theory of time series. In this body of scholarly work, the word 'cointegration' is used to describe the relationship between two or more variables that are themselves non-stationary but that have deviations from an equilibrium condition that are stationary.[4] Since much of economic theory consists of identifying equilibria among economic variables and considering the pervasiveness of time series data, we think the possible applications within economics of this branch of statistics are considerable, and numerous examples can be found. We offer three recent examples from the literature.

In a study of the cointegration of contemporary international financial markets, Goodwin and Grennes (1994, p. 110) argue that while 'real interest rates may wander extensively, certain pairs or groups of such variables should not diverge from one another in the long run'. Economic theory suggests that arbitrage in international money markets should keep interest rates in a relatively narrow band, and any deviations from this relationship should be random and short-lived. In fact, Goodwin and Grennes do find that the deviations from long-run trends among international interest rates are stationary. In other words, shocks to the international financial system that drive interest rates from their equilibrium levels are random (have an expected value of zero) and the differences in rates so generated do not persist indefinitely. Thus interest rates do not wander away from each other. In our work in Chapter 8, we find that while real interest rates across these countries do show some cointegration, apparently there were significant lags in the system in the nineteenth century interfering with the ready identification of the phenomenon. In the same chapter, we find evidence of the operation of these lags in further work that employs tests of 'causality' among interest rates.

Craig and Fisher (1992) use cointegration procedures to test the proposition that there were relationships among the real business cycles of different Western countries in the late nineteenth century. If changes in the real output of, say, Germany, affect real output in the United Kingdom in some systematic way, then we would expect that a shock to the German economy would be felt in the United Kingdom, but that such a shock would be temporary and not disrupt the long-run relationship between the two economies. Indeed, Craig and Fisher cannot reject the hypothesis that the real per capita outputs of France, Germany and the United Kingdom were cointegrated during the period 1870 to 1910. Such a result can be interpreted as evidence of a common business cycle between these countries. For example, a recession in Germany would have had a negative effect on per capita output in the United Kingdom – that is, they would share a common business cycle – and any deviation from this relationship would have been random and short-lived. This integration of business cycles is pursued in Chapter 9, where many additional aspects of the common cyclical experiences of the European countries are examined.

Craig, Fisher and Spencer (1995), in a study of inflation and money growth behaviour across a large set of European countries, show that while inflation is cointegrated, money growth rates are not. This seemingly anomalous result – anomalous because the period was 1873–1913, when the gold standard was in operation across the same countries – is explained as the result of the operation of the 'law of one price level', which in a gold-standard world is disciplined by commodity movements and real capital flows rather than by movements of specie across borders. This prediction comes from what is known as the 'monetary approach' to the balance of payments, as explained for this period by McCloskey and Zecher (1981). These results are extended and explained fully in Chapter 6 of the present study.

Although these examples illustrate the possibilities for testing the relationship between economic time series, and therefore offer a tool for analyzing the integration of the European economy, at least two caveats should be kept in mind. First, these statistical tests only tell us whether we can reject the null hypothesis of no cointegration. They tell us nothing about the mechanism by which integration is established or maintained (though economic theory is certainly useful here); neither do they quantify the extent of integration, the point at which integration could be said to have occurred, nor changes in integration over time. In fact, an important criticism of the way in which these and similar tests have frequently been interpreted is based on the fact that they provide tests of statistical but not economic significance (McCloskey, 1985).

To this charge we plead guilty, but only partially. For one thing, it is our contention that before one seeks to describe the extent of an economic relationship one could clearly profit from the knowledge of whether such a relationship exists in the first place. Furthermore, this time arguing by example, if we were to find that the price levels of two countries – say, the United Kingdom and France – were cointegrated, but that price levels of no other pair of countries were, then that would certainly indicate a lesser extent of international price integration than if, say, the price levels of ten or twenty pairs of countries were cointegrated. In any case, we also look at developments in structural relationships in various ways in this study, the best examples being the structure of production (in Chapter 3) and of financial markets (in Chapters 4 and 5). We also look at demand for money functions in Chapter 7. On the whole, though, because we are looking at macroeconomic and monetary topics only, a good deal of potential structural material is filtered out of this study.

Another potential problem with tests of integration is that statisticians (and economists who use statistics) do not possess a monopoly on the use or definition of words such as 'integration' and 'significance'. The claim that an empire integrated with the mother country produced sufficient profits to propel significantly the Industrial Revolution in Britain refers clearly to economic magnitudes, but may not be doing so in the context of a statistical test (that might contradict such an assertion). In contrast, our definition of integration (cointegration in this case) requires that the link between economic variables pass a statistical test that relies on the *persistence* of the relationship over time. This is a strong test in that the phenomenon could still exist even if it fails to be persistent, but a weak test in that no quantifiable conclusions about the source of the cointegration can be drawn. One hopes that these are convergent research strategies and, as already noted, we do provide considerable material on economic structure with this in mind.

In addition to the cointegration tests, we employ a series of statistical tests to see if some sort of 'causal' relationship can be discerned between economic variables across countries. We do this by testing to see if lagged values of one time series explain contemporaneous values of another (the dependent) series, after netting out the effect of the lagged variables of the dependent series itself. This test of Granger-causality can be performed, for example, by including lagged values of, say, the UK money supply (and the lagged variables of the German money supply) on the right-hand side of a regression explaining the German money supply. If the coefficients on the lagged UK money supply variables are jointly significantly different from zero, then UK money is said to Granger-cause German money.

These tests have been used in a number of studies of European economic history.[5] Sandberg has argued, for example, that while Sweden was a relatively poor country, as measured by per capita output, in the mid- to late-nineteenth century, it was none the less 'sophisticated', as marked by its 'strikingly large stock of human and institutional capital' (Sandberg, 1979,

p. 225), and that the nature of Sweden's sophistication explains its subsequent real economic growth. Fisher and Thurman (1989) test whether or not the sophistication of the Swedish financial sector was responsible for Sweden's real economic growth between 1861 and 1910. Using 'causality' tests as defined in Granger (1969), they cannot reject the hypothesis that growth in real output caused financial sophistication, rather than the other way round, as Sandberg could be interpreted as arguing. Thus, the sophisticated nature of Sweden's financial sector in the late nineteenth century can be attributed to its economic growth and not the reverse, at least based on this evidence. One might further suspect that the influence so identified was very powerful, particularly in view of the magnitude of the income elasticity of the demand for money also identified in the Fisher and Thurman study (as statistically significantly greater than unity); this example illustrates how we utilize structural work in the present study. Indeed, we are interested in both financial sophistication and the demand for money in this study, and both topics offer evidence on the evolving similarity of the financial markets of the European nations. The material appears in Chapters 4 and 7.

Fisher (1992) employs the same time-series technique to test for causality among the money supplies and real output of the United Kingdom, France, Germany and the United States during the late-nineteenth and early-twentieth centuries. The issue involved here is what is referred to typically as the neutrality or non-neutrality of money – that is, whether lagged changes in the money supply cause changes in real output. The neutrality hypothesis states that anticipated changes in the money supply that are unrelated to changes in money demand will have no effect on real economic activity, because buyers and sellers will simply change their price expectations to account for the change in the money supply. Fisher finds overwhelming evidence in support of the neutrality hypothesis, because in none of the countries mentioned above did the money supply Granger-cause real output. We look at this topic again, briefly, in Chapter 4, and again, we find that the European countries are remarkably similar in this respect, having monetary neutrality as the general rule.

1.4 CONCLUDING COMMENTS

As we noted at the beginning of this chapter, integration is a generic term, and it is exactly for this reason that we want to be specific about what we mean by integration, how we test for it, and what the implications of our tests are. We do not reject other definitions or usages, but only want to make clear to the reader the differences between our usage and those of others. Indeed, we often rely on other evidence to support our statistical findings. As McCloskey (1990) notes, narrative, empirical, theoretical and statistical analyses are not mutually exclusive, and indeed, good economic history should rely on all four. In this volume we employ the tools of the economist, the historian and the statistician and in doing so construct a picture of the European economy that shows a surprising amount of interrelatedness even as our story begins in 1850 – that is, before the formal international gold standard emerged, before industrialization can be said to have spread fully across the continent of Europe and before the formal creation of the nation states of Germany and Italy. While a cointegration (or causality) test itself tells us little about the extent of integration between two countries, several sets of such tests covering many countries and series should, in fact, tell us a great deal about the extent of international integration during the late nineteenth century.

We should underscore that since the cointegration (and causality) hypothesis employed here involves testing time series over a period of time, the tests can say nothing about changes in the relationship over time unless the sample can be divided. Here, the lack of adequate degrees of freedom becomes a problem for us. Other evidence that we present, however, supports the argument that the economies grew closer together over time – closer together in the sense that the more backward countries 'caught up' by becoming more like the leaders, at least in the sense that the structure of these economies – in the banking, manufacturing and trade sector – looked more like one another at the end of the period than at the beginning. But each of these countries started at a different point and took a different path, and it is important to account for these factors as well when specific cross-country comparisons are made. Finally, we note that, although the terms 'convergence', 'catching up' and 'integration' often denote different ideas in the literature, they are subsets of a broader concept and are sometimes used interchangeably below.

2 The Political Integration of the European States

2.1 INTRODUCTION

In this chapter we examine the political integration of the modern European nation states, and we relate the process of their political integration to their economic status in 1850. Our story begins in the fifteenth century, in fact, when the Portuguese launched the Age of Discovery in their quest for a sea route to the Far East. At almost the same time, and not entirely coincidentally, the Ottoman Turks conquered Constantinople. Half a century later, the Protestant Reformation began. More than any other, these three events mark the transition from the Middle Ages to the early modern era – the first because it shifted European economic focus away from the overland trade with the East; the second because effectively it destroyed the last political vestiges of the Roman Empire, the decline of which in the West had marked the beginning of the Middle Ages; and the third because it shattered the Roman Catholic Church's control over much of the political, economic and social life of Europe. In terms of economic history, this new era was dominated by an expansion of trade that created a golden age for the merchant capitalist, a development that can be related directly to the above events.

Increases in the growth of per capita income generated by subsequent revolutions in agriculture and mercantile business yielded a rise in the demand for and production of all sorts of commodities, domestic and foreign. Simultaneously, reductions in transportation costs through shorter routes, better ships and fewer political barriers helped yield a growth of domestic and international trade that produced substantial profits for European merchants. In this field, British merchants came to dominate the trade in Indian tea, Caribbean sugar, American tobacco and later cotton. Although in the fifteenth century Italian financiers had dominated the financial side of these markets, followed in the sixteenth century by Germans and in the seventeenth century by the Dutch, from the late eighteenth century, London grew to be the primary securities market in Europe and remained in that position up to the First World War.

Each of the countries under consideration in Section 2.2 had either developed some form of representative democracy prior to 1850 or did so during the following fifty years. The rise of social-democratic parties in many of these countries was, in fact, a political manifestation of both national integration and the increasing wealth and economic and political power of segments of the population below the ruling hierarchy. Most importantly, as these societies progressed, the middle and working classes became increasingly politically powerful; rising wealth was the proximate cause of much of this change, and it is also associated with integration (for example, through trade) and, unfortunately, disintegration (as nations fought over the gains from broader markets).

An aspect of great importance with respect to national political integration lies in the nature of the data upon which we perform our statistical tests. As we noted in the Preface, this volume analyzes primarily national aggregate variables. The most important of these are population, gross national product (GNP), the price level, the money supply, exports and imports. Aside from population, 'satisfactory' values of these variables became part of the goals of national economic policies, and so this provides a major link between the political arena, where the national social goals are framed, and the economic arena, where the public and private sectors determine their actual values. For example, a central bank and a common set of banking laws, designed to promote stability in financial markets, will also partly determine the money supply and the degree of financial sophistication of the country. In addition, laws concerning property and trade, established and enforced by the state, affect the way markets work and thus affect economic growth. There are many other examples in the following pages.

We should emphasize, however, that using the nation state as the economic unit is not without controversy, since it is after all a political unit. In his treatise, *Modern Economic Growth* (1966), Kuznets recognizes this problem, but chooses not to depart from the common practice of making the political unit the economic unit; Gerschenkron follows suit. This approach has not gone unchallenged; Parker, for one, emphasizes in his work subregions that might or might not lie within a single national boundary. His criticism of the national approach is reflected in his critique of Gerschenkron's work (1991a, p. 307):

> Gerschenkron's focus throughout was on the national economy, *its* power structure, *its* organization, *its* controls, *its* position as a mercantilist power relative to its rivals ... [this notion] leaves no room to consider the profound questions of the relation within the capitalist culture as a whole between the growth of knowledge of techniques and resource supplies, on the one hand, and the expansion and focus of final demand, on the other ... [it] is thus a feature of almost no value in

explaining the economic rise of a whole interconnected Continental culture.

Without question, any number of important factors contribute to economic growth – human capital, technological innovation and natural resources – and these may be distributed in ways that transcend national boundaries. But certainly the differences among national states affect economic growth and the national economies in a number of vital ways. National laws determine the structure of the banking system; they set tariffs and import quotas; they subsidize particular industries; they establish tax systems and they control central banks. In short, each of these activities influences the national economy and its relations with other economies, and these activities and relations are manifest in the macroeconomic time series we analyze in this volume; thus, we argue that for some, though certainly not all, issues relating to the economic growth and development of Europe, the nation state is the relevant economic, as well as political, unit of reference.

2.2 COUNTRY STUDIES

We argued in Chapter 1 that the established economic conditions at any particular date can influence the subsequent path of development, and in this chapter we give a brief history of each country that summarizes the initial conditions found in each as our story begins in 1850. What we shall do is to focus on the political integration (consolidation, really) of each country, and in each case we note, where appropriate, the connection between political integration and economic development, focusing on three important issues: the advent and development of financial institutions and markets; the evolution of transportation and trade networks; and the rise of the middle class. We begin with the dominant economy at the middle of the nineteenth century, the United Kingdom, and proceed down the economic ladder, moving roughly, from North to South and West to East.

The United Kingdom

Commodities have long been traded internationally, of course. While the 'exotic' foreign commodities (silk, tea, spices, sugar and tobacco) get a great deal of scholarly and popular attention, the volume of trade in the more mundane European goods (grain, wool and wine) was considerably greater and existed in a broad network dating back to Roman times. In most of these commodities, between the seventeenth and nineteenth centuries the British became the dominant international traders and financiers. As our story begins, in the second half of the nineteenth century, a dramatic increase in the trade in manufactured goods and capital was under way and the British dominated this trade as well, at least initially. Capital flows (investment) and the movement of manufactured products across borders also increased substantially, and the share of these items, as a percentage of national income, also increased. To put British economic dominance in perspective, consider the following: in 1850, Great Britain had more cotton spindles, consumed more raw cotton, produced and consumed more coal, produced more pig iron, and had a greater capacity of steam power than the rest of Europe *combined* (see Chapter 3).

There were many reasons why the British came to dominate as they did, not the least of which, as we shall see shortly, was their political system, which supported the growth of the mercantile and manufacturing classes. During the Wars of the Roses in the late fifteenth century, the Tudor monarchy was established; the early modern effort at integrating Britain began at that time and continued through the Tudor reign. Henry VIII (reigned 1509–47) focused on integrating Wales and the North (the Palatinate of Durham) with England. Although both regions had owed allegiance to the English crown, they were formally brought under the jurisdiction of Parliament and the English court system during Henry's reign. While Henry tried to integrate Scotland with England, the two crowns were not, in fact, united until Elizabeth I died without an heir in 1603. Although the Stuart reign that began then united the two crowns, Parliament did not unite Scotland and England formally under the name Great Britain until 1707. The century that intervened between the accession of James I and the formal union of Scotland and England was one of great political turmoil in England, primarily between the Stuart kings and Parliament. When Charles II died in 1685, his younger brother, James II, a Catholic, became king. James' short rule was one of perpetual conflict with Parliament, and he abandoned the crown and fled to France in 1688. A year later, Parliament offered the throne jointly to the Protestant Prince of Orange, William (William III of England), and his wife Mary, James II's Protestant daughter.

The resolution of the conflict between Parliament and the Stuarts resulted in the two most significant (at least from an economic perspective) political achievements of the early modern era in Britain, namely the perpetuation of Parliament's right to approve new taxes, and the establishment in 1689 of a constitutional monarchy. The establishment of a constitutional monarchy more clearly delineated the separate interests and responsibilities of both the ruler and the ruled, and made the perpetuation of the former's reign formally dependent upon recognition of the prerogatives of the latter. In order to understand the role this played in Britain's subsequent economic growth, it is helpful to contrast it with the continental countries. North (1981, p. 156) puts the issue as follows:

> The rise of Parliament caused the nature of English property rights to diverge from the Continental pattern. The power to grant property rights increasingly fell to a group [Parliament] whose own interests were best served by private property and elimination of crown monopolies.

A stable political system based on individual freedom ensured the property rights of an aspiring middle class, which in turn invested its financial and human capital in industry, trade and an increasingly productive agricultural sector. Indeed, perhaps the most notable property issue of the era was the ever-broadening enclosure movement, which, by ensuring the private return to agricultural innovation, contributed to the agricultural revolution in England and assisted in the flow of resources (relatively) from the agricultural to the industrial sector.

Clearly, the English political system rewarded the capital accumulation and technological creativity upon which the Industrial Revolution was based. At the same time, English domestic prosperity provided a growing tax base to be exploited by Parliament and the crown to further national policies. It is also no accident that central banking in England, in the form of the Bank of England, emerged during the late seventeenth century. The creation of the Bank resulted from a fundamental principle of public finance: given that there are often sharp increases in the demand for funds by the government (especially during wars), and given that such increases would be difficult to finance by means of relatively inflexible tax systems, governments can serve both themselves and the people if they find some way to smooth the flow of tax revenues over time. An obvious solution is to borrow the funds they need and pay them pack with future tax revenues. The central bank is an ideal institution for this purpose, and so Parliament turned to this device in 1694, creating the Bank of England as a private bank with public responsibilities.

In combination, these achievements allowed the rising British middle class to pursue its economic self-interest relatively unencumbered (relative, that is, to continental standards). The spirit of enterprise inherent in the rising mercantile and manufacturing classes contributed to the rising rates of economic growth. In turn, the growing British economy allowed Parliament to carve out a larger role for the government in meeting national objectives while increasing its share of the national product, but, except in war times, without unleashing the negative influence of the 'crowding out' of private investment expenditure.

Despite its mid-nineteenth-century pre-eminence, the United Kingdom's role as the dominant economic power in Europe simply could not have been predicted with any certainty at any time between 1500 and 1750. Portugal, Spain, Holland and France had developed prosperous trading empires before the British, but each had come into conflict with England and had been defeated militarily and eclipsed economically. Since Tudor times, the primary objective of British foreign policy had been, and would continue to be, the prevention of continental hegemony by a single power. Because the British utilized their economic might in trade, finance and manufacturing successfully, and because of the support of their military forces – the navy in particular – this policy succeeded, and established an important link between British political integration and economic success.

Belgium

During the century leading up to the Hundred Years' War, the wool industry in Flanders and the surrounding territories represented one of the most dynamic economic forces in Europe, rivaled only by the diverse interests of the Italian city-states. In addition, the Meuse river valley between Namur and Liège became the most important iron-producing centre on the Continent. With the Italian city-states, Flanders was arguably the most prosperous region in the West at the end of the Middle Ages; Bruges and Antwerp became financial centres of north-western Europe; and the areas around Namur were among the Continent's largest and most technologically sophisticated iron producers. But by the nineteenth century, Belgium's position was closer to the middle of the European countries in terms of per capita output, behind the United Kingdom and France. This is not a large relative decline, to be sure, but it is mostly, we think, the result of an unfortunate political–economic environment.

Much of the same early history as we will relate about the Netherlands befell Belgium, but Belgium remained Catholic and under Austrian, Spanish or French domination for 300 years – not, of course, by choice. The Dutch, as we will see, broke free in 1609. In addition to preventing Belgian political independence, the Spanish Habsburgs were indirectly responsible for the transfer of Belgium's regional financial leadership to the newly independent Dutch state. The Habsburg Empire was expensive to maintain and lenders to the throne frequently became impoverished; in effect, the unsatisfactory risk-return relationship drove both borrowers and lenders out of the Spanish-controlled areas into the northern (Dutch) Netherlands. Thus Amsterdam grew to be a dominant European financial centre and the Belgian cities languished relatively.

The Belgian territories passed from Spain to Austria in 1714. There was an unsuccessful revolution by the Belgians in 1787, and in 1797 Belgium passed to France after Napoleon's victories over the Austrians. Belgium remained part of France until the Congress of Vienna created the Kingdom of the Netherlands by reuniting the northern (Dutch) and southern (Belgian) provinces of the original Spanish Netherlands. The Belgians had many objections to this arrangement, some of them economic. In particular, most of the financial institutions (including the central bank) were Dutch; the public debt was divided equally among the two regions, though that incurred by the northern provinces before the union was many times that incurred by Belgium; and the Dutch tariff system, which the kingdom adopted, did not offer adequate protection for the Belgian textile industry, now at a comparative disadvantage to the ever-more-productive British. Following a revolt, the Kingdom of Belgium was established in 1830, making it one of the last of the modern states in this study to be formed.

The relative decline of Belgian fortunes hinged partly upon its perpetual subordinate political status, particularly since the Belgians were ruled from time to time by monarchs who tried to impose tax policies (and other institutions) on them that were not conducive to economic progress. In addition, the wars were expensive and, worse for the Belgians, they were generally forced to support the losing side. Compared to the Dutch, the Belgians did not do as well during the period of the commercial revolution, partly for these reasons. But the Dutch were eclipsed by the British in trade and finance, and did not do very well in the early industrial revolution, while the Belgians, with good coal and iron resources and a large proto-industrial work force (see Mokyr, 1976) were quick to take advantage of the industrial revolution. In 1850, on balance, the Belgians were just below the British in Europe in per capita income; this was a good position to be in for what was to come.

France

The economic revolutions (especially the agricultural and commercial) of the sixteenth and seventeenth centuries were not as influential in France as they were in England and the Low Countries. In the eighteenth century, however, French economic growth matched that of the British by some accounts, at least until 1780, and it has been argued elsewhere that during the rest of the period to 1850 (in fact, to 1913!), French commodity output per capita also matched that in Britain.[1] Indeed, by the middle of the nineteenth century, France had the largest national economy in Europe, and according to some per capita measures of output, which we discuss in Chapter 3, only the subjects of the United Kingdom and possibly the citizens of Belgium were better off than the average Frenchman. Curiously, earlier generations of economic historians emphasized the relative backwardness of France's economy, but in recent decades the study of French economic history indicates that a slow but steady rate of economic progress seems to have misled some observers as to the true nature of the economic evolution, and ultimately the industrial transformation in France.

By the middle of the fifteenth century, a number of powerful families competed for the dominant political position in France; among the claimants to national power were Brittany, Anjou, Bourbon and Burgundy, as well as those of the ruling house of Valois. One by one over the next century, through marriage, conquest or both, Burgundy, Anjou and Brittany came under control of the French crown, and in 1589 Henry IV established the Bourbon dynasty that lasted until the French Revolution two hundred years later. In the sixteenth century, Spain was the pre-eminent continental power, establishing the first great overseas empire. In the seventeenth century, when Spanish power declined, the United Provinces carved out a global empire as well, but by 1713 the Dutch, in turn, were unable to withstand the British, and so the French, largely under Louis XIV (who ruled from 1643 to 1715) vied with the British for European domination.

The tools of the century-and-a-half-long conflict were military and economic, with mercantilist policies – first used by Louis XIV and later employed by his English rivals – providing much of the latter. In this conflict, leaders of both countries acted as if the economic growth and political hegemony by their rivals necessarily meant the eclipse of their own influence. The wars most notable for this combination of political and economic interests are those that involved the attempt (by Louis XIV) to put a Bourbon on the vacant Spanish throne in 1701, an attempt that, although ultimately successful, expended a great deal of French resources; the support of Austria against Prussia in the Seven Years' War (by Louis XV); and the struggle over who was to dominate in North America (over much of the last half of the eighteenth century). The Napoleonic Wars were the last of these great struggles.

In France, in contrast to Britain and the Netherlands, there was no effective move towards a constitutional monarchy. Rather, the Bourbons financed their reign through the employment of local monopolies enforced by the guilds in return for tax revenues. In addition, the offices responsible for the collection, disbursement and borrowing of revenues were all up for sale. In North's words (1981, p. 150):

> The system of trading property rights for revenue provided a solution but required an elaborate agency structure to monitor the system. The

resultant bureaucracy not only siphoned off part of the resultant income but became an entrenched force in the French political structure.

Of course, this approach was not well suited to finance the extraordinary expenditures of war, so the French crown also borrowed liberally. So did the British, of course, but the French had no central bank and so it is likely that the crown was unable to secure the best terms; in any event, it was the interest rate burden accompanying those efforts that ultimately drove the monarchy to the brink of financial collapse (in 1789). In fact, at that time, Louis XVI called the Estates-General to conduct a much needed reform of the tax system; this effort did not produce a reform but certainly provided a venue for the expression of a common discontent. In the chaos that ensued, the monarchy was destroyed.

At the end of the Bourbon reign, France experienced unparalleled and well-documented political and social upheaval; it is remarkable that it seems not to have cost them their position in the economic hierarchy. This is probably because of the power of the ongoing commercial, agricultural and industrial changes in France. Of course, the internal disruption caused by the Revolution was ameliorated somewhat during Napoleon's rule by the codification of French law and many economic reforms – such as the creation of the Bank of France – and there were many improvements in the transportation infrastructure, but Napoleon Bonaparte's imperial designs and attempts to establish continental dominance again brought him into conflict with the British.

Upon Napoleon's fall, France had nowhere near Britain's command of shipping or finance (private or public), and nothing like the far-flung British Empire to develop and draw upon for resources. Yet the fact that Britannia ruled the waves (and the financial markets), as Britain continued to do throughout the nineteenth century, did not inhibit the French (or any other continental economies) from exploiting their own rapidly-growing internal markets – as well in concentrating on commodities for which they had an international comparative advantage. Importantly, the French domestic economy was the largest and most diversified in Europe. France was never *the* leader in either technological innovation or production in textiles, iron and steel, railroads, or finance, but it was always close behind whoever was the leader. Indeed, by the middle of the nineteenth century, France ranked just below the United Kingdom in per capita output, and French growth rates were in fact higher than British.

By 1850, of course, the road to a prosperous state had shifted from early modern merchant capitalism to manufacturing. While a strong navy and large merchant marine remained important, the production of goods with a high value added provided the wealth of the modern industrial state. During the previous hundred years textiles had been the dominant manufacturing industry, but increasingly steel, metal fabrication and chemicals overshadowed textiles in value added. The innovations in manufacturing technology favoured the production of steel rails, rolling stock, merchant ships, machine tools and, of course, armaments. Later, chemicals, electricity and the automobile reflected the growing importance of manufacturing over mercantile activities. And in each of these areas the French always managed to stay near, though, again, never at the top of the ladder in terms of per capita output, as we shall show in Chapter 3.

The Netherlands

In terms of per capita output, the Netherlands ranked behind the United Kingdom, France and Belgium during the middle of the nineteenth century. The relative economic status of the Dutch owed much to the timing and condition of their political integration, which, like so much of recent European history, resulted as an outgrowth of the Protestant Reformation. The 'Low Countries' of Belgium and the Netherlands, which were previously united to France, passed to the Habsburgs in the late fifteenth century and to Spain (as a part of the Habsburg Empire) in 1516. The Dutch resented Habsburg rule, especially so after the Reformation. The combination of what the Dutch and Belgians considered to be confiscatory taxes, including forced loans, to finance Spanish imperial expansion and the Spanish persecution of Dutch Protestants led ultimately to open revolt in 1568. Drawing on their economic wealth, the Dutch, with help from the English, prosecuted a series of successful campaigns for independence, which they declared as the United Provinces of the Dutch Republic in 1581. Sporadic fighting went on until the Twelve Years' Truce ended it in 1609. By then the Dutch had achieved *de facto* independent status, and Spain finally recognized full independence of the United Provinces with the Treaty of Westphalia in 1648.

In 1609, the same year that the truce between the Netherlands and Spain was declared, the Bank of Amsterdam was founded. Prior to the revolt against Spain, Antwerp had been the financial centre of the region, but during the revolt, and especially after the subsequent success of the northern provinces in securing independence, considerable economic activity moved north, further from direct Spanish control, and Amsterdam became the region's financial centre. The Bank of Amsterdam was a central part of the Dutch rise in the financial world. It was founded as a deposit bank at the behest of importers who complained about the costs of determining the value of the plethora of currencies they encountered. By decreeing that all bills of exchange above a certain value be paid at the Bank with liabilities of the Bank, the city gave it a *de facto* monopoly on the payment of bills of exchange in Amsterdam. The Bank was, and remained, almost exclusively a deposit bank until the late-eighteenth-century, when it was driven to insolvency by unsuccessful loans to the Dutch East India Company.

In many respects, the United Provinces can be viewed as the first modern state. Individually and collectively, the United Provinces had a democratic government dominated at local, provincial and national levels by the Regents, a political entity that drew its members almost exclusively from the economic elite. Though limited to an oligarchy that by today's standards looks like little more than a prosperous clique, it was none the less a nascent republic surrounded by divine-right monarchies, with the notable exception of England's/Britain's constitutional monarchs from 1689. It is clear that early Dutch economic prosperity and growth resulted partly from the fact that the United Provinces had both a representative system of government and one that was dominated by individuals with commercial, rather than landed, interests. In fact, the Dutch economy was based on finance, trade, and a proto-industrial textile industry rather than just on agriculture, yet Dutch agriculture was among the most technologically advanced in the world. With the possible exception of the key Italian city-states and a few German towns, the Dutch had the most sophisticated financial institutions in early modern Europe, and as the Atlantic trade outgrew that of the Mediterranean and the Rhine, the Netherlands replaced Italy and Germany as the financial centre of Europe. As noted, the Bank of Amsterdam contributed to this shift, and such innovations as commercial banking, discounting bills of exchange, insurance and double-entry bookkeeping flourished in the Netherlands. Because of these advantages, the Dutch political and economic systems provided a standard of living that was surpassed only by the British during the next two centuries, to 1850. Even after the Industrial Revolution spread to the Continent and the size of the Dutch manufacturing sector slipped relative to its larger neighbours, the Dutch maintained their per capita standing, though by aggregate measures the Dutch certainly were no longer among the dominant economic powers.

Germany

Of the European states we are examining, the last to take its modern form was Germany, even though the recognition of Germany as a geographical area and the Germans as a people date from antiquity. The Catholic-Protestant split in the Holy Roman Empire during the Reformation played an important role in the nature of Germany's political integration, for it was within the Empire that the Reformation dawned, and it was largely the division of Germanic peoples between the Protestant and Catholic Churches that ultimately divided the Empire politically as well. While there were numerous conflicts in the first century of the Reformation, the greatest was the Thirty Years' War, which ended in 1648. The war was expensive, of course, but for our purposes the chief problem that resulted was the political fragmentation of the German states. In fact, there were more than 300 of these petite princes, dukes, margraves, bishops and counts; it took another 200 years to mould these units into the modern German state.

Even though not politically unified, the German states represented a considerable economic force throughout modern history. Up to the sixteenth century, the north German cities exerted considerable influence on trade in the Baltic through associations known as *Hansas*, the most important of which is commonly referred to as the Hanseatic League (formed in 1377). These associations were typically trading agreements among cities with the objective of gaining and protecting trading privileges, especially the creation and enforcement of monopolies over the trade in particular goods, such as fish, naval stores, and iron. The Hansa declined around the time that trade patterns shifted more towards the Atlantic, in the sixteenth century. Even so, the north German cities remained populous and prosperous throughout the modern period and are part of the base on which the German colossus was built.

Also important to the economic development of the early-modern German states was the banking industry in Augsburg and Nuremberg. The Fugger family of Augsburg was the first great banking house to challenge the financial control of the Italians. By the sixteenth century, the Fuggers had made Augsburg the financial centre of Europe. The early basis of German banking was the Bavarian silver mines but, once established, the German bankers reached across Europe. The Fuggers themselves went bankrupt, having loaned money once too often to the Habsburgs, and the silver mines declined, but the Rhenish area of Germany that was involved contained some of the most economically advanced regions on the Continent and continued to prosper. Commerce along the Rhine and its many tributaries, and the abundant natural resources and agricultural products of the region were the sustaining basis of this prosperity.

From the beginning of the eighteenth century the leading force in the movement to unify Germany was the House of Hohenzollern, the ruling House of the Electorate of Brandenburg. The Hohenzollerns were unlikely candidates to lead unification, since their territory in Prussia and eastern Germany was poorly located for commercial purposes and possessed none of the natural resources that fuelled the early stages of the industrial revolution. This point is somewhat moot, however, since the Prussians advanced economically and politically through conquest and political manoeuvreings.

Between 1720 and 1772, Prussia added, primarily through conquest, the territories of West Pomerania, West Prussia and Silesia, along with several smaller territories in the western part of modern Germany. The most important conquest for economic reasons was Silesia, which Prussia acquired during the War of the Austrian Succession (1740–8). Silesia was a prosperous agricultural region, and through the middle of it flowed the Oder, on both sides of which were coal deposits, and in the heart of the territory was Breslau, a regional centre of finance and manufacturing. Prussia also participated with Russia and Austria in three partitions of Poland (in 1772, 1793 and 1795).

By these means, the Hohenzollerns had, by the beginning of the nineteenth century, propelled Prussia from a lesser principality on the fringe of Europe up to the second tier of European economic power. In this endeavour they were assisted by Prussian taxpayers, who provided the funds through a series of excise taxes. These were relatively evenly distributed, on the whole, across income classes, so the Prussian leaders avoided some of the problems that plagued the French, for example; in this they were helped, of course, by the enlargement of the tax base through conquest. For its decisive role in Napoleon's ultimate defeat, Prussia received, at the Congress of Vienna, a large chunk of territory along the Rhine (Westphalia). This territory included what became the economic heart of Germany's heavy industry, the Ruhr valley, including some of the best coal areas on the Continent, and the city of Essen, an iron (and later steel) centre.

The final political integration of the German states started with the creation of a series of customs unions, of which the Prussian Customs Union of 1828 was the first. It was followed by the most famous, the Zollverein, in 1834, which, in addition to the Prussian territories, included Bavaria, Saxony, Wurttemburg and Thuringia. In 1867 this arrangement was expanded to include Hanover, Baden, Luxemburg, Mecklenburg, and Schleswig and Holstein. The last two were the bone of contention in the 1866 war with Austria that, handily, Prussia won. In 1870 France and Prussia went to war over who would fill the vacant Spanish throne. Prussia's victory over France resulted in the formal unification of all the German states and the creation of the German Empire.

The industrial revolution provided the stimulus that turned all this economic potential into reality. Before that event, Germany was near the middle of Europe economically (see Chapter 3), but by 1870 it possessed an economic bloc that included, among other advantages, the second largest population in Europe, the largest iron and steel industries, a large agricultural producing region, and important financial facilities. It seems clear that political integration and economic integration were intertwined in this period. Indeed, one may never be able to say which dominated in what was ultimately a spectacular economic achievement.

The Scandinavian states

The dominant economies of the late Middle Ages – the Italian city-states, the German trading cities and the Flemish textile regions – all depended to a certain extent on exploiting a favourable geographic location. The Italians were ideally situated to finance east–west trade; the German trading cities controlled the trade along the river valleys of central Europe, and the Flemish textile producers profited from English wool just across the Channel and from large consumer markets to their immediate north and south. The Scandinavian states of Denmark, Norway and Sweden did not enjoy such locational advantages as the regions just mentioned. They were not placed on such good trade routes, nor was their climate as conducive to agriculture, which might have provided the exports for trade with the proto-industrial centres to the south. Thus the Scandinavians never managed to be at the top of Europe's economic ladder by either aggregate or per capita measures during the early modern era, and as our story begins, in 1850, they were clearly below the countries mentioned earlier, though the economic situation varied from one Scandinavian state to another.

From 1387 to 1523, the crowns of Norway, Sweden and Denmark were united. In 1523, however, Gustavus Vasa (the top administrator of the joint kingdom) took Sweden out of the union, and began a series of adventures in Scandinavia and on the Continent that brought to Sweden a 200-year reign as the most powerful economic and military force in the Baltic. During the Thirty Years' War, the Swedes (though they were a Prostestant nation) allied with the French to prevent the Holy Roman Empire from expanding to the Baltic. For their victories, the Treaty of Westphalia granted West Pomerania, Bremen-Verden and Wismar to Sweden, thus extending Swedish power into the Continent. This achievement marked the high-water mark of Swedish power, and although Sweden lost its territories early in the eighteenth century, it never had its sovereignty threatened. It had acquired Finland in the early seventeenth century, but Finland was annexed formally by Czar Alexander in 1809; this established Sweden's modern borders, although it had some control over Norway in the years up to 1905.

In terms of its overall economic development, nineteenth-century Sweden had several important factors in its favour: it was well endowed with two important natural resources, timber and some of the finest (phosphorous-free) iron ore in the world; it had a relatively enlightened ruling class that, by a royal charter of 1611, had a voice in all legislation; it claimed the world's first proper central bank – the Riksbank, taken over by the state in 1668 – and, by the nineteenth century, Sweden arguably had the most educated population in the whole of Europe. Despite these advantages, by 1850 the Swedish standard of living was below that of both Denmark and Norway, and indeed was one of the lowest in Europe.

While much has been written about Sweden as the 'impoverished sophisticate' of mid-nineteenth-century Europe, its relatively poor economic position reflected three things. First, soil and climate conditions meant that no matter what technological innovations occurred, Swedish agriculture would always be at a disadvantage relative to other European (and later New World) producers. The second reason for Sweden's relative economic position was geographic. Although located out of harm's way during the major military upheavals of the period, Sweden was also off the beaten economic path. The Italian city-states on the Mediterranean, the Atlantic ports, the territory on either side of the English Channel, and the river-valley towns of central Europe had all enjoyed locational rents at one time or another. As for Sweden, the Danes controlled the Skagerrak and had easier access than the Swedes to the markets of western and central Europe; the Norwegians had better access to the North Sea for fishing, whaling, and marketing their abundant timber resources; and the countries immediately to the south and east across the Baltic (Prussia, Poland and Russia), Sweden's low-transaction-cost trading partners, were among the poorest and most economically backward in Europe. Finally, being the supplier of one of the most important resources (iron ore) for the industrial revolution did not generate long-run economic growth for the Swedes, mainly because Sweden had almost no coal. This was not a significant disadvantage in world markets until after 1750, when the use of coke in Britain caused the Swedes to surrender the low-cost world iron trade. They retained an export business in high-grade ore, but it was not until large-scale coal imports began in the mid-to-late nineteenth century that Sweden's economic boom began. This depended partly on the development of transportation and partly on technological changes in iron and steel making.

Throughout the period of Sweden's rise and fall as a significant political influence, Norway was under the control of the Danish crown. In 1814 the Danes transferred control of Norway to Sweden, and the Norwegians tried, unsuccessfully, to establish an independent kingdom. In the following year an act of union was ratified in which the Norwegians declared their independence but accepted the Swedish king as their monarch. Almost a century later, in 1905, they renounced their allegiance to the Swedish crown and elected their own king. Denmark, on the other hand, has been an independent state throughout modern times. Apart from losing control over first Sweden (in 1523) and then Norway (in 1814), it tried to annex the duchies of Schleswig and Holstein in 1863 and was badly defeated in a war with Prussia and Austria, both of which challenged Denmark's claims. Ultimately, both duchies were absorbed by the Germans. The loss of Schleswig and Holstein marked Danish national boundaries for the period we are considering.

In 1850, both Norway and Denmark enjoyed greater levels of per capita output than Sweden, although neither was as developed industrially. This situation resulted from the size of the primary sectors in each economy. Although Sweden's industrial sector was both absolutely and relatively (by per capita measures) larger than those of Denmark or Norway, the greater productivity of the other sectors in the other two Scandinavian countries yielded larger per capita output figures overall. Among these other industries were fishing and timber in Norway, and agricultural production in Denmark. Note that these were not the industries likely to provide significant economic gains in the nineteenth century, and none of the Scandinavian countries participated to any great extent in the first stages of industrialization (to 1850).

Austria-Hungary

While never a threat to Britain's overseas empire, Austria, with France, was the dominant military power on the Continent after the decline of Spain in the late sixteenth and early seventeenth centuries. The early modern era, however, was one in which the growth in national wealth depended importantly upon the conduct and finance of trade in international commodities, and here Austria, essentially a land-locked country, was at a comparative disadvantage. Though the ruling house of the Austro-Hungarian Empire, the Habsburgs, had a head start on the rest of Europe in forming a politically integrated state, many of their conquests brought relatively economically backward regions into the empire, thus lowering per capita measures of output. However, such conquests did, of course, raise total output and the tax base.

The dual monarchy of Austria and Hungary dates from 1526, and in 1683 the Habsburgs added Slavonia, Transylvania, Banat, Serbia and Lesser Wallachia to the empire after finally defeating the Ottoman Turks. In the west, Austria had joined England in attempting to keep a Bourbon from the vacant Spanish throne during the War of the Spanish Succession, and in return the Treaty of Rastadt (1714) granted Austria the Southern (Spanish)

Netherlands, the Duchy of Milan, and the Kingdom of Naples. In 1740, as the result of a war over the Austrian succession, the empire lost Silesia to the Prussians. The Austrians did, however, consolidate their hold over Hungary.

By 1740, the Dutch, as well as the French and English, enjoyed standards of living superior to the least backward (Austrian) parts of the empire, even though only France and England had larger aggregate economies. While missing out on the growth of trans-European trade meant that the Austrians had a smaller opportunity to accumulate capital – and much is made of this in the literature – the modern view is that this did not have a substantial effect on the economic status of the empire, even though it did slip to the lower rungs of the European economic ladder in the comparative statistics.[2]

By the mid-nineteenth century the pattern of subsequent economic development within the Austro-Hungarian Empire was evident. Despite relatively underdeveloped capital markets (see Chapter 4) the cosmopolitan regions of Austria, Bohemia and Moravia had developed local centres of the textiles and metals industries, and those regions had a standard of living that surpassed all but Great Britain, France, the Low Countries and Germany. Although the Hungarian economy was more agricultural than Austria, this sector was growing rapidly during the period, and the specialization in agriculture complemented the more modern sectors in Austria. In addition, Hungarian industry was expanding relatively rapidly after 1850. The empire's Balkan territories were another matter, however. Plagued by centuries of invasion and internal conflict, and poorly situated economically, these territories were among the poorest in Europe. Taken together, the per capita standard of living in all these geographical regions place the empire near the middle of the European economic order in 1850.

Italy

With the exception of Spain, Portugal and the Balkan states, Italy was the poorest country in mid-nineteenth-century Europe. However, we need to emphasize that the level of per capita income differed considerably between the north and the south. This north–south difference in living standards dates from the Middle Ages and has more to do with the growth of the north than the decline of the south, at least in absolute terms. The city-states of Genoa and Venice were the centres of the east–west trade in the Mediterranean at that time and thus were established as the leading economic powers of Europe during the late Middle Ages. The key to this power was their physical location, of course, but the development of certain financial products was also very important. In fact, it was credit in general and the bill of exchange in particular that made Italian financiers so effective in international trade.

What the bill of exchange did was bridge the gap between the shipment of products and their final sale; this instrument replaced hard money in this role. In fact, the bill of exchange represented a claim on specie without having to transfer the latter physically. It was in the marketing and clearing of such bills that the Italians specialized, and to broaden the market in these financial instruments they established what were in effect branches in the major trading centres throughout Europe. These banking syndicates were primarily the creation of a number of great banking families, such as the Bardi, Peruzzi and Medici of Florence.

Among the more than a dozen Italian states that had existed since the fifteenth century, Venice was the dominant economic power, unchallenged since its eclipse of Genoa, but two threats, one from the east and one from the west, eventually led to the eclipse of Venice. In the west, Portugal and Spain sought to circumvent Italian domination of the trade in Asian luxuries (and the ever-increasing belligerence of the Turks) by finding either a western or southern sea route to the Orient. Their success weakened not only Venice's but all the other Italian states' long-standing advantage in the financing of both the final legs of that trade and the exchange of goods throughout Europe. In the east, the Ottoman Turks proceeded into Europe after the fall of Constantinople (1453), and their advance through the Balkans brought them into conflict with the Venetians. The other Italian states were also unable to maintain their positions at the top of Europe's economic hierarchy, and among these Venice, the Kingdom of Naples and the Duchy of Milan became pawns in the game among the early modern European political powers.

The Congress of Vienna settled the Italian question for a generation by recognizing the nominal independence of nine Italian states, though they were, in fact, under constant Austrian domination: the Kingdom of Sardinia (Piedmont), Modena, Parma, Lucca, Tuscany, the Papal States, the Kingdom of Naples, the Republic of San Marino, and Monaco. The Congress also incorporated Venice directly into the Austrian Empire. After decades of Austrian control, however, a coalition of states led by Count Cavour, premier of Piedmont, and Giuseppe Garibaldi, who had conquered Sicily and Naples, formed the Kingdom of Italy in 1861. Venice was annexed into the kingdom five years later.

At the time of unification, the northern regions (Piedmont, Lombardy, Tuscany and Venice) were relatively prosperous, with technologically advanced cotton-spinning and silk-throwing industries, and a small but advanced metals industry. The per capita output of these regions was below that of Great Britain, France and the Low Countries, but probably above much of the rest of Europe, so the economic competitiveness of at least part of Italy cannot be doubted. Including the rest of the peninsula and Sicily, however, severely lowers per capita national product, because these were largely agricultural regions, and the agricultural productivity in those regions was low by European standards, making them among the most economically backward regions of the Continent.

Spain and Portugal

Spain was the first major economic power in modern times; it was the first European state to achieve political integration along the lines of its current national boundary; along with Portugal, which it absorbed for some time, it was also the first to establish and maintain an overseas empire. In 1850, however, Spain's days of economic and political leadership were long gone, and Spain's relative decline was well under way. We shall document and offer some explanation for this change in fortune for a country that, through its overseas exploration, must be considered one of the founders of the modern global economy.

The union of Ferdinand of Aragon and Isabella of Castile in 1479 created a united Spain that had a well-documented expansionist orientation. They further consolidated their rule of the Iberian Peninsula through their conquest of Granada (in 1492) and the expulsion of the Moors, while simultaneously conquering new lands in the West Indies and the Far East. The addition of overseas territory meant that the Spanish Empire and the Habsburg-dominated Holy Roman Empire were Europe's two most powerful monarchies at the dawn of the early modern era.

The staples of the early-modern Spanish economy were specie (primarily silver), which was extracted and imported from Spain's American holdings, and wool, which was produced domestically. Although these two activities generated a great deal of Spain's wealth during the early modern era, neither ended up contributing materially to modern economic growth. In the New World, the Spanish conquerors obtained specie in ways that did not expand the economic base. The specie was, in turn, remitted to Spain where it did little but drive up the domestic price level (it was money, after all). Indeed, the specie did not remain long in Spain, since the chronic trade imbalance that the Spanish had with the rest of Europe was financed by a specie outflow. In many ways, the Spanish colonies actually ended up being a drain on Spanish resources, one they could ill afford, given the nature of their own economic base (see Kennedy, 1987). In particular, the crown had to borrow in order to balance its books; the debt issue and its associated interest burden probably crowded out some domestic investment, and the occasional forced refinancing of loans disrupted Spanish financial markets.

This alone did not cause Spain's problems, of course; indeed, there is a plethora of potential explanations for Spain's slide down the economic hierarchy.

Another often-mentioned factor is the way the agricultural sector developed. The production of wool in Spain was controlled by the sheepherders' guild – the Mesta. The Mesta, which had been established in 1273, grew in importance with the consolidation of the crowns of Aragon and Castile and the emergence of a unified Spain at the end of the fifteenth century. Spanish wool, provided by the renowned Merino sheep, was the finest on the Continent, and during the sixteenth century, the booming textile industry consumed a great deal of it, particularly in the Spanish Netherlands. But there were costs imposed on Spanish economic growth by the specialization in wool production that resulted in part from the exceptional treatment the Mesta received from the crown. Because the sheep were herded from the mountains to the lowlands every winter, and back in the summer, they could be taxed easily, as could the wool when it was exported. The crown chose to use such taxes to finance the expansion of its global empire, and in exchange granted (common) grazing rights to the Mesta. During the next three centuries, as other countries increasingly enclosed agricultural land, granting property rights to private farmers and eliminating commons, Spain perpetuated the common property rights of the Mesta until the system was terminated in 1836. The special treatment afforded to the Mesta provides one reason why Spanish agriculture did not experience the agricultural transformation that occurred elsewhere in western Europe in the sixteenth and seventeenth centuries, although, of course, there were substantial agricultural areas outside the control of the Mesta.

We cannot say for certain how the European countries ranked economically in the sixteenth century, but it is not likely that the Spanish were far from the top in per capita income. They clearly did not have the sophisticated financial markets of the Italian city-states, the proto-industrial labour supplies that existed in north-western Europe, or the middle class found in both regions, and these are important factors in Spain's subsequent slower growth. Mention also has to be made of climatic factors, since the broad-based agriculture of the north of Europe is possible only in the northern parts of Spain that remained relatively inaccessible until the arrival of railways. Furthermore, Spain's coal deposits are neither considerable nor well located, and the country possesses few other significant natural resources. Even so, by 1800, as England and France began the process of modern economic growth, Spanish per capita income was only 30 per cent below that of England, and 10 per cent below France's (Molinas and Prados de la Escosura, 1989). Thus events in the nineteenth century are the key to why, by 1900, Spain had fallen much further behind, with a per capita income about a half that of the other two countries. In our view, this puts more weight on lack of resources and the relatively slow development of an appropriate infrastructure and proto-industrial work-force, than one finds in many accounts of the Spanish situation. Of course, political factors are also important, as we have also emphasized in our discussion.

We are not going to feature Portugal in this study, although occasionally we shall include some of the few data that are available for the late nineteenth century, but at this point we should say something about Portugal's background in order to complete our historical survey. Portugal is one of the oldest countries in Europe, with established political frontiers since 1297. Portugal prospered in the fifteenth century, especially with a trading relationship that grew between Portugal and Flanders. Furthermore, during this period, the great age of Portuguese exploration and expansion occurred under the leadership of Prince Henry the Navigator. In 1580, however, Philip II of Spain sent an army into Portugal and claimed the throne as Philip I of Portugal. He undertook to preserve Portuguese autonomy and considered the union of Portugal and Castile as a personal one, much like that of Aragon and Castile under Ferdinand and Isabella. He appointed only Portuguese to the administration and summoned the legislature frequently. However, when succeeding Spanish kings neglected these undertakings, the Portuguese drove the Spanish garrisons from Portuguese soil, and in the Treaty of Lisbon (1668) Spain recognized Portuguese independence.

From the time of the Portuguese overseas conquests, the flow of specie from the new territories did little to improve the domestic economy, still largely rural. The financial position of the late fifteenth century (derived from trade in slaves, gold and spices) did not long survive into the sixteenth century. The expenses of maintaining far-flung and unproductive foreign outposts, and pirate attacks against Portuguese ships, quickly absorbed any surpluses. There were few domestic industries and manufactured goods, and cloth, tapestry, metalware and even basic foodstuffs (salt meat, cured fish and dairy products) were largely imported. In 1703, Portugal joined the Anglo-Austrian alliance against the French in the War of the Spanish Succession. In the same year, the Methuen Treaty was concluded, by which the exchange of port wine for English woollens became the basis for Anglo-Portuguese trade. From 1703, attempts were made to improve the export value of port wine, and government support was also given to the production of woollen goods, linen, paper and porcelain, and to the sardine and tuna fisheries. However, the Portuguese textile industry was unable to withstand mechanized competition. After 1850, public works, railways and ports were given priority, but Portugal had to wait until the twentieth century for any substantive improvement in its economic situation.

2.3 CONCLUSIONS

This summary of the political integration of the European nation states indicates that it had effects on the economic integration and status of each state, and in 1850 provided an important part of the explanation of the differences that existed at that time. Despite these differences in their earlier paths and level of economic development, we note that the economies of the countries we are considering were well on their way towards some broadly defined norm by the mid-nineteenth century.

Prior to the nineteenth century only three countries had anything remotely close to a central bank; credit markets were concentrated in only a few areas; and only Britain and the Low Countries could be said to have prosperous and well-established (both economically and politically) middle classes. But with industrialization came a move towards integration that touched most of Europe. With the exception of Portugal, Spain and the Balkans, all countries saw the significant rise of the middle and working classes; every country had some central institution for controlling finances; and the share of inputs going to the manufacturing sector rose everywhere.

What we have shown in this chapter is that the internal political integration of the European nation states was mainly complete by 1850. While there is no neat correlation between political integration and economic achievement in this period, once one has controlled for the geographic position of countries, the connection becomes more obvious. In particular, a ranking of European countries by the level of their economic and political development would correspond to a line running roughly from north-west to south-east. The unquestioned economic leader of the day was Great Britain, followed by the Netherlands, France and Belgium, though in the aggregate the economies of both Great Britain and France dominated those of the Netherlands and Belgium. The German states and Denmark were at the next, slightly lower, level of development, but the soon-to-be consolidated German Reich was the second largest economy on the Continent, surpassed only by France. Austria-Hungary, Norway and Sweden followed these countries and, other than the Balkan states, Italy, Portugal and Spain were the least economically developed of the European countries in the middle of the nineteenth century. Politically, something like the same order could be established, at least if one were to emphasize the political institutions that contributed to economic proficiency, which we have attempted to do in our survey.

3 The Nature and Causes of Economic Growth, 1850–1913

3.1 INTRODUCTION

From just after 1815 until the First World War, the countries of western Europe experienced unprecedented changes in their economies that both contributed to and reflected their industrialization, which also occurred in this period. By 1914, with the exception of Spain, southern Italy and parts of the Balkans, the entire Continent was experiencing what Kuznets calls 'modern economic growth' – that is, 'a sustained increase in per capita or per worker product' (Kuznets, 1966, p. 1). It is one of the fundamental propositions of this volume that the arrival of modern economic growth in each of these countries within a generation or so of one another is not coincidental. In fact, the economic agents in each country conducted real and financial transactions that built unbreakable economic ties that benefited most economic groups. The resulting integration was driven by trade, real capital flows, migration, technology transfers and the growth of the international financial community, just as it is in the mid-1990s.

During this era the industrial revolution entered a new phase, one in which first iron, coal and railways supplemented textiles as the most conspicuous industries; later, these industries were joined by newer ones, including steel, machine tools, chemicals and electrical power. The growth of these new industries was accompanied by the proliferation of large-scale manufacturing operations – large in both the size of their physical plant and the organizational structures by which they were managed. The water-powered textile mill employing perhaps a couple of hundred workers and financed by a managing entrepreneur – an economic marvel of the previous century – seems quaint in comparison to the industrial works that marked the economic landscape of the late nineteenth century. Richard Arkwright's cotton mill at Cromford, financed in 1771 by the profits of two merchant-manufacturers, employed 300 workers eight years after it opened (Mantoux, 1961, p. 224). A little over a century later, Krupp Steel in Essen employed 1600 workers (Hughes, 1986, p. 235). The technological change that increased the scale of coal and steel production and helped create whole new industries – electrical power, for example – played no small part in the process of modern economic growth and in the catching-up of the later-industrializing countries.

One of the reasons that we have selected 1850 as the starting date for this study is that it is a point at which economic agents in Europe – including the national governments – can be said to have been fully conscious of the existing dimensions of the industrial revolution, though the term itself had yet to be coined. Two years earlier, in 1848, Karl Marx had published his *Communist Manifesto*, which decried the economic system that had, by that point, proved to be history's most efficient at generating economic growth. Marx, of course, did not see it that way, equating the growth and productivity in the manufacturing sector with growing inequality and misery (Marx, 1906, vol. I, p. 470):

> That portion of the working class which machinery has thus rendered superfluous ... either goes to the wall in the unequal struggle of the old handicraft and manufacturing industry against the machine industry, or else floods all the more easily accessible branches of industry, swamps the labour market, and sinks the price of labour-power below its value.

The dour predictions of Marx coincided with the rise of a politically vocal working class. Yet neither Marx's warnings nor the chronicle of complaints by subsequent generations of social democrats can obscure the fact that the mid to late nineteenth century represented a period of previously unparalleled economic prosperity in Europe and the United States.

That industrialization resulted in higher average wages and incomes is not generally disputed today, though the extent and direction of changes in the distribution of income and movements in broader (and more amorphous) measures of welfare or living standards, remain open issues. The literature on this subject has been divided broadly between those who argue that standards of living – variously measured – rose unambiguously as a result of industrialization: the so-called 'optimists'; and those who argue standards of living – again, variously measured – fell: the so-called 'pessimists'.[1] Those among the former group rely primarily on two empirical measures: rising wages and per capita incomes and/or rising per capita levels of consumption. Feinstein (1981) and Crafts (1985) show that in the early nineteenth century the growth of per capita consumption accelerated in Britain. In addition, Lindert and Williamson (1985), and Williamson (1985), show that mean wages and incomes rose during the first half of the nineteenth century; however, Williamson (1985) argues that rising wages and incomes were accompanied by increasing inequality in the distribution of income, a point with which Feinstein (1988) disagrees. Ironically, this finding by Williamson supports one of the main claims by the pessimists, namely that rising means did not translate into rising living standards for the majority of the population because a disproportionate share of the growth went to those in upper income brackets. The pessimists rely on two other sets of measures to make their case. One of these involves quality-of-life measures, such as the infant mortality rate. Huck (1992), for example, shows that infant mortality rose during the period to which the optimists point as one of rising standards of living. The other measure involves biological data, such as heights. Floud et al. (1990) show that cohorts born at mid-century were the shortest of the century, and they conclude that while economic measures of living standards indicate optimism, physical measures indicate pessimism.

It is clear that the conclusion one draws from this debate over what happened to standards of living during the first half of the nineteenth century depends on the measure one employs. It is equally clear that the standard macroeconomic measure of economic growth – real per capita output or income – rose steadily, and, by this measure at least, the economic and social consequences of industrialization were clearly evident by 1850. For those still unsure of the future course of industrialization and agricultural improvements at mid-century, the year 1851 revealed the future with the opening of the Great Exhibition at the Crystal Palace in London. The multitudes of observers from all over the world who streamed past the displays saw a vast cross-section of revolutionary industrial products and inventions. The array included Krupp's gigantic steel block, McCormick's reaper and Whitworth's machine tools. The technological achievements dominated the natural wonders at the exhibition. It was said, for example, that McCormick's reaper 'attracted more visitors than the famed Kohinoor diamond' (Oliver, 1956, pp. 254–6, quoted in Parker, 1991b, p. 17).

Despite the economic growth that had occurred during the first half of the nineteenth century, and the future growth foretold by the Great Exhibition, the period was not devoid of social conflict. While the general impoverishment of broad classes of the population is unlikely to have occurred in this period, particular economic or demographic groups seem to have seen their living standards decline,[2] although it was usually possible for economic agents to change their position (professionally and/or geographically) to attempt to improve living and working conditions. The broad evidence for this, of course, lies in the strong migration and urbanization movements of the period, as discussed below. In any event, change by definition disrupts the status quo, and the economic and political events of both the preceding and concurrent period altered most economic relationships; many of these events are reflected in our macroeconomic perspective.

In Chapter 2 we chronicled the emergence of Europe's modern nation states from their late medieval roots. As these territories evolved politically and socially into large-scale political units with centralized legal systems and policy apparati, the concept of national wealth evolved as well. While the early mercantilists first raised the issue, Adam Smith is credited – in his critique of mercantilist thought (1776) – with the first statement of the modern concept of national wealth. This definition focuses on the per capita real value of the goods and services consumed by the people of a nation; in this, consumption necessarily includes that of both private and public goods. In fact, following Kuznets, in this study we generally define economic growth as the growth of per capita output rather than of per capita consumption. This focus reflects, at least partly, the state of the data, which are generally derived from the production side of the economy.

In any event, per capita measures of real income or output reveal an important view of the actual performance of an economy over time. Further, the construction of these series and their conversion into a common currency allows one to compare rates of growth across countries and over time. Knowledge about the relative performance of each economy allows us to compare their growth rates with their levels of output. As we noted in Chapter 1, much has been written about the 'relative backwardness' and 'catching up' or 'convergence' of these economies over time. To the extent that these ideas focus on per capita income or output, they overlook the historically crucial issue of *how* countries caught up or converged. The path of political integration, institutional change, technological change and shifts among leading industries all differed across national boundaries, and each contributes towards explaining the path of economic growth of a particular country and its integration into the European economy.[3] In other words, a late-industrializing country could substitute *new* technologies and human and physical capital – prerequisites as we used to call them – in place of those employed by an early industrializer. This substitution allowed the latecomers to grow at a more rapid rate and thus catch up.

In this chapter, then, we relate the rate of economic growth during the period 1850–1913 in each country to the structure of its economy. In doing so we show how, and explain why, some countries were able to stay ahead, others were able to catch up, and still others either fell behind or fell further behind. As the leading industries changed over time, for example, some countries were able to substitute into those activities either through a 'natural' comparative advantage based on resource endowments, or by means of institutional changes that permitted entrepreneurs to take advantage of the new situation. Catching the wave of economic change required some combination of political support, a conducive institutional structure, and aggressive behaviour by key economic agents. Our objective is to illustrate how these countries substituted among these requirements depending upon their particular historical experiences, and to show that, despite the differences in the paths, in most cases these countries did, in fact, 'converge' in the sense that their economies looked more like one another at the end of the period than at the beginning. We attribute this convergence primarily to the actions of individual economic agents in their pursuit of profit and utility, although the role played by supportive (and permissive) governments is also very important.

3.2 THE GROWTH OF REAL PER CAPITA OUTPUT

To give the reader an idea of the relative economic ranking of countries during the era in which modern economic growth spread throughout Europe, we begin with Table 3.1. The top panel of the table shows the per capita output or income in 1913 (UK) pounds sterling of twelve European countries and the United States in 1820, 1870 and 1913.[4] The lower panel of the table shows the average annual compounded rates of growth between 1820–1870, 1870–1913 and 1820–1913. In addition, levels and growth rates are ranked from 1 to 13 for each year to help the reader see the changes in the relative economic positions of each country. It needs to be emphasized, at the outset, that the nations at the lower end of the scale had large, in some cases near subsistence, agricultural sectors that tend to obscure the relative performances of their industrial sectors. Austria-Hungary, Italy, Portugal and Spain are the most conspicuous examples of these 'dual economies', and the first two mentioned did, indeed, have strong industrial sectors.

For the European countries, the figures in Table 3.1 show that the United Kingdom was the undisputed leader in terms of output per capita throughout the century, with France and Belgium on the next rung. In the middle of the ladder were the German states (later Germany), Norway, the Netherlands and Denmark, though after 1870 Germany's growth rate was faster than any of the countries with higher levels of per capita output, an observation that is consistent with economic convergence. By 1870, the poorest countries were Austria-Hungary, Sweden, the Italian states, Portugal and Spain, although with the highest post-1870 per capita growth rate, Sweden had moved to the middle rung by the end of the period. While after mid-century the relative growth rates of the upper- and middle-rung countries and Sweden generally support the convergence hypothesis, note that Austria-Hungary, Italy, Portugal and Spain remained the poorest countries in each period.[5] More importantly, their growth rates were quite

Table 3.1 Output per capita: levels and growth rates, 1820–1913 (in £s)

Country	Per capita output in 1913 (£ sterling)					
	1820	Rank	1870	Rank	1913	Rank
Austria-Hungary (GNP)	7.02	13	10.06	13	17.55	11
Belgium (GDP)	13.00	4	33.98	3	56.54	3
Denmark (GDP)	11.76	8	18.54	8	44.75	5
France (GDP)	14.71	3	24.47	4	47.00	4
Germany (GNP)	12.31	6	21.24	6	44.25	6
Italy (GNP)	9.89	11	15.18	9	20.87	10
Netherlands (NI)	11.05	9	22.95	5	35.58	9
Norway (GDP)	12.41	5	20.64	7	41.81	7
Portugal (GDP)	7.56	12	10.99	12	14.94	13
Spain (GNP)	12.00	7	14.31	11	15.74	12
Sweden (GDP)	11.05	10	14.93	10	35.76	8
United Kingdom (GNP)	16.71	2	35.77	2	59.52	2
United States (GNP)	21.14	1	43.42	1	92.16	1

	Coefficient of variation		
European countries	0.22	0.39	0.41
(excluding Spain and Portugal)	0.21	0.35	0.32

Country	Average annual compounded rates of growth (%); and rank					
	1820–70		1870–1913		1820–1913	
Austria-Hungary (GNP)	0.72	11	1.30	7	0.99	10
Belgium (GDP)	1.94	1	1.19	8	1.59	2
Denmark (GDP)	0.91	8	2.07	1	1.45	3
France (GDP)	1.02	6	1.53	6	1.26	9
Germany (GNP)	1.10	5	1.72	4	1.39	4
Italy (GNP)	0.86	9	0.74	11	0.81	11
Netherlands (NI)	1.47	3	1.02	10	1.27	8
Norway (GDP)	1.02	7	1.66	5	1.31	6
Portugal (GDP)	0.75	10	0.72	12	0.74	12
Spain (GNP)	0.35	13	0.45	13	0.29	13
Sweden (GDP)	0.60	12	2.05	2	1.27	7
United Kingdom (GNP)	1.53	2	1.19	9	1.38	5
United States (GNP)	1.45	4	1.77	3	1.60	1

Sources: The income estimates are described in the Data Appendix. We used the measures listed there. The 1820 estimates for each country were calculated using growth rates derived from Maddison (1982). Exchange rates were calculated by converting each currency into gold and then into pounds sterling. The gold content of each currency was found in or calculated from Muhleman (1896).

low as well, with only Austria-Hungary converging on the leaders after 1870.[6] These results imply that certainly Spain, and probably Italy and Portugal, were diverging from the rest of the countries considered though the Italian case is not that clear, since northern Italy contained sizeable pockets of advanced industrialization.

The top panel in Table 3.1 provides an additional piece of information concerning convergence. We have calculated coefficients of variation for the European countries for 1820, 1870 and 1913. A falling coefficient of variation would be consistent with the convergence hypothesis.[7] Given the relatively poor performance of the Portuguese and Spanish economies throughout the period, we have calculated an additional set of coefficients of variation that excludes Iberia, which had the lowest levels and growth rates of per capita output during this era. Interestingly, until mid-century the levels of output per capita in fact diverged considerably, as measured by the coefficient of variation. The United Kingdom's rapid growth from an already impressive level of output no doubt played a part. As the first industrial country, this finding is not surprising. After 1870, as the major continental countries industrialized, the coefficient of variation falls slightly (in the figures that exclude Portugal and Spain). We conclude that the level figures show little convergence among these countries.

Turning then to the growth rates, we note again that for the period 1820–70 the growth rates do not in general conform to the convergence hypothesis. For example, the leading European country (the United Kingdom) has the fastest growth rate, while the countries with three of the four lowest levels of income or output per capita (Austria-Hungary, Spain and Sweden) have the three lowest growth rates. These rates are reflected in the top panel in the increase in the coefficient of variation between 1820 and 1870. For the later period, 1870–1913, however, the growth rate figures show some convergence. The three richest European countries in 1870 – the United Kingdom, Belgium, and France – have relatively slower growth rates, while Sweden, Denmark and Germany all grew relatively rapidly. We consider this clear, if modest, evidence of the long-run process of economic convergence among these countries.

The output figures used in Table 3.1 raise another question, which we now address. Since the output of each country has been converted into British pounds sterling, the estimates reflect to a certain extent the international purchasing power of each currency. We shall see in Chapter 5 that sterling often served as the reserve currency for countries on the gold standard, and in that sense the figures in the table are useful ones for international comparison. But there may have been domestic growth that for some reason is not reflected in the purchasing power parity estimates in Table 3.1, which reflect primarily the value of traded goods. Indeed, the larger the share of a country's output that is not traded internationally, the greater the possibility that the figures in Table 3.1 will measure incorrectly the level of output. For example, Komlos (1983) has shown that the free trade zone created by the Austro-Hungarian customs union formed in 1850 promoted growth within the empire. That growth may be understated when the Austrian currency is converted to pounds, because *all* the output is converted to pounds by our procedure, even that portion that was not traded internationally.

For this reason we have constructed Table 3.2, which shows the growth of real per capita output in the domestic currency of each country. We have chosen 1880, somewhat arbitrarily, as a mid-point for the period in question and have calculated growth rates before and after that date, and for the whole period. The table shows, for example, that while Denmark, Sweden and Germany maintained their places as the most rapidly growing economies during the late nineteenth century (after 1880), Austria-Hungary moves up a couple of places. We see further from the table that only Italy, Portugal, Spain and, interestingly, the Netherlands, experienced domestic growth rates below 1 per cent per annum.

Table 3.2 Annual growth rates of real per capita output in domestic currency for selected European countries and the United States, 1850–1913 (per cent)

Country	Start year	To 1880	1880–1913	Full period
Austria-Hungary	1867	0.47	1.61	1.30
Belgium	1850	1.66	1.02	1.35
Denmark	1850	0.74	1.93	1.36
France	1850	1.17	1.55	1.37
Germany	1850	1.52	1.71	1.62
Italy	1861	1.04	0.79	0.88
Netherlands	1850	0.81	0.57	0.70
Norway	1870	0.86	1.39	1.27
Portugal	1850	0.75	0.65	0.69
Spain	1860	1.48	0.46	0.97
Sweden	1861	1.90	2.10	2.03
United Kingdom	1850	1.48	1.21	1.34
United States	1869	2.48	1.55	1.77

Notes: The growth rates were calculated from three-year moving averages. The Spanish growth rates are calculated to 1890 and 1910.

Sources: See Data Appendix.

This overview of the aggregate economic growth of the European states between 1820 and 1913 indicates that by the end of the period all of them – except possibly Spain and Portugal – had achieved levels of output and growth rates that were consistent with 'modern' economic growth. Between 1850 (or the other starting years in Table 3.2) and 1913 only one country other than Portugal – namely, the Netherlands – experienced a real growth rate substantially below 1 cent per annum, and its per capita output was more than twice that of the poorest countries. Thus, while Iberia, southern Italy, and the Trans-Danubian regions of the Austrian Empire (and the Balkan states) were still backward by any contemporary measure, the rest of Europe was on its way to becoming a collection of modern industrial nation states. Furthermore, there is some evidence of convergence in real output per capita among these countries towards the end of the nineteenth century, but the paths they followed differed considerably, as we argue in the following sections.

3.3 POPULATION GROWTH AND MIGRATION

When considering the growth of per capita output, it is natural to inquire about the growth of the population. Few topics in the study of economic growth have yielded as much debate as the role of population. During the nineteenth century, all the countries listed in Table 3.1 experienced what demographers often refer to as 'the demographic transition' – the movement from historically high birth and death rates to considerably lower levels of both. Although the timing of the transition differs from country to country, by the end of the period they had all moved from crude birth rates in the neighbourhood of 45 to 50 per thousand to rates of around 20 per thousand. Crude death rates fell as well and, in addition, all European countries experienced considerable migration – much of it to the United States – though again, the timing and extent differed from country to country. This transition had potentially enormous effects on such economic variables as consumption, savings and labour supply, though the net effect on output is unclear.

While it is perfectly obvious that population growth causes aggregate demand to grow, the debate that has arisen concerns whether *effective* aggregate demand also rises. This question revolves largely around whether the supply-side effects of population growth, mainly in the form of a larger work-force that is actually employed, exceed or fall short of the demand-side effects. To complicate the issue, of course, there are independent supply-side effects – most notably in the form of increasing skills and technological change – potentially balanced by demand-side effects that could make demand less effective – such as increasing inequality in the distribution of the proceeds of growth. Thomas Malthus serves as an able spokesman for the negative position, although he concentrated on the agricultural aspects of the problem, and for Europe, at least, the two centuries since Malthus wrote have been ones of tremendous technological change and productivity advance.

More recently, a generation of growth theorists, primarily addressing population growth in the developing world, has argued, not unlike Malthus, that the negative effects of population growth dominated the positive effects, and that population growth strained economic growth. The other side of the story appears in the form of the neoclassical growth model, which describes equilibrium growth in terms of population growth plus an enhancement factor largely attributable to technological change.[8] Some writers, indeed, have gone so far as to argue that by adding to the stock of human capital and spurring technological change, population growth is the primary source of economic growth (Boserup, 1965, 1981; and Simon, 1981). Recently, Kelley (1988) has surveyed the empirical literature on both sides of this debate and reports that in fact one can identify no iron law of the effects of population growth on economic growth.

For the period of time and place we are considering, the rate of technological change was quite rapid by historical comparison, and whatever negative population effects there might have been in the short run were mostly suspended in the long run. As the lower half of Table 3.1 shows, per capita growth rates for these countries are always positive, even taking the poorest of the European countries (leaving out the Balkans for lack of data, unfortunately). Thus the neoclassical model would 'fit' this experience quite well, since the growth of real output exceeds population growth for these countries throughout the period. This conclusion says nothing about the distribution of the proceeds (which is *assumed* to be constant in the neoclassical model). We will have nothing more to say about this topic in this study, though interested readers should refer to the review in Mokyr (1993) cited above.

Table 3.3 shows the size and the growth rates of the populations of these countries from roughly 1850 to 1913. Note that the two outliers at either end of the distribution are France – arguably the first country to experience the demographic transition – and the United States – the country experiencing the greatest immigration. Aside from those two important countries, the differences among nations are still considerable. For example, the growth of population in Spain is only half that in the Netherlands and Denmark; and for another example, Germany's population growth is more than 50 per cent larger than Italy's.

Table 3.3 Population size and growth rates for selected European countries and the United States, 1850–1913

Country	Start year	Start year population (000s)	Population in 1913 (000s)	Growth rates (%) Pop.	Output PC	Non-PC
Austria-Hungary	1867	33 040	47 510	0.79	1.30	2.09
Belgium	1850	4 414	7 605	0.87	1.35	2.22
Denmark	1850	1 424	2 833	1.10	1.36	2.46
France	1850	35 630	39 771	0.17	1.37	1.54
Germany	1850	35 312	66 978	1.02	1.62	2.64
Italy	1861	24 971	35 192	0.66	0.88	1.54
Netherlands	1850	3 057	6 213	1.11	0.70	1.81
Norway	1870	1 735	2 447	0.80	1.27	2.07
Portugal	1850	3 850	6 004	0.71	0.69	1.40
Spain	1860	15 645	21 121	0.57	0.97	1.54
Sweden	1861	3 889	5 622	0.71	2.03	2.74
United Kingdom	1850	27 550	45 649	0.81	1.34	2.15
United States	1869	39 051	97 225	2.09	1.77	3.96

Sources: See Data Appendix.

Clearly, if population growth and real economic growth are similiar for a given country, then in a fundamental sense, because per capita income is not changing, the citizens of the country are not better off, on average. What we have seen, though, is that per capita incomes have, in fact, increased for all these countries in this period. In the neoclassical model, to which we are not bound by any means, such growth would be attributed to technological change (Phelps, 1965), by default if nothing else. There are two questions, then. First, is population growth somehow itself responsible for greater per capita growth, perhaps by permitting the operation of economies of scale? Second, is economic growth faster for countries with faster rates of growth of population? The first question can hardly be answered with the present state of the data, but we can certainly look at the second.[9] It is worth pointing out that the second positive relationship is an implication of the neoclassical model that is very likely to hold in this period.

To see the relationship between population growth and economic growth, we have also computed the change in real national product (variously measured as in Table 3.2) and included it in the last column of Table 3.3. Note that this comparison is between the growth rate of real income (not adjusted for population growth) and the growth rate of population. In fact, the

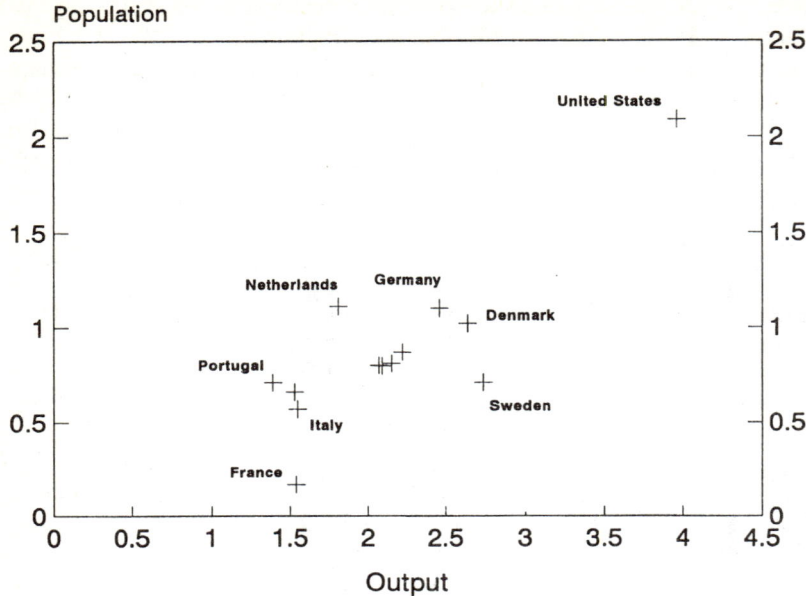

Figure 3.1 Population and output growth rates compared, Europe and the United States, c.1850–1913

correlation here is a strong 0.81. To see the relationship a little more clearly, we have constructed a simple scatterplot of the two series, taken directly from Table 3.3; this appears in Figure 3.1.

As noted, the relationship is strongly positive, with faster-growing countries having faster-growing populations, at least in a general sense. Of course, there are outliers in the data, and there are many other things to consider in explaining the growth rate of a country; so the true force of this influence is not really shown here. There is, though, no reason to exclude the United States or France from these calculations, even though they are outliers that strongly influence the correlation coefficient, since they are valid examples of the proposition. It is also worth considering Sweden and the Netherlands, which are marked in the figure; Sweden grew faster and the Netherlands more slowly (relative to population growth) than other countries, primarily for structural reasons (not directly related to population) as we have suggested and will further explain below.

There are two other aspects to population growth in this period that attest to the growing integration of the European economies. One is explicit: there was considerable migration among these countries before 1914, and this helped to establish the basis of a 'common' labour market that all could draw upon. We do not want to exaggerate this influence, but the scattered data that we have suggest that it is an underrated factor in tying these countries together. Of course, migration also means emigration, from Europe to (mainly) the former colonies, and this is not only sizeable, but also establishes an integration in a global sense that goes beyond our study (although we will look at a few numbers). The second topic is more implicit: all of these countries experienced comparable urbanization rates (in the industrial and commercial parts of the country) as the second industrial revolution continued, which also attests to the changing structure of the European economy.

Migration out of Europe plays a particularly notable role in the economic history of this period, and these countries lost population to territories conquered and settled by Europeans in the previous three centuries. Like population change in general, emigration had potentially conflicting effects on output, which we have already considered. There are several additional aspects to migration, though. For one thing, the dominant emigrants were prime-aged males who had spent their childhood in their native countries accumulating human capital and contributing little in the form of net output. The loss of these individuals clearly had a potentially negative impact on economic growth in the countries with high emigration rates. On the other hand, to the extent that the people who left had below-average human capital and wealth, and expected below-average rates of growth over their working lives, it is possible that their migration benefited both the country they left and the one they entered.[10]

Table 3.4 contains the net emigration rates from the European countries we are considering. In comparison with our earlier data on national product, the table shows little correlation between net migration rates and either the level or rate of per capita economic growth. For example, after 1880, Italy, Sweden, the United Kingdom (even excluding Ireland) and Denmark had the highest net emigration rates. Italy had a relatively low per capita growth rate, and Sweden and Denmark had high rates. We think a partial explanation is that the population that emigrated to the United States, at least, was often agricultural, in the first instance. It was attracted to the United States because of the abundant land (and for many other reasons) and was driven from Europe because of poorer opportunities there; probably the pull was stronger than the push, although this conclusion is in dispute in the literature and, in any case, varies from country to country. Notice that the agricultural opportunities in Europe were poorer partly because of the growth of the agricultural sector in the United States.

Table 3.4 Net emigrants from Europe per 1000 population, 1850–1913

Country	1850s	1860s	1870s	1880s	1890s	1900–13
Belgium	0.66	0.17	−0.93	−1.06	−1.80	−2.88
Denmark	–	–	1.95	3.68	2.55	2.58
France	–	0.11	0.09	0.19	0.11	0.01
Germany	–	1.61	1.35	2.89	1.12	−2.45
Italy	–	–	–	–	6.78	13.01
Netherlands	–	–	0.10	0.81	1.16	0.31
Spain	–	–	–	0.98	0.42	2.50
Sweden	–	–	–	7.30	3.77	2.93
United Kingdom	–	1.29	1.52	3.23	0.93	3.31

Note: United Kingdom figures exclude Ireland.
Source: Hatton and Williamson (1992, Table 1).

Urbanization played an important role in the economic transformation of Europe during the late nineteenth century. While others have focused on the social and political aspects of this migration, we argue that it offers strong evidence of an economic transformation that coincided with the timing and paths of economic growth described above. In 1850, for example, other than the United Kingdom, only one European country – Belgium – had more than 30 per cent of its population residing in urban areas, and Austria-Hungary, Norway, Spain and Sweden all had rates of urbanization below 20 per cent (see Table 3.5). By the end of the century, however, only Austria-Hungary had a rate below 20 per cent, and every other country except Norway and Sweden had an urban rate above 30 per cent. This dramatic shift occurred in one generation. In most of the countries in the table, the urban share of the population was growing faster than the population as a whole (see Table 3.3), which would imply that there must have been a great deal of economic migration from rural – predominantly agricultural – regions to urban industrial areas.

During this period, then, we have found some mild evidence of convergence of national products, especially in a per capita form; this finding, however, is conditioned by many factors, some of which tend to obscure the basic drive to convergence. We have more to say about this statement in the next section. We have also found the European economies growing alike in several other respects. All these countries had growing populations, and many had significant emigration, either to other European countries or out of Europe entirely. Furthermore, all these countries were

Table 3.5 Percentage of the population residing in urban areas for selected European countries and the United States, 1850–1910

Country	1850	1860	1870	1880	1890	1900	1910
Austria-Hungary[a]	9.0	10.2	10.9	13.7	16.0	–	–
Belgium[b]	32.6	34.8	36.9	43.1	47.7	–	–
Denmark	20.9	23.4	24.9	28.1	33.2	38.2	40.3
France	25.5	28.9	31.1	34.8	37.4	40.9	44.2
Germany[c]	26.8	29.4	32.5	35.6	39.4	–	60.0
Italy[d]	–	25.2	24.9	27.0	–	–	–
Netherlands[e]	29.0	–	–	–	43.0	–	–
Norway	12.3	19.8	25.7	18.3	23.7	–	–
Spain[e]	–	16.2	–	–	29.6	–	–
Sweden	10.1	11.3	13.0	15.1	18.8	21.5	24.8
United Kingdom[f]	50.2	54.6	61.8	67.9	72.0	77.0	78.1
United States	15.3	19.8	25.7	28.2	35.4	39.7	45.7

Notes: In cases where no data were available for the years listed at the head of the column, we have reported figures for the next closest year.
[a] The urban population for Austria is cities with 10 000 or more inhabitants; for Hungary it includes 'free' and 'small' cities; [b] The urban population includes cities with 5000 or more inhabitants; [c] The 1910 figure comes from Trebilcock (1981, p. 54); [d] The urban population includes cities with 6000 or more inhabitants; [e] The urban population includes cities with 10 000 or more inhabitants; [f] The figures for the United Kingdom include England and Wales only.
Sources: Austria-Hungary, Germany, Italy, Netherlands, Norway and Spain (Weber, 1899, pp. 82, 95, 101, 111, 115, 116, 118, 119); Denmark, France, Sweden, United Kingdom and the United States (Berry and Horton, 1970, p. 75).

urbanizing rapidly, as their commercial, industrial and service sectors expanded, and urbanization represents another way that they were converging on the European leader (the United Kingdom) in this respect. But we are only part way along in our summary of the structural similarities across the European countries; the next section considers the details of changes in the agricultural and manufacturing sectors.

3.4 IMPORTANT INDICATORS OF MODERN INDUSTRIAL EXPANSION

Kuznets (1966) placed a great deal of emphasis on what he calls the 'sustained character' of both the growth of per capita product, and on 'structural change'. By sustained character he means that the long-run rate of growth was such that living standards could not be 'overshadowed' – his word – by short-run fluctuations. In other words, the long-run trend of average living standards, as measured by per capita output, was not only upward, but also temporary downturns in the levels were made up relatively quickly. According to Kuznets, the structure of a nation's industries plays an important role in ensuring this result. In particular, he focuses on the shift of capital and labour from agriculture to manufacturing and services in this period. Because of the shift of resources to the more productive sector – that is, the sector with the greatest value of output per unit of input – real per capita output grew.

One way to see this change is to look at growth rates of industrial production compared to those for the economy as a whole. We have industrial production indices for eight countries, and the growth rates of those are shown in Table 3.6, which is set up exactly as Table 3.2 to facilitate comparisons. The manufacturing sector offered higher wages and higher rates of return on capital throughout the period; thus, capital and labour were attracted to manufacturing, leading to growth rates in industrial production that were greater in each country than those for the economy as a whole. This sector thus led the way towards a European economy.

A more dramatic way to visualize the changes wrought in this manner is to look at yet another measure of structure, the ratio of agriculture to manufacturing in the national product. Each of these countries was

Table 3.6 Annual compounded growth rates of indices of industrial production (per cent) for selected European countries and the United States, 1850–1913

Country	Start year	To 1880	1880–1913	Full period
Austria	1880	–	3.68	3.68
France	1850	2.82	2.25	2.52
Germany	1850	3.52	4.08	3.82
Italy	1861	1.83	2.91	2.52
Spain	1850	2.81	2.17	2.47
Sweden	1861	2.81	4.28	3.75
United Kingdom	1850	1.88	2.04	1.97
United States	1884	–	4.02	4.02

Note: The growth rates were calculated from three-year moving averages.
Sources: Mitchell (1978) and Miron and Romer (1990).

experiencing a relative 'decline' of its agricultural sector in this period, although we are not in a position to document this completely. We do have appropriate agricultural and manufacturing data for six countries, and Figure 3.2 presents those data. What we have here is the ratio of industrial to agricultural output, measured variously. This picture illustrates the early lead and continuing shift out of agriculture by the United Kingdom.

In the figure, France, a relatively early industrial country, displays almost equal growth in its agricultural and industrial sectors, while Italy, at a much lower level of industrial production, similarly shows comparable rates of industrial and agricultural growth. The figure also shows the catching up of three *relatively* backward economies, Germany, Sweden and Austria-Hungary. Note that their path of acceleration follows their degree of relative backwardness, with Germany the least backward of the three beginning its transition out of agriculture earlier than the other two, followed by Sweden and Austria-Hungary, in that order.

As important as the shift out of agriculture was, changes in the composition of industrial output were equally important, though less attention has been paid to them. During the early days of the industrial revolution, the technological innovations in textile production made raw fibre

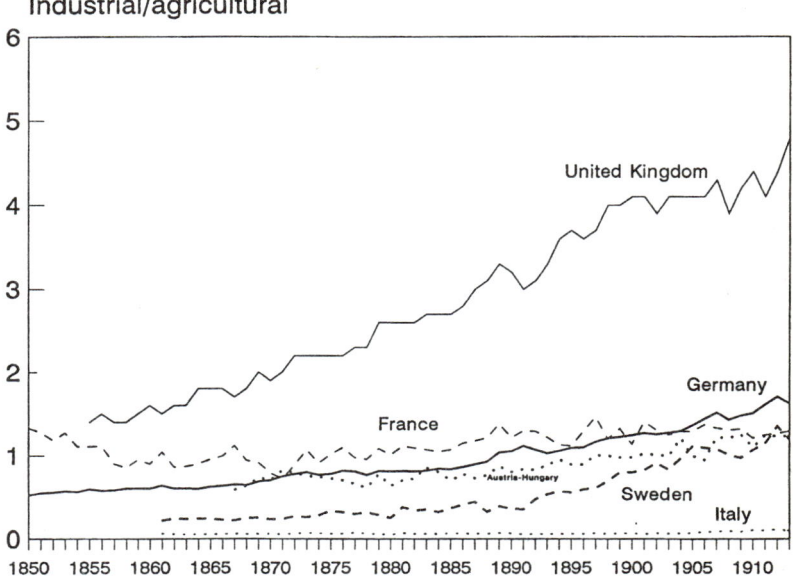

Figure 3.2 Ratio of industrial to agricultural production, 1850–1913

the petrol upon which the industrial revolution ran. The mechanization of the carding, spinning, and weaving of cotton and wool made textiles the first modern industry, and nowhere did textile production grow as fast and as early as in Great Britain. Almost simultaneously, there sprang up a machine tool industry to construct the instruments of the now mechanized industry. These machines were made at least partly of iron and later driven by steam; thus, textile production contributed to the growth of the iron, coal and machine tool industries. Later, railways were built to haul the stuff around, which in turn further increased the demand for iron and coal, and in this way did the British become, in the words of Mathias (1983), the 'first industrial nation'.

As noted in the previous chapter, by 1850 the British consumed more raw cotton and produced more iron and coal than the rest of Europe combined. They also had one of the densest grids of railway tracks. The extent of British domination at the middle of the century is illustrated in per capita terms in Table 3.7. While the starting years differ from country to country and industry to industry, Table 3.7 shows that in almost every case the

Table 3.7 Measures of industrial activity for selected European countries and the United States, 1850 and 1913

Country	Cotton consumption (tons per mil. pop.)		Pig iron production (tons per mil. pop.)		Coal production (tons per mil. pop.)		Railroad track (km per mil. pop.)	
	Start year	1913	Start year	1913	Start year	1913	Start year	1913
Austria-Hungary	1.08	4.49	6.55	48.14	53.15	1 095.18	45.20	485.29
Belgium	2.27	18.01	32.85	302.24	1 318.76	3 252.79	193.48	621.15
France	1.76	6.71	12.80	122.75	128.71	1 018.07	91.39	1 026.69
Germany	1.67	7.16	6.64	232.64	220.83	3 865.39	174.14	947.65
Italy	0.24	5.02	1.06	10.57	1.50	18.32	127.30	532.80
Netherlands	0.32	5.44	–	–	9.24	276.29	56.52	531.41
Norway	–	–	3.46	2.89	–	10.85	45.95	1 273.13
Spain	1.33	4.50	4.18	20.55	22.97	204.32	53.93	746.29
Sweden	0.83	3.82	47.09	123.16	7.78	61.85	210.36	2 537.44
United Kingdom	10.94	20.66	91.42	212.61	1 822.14	6 107.58	370.80	712.17
United States	12.49	32.77	39.51	298.15	980.28	6 156.98	1 786.36	4 677.60
Coefficient of variation	1.37	0.90	1.17	0.85	1.46	1.22	1.78	0.99

Notes: Where possible, the figures were calculated from three-year moving averages. The starting years for each country are as follow: Austria-Hungary (1852); Belgium (1850); France (1850); Germany (1850; cotton, 1858); Italy (1861; cotton, 1866); Netherlands (1850; coal, 1870); Norway (pig iron, 1866; coal, 1907; and rail, 1854); Spain (1857; pig iron and coal, 1860); Sweden (1861); United Kingdom (1850); and the United States (1867).
Sources: Authors' calculation from Table 3.3 and Mitchell (1978).

United Kingdom dominated all the other European countries by a multiple greater than two, and in most cases it was several times that. By the end of the period, however, the United Kingdom maintained its earlier overwhelming pre-eminence only in coal production, and even there every country but well-endowed Belgium was gaining rapidly.

In addition to showing the relative erosion of British economic dominance, Table 3.7 illustrates another important feature of late-nineteenth-century European industrialism. At the bottom of the table we have calculated coefficients of variation for each industry in the starting year and in 1913. Note that in each industry the coefficient drops substantially between the starting year and 1913. These steep declines indicate that in terms of industrial structure not only were the other countries catching up with the leader, at least as measured by per capita output, but that the economies of these countries were also becoming more alike over time, a form of convergence that often goes unrecognized.

The changes in the levels of per capita output in Table 3.7 reflect the various growth rates experienced across countries. Table 3.8 contains the annual compounded rates of growth of each industry in each country listed in Table 3.7. Table 3.8 illustrates two important features of the European economic order during the period 1850–1913. First, with a couple of exceptions, most notably Belgian coal, between 1880 and 1913 every country experienced faster rates of growth in each industry than did the United Kingdom. It is hard to imagine more convincing evidence of convergence of the structures of these economies. Second, for most industries in most countries the growth rates during the second period, 1880–1913, were slower than those for the earlier period, base year–1880. This observation is interesting, because at first glance it contrasts with the industrial production indices discussed above and shown as the numerator to the figures shown in Figure 3.2. Clearly, what was happening in most of these economies was a relative substitution towards other newer, faster-growing industries.

These new leading industries offered the later industrializing countries the opportunity to accelerate the process of catching up with the United Kingdom. The integration that had already occurred in technology, and human and financial capital, allowed them to begin at the top of the technological ladder in those newer industries. We illustrate this process and conclude the presentation of data in this chapter with Table 3.9, which shows the per capita output of steel, sulphuric acid (representing the chemical industry), and electric power. Note that the starting year for each of these industries is later than the earlier leading industries, and that the growth rates are in general quite a bit higher than those for the established industries. Also

Table 3.8 Average growth rates of per capita industrial activity, selected European countries and the United States, 1850–1913
(per cent)

Country	Cotton consumption		Pig iron production			Coal production			Railroad track in use		
	1850–80	1880–1913	1850–1913	1850–80	1880–1913	1850–1913	1850–80	1880–1913	1850–1913	1850–80	1880–1913	1850–1913
Austria-Hungary	2.09	2.74	2.44	2.63	4.13	3.44	8.25	2.81	5.26	7.55	1.28	4.11
Belgium	2.34	4.40	3.40	3.85	3.45	3.64	2.75	0.27	1.47	4.60	-0.57	1.90
France	1.30	3.05	2.22	4.40	3.22	3.78	4.79	2.24	3.45	6.82	1.59	4.05
Germany	2.74	2.81	2.78	7.36	4.78	6.00	6.27	3.49	4.80	5.17	0.73	2.82
Italy	7.83	6.61	6.96	-2.50	8.99	4.71	6.66	4.28	5.14	5.38	1.54	2.90
Netherlands	7.67	2.21	4.77	–	–	–	0.15	11.05	5.73	7.52	0.43	3.74
Norway	–	–	–	-13.53	-5.50	-0.40	–	–	–	10.49	2.62	6.00
Spain	2.94	1.84	2.29	2.93	3.22	3.17	4.79	3.98	4.38	10.03	1.65	4.99
Sweden	4.71	2.21	3.11	3.41	1.13	1.94	6.32	3.08	4.23	10.62	2.13	5.11
United Kingdom	1.57	0.57	1.05	2.98	-0.02	1.39	2.87	1.14	1.97	2.34	-0.05	1.08
United States	3.51	1.75	2.22	5.16	4.53	4.70	4.72	4.09	4.26	4.40	1.40	2.21

Note: For specific starting years, see the note in Table 3.7.
Sources: Authors' calculations from Table 3.7.

note that while the United Kingdom was a leader in steel and sulphuric acid in 1870 and 1880 respectively, its growth rate in these two industries was the slowest of any country, and it was never the leader in electric power. By 1913, Germany was second to the Belgians in steel and sulphuric acid production, and second to the Swedes in the production of electric power (all in per capita terms, though). Although it is interesting to note that the British were either the leader or among the leaders in these industries, again, as the industries developed, the British surrendered their leadership within a generation. The rate at which other countries 'caught up' in the new industries was much faster than had been the case with the older industries. This observation leads us to assert the presence of economic integration behind these figures.

The data summarized in the tables in this section tell us something fairly obvious to the historically literate; namely, that certain industries were expanding faster than others during the late nineteenth century, and these fast-growing industries included steel, chemicals and electric power. When we compare the figures in Table 3.9 with those in Tables 3.7 and 3.8,

Table 3.9 Output per capita and annual growth rates of steel, sulphuric acid and electric power for selected European countries before 1913

Country	Steel production (tons per mil. pop.)			Sulphuric acid production (tons per mil. pop.)			Electric power generation (gigaWatt hrs × 100)		
	1870	1913	Growth rate (%)	1878–80	1913	Growth rate (%)	1900	1913	Growth rate (%)
Austria-Hungary	1.10	54.22	9.98	0.65	7.37	7.18	–	–	–
Belgium[a]	14.68	306.88	8.81	5.55	55.26	6.79	–	–	–
France	2.67	108.78	9.47	5.38	22.63	4.19	0.97	3.79	14.56
Germany	3.72	243.00	10.73	2.08	25.78	7.46	2.16	10.77	15.71
Italy[b,c]	0.08	24.65	20.21	1.91	18.32	11.97	0.38	5.05	26.27
Spain[d]	1.91	14.88	8.21	–	1.02	–	0.73	2.29	10.93
Sweden[e]	2.94	94.13	8.82	2.11	14.94	7.82	1.94	20.57	23.95
United Kingdom	13.92	155.86	6.23	25.99	23.70	–0.28	1.20	5.13	14.10
Coefficient of variation	1.13	0.83		1.43	0.77		0.56	0.86	

Notes: Where possible, the figures were calculated from three-year moving averages. [a] The starting year for Belgium steel production is 1875; [b] The starting year for Italian steel production is 1880; [c] The starting year for Italian sulphuric acid production is 1893; [d] The starting year for Spanish steel production is 1885; [e] The starting year for Swedish sulphuric acid production is 1887.
Sources: Authors' calculations from Mitchell (1978).

however, they tell a less obvious story, which is how countries catch up or converge based on the timing of their industrialization. This story reveals that convergence and catching up as measured by per capita output are manifestations of the industrial structure that composes measures of aggregate output. A country displaying moderate backwardness, such as Germany, which had participated with a lag in the economic modernization associated with the 'old' leading industries: textiles, iron, coal and railways, and which subsequently embraced the 'new' industries, moved to the top rung of the economic ladder. With respect to the more backward countries, they leapt to a higher rung, as did Sweden; saw tremendous growth in isolated regions, as was the case in Italy and Austria-Hungary; or fell behind, as did Spain.

3.5 CATCHING UP: A NEW INTERPRETATION OF AN OLD DEBATE

It is our contention that the integration of the European economy that was in place during this period explains the timing and the course of the catching up that occurred among the later industrializing countries. The nature of the leading industries – their underlying technological structure, if you will – of the late nineteenth century differed from the earlier leading industries in one of two ways, and sometimes in both. The scale of production was larger and/or their production involved relatively complex technical features absent from the early leading industries. Together, these two characteristics of late-nineteenth-century industrialization rewarded the capacity to attract or supply financial and human capital on an unprecedented scale: the former to finance the scale of production and the latter to organize it.

Here, then, were the returns to an integrated international economy. Certainly, the United Kingdom had a great deal of financial and human capital, both absolutely, and relative to a latecomer like Austria-Hungary or even a continental power like Germany, but the United Kingdom also had a great deal of capital invested in older technologies. At the margin, British capitalists would not have found it profitable to scrap entire industries to create new ones. Once an innovation occurred, however, the entrepreneurs, financiers and politicians in countries such as Germany – which had lagged in the development of the earlier industries – learned how other countries had prospered from earlier innovations and were now themselves in a position to capitalize on the new opportunities. And importantly, it was the integration of the European economic order that made these opportunities possible. Without the transfer of technology and the access to capital, the latecomers would have been 'non-comers'. Thus to understand the process of convergence in its broadest forms, as we have done in this chapter, one must understand that the formal economic integration for which we test in the rest of this volume rests in some sense on a less specific form of integration that allowed entrepreneurs and financiers in a country such as Germany to take advantage of new technologies and industries, and thus to catch up with the United Kingdom.

As we have seen, Gerschenkron emphasizes the role of banks and the state in organizing late-nineteenth-century industrial expansion. But our point is that, without integrated technological and financial systems, the capacity for the latecomers to take advantage of the knowledge and savings accumulated indigenously and elsewhere, and required to catch up, would have been impeded. In the next two parts of this volume we test the hypothesis that international integration, both real and financial, marked the late-nineteenth-century European economy, and this integration played an important role in the economic growth of the participating countries. Without this integration in this early version of the 'global economy', the concepts of convergence and catching up are hollow metaphors analogous to describing the progress of horses in different races.

Part II

The Financial System

4 Money, Banking and Financial Sophistication

4.1 INTRODUCTION

During the period 1850–1913, the banking systems of Europe grew very rapidly by historical standards. The typical pattern was for the money stock to grow considerably faster than nominal gross national (or domestic) output, as we illustrate below, and as we noted in Chapter 3, real gross output also grew rapidly by historical comparison throughout much of Europe during this period. Indeed, the money supply grew more rapidly than nominal output in every country for which we have the appropriate data, except the United Kingdom. This finding implies that velocity – that is, the average number of times a unit of domestic currency changes hands – fell during the period 1850–1913.[1] The period also features price levels that fell about as often as they rose, so that growth rates of money were also generally much in excess of rates of inflation. It follows that the rapidly expanding banking systems on the Continent were filling a need, at the same time many of the economies were industrializing at unprecedented rates, by providing new financial services at an equally unprecedented rate.

We begin our work in this chapter with Section 4.2, which covers the data, including the money stocks, the inflation rates and the velocity of money for each country. The idea here is to see just how alike in their uses of money these countries became over time. In particular, we look at the development of the financial sector by means of what we call a 'financial sophistication index', the calculation of which yields the number of weeks of national income held in the form of money.[2] This index shows increasing financial sophistication generally, except for the United Kingdom. Since, as we argued in Chapter 2, the British had the most sophisticated financial sector in the world in 1850, the more rapid financial development of the continental economies is consistent with our characterization of the period 1850–1913 as one of convergence upon the leaders by those formerly trailing. In a way, this is obvious, since much of the structural convergence we discussed in Chapter 3 was financed by the expansion of the banking systems reviewed below. The pattern of increasing financial sophistication varies across countries, however, and the story is as interesting for that which is unique as for that which is similar across countries.

In Section 4.3 we discuss the banking systems of the twelve countries that we are examining in this study. This material spells out the details of the expansion of financial services, country by country. Although we distinguish considerable variation in the initial institutional structure and path of financial growth among these countries, by the end of the period we identify what to us appears to have been a remarkable degree of similarity in the banking systems of the countries in question. In short, we find that by 1914 almost all European countries – certainly every major economy – and the United States had 'mixed' banking sectors, with institutions accepting deposits that could be drawn upon, discounting notes and providing long-term credit (or underwriting) for industrial and commercial activities. That is, each country had what are typically called savings, merchant, commercial and investment banks.

In Section 4.4, finally, we look at fresh evidence on monetary neutrality within each country. Here the issue is testing one of the most contested propositions in monetary theory: do changes in the domestic money supply cause changes in real economic activity? Answering this question involves testing for causality between movements in the money supply and real output within each country. While the discussion of the institutional aspects of banking covers much of Europe, in the discussion in Section 4.4, we work with a smaller set of countries, in view of the need to have both money and real output in these tests. Incidentally, we also investigate the role of financial sophistication in this section, as an influence on (or of) real activity, a topic that has come up in the literature in a variety of ways. In this last section, then, countries appear to be similar as far as our data take us: real activity 'drives' financial activity and the converse, while money apparently 'drives' price levels only in a few cases. But there are many exceptions and qualifications that go with these generalizations, and statistically the tests are of low power.

All the evidence outlined above and discussed in detail in the present chapter might seem to imply that there is considerable monetary interaction among these countries. As we shall see in Chapters 5 and 6, however, this is not as obvious as it was once thought to be in this gold-standard-dominated world. In Chapter 5, for example, we show that the gold standard might have been subverted routinely by countries supposedly playing by the rules of the system, and that the high-powered money stocks of these countries are not firmly linked together (in a statistical sense) in this period – at first glance, a somewhat surprising result in a gold-standard world. In Chapter 6 we report and discuss the same type of test for the money stocks and price levels of these countries; we find that money stocks do not interact but prices do in these tests. In both Chapters 5 and 6 we attempt to reconcile our findings with the major theories of how the gold standard in fact worked.

4.2 MONEY, PRICES AND NATIONAL INCOME

In this section we review the data on money, prices and income on a country-by-country basis. Table 4.1 summarizes the data on money, and the associated data on real national product and prices in each country. It should be emphasized that the measure of output is not the same for every country and, in any case, the series are dated differently, generally but not always depending on the dates that the money supply series begins. In this table, the money stock generally grows faster than real output, making due allowances for the slight differences in periods, while inflation rates are considerably lower, particularly before 1890 (which one can deduce, of course, from the numbers in the table).

The first thought one might have is that the quantity theory of money was suspended in this period, since the growth rates of money and prices are so dissimilar. Indeed, as we show in Chapter 6, this pattern holds up for all measures of prices available: wholesale prices (as in Table 4.1), consumer prices and gross product deflators. Since these results, particularly those for

Table 4.1 Growth rates of money (M), prices (P) and real income (y) various dates to 1913

Country	Date	Date to 1913			1890 to 1913		
		M	P	y	M	P	y
Austria/Hungary	1867	5.69	−0.23	1.97	5.65	1.07	1.93
Denmark	1870	5.39	0.25	2.62	4.41	0.73	3.05
France	1850	2.47	0.07	1.52	3.03	0.64	1.82
Germany	1850	5.01	0.54	2.60	5.88	0.63	2.77
Italy	1861	4.44	0.05	1.58	3.60	0.57	1.86
Norway	1850	5.49	0.72	2.10	5.49	1.33	2.44
Spain	1874	1.98	0.51	–	1.92	1.31	–
Sweden	1850	5.89	0.02	2.74	6.35	0.86	3.25
United Kingdom	1871	1.72	−0.35	1.72	2.07	0.51	1.83
United States	1867	5.45	−1.01	3.90	6.04	0.94	3.75

Notes: The dates for all series are for the beginning of the money stock series, except as follows. The prices in the table are wholesale prices except for Denmark and Norway, where they are national product deflators. The prices for Austria/Hungary terminate in 1909, while those for Norway start in 1865, and for Sweden start in 1860. Real product begins in 1865 for Norway, in 1861 for Sweden and in 1869 for the United States.
Sources: See Data Appendix.

1890–1913, come from a period when the gold standard was operating, and since the gold standard formalizes the connection between domestic monetary bases and monetary gold, this might seem paradoxical. In particular, under purchasing power parity, gold should move from high-inflation to low-inflation countries. These gold flows cause countries to experience roughly similar rates of inflation, at least in the long run. In fact, in Table 4.1, countries do experience similar inflation rates, which are quite low by more recent standards in both periods, with a rather narrower distribution of inflation rates in the 1890–1913 period than overall. But why are inflation rates so low compared to money growth?

In fact, employing the equation of exchange ($MV = Py$ in its static form), the income velocity of money is the residual in Table 4.1. Clearly, to reconcile the figures, velocity must be falling, and falling pretty substantially, for all countries but the United Kingdom. Is this an exception to the quantity theory of money? We think not, since, as explained by Friedman (1956), while the quantity theory of money is certainly obtainable in a world with constant real income and constant velocity, that is not the essence of the theory, which holds *ceteris paribus*. What *is* important to establish, to underscore the relevance of the theory, is the stability of the demand for money (or a 'velocity function') for each country. We discuss this issue in Chapter 7.

Changes in velocity are consistent with the quantity theory, provided that the changes are explainable either in terms of a stable demand for money (or velocity) function or in terms of institutional changes that affect velocity. In modern times, velocity often rises, and we think this is because of the invention of new forms of money, new ways to purchase goods and services (such as with credit cards), and the relaxation of restrictions on interest rates on the components of the monetary aggregate. In the period we are examining, though, we see a velocity *decline*, not a rise, and, we suspect, the effect of the invention of monetary substitutes is not very important in this period. Instead, the use of money was extended dramatically in this period through the significant extension of both specific financial instruments and the geographical territory receiving up-to-date banking services in all countries except the United Kingdom, which, we believe, was already quite advanced financially as the period began. Indeed, the decline of velocity towards the British level (or thereabouts) is part of the catching up of each of these countries to the most advanced country in terms of its banking structure. By 1913, most countries had velocities of money similar to that in the United Kingdom, and this is yet another way that the economies of these countries converged in this period, becoming much more similar to each other in terms of the shape of their financial system, at least when judged in this way.

In their study of the behaviour of velocity, Bordo and Jonung (1987) argue that the declining velocity of the period is the result of the monetization process, whereas rising velocity in later periods is the result of increasing financial sophistication. 'Financial sophistication', as Bordo and Jonung use the term, is defined as *both* the emergence of a large number of substitutes for money *and* the development of various methods of economizing on money balances. We are, of course, suggesting that, initially at least, monetization itself is a form of financial sophistication and, in any case, we study only the period of declining velocity. Of course, there were other forms of money at the time. For example, the use of commercial bills certainly increased in this period, although in the absence of really good figures on their volume, we can only conjecture that their use does not disrupt our proposition.

A way to visualize the relative financial development of countries – and how this concept changes in this transitional period – is to use the 'financial sophistication index' suggested by Friedman and Schwartz (1982). This index is calculated by multiplying the inverse of velocity (that is, M/Y) by 52 (the number of weeks in the year). The result is the number of weeks of national income financed by (or covered by) money balances. Friedman and Schwartz compare the United States and the United Kingdom, and their analysis illuminates the contrasts between two countries with differing levels of financial development. They note that the income elasticity of money demand is considerably higher in the United States than in the United Kingdom (where it is around unity), and they associate this with a lack of relative financial sophistication in the United States. By this they mean that the general lack of financial services makes those that do exist relatively valuable to Americans. In the United States an increase in income of a dollar led to a more than one dollar increase in the use of money. This finding implies that monetary services are less widely used in the United States than in the United Kingdom, reflecting, it can be argued, a relative scarcity of such forms of payment (and of the accompanying banking services). Comparing the United States in the 1870s with the United Kingdom, Friedman and Schwartz note (1982, p. 146):

> The United States, by contrast, though wealthier and more populous, was still financially backward, conducting its international trade largely in sterling. Nearly three-quarters of the population was classified as residing in rural areas, and half of the working force (male and female) was still in agriculture ... These differences meant a much higher demand for money relative to income by United Kingdom than by United States residents.

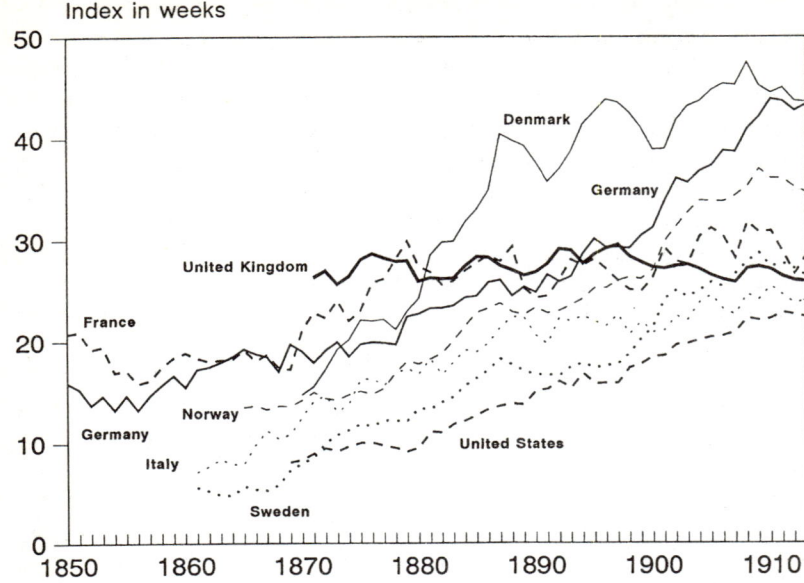

Figure 4.1   Financial sophistication indices, 1850–1913

Indeed, Friedman and Schwartz argue that in the United States much of the conversion to a more financially sophisticated economy occurred between 1870 and 1906.

In Figure 4.1, we plot the financial sophistication indices for the eight countries listed in Table 4.1.[3] Here we see what is perhaps the greatest advantage of the approach: the index is in units (weeks) that mean the same thing in each country, so that comparisons can be made across countries. Of course, both monetary and nominal income figures are not produced by similar procedures in each case, so one should not expect this compilation to provide more than a general picture of this phenomenon. In any case, Table 4.2 provides more exact numbers for the same concept, taken at five-year intervals. This table is included to make the following discussion more numerate.

The *United Kingdom* comes across as the only country in the sample that does not show a rise in its financial sophistication index. In other words, as measured by this index, in the United Kingdom monetary and banking services were added at the same rate as the economy expanded from 1870 to

Table 4.2 Financial sophistication indices, 1851–1913

Date	Denmark	France	Germany	Italy	Norway	Sweden	UK	USA
1851		20.9	15.3					
1856		15.8	13.3					
1861		18.3	17.2	7.1		5.5		
1866		18.1	18.8	9.9	13.7	5.3		
1871	15.6	22.8	17.9	14.2	15.0	8.6	26.3	9.0
1876	22.0	25.8	19.9	16.3	14.8	11.7	28.6	10.1
1881	28.5	26.9	23.2	18.3	18.2	13.4	26.3	11.1
1886	34.9	28.4	25.8	19.8	23.2	17.2	28.3	13.4
1891	35.7	24.5	26.6	19.7	22.8	16.7	27.6	15.3
1896	43.8	27.1	29.2	21.5	25.2	17.6	29.2	15.9
1901	39.0	29.2	33.8	21.0	29.8	24.2	27.2	18.5
1906	45.4	30.4	38.8	23.2	33.8	25.4	26.1	20.5
1913	43.5	28.4	43.3	24.0	34.6	26.4	25.9	22.4
Annual growth rates, 1871–1913	2.44	0.32	2.10	1.12	1.99	2.67	–0.04	2.17

Sources: See Data Appendix. The UK income data are from Solomou and Weale (1991), while those for the US are from Balke and Gordon (1989).

1913. This finding is hardly surprising, really, because the United Kingdom already had a well-developed financial sector by 1850. But it may also suggest a growing use of money substitutes in the United Kingdom, since the growth of commercial bank liabilities in this period (at least to 1880) was very rapid. In this case the index would be misleading, as it would be after the velocity increase occured, later in the twentieth century.

From the figures provided, *France* shows only a modest change over the period, with the bulk of the effect over by 1886. France also has a relatively high index in 1851 (at 20.9 weeks of gross national product (GNP) in the form of money). Thus, the subsequent convergence of the French toward the UK standard is not remarkable, attesting to the relative financial sophistication of France throughout the period. The *Germans* show less financial sophistication in 1850 than do the French, but their financial development accelerates sometime in the mid-1870s; indeed, by 1890 they have surged ahead and finish (along with *Denmark*) at the top of the table at 43 weeks of GNP in the form of money. The rapid growth of German financial sophistication is somewhat surprising, but, as we shall discuss in Section 4.3, it can be explained partly in terms of the large compensating balances that the German banks required of their large corporate customers (which allowed the banks to expand their liabilities accordingly), and partly in terms of the lending policies of the Reichsbank, which were quite liberal by the standards of the day. We shall also comment in that section on the Danish and Norwegian situations.

Sandberg (1978) employs the concept of financial sophistication in the context of suggesting that the *Swedish* financial sector was well-developed around 1850 compared, let us say, to a European average. Sandberg appears to be arguing that in 1850 Sweden may have had 'excess financial capacity' in some sense, but the notion that Sweden was financially well developed at this time runs counter to the existing tradition in the literature (see Heckscher, 1963 and Kindleberger, 1982). Although this is not the only way to measure financial factors, we note that the Swedish financial sophistication index is the lowest in the table, at its inception, so our measure does not support Sandberg's view. In fact, the index rises rapidly until the twentieth century, finishing up very near the UK figure.

Given the fact that Italian bankers were once the leading bankers of Europe, and can be said to be the principal early developers of many of the tools of finance, we might expect *Italy* to exhibit considerable financial sophistication, especially compared to the less developed European countries and possibly even to countries that possessed considerably larger per capita income and wealth. Yet this is not the case in our exhibits, probably because our measure of sophistication covers the entire country, and much of Italy was agricultural, even in 1913. We would, then, expect increased industrialization to coincide with an increase in the financial sophistication index in Italy, as it does with all but the United Kingdom during this period. Indeed, that is what happened after 1861, and the Italians ran roughly parallel to the Swedes in this period, the two of them eventually converging on the United Kingdom. The percentage change for Italy is actually larger than for all countries in our tabulation except Sweden. Since these are two of the latecomers in European industrialization, such a finding is clearly in line with our discussion of real convergence in Chapter 3.

We conclude this section with the presentation of two other measures of the growth of the financial sectors in these countries. These are growth rates for assets, in the top half of Table 4.3, and the ratio of assets to national product, in the bottom half. The numbers in the top part of the table are remarkably similar across countries, and all are growing quite rapidly, by any standard; the first two columns of the second table illustrate this in another way, although in this part of the table there are large differences having to do with the fact that nations started off the period at dramatically different levels. Spain stands out in both tables, with very low numbers for financial assets in comparison with the other European countries, and a very low growth rate of assets in the 1900–1913 period. Spain, of course, is the only country in this

Table 4.3 A Average growth rates of assets held by financial institutions in Europe, 1854–1913 (per cent)

Country	1854–73	1873–1900	1900–13
Belgium	8.7	5.6	6.4
Denmark	–	5.1	5.9
France	6.2	4.4	3.8
Germany	–	2.5	2.7
Italy	–	3.6	8.0
Netherlands	–	3.3	5.8
Norway	–	4.2	5.7
Spain	7.4	4.6	0.6
Sweden	–	4.5	5.5
United Kingdom	10.0	4.2	5.7

B Ratio of assets held by financial institutions to national product in Europe, 1880–1913

Country	1880	1900	1913
Belgium	73	114	158
Denmark	95	147	184
France	50	96	104
Germany	95	93	103
Italy	36	61	97
Netherlands	46	62	83
Norway	107	136	166
Spain	31	39	33
Sweden	89	123	136
United Kingdom	71	94	109

Source: Goldsmith (1969, Tables 4.4–4.7).

set that is not really experiencing much of an industrial transformation in this period. Denmark and Norway also stand out, at the other end of the scale (in the bottom part of the table), showing very large ratios of financial assets to national product.

Across nations, then, while neither measures of money nor measures of national income are strictly comparable, the figures we have presented on financial sophistication suggest another way countries grew to look alike in this period. In 1870, the UK economy was the most financially sophisticated in Europe, while in 1913, every country had gained on the United Kingdom, with many even showing higher measures of financial sophistication. Indeed, all but the relatively developed French more than doubled their use of banking and monetary services as a percentage of income, with the Germans, Danes and Norwegians ultimately surging ahead of the pack. The main point is that all but the leader grew substantially and at rates suggested at least in part by how far behind they were in 1850. It is important to appreciate that we are not saying that all countries look exactly alike by this measure but, rather, that all countries shown here had modern banking systems in place in 1913 that were roughly comparable to that in the United Kingdom. This was not the case in 1850.

4.3 THE EVOLUTION OF BANKING

In this section we chronicle the financial development of twelve European countries. We begin with the United Kingdom, which by all accounts had the most sophisticated financial system in the world in 1850, though – and this is one of our themes – the lead was in a particular type of banking, which proved to be somewhat less effective in the provision of the capital required by the large-scale industrial enterprises that proliferated during this period. The other countries we consider, in order, are France, Germany, the Netherlands, Belgium, Austria and Hungary, Sweden, Denmark, Norway, Italy, Spain and Portugal.

United Kingdom

To begin with we note that the United Kingdom was on the gold standard throughout the period, and because of its economic and military dominance (see Chapter 2), sterling was an international currency. 'The whole liability for ... international payments in cash is thrown on the Bank of England', wrote Walter Bagehot in *Lombard Street* (1873, p. 16). The central banks of several countries maintained sterling as a reserve much like gold. As the

Money, Banking and Financial Sophistication 75

reserve-creating country, the United Kingdom enjoyed simultaneously the advantages of the system while being unencumbered by its manifest inflexibility. As long as foreign bankers and policy makers believed that the Bank of England could and would maintain convertibility, sterling was 'as good as gold'. Faith in British finance in general, and the Bank of England in particular, was based on Britain's economic might, gold discoveries in Britain's dominions in Australia and South Africa, and, in the words of Hughes (1983, p. 409), her 'gunboats at the fringes of the system'.

The UK money supply, primarily specie and bank liabilities, was determined jointly by endogenous factors – that is, by the decisions of commercial bankers (when they determined the quantity of reserves they held against their notes and deposits), by the actions of individuals (when they determined the quantity of gold and currency they held relative to their bank deposits), and by the portfolio decisions of the Bank of England (which were a combination of profit-maximizing and policy-orientated decisions). Of course, all these were influenced by the institutional structure of the British banking system.

The English banking sector from 1850 consisted of a wide variety of institutions in addition to the proto-typical joint-stock banks (London and provincial). The list includes building societies, merchant banks, savings banks, discount houses and foreign banks. Collectively, they participated in all banking activities, including in some cases the issuance of bank notes, though this practice was restricted over time and prohibited to all new banks by the Bank Act of 1844. These restrictions gave the Bank of England essentially a monopoly of note issue, which strengthened the Bank's ability to function as a central bank (see Chapter 5).

The role the banking system played in Britain's industrial development has been debated among economic historians for some time. Before explaining the issues involved, however, it is important to keep in mind that there is little question concerning either Britain's early financial dominance or the important role that position played in Britain's early economic dominance. The service of clearing and discounting of bills was crucial to the development of Western trading networks, and London eventually became the centre of these activities. So the role of British banking in Britain's economic development is not an issue; rather, it is the actual or perceived lack of lending by the financial sector to the manufacturing sector that is at issue. It is worth taking a moment to consider the debate on this topic, because, given the nature of ninteenth- century financial intermediation, it is one that occurs in other countries as well.

Broadly speaking, we can identify two schools of thought on the role of British banking in industrialization. We call these two schools the 'original accumulation' school and the 'roll-over' school. Karl Marx conceived the term 'original' or 'primitive' accumulation to describe the process by which early merchant capitalists and, what modern economic historians call proto-industrialists, invested profits in new technologies that led directly or indirectly to the factory system. Whether these profits were invested by the capitalist, or borrowed directly from him, does not matter. The key to this view of early industrialization is that little intermediation between a lender (saver) and a borrower takes place; thus there is a relatively small role for the banking system in the financing of manufacturing. It follows that Great Britain, as the first industrial nation, financed its early industrial development largely in this way – that is, with little use of bank lending for long-term investment. While this view of early British manufacturing development originates with Marx, it has been given much support in the work of Gerschenkron (1962) and Cameron (1967a and 1972).

Empirical support for the 'original accumulation' view comes largely from comparing the composition of assets of UK banks with those of a country such as Germany, where banks took a more active role in financing – and managing – industry (see below). While we do not have exact numbers available, Kindleberger (1993) suggests that a typical UK bank held only 20 per cent of its assets in loans and advances in the nineteenth century. Contrast this figure with those provided by Tilly for Germany: excluding the Prussian Bank, the rest of the North German banks held on average 40 per cent of their assets in loans and advances (1967, p. 64). In any case, the original accumulation school equates the emphasis of English banks on short-term credit, manifest in the discounting of bills, with an absence of the supply of long-term credit to manufacturers.

The 'roll-over school', led by Mathias (1973 and 1983), argues that British industrialists could, and frequently did, roll over their short-term bills as they came due, and that the banks participated actively in converting these ostensibly short-term loans into long-term loans. If firms could roll over short-term loans perpetually, even if the loans were ostensibly for working rather than fixed capital, then they could invest the resulting funds in physical plant and equipment. In addition, Pollard (1964) and Cameron (1967a) argue that the ratio of working to fixed capital in industrial firms was quite high; thus, short-term loans would have been particularly important in financing British industry even if the loans were not directly invested in plant and equipment. We conclude that it is not at all clear that the English banking system played little or no role in financing the first industrial revolution, though the size of that role was arguably small relative to that played by banking in some later industrializing countries, as we shall see.

Although the British banking sector evolved during the late nineteenth century, it was slower than many continental countries to adopt the 'mixed' form of banking, which combined investment and commercial banking activities in one institution. Partly, this may have been related to the scale at which British financial institutions operated. As late as 1870, the English banking industry 'still consisted largely of unit banks, both private and joint-stock, and a national banking system only developed from the 1890s as a result of amalgamation and branch expansion' (Cottrell, 1991, p. 26), and when British banks did participate in underwriting new issues it was often for foreign rather than for domestic firms.

The relatively small role played by the British banking sector in the founding, underwriting and managing of industrial concerns in the late nineteenth century resulted partly from constraints found in the common law concerning economic combinations. Chandler (1994) argues that, as much as any other single item, the prohibition against combinations separated British banking from that of Germany. In particular, as we shall see below, the ability of German firms to enforce cartels by legal means created scale opportunities for German financial intermediaries that, because they were illegal, were unavailable to the British. Thus the so-called 'failure' of the British banks to finance large-scale industry to the same extent as their continental counterparts in the late nineteenth century may actually have been a manifestation of British institutional arrangements embodied in the common law, which presumably served the country well in other respects.

We can summarize the evolution of the British banking sector during the period 1850–1913 with three observations. First, at the outset, British banks probably did not play as direct a role in financing long-term (and large-scale) capital investment or managing industry in Britain as did the continental banks (later). Even so, British banking was evolving, and the technology of banking from the middle of the nineteenth century and later differed from that found earlier in England, just as the leading industries and scale of operations were changing over time. Second, despite Parliamentary regulations and perhaps as a result of them, the banking system developed as a widespread and diversified financial system that included a number of characteristics that mark banking to this day. These include the creation of building associations and the use of deposit banking and cheque writing on a large scale. Finally, the Bank of England served as a central bank in the modern sense of the term – that is, it controlled the money supply and served as a lender of last resort (see Chapter 5). Although its policies were not very aggressive (compared to modern practice), it none the less became the model for late-nineteenth-century central banks.

France

Modern banking in France begins with the Bank of France, which began operations in February 1800.[4] It was created by Napoleon Buonaparte and operated primarily to discount bills of exchange for, and make advances to, the government. For a time it had a national monopoly of bank note issue (from 1803 to 1814), which was subsequently restricted to the Paris area until 1848, when it once again obtained the national monopoly of issue. From 1817 to 1838, a small number of private banks were chartered in France, mainly in other economically important cities (for example, Bordeaux, Lyons), and in 1836 the Bank itself began to spread out, with thirteen branches in operation by 1848. In the financial crisis brought on by the Revolution of 1848, all other banks suspended, and almost all of them perished.

We shall explore the performance of the Bank of France as a central bank in Chapter 5, but here we note that the Bank followed a very restrictive discount policy, and so there were quite a few private discount operations in place around the country. In addition, the Bank was closely tied to the government and, in return for credit, the Bank typically persuaded the government to be less supportive of potentially competing financial institutions. Following the financial crisis of 1848 in which many private banks failed, the government permitted the establishment of *'comptoires d'escompte'*. These discount branches or offices were linked formally to the Bank of France in that they served as intermediaries between local merchants and industrialists and the Bank. Although created initially to ease the financial crisis brought about by the Revolution of 1848, several *comptoires* survived in one form or another and became permanent financial institutions.

In 1851, Napoleon III became Emperor, and in an attempt to support French economic growth and to offer a counter to the political influence of older financial establishments, such as the Bank of France, his government created several new financial institutions. Over the next fifteen years, several important banks of one form or another were created. In 1852, a nationwide mortgage bank (Crédit Foncier de France) and the famous Crédit Mobilier were founded. The latter, which itself was modelled on Belgian investment banks, became in some respects a prototype for many subsequent ventures in investment banking throughout Europe. The Crédit Mobilier sold bonds and granted loans primarily for public projects, especially railways, but also for ports and public water and gas works. Interestingly, the Crédit Mobilier did not provide capital directly to the manufacturing sector, though many of its imitators did, and it was forced eventually to liquidate in 1867 because of an unsuccessful venture into real estate loans. In addition to the mortgage and public works financing of the Crédit Foncier and the Crédit Mobilier, in 1860 the former was directed to extend its lending into agriculture, and to do so it created the Société de Crédit Agricole.

The government was still hostile to British-style deposit banking after 1851, and while prior to the early 1860s other banks were also founded, cheque writing, a speciality of British banks, was slow to develop, being formally legalized only in 1865; so the discount banks, as earlier, filled the gaps. Three banks which countered this trend were the Crédit Industriel et Commercial (founded in 1859), the Crédit Lyonnais (1863), and the Société Général (1864). Each was national in scope and offered demand-deposit accounts. Although each of these banks did some lending to the manufacturing sector, particularly during their early years, as did the English banks upon which they were modelled, their lending functions were concentrated in short-term securities – typically either high-grade government bonds or commercial bills secured by commodities – rather than long-term capital projects. Unlike the British banks, which, as we noted above, often held short-run manufacturing assets that could be rolled over into *de facto* long-run loans, these French banks dealt almost exclusively in government securities, both domestic and foreign.

Given its size and monopoly over note issue, it is not surprising that the Bank of France continued to expand throughout this period, reaching 60 branches by 1870 and 411 by 1900. Cameron (1967b) claims that by 1870 one could refer to the French financial system as being 'mature' (p. 109):

> by 1870 the basic pattern of the modern French banking structure had been fixed. It included the Bank of France in the centre, the sole source of paper currency and supreme regulator of the system; a relatively small number of large joint-stock deposit banks – four or five – operating on a national scale; a much larger number of small local and regional banks in the provinces; a few *banques d'affaires* [investment banks] and a number of specialized institutions for foreign commerce, mortgage credit, etc., some of which ... had quasi-official status.

As we have seen, our financial sophistication index confirms that at some time within a decade or so following 1870, the French financial system could be referred to as being mature, at least in this restricted sense.

We can summarize the evolution of the French banking sector during this era with three observations. First, the French were slower than the British in developing widespread deposit banking, and this probably had some, albeit small, effect on French economic development. Second, the French developed the joint-stock investment bank earlier than, and to a greater extent than, just about every other country apart from Belgium, though, with respect to both deposit and investment banking, France and the United Kingdom were much more similar by the end of the period than at its beginning. Finally, while the Bank of France had a monopoly of the note issue and could therefore control the money supply, and while it did serve as a lender of last resort during a number of crises, only towards the end of the period did it do so in a manner comparable to the central banks of other major European economies.

Germany

Modern-style banks of issue first appeared in Germany in the 1830s; the first was the Bavarian Mortgage and Discount Bank. The more important Prussian Bank of 1846 took over the assets and liabilities of the Royal Bank of Prussia; it was privately owned but regulated by the government – a style that marked most European central banks of that period. While it never held a monopoly of note issue, the Prussian Bank's note circulation dominated the total, reaching 40 per cent by 1865 and almost 90 per cent by 1896 (Muhleman, 1896, p. 110). Other states set up note issuing banks from 1847. Even so, private banks were the dominant form of banking enterprise, and they were ubiquitous throughout the period 1815–1870. In Prussia alone there were 330 of these institutions in 1820–21 and their number grew to 642 by 1861 (Tilly, 1967, p. 161). These banks did not issue notes but they did considerable business in banker's acceptances and discounts. They also dealt with the government, sometimes on a very large scale (for example, the Rothschilds of Frankfurt). But their direct contribution to industrial fixed capital was probably quite small. The banks that did lend to industry were the so-called Kreditbanken, the first of which was the Schaaffhausen'schen Bankverein in Cologne, which was founded in 1848. Subsequently, attempts to emulate the apparent success of the French Crédit Mobilier motivated growth in this type of bank after 1852, and their growth in the 1860s was quite rapid. By 1865 there were fourteen such Kreditbanken in north Germany, and they controlled more than 20 per cent of all joint-stock bank assets (Tilly, 1967, p. 164).

The antecedents of the unique character of late-nineteenth-century German banking can be found in these earlier institutions, but the passage of an act of general incorporation in 1870 led to tremendous growth in both the role and the concentration of universal or 'mixed' banks. These banks derived their name from their combination of investment banking – that is, underwriting – and commercial banking. Tilly (1986) argues that the German mixed banks evolved naturally from financial institutions that handled almost exclusively a small number of large state accounts into ones that handled large industrial accounts. German bankers guided (or even controlled) the finances of many major enterprises, in some cases involvong themselves explicity in capital projects, and in return demanded seats on the boards of the borrowing firms. They also required that these enterprises maintain relatively large compensating balances in the banks. Part of the aggressive behaviour of German banks resulted from the discounting policies of the Reichsbank, which were quite liberal and were not marked by rationing to the extent of those of other central banks – such as the Bank of France or the Austrian National Bank. This policy allowed German banks to 'lend to the hilt' without fear of liquidity constraints. The practices of German banks were also influenced by the technology of a number of major late-nineteenth-century industries (coal, steel and electrical power) which was such that their optimal scale was quite large, as were their financial requirements. These conditions led to consolidation, often through cartelization, in both product and financial markets.

The welfare implications of monopoly power embodied in the cartelization of German banking and other industries has led some to question the proposition that the structure of German banks contributed to long-run economic growth. Neuberger and Stokes (1974), for example, argue that because the banks came to dominate the firms to which they lent, the resulting allocative inefficiency produced an over-building of large-scale capital (and, of course, overly large commercial bank liabilities). This point is countered by Tilly (1986), who demonstrates that the portfolio of the German banking sector appears to have been relatively close to an efficient portfolio, in fact closer than the British banking sector, and Tilly (1967, 1986, and 1991b) is, on the whole, very positive about the role of German banking in this period, taking 'banking' in a very broad sense. Even when they served as merely discounters of bills of exchange prior to the emergence of the mixed banks, he argues, banks became heavily involved in shaping the capital markets. We should add that they certainly played a major role in providing information on the credit-worthiness of their customers to the general capital markets, whether they were directly involved in long-term capital projects or not. Once the great banks became involved in long-term capital finance, Tilly argues, their portfolios became specialized in certain risky ventures as they served their main customers – the large industrial enterprises; thus the relatively secure banks promoted industrialization and German economic growth by financing risky ventures and, in the process, reduced the overall risk of these activities.

Whether one disagrees with Tilly's arguments or not, these observations provide a clear explanation of why the German financial sophistication index moved so high after 1895, and we can summarize the role of the German banking sector in industrialization in four respects. First, the German banks emphasized investment banking in manufacturing to a greater degree than did banks in other countries. Second, German bankers provided a larger array of entrepreneurial services, such as structuring mergers and organizing cartels, than did others. Third, German banks placed senior executives on the boards of corporations in order both to control decisions and to obtain information. Finally, the size of both financial institutions and the firms they financed were large by international standards. By the twentieth century these characteristics of the German financial sector were similar to those of other countries, most notably the United States, France and even the United Kingdom.

Belgium

Following the Congress of Vienna, Belgium was unified with the Netherlands. In 1822, the unified states chartered the Société Générale de Belgique. This institution was the world's first joint-stock investment bank. Indeed, its charter gave it the ability to perform every major banking service: it could discount bills of exchange, issue notes, accept deposits, make loans (personal, industrial, and real estate), manage royal estates, and sell bonds to finance industrial investment. In short, the Société was the first great mixed bank, and potentially the most sophisticated financial institution in the world. We say *potentially*, because it was not until the following decade, after Belgian independence, that the Société really expanded into a powerful financial intermediary. Between 1835 and 1850 its portfolio of industrial loans grew from 3.8 to 54.8 million francs (Van der Wee and Goosens, 1991, p. 115). By the latter date there were three other joint-stock banks in Belgium: the Banque de Belgique, the Banque de Flandre, and the Banque Liégeoise. In the same year, 1850, the state chartered a central bank, the National Bank of Belgium, to handle state accounts, control the money supply and serve as a lender of last resort.

With the passage of a law of general incorporation in 1873, the number of banks grew rapidly. According to Cameron (1961, p. 138), the number of joint stock banks grew from 4 in 1850 to 21 in 1870 and 47 in 1875, and the per capita assets of those banks grew by a factor of five between 1850 and 1875. With respect to the growth of mixed banks in particular, Van der Wee and Goosens (1991, p. 115) claim that in 1870 six were of the mixed type, and by 1913 at least 30 of Belgium's 250–300 financial institutions could be considered to be mixed banks. These institutions focused on industrial development, at home and abroad, and were led by the Société Générale, which by 1879 held almost 50 per cent of its assets in the coal and metals industries (Van der Wee and Goosens, 1991, p. 119). As we saw in Chapter 3, Belgium was a leader in both industries.

In addition to its well-deserved reputation as a leader in industrial finance, Belgium had an assortment of other financial institutions that provided financial services to smaller-scale savers and borrowers. These included mortgage banks, savings banks and mutual credit societies. Table 4.3 shows the relative growth of the Belgium banking sector. Its assets expanded at one of the fastest rates in Europe during the period in question, and by 1913 only the Scandinavian countries had higher ratios of assets to national product. In short, Belgium had a relatively sophisticated banking system earlier than did many other countries, with a modern central bank at its head, a number of large mixed banks, and a diversified set of smaller institutions.

Netherlands

For a country that had been among the leaders of early modern finance, the Netherlands had a surprisingly undistinguished banking sector. Although much of the initial Belgian lead in banking came while the country was under Dutch rule, the Belgians managed to maintain their lead, and even by the end of the period the Dutch had not caught up. Except for Spain, the Netherlands had the lowest ratio of assets held by financial institutions to national product of any European country, and the growth of total assets was quite low as well (Table 4.3). Furthermore, there were only thirteen banks in the Netherlands in 1896 with a total capital of 7 million florins. At contemporary exchange rates that was less than one-thirteenth the value of Belgian bank capital (Muhleman, 1896, pp. 104, 115).

At mid-century, the Dutch financial system was dominated by the central bank, the Nederlandsche Bank, which was founded in 1814 along the lines of the Bank of England. In addition, there were a small number of elite private firms that handled government paper, and there were a larger number of general discount operations. According to Cameron (1961, p. 121), with the development of the Mobilier-type banks in France and neighbouring Belgium, it became clear to the Dutch commercial and political leadership 'that a major obstacle to the development of Dutch commerce and industry lay in its antiquated banking system'. It was not until 1863, however, that the state chartered four new 'Mobilier' banks, the first of which was the Nederlandsche Credit-en Deposito-Bank of Amsterdam. Despite the motivation behind its creation, the bank served primarily as financial intermediary between foreign lenders and foreign borrowers. Only its charter was Dutch. The most notable of these early banks was the

Algemeen Maatschappij voor Handel en Nijverheid. Although it was liquidated in 1868, in its first year of operation this bank created the Nederlandsch-Indische Handlesbank, the State Railway Operating Company, and the Netherlands-Indies Railway Company, each of which contributed in various ways to Dutch development. In addition to these investment banks, the Rotterdamsche Bank and the Amsterdamshe Bank handled commercial banking in those urban areas.

Austria-Hungary

The structure and performance of the banking sector in the Austro-Hungarian Empire has generated a great deal of debate since the 1970s. To understand the issues involved one must recall from Chapter 3 that during the nineteenth century in terms of output per capita, Austria-Hungary gained little on the United Kingdom and fell further behind Germany. The debate concerning the Austro-Hungarian banking sector revolves around the following issue: did banking practices contribute to the country's relative economic 'failure', or did they in fact prevent the situation from being worse than it was? While this issue can probably never be resolved in a way that would satisfy the participants in the debate, a review of the empire's banking sector and a comparison with other countries will at least illuminate the different views.

Modern banking in the Austro-Hungarian Empire began with the founding of the Austrian National Bank (1816), which was part of the reorganization of imperial finances following the Napoleonic Wars. The bank handled state accounts and possessed a monopoly of note issue, but it never served as a lender of last resort in the contemporary sense of the term (see Chapter 5). Indeed, throughout much of the nineteenth century it discounted high-grade bills for only a handful of the élite private Austrian banks (Rudolph, 1972, p. 34). These banks, in turn, lent almost exclusively to the state and the nobility, and while the latter often had industrial interests, in general the banks did little to promote industrialization.

This situation changed in the 1850s. Following the revolution of 1848, the state decided to accelerate its investment in railroad construction. Accordingly, it chartered three joint-stock credit institutions: the Niederösterreichische Escomptegesellschaft (1853), the Banca Commerciale Triestina (1854), and the Creditanstalt fur Handel and Gewerbe (1855). The first two were traditional merchant or commercial banks, specializing in short-term credit on trade. The esteemed Creditanstalt was Austria's first mixed bank, performing the traditional discounting services while also serving as a 'Mobilier' investment bank. By 1883 there were thirteen such banks in the empire. Between the founding of the Creditanstalt and the

Crash of 1873 more than a thousand non-financial joint-stock companies were chartered, and the investment banks played an important role in providing short-term credit, long-term capital financing, and in some cases outright ownership of the new industrial ventures. Few of these firms survived beyond 1873, however, and only 43 new firms were chartered between 1873 and 1880; indeed, between 1880 and 1900 only 123 new joint-stock firms were created. Over the following decade, however, the net growth of new firms nearly tripled, from an average of roughly six a year before 1900 to eighteen a year in the subsequent decade. Still, for a comparison of the expansion of new enterprises, consider that by 1907 Germany had eight times as many joint-stock companies as had the Austro-Hungarian Empire (Rudolph, 1972, pp. 39–41). For another comparison, note from Table 4.3 that the Austro-Hungarian ratio of assets held by financial institutions to national product was quite low, though it grew rapidly during the last three decades of the period. In short, the empire's banking sector was underdeveloped relative to its closest neighbour, though at least in some respects it was catching up with Germany.

The relatively small role the banking sector played in promoting Austro-Hungarian industrialization has been attributed to various factors. Among these, we consider four: the preferences of savers, the role of foreign capital, the portfolio decisions of lenders, and imperial tax laws.[5] The first of these can be dispensed with relatively easily. There is no reason to believe that domestic savers should have been any more risk averse than those in other similarly situated countries. Besides, if (risk-averse) domestic lenders refused to lend to industry, then (risk-taking) foreign investors would have provided an important ingredient in the empire's economic development. Furthermore, foreign investment *per se* is neither good nor bad and, in fact, the emerging economic power of the day, the United States, relied heavily on foreign capital. With respect to the composition of the banking sector's portfolio, it was relatively heavily weighted with mortgage loans, but as Komlos argues, these supported the agricultural boom – primarily in Hungary – which itself contributed importantly to the empire's economic development. In fact, if anything inhibited the role of the empire's banks in its industrialization, it was the restrictive laws concerning incorporation. As late as 1903–4 the empire's tax laws were structured in such a way that incorporated firms paid two to four times the amount of taxes that identical private firms would have paid (Rudolph, 1972, p. 40).

Given the performance of the Austro-Hungarian banking sector between 1855 and 1873, and again in the decade before the First World War, it is difficult to maintain the proposition that it 'failed' in some absolute sense. Although its central bank served neither as a lender of last resort nor as a promoter of economic growth, the investment, commercial and mortgage banks of the empire were modern and, by most accounts, competent financial intermediaries, though the banks did often have to turn to foreigners for bank capital (Trebilcock, 1981). The problem, then, lies in the extent of financial intermediation rather in than the performance of the institutions that existed. While some authors have argued that the preferences of Austrian lenders or foreign ownership of several of the more important of these institutions hindered the empire's economic development, as we noted above, the attraction of foreign capital during the early stages of industrialization has often been a positive rather than a negative influence on growth. We conclude that the relatively low level of per capita real output in the empire could not generate the surpluses required to support a robust financial sector, and indeed probably resulted in the relatively large role of foreign capital in the banking sector. In addition, misguided state policies on incorporation and taxation led to the small role that financial intermediation played in the empire's industrialization.

Scandinavia

The extent of Sweden's financial sophistication in the mid to late nineteenth century has been debated in the literature. Sandberg (1979) has labelled Sweden the 'impoverished sophisticate', by which he means a poor (in terms of per capita output) country, but one with a literate society and advanced financial intermediation. Kindleberger (1982) challenges this view, arguing that Sweden was not financially sophisticated at mid-century. The data shown in Tables 4.2 and 4.3 indicate that by 1850 Sweden was not financially sophisticated relative to other European countries, but that by 1913 it had caught up with the rest of Europe. Furthermore, Sweden did have in place a financial system that featured most of the technology of modern banking of the time, although it was concentrated geographically, and possibly not very impressive when judged in per capita terms. As Nygren (1983, p. 45) puts it:

> the Swedish commercial banking system prior to the middle of the nineteenth century was notable for solidity and profitability, but it did lack liquidity ... Deposits were negligible ... the 1850s were the first decade to feature banking innovations and structural changes of significance for the future.

Indeed, the impression we get from Nygren's work is that a significant contribution from bank development is more obvious from the 1870s onwards than from the 1850s. We saw this, really, after 1866 in Table 4.2. In addition, while the growth of assets held by Swedish financial institutions was unremarkable during the latter half of the century, of the non-Scandinavian countries, only Belgium had a higher ratio of assets to national product than Sweden in Table 4.3.

In the 1830s, private (*enskilda*) banks, began to issue currency and these issues grew to 43.2 per cent of the total note issue by 1859. These banks were not limited liability joint-stock companies; they were also inhibited by regulation of the interest rates they could charge and their deposit business was small. In 1863 the Bank Reform Act established private banking on the joint-stock principle and permitted banks to lend at market interest rates. In return, however, the *enskilda* had to choose between limited liability or note issue. While a number of banks continued to issue notes, others turned to deposit banking, and eventually the central bank (the Sveriges Riksbank, chartered in 1656) acquired a monopoly of the note issue (1897–1903, see Chapter 5). In 1864, the year after the Bank Reform Act was passed, there were 24 unlimited liability or note-issuing banks and 4 limited joint-stock banks. A decade later there were 27 note-issuing and 8 limited liability banks; by 1895 there were 45 banks of both types; and by 1908 there were 83. Because of the act granting a monopoly of note issue to the Riksbank (beginning in 1897), all *new* banks were limited liability banks. In addition to these institutions, there were 300 savings banks, more than 40 mortgage companies and numerous other financial institutions. Altogether, these smaller institutions held more than half of the assets of the Swedish financial sector until the 1890s (Lundström, 1991, p. 178).

By most empirical measures Denmark and Norway were moderately financially sophisticated by 1870 and became increasingly so over the following forty years (Table 4.2). By 1900 these two countries had the highest ratios of assets held by financial institutions to national product of any European country (Table 4.3). Besides their national banks (see Chapter 5), Norway had 36 incorporated banks in 1896 (Muhleman, 1896, p. 113) and a single large mortgage bank; and Denmark had 18 banks in 1870, 40 in 1896, and 140 in 1913/14.

The Danish central bank, the Nationalbank, was founded in 1818 and possessed the note-issuing monopoly (see Chapter 5). According to Hansen (1982, p. 577), it was the *only* bank in Denmark until 1846, though he defines 'banks' fairly narrowly, because elsewhere he notes that 'The first Danish savings banks were founded in 1810, and by 1830 there were already 30 such institutions' (p. 582). By the 1850s these banks furnished 35–45 per cent of Danish lending. Even after the establishment of other financial institutions, however, the bulk of lending went towards financing agriculture and trade. The demands of the former were met primarily by savings banks and credit associations, and those of the latter were handled by a small number of large banks. Indeed, late in the century three banks held roughly half the balances in the Danish financial system (Johansen, 1991, pp. 166–7): the Privat bank, a mixed bank founded in 1857; the Landsmanbank, also a mixed bank founded in 1872, which had a traditional commercial division and a rural mortgage division; and the Handelsbank, a merchant bank founded in 1873.

From the 1870s the Danish financial sector grew quite rapidly, both in absolute size (Table 4.3) and in its relative importance to the Danish economy. These developments resulted from two factors. First, the long-run decline in world grain prices led to a shift in Danish agriculture to livestock and related products, and the modernization of agricultural production accompanied this shift. To a large extent, these changes were financed by Danish lenders. The second factor affecting Danish financial growth was the emergence of the three banks mentioned above as important financial intermediaries. Hansen (1982, pp. 586–7) argues that, like the German Grossbanken, the Privatbank provided a broad range of financial services, including entrepreneurship, underwriting, discounting, management and aid in cartelization, though the Privatbank performed the first two functions to a lesser degree than did its German counterparts. Thus, by most measures, the Danish banking sector was well developed by the end of the nineteenth century.

The Norwegian central bank, the Norges Bank, was founded in 1816 (1817 according to Bloomfield (1959)). It held the note-issuing monopoly from the outset, and it also provided commercial credit. Because of the dominance of primary industries in Norway's economy, for example, fishing, timber, mining and agriculture, the assets of the Norges Bank were dominated by mortgage loans. Egge notes that as late as 1850 the mortgage share of 'outstanding claims' was 'almost 80 per cent' (Egge, 1983, p. 274). By that time there were also a number of private discount houses and 90 savings banks. In addition, the government created 'Discount Commissions' which loaned state funds directly to the private sector. The government's share of total financial assets declined from more than 40 per cent in 1850 to less than 20 per cent by the end of the century (Egge, 1983, p. 277).

Much like Denmark, there was a fundamental change in the Norwegian financial sector around 1850. Two years earlier the first commercial bank had been opened, and in 1851 the government founded the Kongeriket Norges Hypotekbank, which served as a government-owned mortgage bank. The assumption of the mortgage business by the Hypotekbank freed the Norges Bank to assume other lending activities, and by 1895 its 'advances against real property had fallen to 16.3 per cent of the Bank's total lending' (Egge, 1983, p. 278). In addition, between 1850 and 1895 the value of assets held by Norwegian financial institutions increased by a factor of eight. While the growth experienced by the Norwegian financial sector was rapid relative to much of the rest of Europe, Norway's financial growth (and, as we saw in Chapter 3, its economic growth) was slower than either Sweden's or Denmark's. Egge argues that the Norway's geography played a large role in this outcome. Specifically, its capital markets were poorly integrated, due at least partly to the sheer cost of dealing between locations, and its economy was based on sea and forest resources and was poorly suited to take advantage of the sweeping economic changes of the time.

Italy

Prior to the unification of Italy, each of the major constituent states of the country had a central bank of issue; indeed, some had other banks of issue and there were numerous discount houses and other lending institutions. After unification there were five banks of issue in Italy, and a sixth was added when the Papal States joined the Union in 1870.[6] This number was subsequently reduced to three with the formation of a central bank in 1894 (see below). After unification there were 3 non-note-issuing joint-stock banks, which grew to 13 in the following five years. Most of these were started with foreign capital. Among the most notable of these were the Credito Mobiliare and the Credito Italiano, both of which were started with French funds; the latter was eventually taken over by the former. In 1871 came the Banca Generale, which was partly financed with German capital. These 'Mobilier'-type banks did not lend directly to Italian manufacturing industries, but invested primarily in railways, canals and state securities. Both the Credito Mobiliare and the Banca Generale failed in the crisis of 1893. They were replaced by two German (and Swiss) financed and managed institutions, the Banca Commerciale and a new Credito Italiano. These firms operated along the lines of the great German mixed banks described above, and a similar debate concerning their effect on industrialization and Italian economic growth has ensued (Frederico and Toniolo, 1991).

Including the major institutions mentioned above, in 1880–84 there were 115 commercial and industrial banks that performed the roles of discounting and underwriting; 190 savings banks that were restricted in the amount of commercial and underwriting they could perform, and 217 co-operative or mutual lending institutions. By 1910–14, these had grown in number to 126, 186 and 377 respectively. Their assets grew even more rapidly, from 12 billion lire in 1880 to 40 billion lire in 1910–14.[7]

Despite being a charter member of the Latin Monetary Union, Italian banks were unable to maintain convertibility during the 1860s and 1870s. Italy was on the gold standard from 1884–93, but the crisis of 1893–4 resulted in suspension, and it was not until 1902 that the country returned to gold. It was no coincidence that the Bank of Italy was founded during the crisis of 1893–4. In 1893 the Banca Romana failed and the precarious shape of the financial system in general caused the Italian Parliament to consolidate the Banca Nazionale del Regno, Banca Nazionale Toscana, Banca Toscana di Credito e d'Industria, and the Banca Romana to form the Banca d'Italia (1894). According to Cohen (1972), the Bank of Italy was an effective central bank from its inception, providing day-to-day credit for the other joint-stock banks and responding to subsequent crises by direct lending or by creating consortia to provide liquidity. These policies allowed the leading commercial and investment banks to follow the German practice of 'lending to the hilt'. Commercial and industrial assets nearly doubled between 1900 and 1913.

In the two decades following unification, Italy had, with the exception of Spain and the Balkan states, the most backward financial sector in Europe. After 1900, however, Italy's banking sector grew faster than that of any other European country, at least as measured by financial assets – and narrative evidence provided by Cohen and others supports this conclusion. In addition, whereas in 1880 Italy's share of financial assets to national product was the second lowest in Europe (again, Spain had the lowest ratio), and less than half that of Britain and Germany, by 1913 it had almost caught up with both of the latter (Table 4.3).

We may conclude by comparing the Italian banking system with that in Austria-Hungary. Despite many similarities, the evolution of Italy's financial sector differed from the empire's for three reasons. First, the Italian government did not impose confiscatory taxes on corporations relative to private firms. Second, the German-style entrepreneurship displayed in the control of the major Italian investment banks was more effective than in Austria. Finally, the Italian central bank was a much more effective lender of last resort than was the Austrian National Bank. So while the transaction costs associated with unification and the persistence of a large, near-subsistence agricultural region hindered Italy's financial and economic development, during the first decade of the twentieth century the country was clearly catching up with the rest of the Europe with respect to its financial sector.

Spain

As we saw in the previous chapter, Spain had the slowest growth of per capita output of any European country throughout the period in question. In addition, by all the measures we employed, it was the least industrialized. It might not be surprising, then, to find that Spain also had an underdeveloped banking sector as well – at least by European standards – though at this point we shall not speculate on the direction of causality between these factors. In any case, Spain's banking sector was small and not particularly effective at promoting industrial development. For example, it had the lowest ratio of assets held by financial institutions to national product in Europe (Table 4.3) and, perhaps more importantly, the growth of assets was the slowest in Europe as well. So, as with its major industries, the Spanish financial sector was falling behind much of the rest of Europe.

This was partly a result of very strict laws of incorporation. In 1848 a law was passed that required government approval of all incorporations. According to Tortella (1972, p. 95), the process to obtain a charter was 'very long'. In a series of acts in the 1850s these laws were relaxed somewhat for banks, mines and railways. This preferential treatment led to a disproportionate amount of bank assets being concentrated in mining and railways, the latter in particular. Because the demand for transportation services failed to grow as rapidly as the transportation sector over the following decade, the railways defaulted on their bonds in 1866, and as a result more than a third of the joint-stock banks went out of business in the following year (Tortella, 1972, p. 93). Indeed, bank capital declined steadily until 1874, which, as we shall see, was a crucial year in the history of Spanish banking.

The key to the Spanish banking system was the Bank of Spain (founded in 1829), which served as a central bank in the nineteenth-century sense of the term, but not in the modern sense (see Chapter 5). As late as 1843 it was the only joint-stock financial institution in the country! The liberalization of Spanish policy during the 1850s and 1860s led to tremendous growth in the banking sector. For example, including the Bank of Spain, there were three banks of issue and one other credit company in the whole of Spain in 1850. After the decline caused by the crash of 1866, the number of banks began to rise again, and by 1873 there were 16 banks of issue and 17 other joint-stock credit institutions (Tortella, 1972, p. 93). In the following year the Bank of Spain was granted the note-issuing monopoly in return for loans to the government, and 11 other note-issuing banks merged with the Bank of Spain. In Tortella's (1972, 1977) view this move was a disaster for Spanish economic development, as it led to a concentration of financial control in the hands of an institution that was a tool of the state (which itself apparently had little interest in promoting growth). Consider that as late as 1900 the Bank of Spain claimed more than two-thirds of the assets held in Spanish financial institutions (Anes, 1974), and at the same time the ratio of the bank's public-to-private assets was four to one (Trebilcock, 1981, p. 370).

Much like Austria-Hungary and Italy, the causes of the relatively dismal performance of the banking sector fall into three categories: low levels of demand for industrial credit, foreign control of capital, and government policy. As we noted in the sections dealing with Austria-Hungary and Italy, foreign capital *per se* does not retard economic growth, and indeed compared to a situation with no investment funds, foreign capital must be expected to contribute to growth. We also mentioned above that identifying a causal relationship between the supply and demand of loanable funds is in practice a very tricky exercise. Government policies, on the other hand, can clearly have a negative effect on the financial intermediation between savers and industrial firms by raising the transaction costs of financial intermediation and by crowding out private investment. In Spain, laws against incorporation and heavy borrowing by the state that ended up on the books of the Spanish banks impeded the financial sector's support for private industry. Again, government borrowing in and of itself is not necessarily good or bad, and could even be very important for a relatively backward country like Spain, but in Spain the loans were used to secure internal political control, protect an antiquated empire and over-invest in railways. As a result of these policies, the Spanish banking sector contributed little to the small amount of economic development that did occur during this period.

Portugal

Portugal's banking system was dominated by its central bank, the Bank of Portugal, founded in 1822. As we shall see in the next chapter, the Bank of Portugal was a central bank only in the sense that it handled the government's accounts. While it could exert some control over the money supply because of its size, there is no evidence that it served as a lender of last resort. Although in 1896 there were 7 banks of issue other than the Bank of Portugal, and 30 other non-issuing banks as well, the Bank of Portugal's capital was almost twice that of all other banks combined (Muhleman, 1896, pp. 119–20). Compare this to a country such as Sweden, where the ratio was almost exactly reversed (Muhleman, 1896, p. 112) or even Austria-Hungary, where the capital of other banks was six times that of the central bank, and one sees the potential effect of concentrating credit in one government-controlled institution. Interestingly, the Bank of Portugal maintained a relatively large share of its assets in loans, though these were probably state loans, perhaps further supporting the point just made.

4.4 MONETARY NEUTRALITY

In this section we propose to conduct three tests of the data utilized in earlier parts of this chapter, using the Granger-causality test. The narrative accounts of the rise of modern banking in each of these countries, which we presented in the previous section, correspond with the growth of money and financial sophistication in these countries. What we are interested in is the role of money (and financial sophistication) in these economies, by which we mean the influence of money (and financial sophistication) on real income and/or prices. The quantity theory of money, if it is correct, implies that changes in the quantity of money, *ceteris paribus*, drive price levels but in the long run not real income – that is, the quantity theory suggests monetary neutrality in the long run. It follows that real income is determined by real factors, by spending and saving decisions, while the role of money is to set the level of money prices. The *ceteris paribus* condition, of course, warns us that when output or velocity is changing, the relationship would not hold.

We have already seen that money growth rates – which are strongly positive for these countries – are not similar to inflation rates, which fluctuate around zero for most of these countries. We have also seen that velocity, in the form of the financial sophistication index, is definitely not constant in this period, but declining, as money growth rates exceed the rate of growth of the economy. What appears to be going on is that these economies, with the exception of the United Kingdom (which probably experienced the phenomenon earlier), are 'monetizing'. By this we mean that real banking resources are being produced at an especially rapid rate, so that actual changes in the money stock are dominated by increases in the demand for banking (and monetary) services.

Utilizing the equation of exchange, $MV = Py$, we see that the price level is driven by V, M and y. Since inflation rates are zero, more or less, for these countries, it is apparent that changes in V and y have, in effect, neutralized the effect of the rapidly-growing money stocks on prices. One would therefore not expect to obtain much success for a causality test of money on prices in this period. As we shall see, this was the case. We should note at this point, however, that there is more to the relationship between money, prices and income than the results given in this chapter, as will be discussed in Chapters 5 to 7.

We are in this chapter interested mainly in how the financial sectors of these economies grew, and what the macroeconomic effects of that growth were. In this section, this interest translates into questions about whether money, or the financial sophistication index, drive – or are driven by – real income. If, for example, the financial sophistication index drives real income, then an important determinant of the latter is revealed. This result would establish a connection that highlights the growing similarity of these economies and the role that increasingly similar banking systems played in that result. If real income drives financial sophistication, we are still talking about growing similarity, since these countries all appeared to be approaching or exceeding the norm established by the United Kingdom for financial sophistication. In this case, however, what is driving the process is the convergence of real growth rates, itself driven by industrialization. We shall also offer some results for money and real income, but believe that little would be expected in that area, under circumstances to be explained in Chapters 5 to 7.[8]

Let us begin, though, with a brief review of the literature on these issues. In the literature, there are causality-style tests of monetary neutrality for several of the countries in our sample, as well as other kinds of test that bear on the same issues. Relying to some extent on the survey by Bordo (1986), we begin with the United Kingdom. For that country, Mills and Wood (1978), employing Sims' version of the Granger-causality test, find that output Granger-causes money in this period, but not the converse. Similarly, employing Granger-causality tests based on multivariate autoregressions, Dwyer (1983) and Mills and Wood (1978) finds that for the period 1870–1913 the money supply is demand-determined. In contrast, studying the UK cycle for 1833–1913 by methods similar to Dwyer's, Eichengreen (1983) finds real factors more important before 1880 and monetary factors after that year. He employed high-powered money in these tests. These results suggest, on balance, that monetary neutrality may hold in the United Kingdom, but that a closer examination of subperiods is clearly warranted.

For the United States, Brillembourg and Khan (1979), using Sims' test procedure, find no Granger-causal relation between money and output (although they do establish a contemporaneous one). For Sweden, similarly, Fisher and Thurman (1989), for a variety of financial instruments, find no Granger-causality running from nominal instruments to real income (but do find the converse). Results for Italy appear to conflict with these. Fratianni and Spinelli (1984), for example, argue that the monetary base Granger-causes real GNP, but not the converse, during a roughly comparable period.

A way to explore the interaction of money and price levels is to employ a test of Granger-causality to search for signs of one-way or bi-directional 'causation' among the nominal variables being considered. The test itself considers the distinct influence of lagged values of the independent variable (the proposed 'causal' variable) and so it is, strictly, a test of what is often called the 'temporal ordering' of the data. The procedure is to regress a variable in which we are interested – let us say British real income – on its own lags and on the lags of a potential 'causal' variable – say the British money supply. If the lags of the other variable add significantly to the explanation of the dependent variable, then it is said to Granger-cause that variable. The model used in this exercise is

$$\ln y_t = \alpha + \sum_{i=1}^{p} \beta_i \ln y_{t-i} + \sum_{i=1}^{p} \delta_i \ln x_{t-i} \qquad (4.1)$$

where p is the arbitrary length of the lag. This lag is assumed to be the same for each variable in these tests. The statistical test, an F-test, is used to see whether the exclusion of all of the x terms in Equation 4.1 would significantly reduce the explanatory power of the regression. Conventionally, we shall argue that Granger-causation is established if the probability that the proposed causal agent is not influential is 0.05 or less. Note that a more complete discussion of the properties of the model, and some important caveats, are discussed in the Technical Appendix to this study.

Before conducting these tests, though, we have to deal with a problem that arises because these data are dominated by trends. In particular, if the data contain unit roots in the levels, then, as an implication of having non-finite variances, certain test procedures would be invalid. The Granger-causality procedure is one such, and, since the data, in general, do contain unit roots, we must test for Granger causality in first difference form. The procedure for testing for a unit root, the Augmented Dickey–Fuller test, is explained in Chapter 5, where the results are also provided (for the monetary base). The results for the money stock series used in the present chapter appear in Chapter 6. Note that a full description of the unit root test procedure, along with some important caveats, also appears in the Technical Appendix.

In Table 4.4 we present a complete set of results – typical results, that is to say for the Granger-causality test for the influence of real income on financial sophistication. This is our main interest and, as well, the strongest set of results obtained by this test procedure. Again note that the data appear in growth rate form in these tests. The p-values in the table are the probability associated with rejecting the null hypothesis of no causation, at the 5 per cent level of significance. Thus there is only a 1 in 20 chance that the statement that Granger-causality is revealed is incorrect. Here we see that six of the eight cases show the influence of real income on financial sophistication, in the sense that the former occurred, systematically, before the latter. Again, this result is expected, since it is probable that growth and industrialization spurred the development of financial services.

Table 4.4 The Granger-causal influence of real income on financial sophistication

Country	\multicolumn{5}{c}{p-value for lags of}				
	1	*2*	*3*	*4*	*5*
Denmark	0.58	0.36	0.70	0.03*	0.13
France	0.00*	0.00*	0.00*	0.05*	0.03*
Germany	0.00*	0.04*	0.07	0.21	0.25
Italy	0.00*	0.00*	0.00*	0.00*	0.01*
Norway	0.22	0.36	0.33	0.33	0.43
Sweden	0.94	0.87	0.91	0.98	0.97
UK	0.00*	0.02*	0.00*	0.01*	0.03*
USA	0.05*	0.08	0.08	0.10	0.33

Notes: * A p-value of 0.05 or less indicates significant Granger-causality.

When we test for the Granger-causal influence of financial sophistication on real income, there are in fact five cases, including four of the above, in which this occurs significantly. These are for the following countries: Denmark; France; Sweden; the United Kingdom; and the United States.

It is a little odd that the test shows Granger-causality running both ways, but in fact, since it occurs at different lags in general, this is probably not a problem. In any case, because it is a diagnostic test, we do not know which direction is the stronger. We can conclude, then, that there is a link between financial sophistication and real growth in seven of these eight countries.[9] This result, indeed, supports what we have been saying in this chapter, without taking a stand on the causal direction.

We expect poor results between money growth and inflation in this period, partly because of the fact that inflation and money growth had two distinctly different trends in all these countries. The results for direct Granger-causality between money and prices show that only for Italy, the United Kingdom and the United States does money Granger-causes prices.[10] We believe this is not damaging to the quantity theory of money in this period, although one might have expected all countries to show this result in a gold standard world. Finally, we note that there is, in any case, a significant breakdown of neutrality in three of these countries. That is, in the following countries, money Granger causes real income: Denmark; Germany; and Italy.

In our review of the literature already reported on, we noted that Fratianni and Spinelli obtained this result for Italy. For Germany, something like this is also reported in Fisher (1992). Denmark is a new result. This test is not a particularly powerful one, nor is it a strong refutation, but it is certainly clear that simple-minded notions of the relationship between money and the economy, even under the aegis of the gold standard, are inadequate.

4.5 CONCLUSIONS

We began this chapter with a discussion of the definition and potential role of financial sophistication in economic development. Our measure of financial sophistication in fact indicates the extent to which economic activity in a country is monetized. Clearly, the financial sophistication of a country is determined to a large extent by the institutional structure of its banking sector. Over time, as the banking sectors of the European economies converged towards a universal or mixed system, the financial sophistication indices converged as well. Moreover, financial sophistication can either be a cause of, or itself be caused by, real economic growth, and our empirical results show that, in fact, a case can be made for both outcomes during the period in question. Only one country (Norway) did not experience any significant 'causal' relationship between financial sophistication and real output.

With respect to the banking sectors of the European countries, three general statements can be made. First, at the beginning of the period, the extent and types of banks and banking services offered varied greatly from country to country. Although the United Kingdom had the largest and most sophisticated money market in the world in 1850, it lagged behind several continental countries in the development of joint-stock investment banks and mixed or universal banks. Second, by the end of the period, every country had a mixed banking system, even though the means by which the various banking activities were carried out still differed among countries. Finally, the path to this convergence varied across countries as well. While the British led the way in discounting bills, the Belgians and French pioneered the joint-stock investment bank, and the Germans and Austrians developed the universal bank.

Finally, it would seem that the general neutrality of money is pretty firmly established, particularly as the nineteenth century ended and Europe moved into a more closely integrated international economy. Real causes dominated financial causes in the determination of fluctuations in real output, and, as we shall see in subsequent chapters, in this economy, business cycles were increasingly similar across nations. Of course, the overall conclusions one might draw at this point have to be stated as conditional on the state of the data, on the arbitrary choice of time period and on the choice of the Granger-causality test for testing neutrality. Even so, we believe the results are strong enough and pervasive enough to warrant such conclusions.

5 Central Banking before 1914

5.1 INTRODUCTION

In this chapter we address questions relating to the evolution of central banks during the period 1850–1913. While the operation of the gold standard gets the most attention in the literature, there was considerably more to central bank behaviour than merely adhering to the gold standard. As we show below, the monetary authorities of individual countries sometimes pursued what might be characterized as domestic monetary objectives from time to time. They also supervised their domestic banking systems, at least in some cases. It will be the main task of this chapter to discuss the institutional details of the financial sectors of the major European economies, keeping one eye on the operation of the gold standard (or its failure to operate as designed) and one eye on the evolving nature of central banking itself.

In addition to the discussion of the changing institutional structure in which central banks operated, we include a series of correlation, Granger-causality and cointegration tests on the high-powered money stocks (the monetary bases) of the countries for which we have such data. What we find is that, the gold standard notwithstanding, high-powered money stocks are not integrated closely across countries. The objective here is to try to get a statistical measure of central bank interaction during the period in which most of the countries in our sample were, at least nominally, on the gold standard. The material in this chapter adds to an extensive literature that has most often concerned itself with the details of changes in central bank balance sheets. That literature is relevant and will be addressed briefly in this chapter, but the statistical tests provided here are designed to explore matters of integration in a (non-structural) way that can shed additional light on questions surrounding the actual operation of the international central-banking community.

Historically, central or national banks were created to handle the accounts of the states that chartered them. Over time, the role of European central banks evolved, and they came to undertake their modern tasks of controlling the money supply and serving as lender of last resort. Many of the changes occurred in the nineteenth century. With respect to controlling the money supply, three considerations define their operations in the period covered by this study. One is the acquisition of a monopoly of note issue; another is the restraint imposed by the gold standard (in maintaining convertibility), and a third is any legislated constraints on note issue, such as reserve requirements.

As for serving as a lender of last resort, before a nineteenth-century central bank could perform such a role its directors had to reconcile this function with the fact that they were, in most cases, directors of a privately-owned institution with a public role.

With respect to the note issue, the simple fact is that during this period most banks either had a monopoly of the note issue or were in the process of acquiring it. There has been considerably more discussion of whether central banks played by the 'rules of the game' of the gold standard, an issue which affects both roles of a central bank. A set of rules is defined by Bloomfield (1959) in terms of whether central bank liabilities were adjusted to permit the domestic price level to stay in line with world prices. In this scheme, central bank policies (foreign exchange transactions, open market operations and discount rate changes) would be judged in terms of whether they reinforced the effects of gold flows on domestic money supplies (played by the rules) or counteracted them (broke the rules) (Dutton, 1984).[1] In fact, the cost of playing by the rules would be to limit the central bank's ability either to regulate the money supply or to serve as a lender of last resort.

In this chapter we have set ourselves the task of explaining how European central banks operated their (macroeconomic) policies. Our only statistical tests here involve the analysis of the behaviour of high-powered money stocks across nations. This exercise establishes no firm connections across countries. In other words, our evidence is consistent with a world in which countries were not playing by the rules of the gold standard in this period. We do not, however, draw this conclusion, although we shall not complete our argument in the present chapter. In Chapter 6, for example, we look at how prices and money stocks interacted in this period, dividing the overall period in order to highlight the influence of the gold standard. The results there show that money stocks also are not integrated across countries, but that price levels are. Returning to the present chapter, then, our theoretical work here contains a model (that of Barro (1979)) that explains how these elements are reconciled in a gold-standard world. In this model, price levels are determined by gold stocks, the domestic demand for money and the institutional structure of the financial system. This model leaves out consideration of exactly *how* international prices were brought into line; we think it was through a process explained by the 'monetary approach' to the balance of payments, which we discuss further in Chapters 6 and 7.

5.2 CENTRAL BANKING, 1850–1913

In this section we undertake a country-by-country survey of the institutional structure of European central banks in this period. Our survey covers quite a few countries, so we have taken some steps to condense our material, without losing the institutional flavour. Here we focus on the performance of the two roles of a central bank noted above, with particular attention paid to the first appearance of a central bank's execution of those roles. We develop the important theme that during this period central banking practices evolved to the extent that by the end of the period there is clearly convergence in the structure and operation of European central banking.

United Kingdom[2]

Because the international financial system in this period is dominated by the United Kingdom, a discussion of that country will help to establish the nature of the system and how it operated. First, we need to recall that the Bank of England – established in 1694 to help finance the war with France – was a wholly private bank with public responsibilities. From 1742, the Bank of England enjoyed a monopoly of the note issue over all except private banks with six partners or less (Kindleberger, 1993, p. 78). After 1772 only the so-called 'country banks' continued the practice, and even this was prohibited after the Bank Act of 1844 (Dowd, 1989, p. 5). Throughout the banking system, the liabilities of the Bank of England were the principle reserve of the other banks. This fact meant that even though the Bank of England did not have a monopoly of the note issue, it had considerable control of the money supply. Furthermore, the bank often operated as the lender of last resort in order to protect its own interests, if for no other reason, since in a general crisis other banks would try to redeem Bank of England liabilities for specie.

Still, the United Kingdom's currency supply was relatively inflexible, partly on account of the restrictions of the Bank Charter Act of 1844, which divided the Bank of England into two departments: an Issue Department and a Banking Department. Following the arguments of the currency school, which greatly influenced the Cabinet at that time, the Issue Department maintained a 100 per cent reserve against all notes above a small initial volume backed by government securities. These restrictions contributed at least partly to liquidity crises – and bank failures – in 1847, 1857 and 1866. Beginning with the Crisis of 1857 – that is, for most of the period we are looking at – the Bank of England operated effectively as a central bank. By suspending the note restrictions in the 1844 Act, it controlled the money supply and used both lender of last resort functions and discount rate policy, but always with one eye on its profits. The discount rate policy was used primarily to produce a quick increase in the gold reserves of the bank (drawing from domestic and foreign sources), but this policy did have a tendency to undermine bank profits and so was not employed in a routine fashion.³ With respect to this last point, Hinderliter and Rockoff (1976) note that the bank consistently maintained a level of gold reserves that, while consistent with its profitability, undermined its ability to serve as a lender of last resort, an issue to which we now turn.

Of course, all the above must be considered in the light of Britain's commitment to the gold standard. Bloomfield does not give high marks to the Bank of England for its adherence to the gold standard rules. Studies of interest rate policy by Dutton (1984) and Goodhart (1972) suggest pretty strongly that Bank responses were stabilizing. With regard to Bank of England portfolio adjustments, however, Goodhart, Dutton, and Pippenger all argue that these responses were in fact procyclical. For example, Goodhart (1984, p. 223) takes the position that the Bank 'accommodated the demand for cash by buying more securities at times when the reserves were low and interest rates were high'. Presumably, this suggests that they were following the domestic objective of trying to smooth nominal interest rates. Pippenger (1984, p. 209) suggests that 'The Bank systematically reduced liquidity in order to earn income.' This last view reflects a continuing suspicion that the bank's private ownership influenced its decisions – which is certainly likely – at the cost of policy effectiveness. Of course, the interest-rate stabilizing policy detailed by Goodhart could produce the higher profits noted by Pippenger.

Much debate revolves around the use of the term 'lender of last resort' when it is applied to nineteenth-century central banks. In particular, Ziegler (1992) attacks Collins' (1989) claim that the Bank of England consciously played such a role during the banking crisis of 1878.⁴ In question are two issues pertaining to nineteenth-century central banking, which, although not unrelated, differed to varying degrees among the European central banks. Because each central bank faced these same issues, we explore them here to avoid repetition below. The first issue revolves around how a central bank meets the credit needs of the banking system. For example, the central bank could stand ready to meet the day-to-day borrowing needs of the banking system, which would include a broad array (in terms of size, location and function) of financial institutions. On the other hand, the central bank could deal on a daily basis with only a relatively few banks (usually large commercial banks, located in the financial centre) but stand ready to meet the borrowing needs of the banking system during a crisis, either directly or through the creation of loan-granting consortia. The second issue revolves around the central bank's willingness to announce its intentions explicitly and to make them formally part of its policy. In *Lombard Street*, Walter Bagehot excoriated the bank for its failure to declare that it would serve as a lender of last resort *ex ante*, so that rather than ameliorating crises on a case-by-case basis, such crises could be averted.

With respect to the operations of the Bank of England during this era, Ziegler points out that the bank did not serve as a lender of last resort in the modern sense, because it failed to adopt explicity the doctrine that it would always provide liquidity to the banking system (the second issue above). Even so, when we, like Collins, refer to a nineteenth-century European central bank behaving as a lender of last resort, we usually mean taking actions in specific episodes. Most central banks at that time were private banks and thus could not unambiguously declare their intention to bail out the financial system during every subsequent crisis. By this standard we find that most European central banks at one time or another behaved as a lender of last resort, at least by the end of the period in question.

One way to appreciate the extent of Bank of England domestic policy operations is to document their best-known stabilizing operations. In 1857 and 1858, for example, there was a recession (see Chapter 9) that quite possibly began with a financial crisis that erupted in October 1857 in the United States and spread to British firms with substantial interests in American markets. Apparently, the bank of England almost exhausted its reserves as it expanded its lending, with the consequence that the defined limits on the bank's note issue embodied in the Bank Charter Act of 1844 had to be suspended. This example illustrates the bank's willingness to provide, under duress, an 'elastic currency' in the presence of a liquidity crisis.[5]

The next financial panic occurred in 1866 upon the failure of the prominent brokerage firm of Overend, Gurney (on 10 May). The bank refused credit to the firm, because of the latter's lack of security. Other firms, many of which held Overend's liabilities, panicked, and Black Friday (11 May) ensued in which there was an enormous general sell-off of securities. In this case, the government acted immediately to suspend the note restrictions of the Bank Charter Act (on the same day, in fact) so that while there were some business failures, quite possibly not as a direct result of the financial disruption, the overall disturbance was relatively slight. Indeed, in Chapter 9, we do not locate a recession at this time.

Finally, in November 1890, another crisis resulted when the Barings Brothers investment firm came close to collapse. Barings was heavily involved in the underwriting of Argentinian loans, and, for reasons still debated in the literature (see Kindleberger, 1989, p. 121), other European houses had been refusing Argentinian assets for two years. In order to support their client, Barings resorted to direct loans, but in 1890, when the wheat crop failed and a coup produced a new regime in Buenos Aires, Argentina defaulted. In this case, the Bank of England played a less dramatic role in that the Bank Charter Act was not suspended, but the Governor called a meeting of London banks and 'persuaded' – to borrow Dowd's (1989, p. 31) word – them to guarantee Barings' liabilities. In addition, the bank arranged for credit from the Russian State Bank and the Bank of France. (Note the presence of international co-operation among central banks.) Probably as a result, the disruption to the financial community was again slight, and there was no general panic or depression.

We can see, then, that during this period the Bank of England took on the role of a central bank in the modern sense of the term. Indeed, in the course of the nineteenth century the bank acquired the two roles typically associated with modern central banks – controlling the money supply and serving as the lender of last resort. As guardian of the money supply, its role was defined by the Bank Act of 1844, restricting future note issues by other institutions. It fulfilled the role of lender of last resort, partly to protect its own balance sheet, but when the government suspended the restrictions on the note issue during a financial crisis, the bank became responsible for meeting the increased demand for liquidity. In these activities the bank served as a model for other central banks, whose practices became increasingly similar to those in the United Kingdom.

France

As we noted in Chapter 4, the Bank of France began operations in February 1800. Like the Bank of England, the Bank of France was originally created to secure a loan to the government to finance military expenses. In addition to these public duties, the bank discounted bills of exchange. It had a national monopoly of banknote issue from 1803 to 1814, which was subsequently restricted to the Paris area until 1848, when it once again obtained the national monopoly of issue. (Note that this pattern followed roughly that of the Bank of England.) Although the government did not own any of the stock of the bank, its officers were appointed by the French head of state, and the bank handled state accounts.

After 1850, the Bank of France followed a generally conservative discount policy, creating, as in England, the opportunity for other private discount operations. Still, the bank expanded throughout the period, reaching 60 branches by 1870 and 411 by 1900. In general, however, because of its conservative policy and the recourse of French businessmen to other near-monies, the Bank of France seems to have played a lesser role than the Bank of England in regulating the money supply and mitigating financial panics during the nineteenth century, though by the end of the period the Bank of France had acted as a lender of last resort during certain episodes.

Central Banking before 1914

As just described, in all likelihood the French money stock was relatively inflexible in the face of cyclical and/or sudden changes in the demand for money. Its note issue, originally placed at 350 million francs, was raised only periodically, and by the end of the nineteenth century stood at 4 billion francs (Muhleman, 1896, p. 102). With reference to particular cycles, Marczewski (1988) argues that the inflexibility of the money supply was responsible for repeated episodes of 'stagflation' – meaning falling real output and a rising price level – in France; these were in 1853, 1859, 1870–1, 1900–2.[6] This stagflation presumably occurred because the money stock did not, in these periods, decline along with its demand. The opposite, presumably, happened frequently during expansions.

Turning to particular financial crises, as noted in Chapter 4, there was a severe downturn in 1848 that wiped out the newly-formed '*caisse*' style of commercial banks. The causes of the collapse were real, however, in that the failure of the wheat crop in that year followed two years of potato blight, and the uncertainty produced by the Revolution of the same year also contributed to the financial crisis. The failure of most of the other banks in France provided the Bank of France with the opportunity to consolidate its power and to secure its note-issuing monopoly. Thus we have an early example of the bank putting its private objectives before its public responsibilities, although this behaviour could be rationalized in terms of bringing order to a chaotic market.

In 1867, the much publicized Crédit Mobilier collapsed, because of its ill-advised venture into mortgage lending, but there was no ensuing financial distress and no strong pressure on the Bank of France, probably because the liabilities of the Crédit Mobilier were not primarily deposits. The Franco-Prussian War, the subsequent five-billion-franc indemnity, and war-induced depression in 1870–1 all put considerable strain on the French financial system. The bank's role during this period was mixed. It advanced the government almost a billion francs during the war, and loaned another 200 million francs to the city of Paris to pay a separate indemnity, and during the subsequent crisis the bank tried to circulate banknotes rather than coin in France. The bank adopted this policy only because it could not maintain convertibility because of the drain of specie to pay off the war indemnity.

Prior to the Franco-Prussian War neither France nor Germany was on the gold standard. The German states were primarily on silver, and France, as a founding member of the Latin Monetary Union of 1865, was bimetallic.[7] The reparations payments from France, however, eased the new German Reich's entry to the gold standard. When the Germans stopped coining silver, silver began to flow into France (and into other silver or bimetallic countries as well), at the same time that gold was flowing out to pay the war indemnity;

thus the French monetary system was subjected to inflationary pressures, which neither the government nor the Bank of France was willing to accept. As a result France limited its silver coinage in 1874 and suspended it in 1878. These events ended what Friedman (1990) argues was history's most successful bimetallic regime, one in which both metals circulated for decades. Ironically, this success may well be an indicator of France's relatively underdeveloped banking system, marked particularly by the lack of deposit banks, as the French money supply was the most heavily specie-driven of any major country. In any case, there were advantages to the abundance of gold, as in the claim by Hinderliter and Rockoff (1976) that the Bank of France's large specie reserve allowed it to perform the duties of a lender of last resort better than did the reserve-poor Bank of England.

From 1878 there was a financial boom that has been attributed by Levy-Leboyer and Bourguignon (1990) to rapid industrial growth, and by Trebilcock (1981) to ill-advised foreign loans. In any event, a financial collapse in 1882 weakened the Bank of France severely, and numerous (newly-created) banks failed. Under the circumstances, the bank found it impossible to loosen credit and maintain convertibility simultaneously. This situation was not unusual, of course, but the bank was itself heavily committed to discounts, and so it was severely restricted in its ability to act as a lender of last resort. In any case, succeeding downturns to 1913 do not seem to have had a strong financial component, which implies that the Bank of France probably was not exacerbating any distress experienced by the financial system, and certainly there is evidence that it often helped to smooth financial disturbances in other ways.

The Bank of France was founded more than a century after the Bank of England, and the Bank of France was the slower of the two to become an effective central bank by today's standards. Still the bank's evolution as a central bank during the nineteenth century was in some respects similar to that of the Bank of England. Both were created as private banks with public responsibilities, with all the conflicts inherent in such a creature; by mid-century, both essentially had a monopoly of the note issue (with rules that led to relatively inflexible note issue), and at times both served as a lender of last resort. While the Bank of England served quite early explicitly in that role, the Bank of France was doing so by the 1880s, at times putting together loans to aid the private banks; for instance, this happened with the Union Général in 1882, the Comptoir d'Escompte in 1888 and the Societé Dépôts in 1891. In addition, there is no evidence that its own profit-seeking behaviour worsened any stress placed on the system (Kindleberger, 1989, 1993). The bank's relative performance was no doubt related to the government's hostility towards deposit banking, the growth of which in Britain alleviated

Central Banking before 1914   107

the monetary restraints embodied in the acts regulating the Bank of England. In France, the similarly conservative policies of the Bank of France were not mitigated by other intermediaries to the same extent that they were in Britain.

Germany

Following the Seven Years' War, the Prussian government established the Königliche Giro- und Lehnbanco Royal Bank in 1765, which became the Royal Bank of Prussia. In 1846 this bank was reorganized as the Prussian Bank, which took over the assets and liabilities of the Royal Bank. Although the Prussian Bank was privately owned, the government exerted considerable control over its operation. At this time it did not possess a monopoly of note issue, though by 1865 the bank's note circulation dominated, reaching 40 per cent of the total.[8] In 1875, four years after unification, the Prussian Bank became the Reichsbank – like the Banks of England and France, a private bank with public duties. At that time, 33 other banks maintained the right of note issue; as they went out of business or surrendered that right, however, no new note-issuing banks were chartered.

With political unification came monetary unification as well, and in 1871 the new German Empire effectively went on the gold standard, defining the mark in terms of gold and thus converting the German states from silver to gold. Bloomfield (1959) claims that subsequently the Reichsbank did not play by the rules of the system, but, according to Sommariva and Tullio (1987, 1988), the evidence suggests that the German central bank did, in fact play by the rules.[9] On the other hand, McGouldrick (1984) argues that gold inflows were cyclically neutral in Germany and that base money (p. 321) 'grew at a remarkably stable pace over German business cycles'. Indeed, base money actually had a slightly countercyclical tendency. He argues that the Reichsbank stabilized gold inflows in this period by means of a bill discount rate policy. He concludes (p. 346):

> The contrasting relative stability of the monetary realm therefore stands as strong testimony to the advantages of the pre-1914 gold standard when properly ruled by a central bank.

In either case, Germany grew very rapidly during this period, with substantial export earnings. The Reichsbank was never threatened with suspension, and it is certainly hard to believe that the gold standard exerted any real pressure on the monetary authorities.

With the possible exceptions of the Bank of England, and on a smaller scale, the National Bank of Belgium, the Reichsbank came the closest of the nineteenth-century central banks to a modern central bank. At one time or another it used all the tools available to control the money supply and smooth economic activity. With respect to the money supply, although the Reichsbank did not have a monopoly of the note issue, by the end of the nineteenth century it issued roughly 90 per cent of German banknotes (Muhleman, 1896, p. 110). More importantly, Germany had a relatively flexible money supply because of the laws regulating the Reichsbank note issue. The bank's note issue was limited to three times the value of its specie reserve, with the provision that the value of uncovered notes must not exceed 250 million marks. When the bank wanted to exceed this limit, during a crisis for example, rather than requiring legislation or executive permission – as was required of the Bank of England – it could do so by paying a 5 per cent tax on the subsequent note issue.

In addition to issuing notes, the Reichsbank, like any large financial institution that deals with smaller ones, used 'moral suasion' to encourage responsible behaviour on the part of its customers (Bloomfield, 1959, p. 45). It also served as a lender of last resort both on a day-to-day basis (Tilly, 1991b, p. 183) and by rescuing major commercial banks during financial crises, much like the Bank of England did on a number of occasions. The most notable example of the Reichsbank rescuing commercial banks was the case of the Leipziger Bank in 1901. While large rescue operations typically attract much attention, the commercial banks relied on the Reichsbank to stand ready to rediscount their assets. In the words of Borchardt, the 'German credit system rested on the assumed liquidity guarantee of the Reichsbank' (quoted in Tilly, 1991a, p. 92). Finally, just after the turn of the century, the Reichsbank was engaged in the most conspicuous activity of modern central banks – namely, open market operations. On at least four occasions between 1901 and 1910 the bank sold bills in the open market to raise interest rates, and presumably to moderate the rapid rate of German economic expansion. Thus by the end of the period the three largest economies in Europe – Britain, France and Germany – had central banks whose operations had converged towards a common standard that corresponded roughly with the modern conception of a central bank.

Belgium[10]

As we saw in the previous chapter, Belgium was the first country to develop the investment bank, and its banking system in general was quite advanced. Similarly, central banking in Belgium was advanced as well. Indeed, of all the European central banks we review in this chapter, Belgium's, the Banque Nationale de Belgique (National Bank of Belgium), was the earliest to conduct all the functions of a modern central bank. Founded in 1850, the

National Bank was privately owned, but the government appointed the bank's governor and a special commissioner to oversee the bank's operations and report to the finance minister. Belgium had followed the French monetary system since 1832 and was a charter member of the Latin Monetary Union. Like France, Belgium was bimetallic until the suspension of silver coinage in 1878 placed it *de facto* on gold, and it remained on gold throughout the rest of the period.

From its founding, the National Bank of Belgium handled the government's accounts, possessed a monopoly of note issue, and served as a lender of last resort. The latter two functions were related to one another in that the Belgian banking system had come under considerable strain during financial panics in 1838 and 1848, with the result being general suspension in both cases. The government responded to the second panic by creating the National Bank, giving it a monopoly of the note issue and making expansion of the note issue relatively flexible. This last goal was achieved by allowing the Bank to issue notes at its discretion, with the provision that all issues above a fixed amount (275 million francs) were taxed at a rate of 6 per cent. (Note the similarity to the regulations concerning the Reichbank's note issue 25 years later.)

From the beginning, the bank stood ready to purchase high-quality bills from the Belgian banking system, and provide for the day-to-day credit needs of the financial system; like the Reichsbank, it did not ration credit to the extent that other central banks did. In addition, Bloomfield notes that the bank 'planned' to use open market operations – that is, it intended to sell bills from its portfolio in order to raise interest rates, presumably to slow down economic expansion and thus smooth output over the business cycle – but that it never did so in practice. There is no evidence in the literature relating the bank's behaviour to particular episodes or financial crises during this era, but it may well be that the efficient operation of the bank throughout the period in fact resulted in the dearth of such crises in Belgium.

The Netherlands

The Bank of the Netherlands was founded in 1814 in anticipation of the re-creation of an independent country after the period of French rule. Although the state owned no part of the bank, its chief officers were appointed by the king. As late as 1896, the bank did not possess a monopoly over the note issue in the Netherlands, though nearly two-thirds of all the notes circulating in the country were Bank of Netherlands notes (Muhleman, 1896, pp. 114–15). Of the rest, 80 per cent were liabilities of other issuing banks. In addition to the Bank of the Netherlands notes and other bank notes, the Netherlands was one of four European countries that issued treasury notes that were direct liabilities of the state; the others were Germany, Austria-Hungary, and Italy. These notes were backed 100 per cent by specie and made up about 20 per cent of all notes not issued by the Bank of the Netherlands. These treasury notes were retired by 1909 (Bloomfield, 1959, p. 19).

There were no restrictions on the volume of the bank's note issue; however, 40 per cent of the combination of its notes and deposit liabilities had to be backed by gold or silver. The Netherlands was on a bimetallic system from 1816 to 1847, at which time it went solely on silver. It returned to a bimetallic system in 1875, but the state ceased minting silver in 1877. In 1883-4 the Bank was threatened with suspension because its gold reserves fell perilously low. The treasury was authorized to remove silver coins from the market, melt them down, and have the Bank of the Netherlands sell the bullion on world markets for gold. As it turned out, this action was never taken. In terms of the Bank of the Netherlands' behaviour as a lender of last resort, Bloomfield argues that it was performing the two primary duties of a central bank by the end of the nineteenth century (1959, p. 13), though he offers no evidence to support this claim.

Austria-Hungary

Given its early start at political integration (see Chapter 2), it is not surprising to learn that the Austro-Hungarian Empire also had one of the earliest starts at central banking, a unified currency being one of the economic milestones of its political integration. The Austrian National Bank (later the Österreichisch-ungarische Bank) was established in 1816 (1817 according to Bloomfield (1959, p. 13). The empire had financed its participation in the Napoleonic Wars through the time-honoured means of borrowing and money creation, in the process driving the National Bank's forerunner, the Bank of Vienna, to insolvency. The government supported its subsequent credit rating with an indemnity from France and new loans from the new National Bank. Although privately owned, the bank maintained state loans (repayable on demand) on its balance sheet, and handled imperial accounts. In return, it was granted the note issuing monopoly from the date of its charter, making it among the earliest of all European central banks to have such a monopoly.

The empire was on a silver standard from 1857, but the currency was never strictly convertible (Muhleman, 1896, p. 116), and the world financial crisis of 1873 precipitated a permanent suspension of silver redemption. By the end of the decade, however, paper money was circulating at par because of the decline in the world price of silver (Hawtrey, 1931, p. 71), and silver ceased to be coined, except on government account, after 1879. In 1892, Austria-Hungary formally joined the gold standard countries, though, again, convertibility was a problem and proceeded gradually before full convertibility was obtained in 1900. Interestingly, the movement to gold was financed by a foreign loan handled by private Austrian banks rather than by the central bank (Kindleberger, 1993, p. 131).

Little has been written about the performance of the National Bank as a lender of last resort, probably because it did not fulfil this role to any large extent, if at all. According to Rudolph (1972, p. 34), the bank:

> dealt primarily with high-grade paper, and its lending and discount operations were based upon criteria which excluded all but the most reliable and wealthy clients. In effect, the bank only served the government and several of the large private banking houses.

The fact that the bank did not operate as a lender of last resort cannot be blamed entirely on the laws restricting its note issue, since the National Bank had the potential of a relatively elastic currency, and the renewal of its charter in 1887 was accompanied by the establishment of a fractional reserve system similar to that governing the German Reichsbank. So, the Bank's performance reflects more the conservative policies of its directors rather than any political constraints placed upon them.

Scandinavia[11]

As we saw in Chapters 2 and 4, Sweden has the world's oldest continuing central bank, the Riksbank, which was founded in 1656 and taken over by the state in 1668. The other two Scandinavian countries, Norway and Denmark, founded central banks in 1816 (the Norges Bank or Norwegian Centralbanken) and 1818 (the Nationalbank of Denmark). Sweden and Denmark went on the gold standard in 1873, and in 1875 they were joined by Norway, and the three of them formed the Scandinavian Monetary Union based on the Swedish krone. This confederation of countries remained successfully on the gold standard until 1914, and there was good deal of financial integration. From the 1870s, for example, the Riksbank accepted the notes of the Danish and Norwegian central banks, and in 1901 the three formally agreed to reciprocate the arrangement. Although the explicit role of the state in the ownership of the central bank differed in each country – in Sweden the state owned 100 per cent of the stock, in Norway a majority, and in Denmark none – by the end of the period each was performing as a modern central bank, possessing a monopoly of note issue and serving as a lender of last resort.

Although it was the oldest of the three Scandinavian central banks, the Riksbank was in fact the last to obtain a monopoly of note issue; the legislation was passed in 1897, and came into force in 1903. Even before that time, however, the size of its note issue was almost twice that of all other issuing banks combined, and its notes were the only legal tender (Muhleman, 1896, p. 112). The Riksbank assumed lender of last resort functions in the 1890s, making it a central bank in the modern sense of the term. It managed to do so for two reasons. First, the legislated limits on note issue were raised over time and never became a binding constraint; thus the bank could easily accommodate fluctuations in the demand for its liabilities. Second, the rapid growth of Sweden's exports during this period gave the bank the opportunity to accumulate adequate reserves of specie (and sterling).

In addition to these characteristics, two other factors made the job of the directors of the Riksbank easier than it might otherwise have been. First, due to its stable political climate and its rapid economic growth, the Swedish banking system was never confronted with a financial panic during this period, though this may, of course, have been an endogenous characteristic that itself was a result of the strong banking system. Second, even prior to granting the Riksbank a monopoly of note issue, Swedish law prohibited joint-stock banks (with limited liability) from issuing notes; thus, in addition to the Riksbank, only private banks (the unlimited liability *enskilda* banks) could issue notes, and this made them quite conservative in practice.

Unlike the Riksbank, the Danish central bank – the Nationalbank – possessed a monopoly of the note issue from its founding in 1818 – that is, several decades before the Riksbank – and, unlike the Riksbank, it was not owned by the government. Still, in other respects the experience of central banking in Denmark mirrored that of Sweden: the Nationalbank (founded in 1818) handled the Danish state accounts; Denmark decided to go off silver and on to gold at the same time as Sweden, easily remaining on the standard throughout the era; and over time the government lifted the restrictions on the volume of notes the Nationalbank could issue, so that the bank could meet short-run surges in the demand for bank liabilities. Hansen (1982) notes that the growing use of cheques after 1890 diminished the influence of the Nationalbank over Danish credit markets, but a decade later it consciously served as a lender of last resort when it rescued the commercial banking sector during the international financial crisis of 1907–8.

The Norwegian central bank, Norges Bank, was founded in 1816 (1817 according to Bloomfield (1959, p. 13)) according to Egge (1983). From its foundation it possessed a monopoly of note issue, and it dominated

Norwegian banking until mid-century (see Chapter 4). From the 1850s the growth of other commercial banks relieved some pressure on the Norges Bank while reducing its influence in the Norwegian capital market. Egge claims that as late as 1895 'the Bank still undertook little in the way of central banking functions but operated largely as a commercial bank in competition with the newly-established private commercial banks' (Egge, 1983, p. 278). After that date, however, the bank behaved increasingly like a central bank with a larger discount business, and even behaved like a lender of last resort during crises. But the Norges Bank continued its commercial lending in competition with other banks, and as a result a number of private and foreign banks created the Centralbanken for Norge, a private central bank, to provide discounting and lender of last resort services. This bank quickly became the largest bank in the country, and in 1907 resulted in a conflict between the Norges Bank and the private banks over the latter's submission of monthly reports to the Norges Bank. After that time, however, the Norges Bank gave up its commercial banking activities and served solely as a central bank.

Italy

As mentioned in Chapter 2, the Italian state was formed in 1861 – although its approximate modern borders were not established for another decade – and had at that time an elected Parliament that oversaw monetary matters. In 1862, the lira was established as legal tender, and in 1863 the official exchange rate of the lira with the British pound was set at 25.3 lire. This rate ruled during the intervals in which Italy had a fixed exchange rate in the succeeding fifty years. In 1865 Italy joined the Latin Monetary Union and adopted the coinage convention of the Union (see above), but in the following year Italy went to war with Austria over control of Venice, and from that time until 1884, the lire was inconvertible.

After unification there were five banks of issue in Italy, and a sixth was added when the Papal States joined the Union in 1870. In 1893 a financial crisis in general and the failure of the Banca Romana in particular prompted the Italian Parliament to consolidate the Banca Nazionale del Regno, Banca Nazionale Toscana, Banca Toscana di Credito e d'Industria and the Banca Romana to form the Banca d'Italia in 1894 (1893 according to Bloomfield (1959, p. 13))

This reform left the Banca d'Italia, Banco di Napoli and Banco di Sicilia with note-issuing privileges, a situation that survived beyond 1913. Thus the Banca d'Italia did not possess a monopoly of the note issue; therefore a co-ordinated monetary policy was difficult to maintain, though the Italian government may well have attempted to adhere to the rules of the international gold standard through legislation and treasury operations (see below). Furthermore, Cohen claims that the Banca d'Italia 'supplied the banking system with a true lender of last resort' (Cohen, 1967, p. 83), at least after 1900. It is true that, much like earlier domestic operations by the Bank of England and Bank of France, the Banca d'Italia organized loans that rescued other Italian financial institutions in 1907 and again in 1911. As we saw in Chapter 4, Italy had a comparatively safe and sophisticated banking system during the post-1894 period, and, aside from the difficulties in 1892–4, financial crises involving bank failures were not an issue for the Italians; the Banca d'Italia probably played a positive role in these matters.

Even though it often was not on the gold standard, Italy may well have been a *de facto* gold-standard country for much of this period. According to Fratianni and Spinelli (1984, p. 408):

Despite the fact that Italy adopted the gold standard intermittently and for brief periods of time, her experience was not different from what it would have been had she adhered to the standard throughout, particularly from 1900 to 1913 ... Briefly put, Italy was guided by the norm of the gold standard.

By 'intermittent', then, is meant inconvertibility from 1866 to 1884, a situation precipitated by the Austrian war effort (1866), and from 1894 to 1902, following the period of general financial crisis and many bank failures, and the reorganization of the banking system. The Italian authorities attempted to control the size of the currency issue and thus 'adhere' to the gold standard by legislating a 22 per cent decrease in the value of notes issued between 1897 and 1911 (Muhleman, 1896, p. 105), and the treasury issued notes as well that to some extent were backed by government holdings of gold.

At the same time, according to Fratianni and Spinelli, examination of the determinants of the monetary base, following the procedure employed by Cagan (1965), suggests that the commercial banks that carried out the policy were actually *sterilizing* foreign-exchange flows, a practice that is decidedly not in keeping with the gold standard rules. Their interpretation is that Italy's apparent adherence to the gold standard is explainable under the monetary approach to the balance of payments, by which means gold flows that alter the money supply are unnecessary, their place being taken by goods flows and adjustments in the demand for money.[12] In either case, the Italian central bank, while a latecomer, was behaving like a modern central bank in the decade before the First World War.

Spain

To finance its alliance with France against Britain during the American War of Independence, the Spanish Crown created the Banco Nacional de San Carlos. In 1829 this bank was reorganized as the Banco Español de San Fernando, commonly referred to as the Bank of Spain, though it did not formally take this name until 1856 (Vicens Vives, 1969, pp. 727–8). While the bank was privately owned, the government appointed its governor and two subgovernors, and in return for a monopoly of the note issue granted in 1874, the bank was rechartered with a capital of 100 million pesetas. At that time it was granted a note issue of up to five times that amount, and it in turn granted the government a 125 million peseta loan. In the words of Vicens Vives, 'the banking business was centralized and the Bank officially linked to the State, to the point that their mutual histories became inseparable' (1969, p. 730).

Tortella (1977, p. 524) argues that before receiving a monopoly of the note issue, the Bank of Spain was clearly not serving as a central bank. More importantly, he notes that the bank's behaviour was in fact 'destabilizing' (p. 428), and that the banks of issue in general and the Bank of Spain in particular 'followed a conscious deflationary policy' during downturns, and that their behaviour typically 'tended to make the crisis worse rather than alleviate it' (p. 433). With respect to the Bank of Spain itself, its role as agent of the state meant that its circulation fluctuated with the credit needs of the government. The economic reforms of the late 1860s, which followed political revolution, involved the informal adoption of the policies of the Latin Monetary Union and the liberalization of the banking laws, including the eventual expansion of the number of banks of issue. These particular reforms were wiped out by the state's exchange of the note-issuing monopoly for credit in 1874, and the bank's policies during the rest of the century were typically conservative (Tortella, 1977, pp. 541–6).

Although never formally a member of the Latin Monetary Union, in 1868 Spain adopted the Union's monetary standards, substituting the peseta for the franc; however, like the other countries in the Union, Spain ceased coining silver in 1878, except on government account. With a large public debt, the interest on which was paid in gold, and an eroding balance of trade in the early 1880s, Spain found it difficult to maintain convertibility, and in 1883 the Bank of Spain suspended the convertibility of its notes into specie. Convertibility was not resumed for the rest of the century, and the value of the peseta steadily eroded relative to the other major currencies. By the end of the century the peseta had fallen to half its original buying power in terms of the pound (Vicens Vives, 1969, p. 719).

During the 1890s, the Bank's most noticeable role was its monetization of the government's debt, which was incurred fighting colonial wars, the most disastrous of which was that against the United States. Overall, then, we must conclude that the Bank of Spain was one of the few nineteenth-century European central banks that was not functioning as a modern central bank by the start of the First World War. Indeed, Martín-Aceña (1994) argues that if the monetary authorities had placed Spain on the gold standard in the 1880s, the subsequent Spanish rate of growth would have been closer to the European mean. Although the positive effects of sound monetary policy are clear, this seems a strong claim in view of the many factors found in the literature concerning Spain's relatively slow growth in the nineteenth century.

Portugal

Following the revolution of 1820, in 1822 Portugal adopted a constitution, and that same year the Bank of Portugal was created to handle the finances of the new political regime. Although the bank did not have a monopoly of the note issue (as late as 1896 there were seven other banks issuing notes), its notes alone were accepted for payment of public debts (Muhleman, 1896, p. 119). In 1854 Portugal went on the gold standard, making it nominally one of the earliest states to do so; we say *nominally*, because, according to Muhleman, who was writing at the end of the century, 'specie payments were suspended some years ago and irredeemable notes circulate' (Muhleman, 1896, p. 120). According to Bloomfield (1959, p. 15), suspension occurred in 1890. Thus while Portugal had a central bank in the sense that the Bank of Portugal served as the financial agent of the state, it did not perform the tasks of a modern central bank.

United States

The United States had no central bank before the creation of the Federal Reserve System in 1914. Thus the United States was the only country in this study that had no financial institution which controlled the money supply, served as a lender of last resort or, at the very least, handled the states financial accounts. It was left to the Congress to regulate the money supply through legislation, a cumbersome and blunt instrument that, until the Aldrich-Vreeland Act of 1908, left little room for either the short-run management of the money supply or the intervention of a lender of last resort. Even so, the US Treasury maintained the gold standard after 1879. We forbear from a further discussion of US central banking since our interest is only in how that country interacted with European financial markets.

Summary

Table 5.1 contains a summary of the history of European central banking up to 1913. By the 1890s every European country in our sample had a central bank that handled state accounts. With the exception of Italy, the Netherlands and Portugal, the central bank of every country either had, or was in the

Table 5.1 Summary of European central banks before 1914

Country	Bank	First founded[a]	Note issue monopoly[b]	First decade as lender of last resort[c]	First year on gold standard
UK	Bank of England	1694	1844	1850s	1819
France	Bank of France	1800	1848	1880s	1878
Germany	Reichsbank	1875[e]	1875[f]	1870s	1871
Belgium	National Bank	1850	1850	1850s	1878
Netherlands	Bank of the Netherlands	1814	No[f]	Unknown	1877
Denmark	National Bank of Denmark	1818	1818	1900s	1873
Norway	Bank of Norway	1816[e]	1816	1900s	1875
Sweden	Riksbank	1668	1897	1900s	1873
Italy	Bank of Italy	1893	No[f]	1900s	1884–93, 1902
Austria-Hungary	Austro-Hungarian Bank	1816[e]	1816[f]	No	1900
Portugal	Bank of Portugal	1822	No	No	1854–90
Spain	Bank of Spain	1829	1874	No	No
USA	None	–	–[f]	–	1879

Notes and sources: [a] This date refers to the bank's original charter or recharter as the central bank. In those cases where an earlier institution was rechartered as the central bank, for example, the Reichsbank, we have given the recharter date. Unless otherwise noted, these dates are from Muhlĕman (1896). [b] This date refers to the state's granting the central bank a monopoly of the note issue. For the Bank of England, the Reichsbank and the Riksbank this date refers to the beginning of the conversion from multiple banks of issue to the central bank's monopoly. For the sources of these dates, see text. [c] The decade reported here refers to the one in which central bank policy could clearly be linked to providing liquidity to commercial banks during a financial crisis – either through lending to the banking sector directly or by putting together consortia of banks for the same purpose. The primary sources of this information are Bloomfield (1959), Kindleberger (1993), and the articles and volumes cited in the text referring to particular central banks. [d] This date refers to when the country went on the gold standard, *de facto*. Although some countries, like those in the Latin Monetary Union, continued to define their currencies in terms of both silver and gold after this date, the 'demonetization' of silver placed them *de facto* on gold. [e] Bloomfield (1959, p. 13) gives a different date for the founding of the central banks of Germany (1876), Norway (1817) and Austria-Hungary (1877). The date for Norway is from Hansen (1982). [f] The governments of these countries also issued notes that were liabilities of the treasury.

process of acquiring, a note-issuing monopoly. In addition, by the first decade of the twentieth century, every central bank except those of Austria-Hungary, Spain and Portugal was behaving as a lender of last resort at least during crises. Finally, after 1902, every country except Portugal and Spain was on the gold standard. The United States remained an outlier in these matters, forming a central bank only in 1913.

5.3 MAINTENANCE OF THE GOLD STANDARD

Since antiquity mankind has employed commodity and commodity-backed monies as media of exchange. By the early modern period in Europe, gold and silver were well established as the dominant commodities for such purposes. The appeal of commodity monies in general and these two metals in particular derived from their value in alternative uses; that is, because of the risks in accepting and the costs of ensuring the value of non-commodity currencies, traders preferred media that maintained an intrinsic value separate from that of exchange, and a value that was high relative to its weight. While the use of commodity monies survived countless wars, political upheavals and debasements through the ages, during the twentieth century gold- and silver-backed currencies have been replaced by fiat money.

Since the demise of the Bretton Woods system there has been considerable interest in reviving a commodity-based exchange system. Events in Europe in recent years, focused on the efforts of the European Economic Community (EEC) to establish a common currency, have also led some to consider the experiences of European countries during previous flirtations with monetary co-operation. More generally, the increases in the price level and periodic bouts of severe inflation that Western countries have experienced during the years since the Second World War have led policymakers and academics to reconsider the workings of the classical gold standard. A recent effort by Backus and Kehoe (1992), for example, compares rates of inflation during the gold standard period of the late nineteenth and early twentieth centuries with more recent experience. A key finding, and one that appears often in the literature, is the dramatic increase in inflation rates (and their variances) for more recent periods.

To deal with the issues raised here, we revive Barro's (1979) model of the determination of price levels in a gold standard regime. The gold standard, as it was employed in the late nineteenth century, relied on a mint to coin bullion into legal tender at a fixed price, and a monetary authority to support the nominal price of gold by standing ready to exchange gold for the liabilities of the banking system. As we saw above, this latter function typically was performed by a central bank. Thus, within a country one could buy and sell gold at a fixed price and this arrangement fixed the exchange rates among countries on the gold standard. Under such a regime, the relative price of gold determined the price level, and while such events as changes in the reserve ratio and velocity could also affect the price level; as Barro (1979, p. 13) argues 'the system possessed an important nominal anchor in the fixed price of the reserve commodity'. *In the long run*, arbitrage led to a common relative price of gold in each country on the standard.[13] In contrast, a fiat currency system contains no such anchor. In the latter case, one then looks to other determinants of the domestic price level, among which central bank management of the money supply stands out.

Barro's paper on the determination of the price level in a gold standard regime presents the following system. The *money supply* equation is given by

$$M^s = \frac{1}{\lambda} P_g G_m \tag{5.1}$$

where P_g is the (pegged) price of gold, G_m is the quantity of official holdings of gold, and $1/\lambda$ represents the multiplier attached to the nominal value of high-powered money. The *money demand* equation is

$$M^d = k(\pi)Py \tag{5.2}$$

where P is the price level, y is real income,[14] and π is the expected inflation rate representing the opportunity cost of holding money. The k function is the reciprocal of velocity. More generally, we can write Equation 5.2 as

$$M^d = Pk(\mathrm{i})f(y) \tag{5.3}$$

where we substitute the nominal interest rate for the expected rate of inflation.[15]

By equating Equations 5.1 and 5.3 we obtain the equilibrium money stock, and, by rearranging, a solution for the price level in equilibrium as well as an equilibrium for the *j*th individual country.

$$\frac{P}{P_g} = \frac{P_j}{P_{gj}} = \frac{G_{mj}}{\lambda_j k_j(i_j) f_j(y_j)} \tag{5.4}$$

Equation 5.4 also shows that in the long run the ratio of an individual country's price level relative to its nominal gold price will be forced into equality with world prices. In the short run, however, P_j can deviate from P.[16] These short-run deviations depend positively on monetary gold stocks and nominal interest rates, and negatively on real income as well as on any shifts in the functions k and f, and changes in λ, for that matter. From this equation we obtain the following predictions.

First, gold production will raise domestic prices. Although a new discovery of gold initially affects only the domestic economy, it eventually leads to increases in the price levels of all countries. While the gold standard tends to push countries towards the one price equilibrium of Equation 5.4, periodic new discoveries will move the system away from equilibrium. Accordingly, purchasing power parity may not hold at any particular point in time.

Second, an increase in real income (or, in the steady state, in the growth rate of real income) would lower domestic prices, *ceteris paribus*. The lower prices lead to gold inflows from abroad, which lower foreign prices and raise domestic prices, and, again, the result is purchasing power parity internationally. Again, differences in the short-run rates of growth across countries, and changes in rates of growth over time will tend to keep the system from equilibrium.[17]

Third, an autonomous increase in money demand would decrease the price level; conversely, a decrease in money demand would increase the price level. Furthermore, differences among countries and changes over time in money demand within a country could prevent the system from yielding the purchasing power parity at any particular point in time in Equation 5.4.

Fourth, substituting paper money for gold (on the gold standard) would not lead to inflation in the long run, but would in the short run. This result occurs because paper money drives gold out of the system (and because of its adverse effect on gold production). The substitution of paper for gold occurs in the model through a decrease in λ. A decrease in the gold backing of the currency may not have been a major factor during the period under study, but it is likely to have been at least a minor influence, especially in the most financially advanced country, the United Kingdom. Moreover, λ may have been endogenous. For example, countries in which the commitment to gold was questioned (as in Italy) may have found it more difficult to maintain convertibility. Policymakers confronted with falling monetary gold stocks caused by a lack of confidence in their commitment to the system, would have had to alter λ, or allow the money stock to decline.[18]

Fifth, and finally, if new countries come into the system, then one result will be an increase in the demand for monetary gold and a decrease, worldwide, in the amount left for everybody else, which would reduce world prices. Indeed, this probably happened during the deflationary period of 1873–95.[19] But the initial effect would be felt more strongly in those countries that were the largest traders with countries coming on the system; thus in the short run the equilibrium price would be disrupted.

This theoretical discussion of the gold standard leads us to conclude that the long-run and short-run effects of the system on money and prices will be different. In the short run – defined here as the time period covering one data point, which in our sample is one year – any number of forces could lead to a divergence of money and prices from levels consistent with some long-run equilibrium. In the long run, however, assuming that a country remained legally on the gold standard, its monetary authorities could not avoid the constraints imposed by the system. These constraints were, in Barro's words, the 'anchor' of the system.

5.4 INTEGRATION AMONG MONETARY BASES

To understand the working of the gold standard, one might employ the 'money stock determinants' approach of Cagan (1965). In this approach, the contributions to the money stock of the currency–money ratio (C/M), the reserves–deposit ratio (R/D) and the monetary base or high-powered money (H, generally defined to be bank reserves plus currency in the hands of the public) can be calculated as follows. If the money stock is defined as currency plus deposits $(C + D = M)$, and if the stock of high-powered money is defined as currency plus bank reserves $(C + R = H)$, then the ratio of M to H can easily be shown to be

$$\frac{M}{H} = \frac{\frac{C}{D} + 1}{\frac{C}{D} + \frac{R}{D}} \qquad (5.5)$$

The reason that the sum of currency and reserves (H) is called high-powered money is that it is capable of supporting a larger number of deposits (+ currency) in a fractional reserve system. In fact, if the central bank is the only issuer of currency, and banks hold their reserves in the central bank, then the total of $C + R$ represents the main items on the liability side of the central bank's balance sheet. This total can be determined uniquely by the central bank, either by setting reserve requirements or through open market operations. The money supply presumably follows suit, although generally with a lag. In any event, this is the source of the central bank's control over the money stock, and consequently is the lever it employs to control the domestic price level and thus to play by the rules (or not) of the gold standard.

Quite naturally, in a functioning gold standard world in which all money stocks are driven (through the co-operation of the central bank) by world production of gold (compared to the demand for it), one would expect the

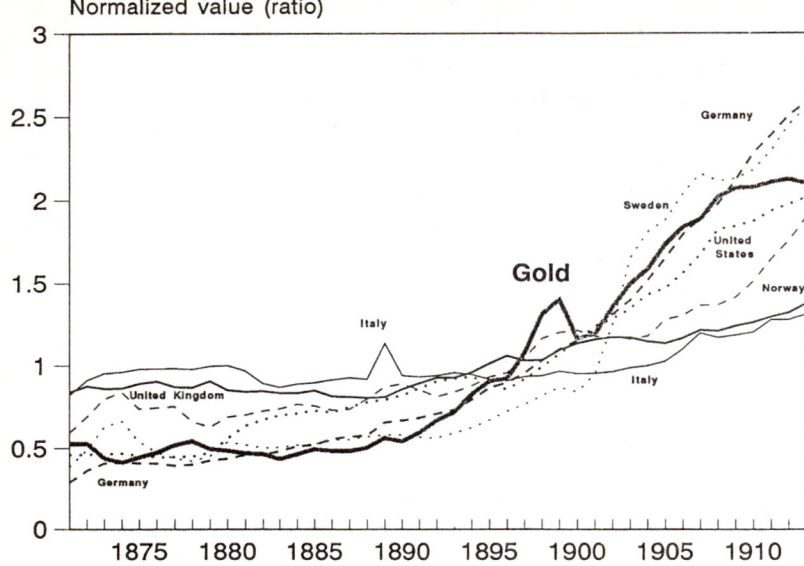

Figure 5.1 Monetary bases and world gold, 1871–1913, normalized

monetary bases of the various countries to be highly correlated. In Figure 5.1 we show the monetary base data for the countries for which such numbers have been provided in the literature. The data period is 1871–1913.[20] This period is the longest for which these numbers are complete; it is also approximately the period for which the gold standard functioned for a number of countries, although in later chapters we shall argue that a better starting date might be 1873.

The data in the figure are normalized (divided by their respective means) in order to facilitate comparisons. What appears to be a rather close correlation breaks down somewhat after the turn of the century. This impression can be confirmed with reference to a set of correlation coefficients for the entire period (1871–1913) versus just the end (1900–13) – these are listed in Table 5.2. The table also contains correlations among the growth rates of these numbers, in anticipation of some results to be provided below.

In the graph it is noticeable that the United Kingdom and Italy show virtually level monetary bases throughout the period. Both operated basically conservative monetary policies. The two rapidly expanding economies of Sweden and Germany show the two lowest (normalized) monetary bases in

Table 5.2 Correlations among monetary bases and gold, logarithms of the data

	Germany	Italy	Norway	Sweden	UK	USA	Gold
1871–1913 (Levels)							
Germany	–	.751	.971	.953	.938	.981	.966
Italy		–	.773	.804	.720	.690	.709
Norway			–	.944	.943	.932	.947
Sweden				–	.924	.919	.938
United Kingdom					–	.880	.968
United States						–	.928
1871–1913 (Growth Rates)							
Germany	–	.524	.515	.611	.140	–.038	–.001
Italy		–	.269	.250	–.078	–.077	.175
Norway			–	.462	–.115	.106	–.085
Sweden				–	–.098	.177	–.060
United Kingdom					–	–.297	–.006
United States						–	–.076
1900–1913 (Levels)							
Germany	–	.976*	.912	.913	.876	.992*	.965
Italy		–	.929*	.853*	.902*	.973*	.922*
Norway			–	.710	.957*	.881	.782
Sweden				–	.682	.911	.966*
United Kingdom					–	.860	.738
United States						–	.970*

1871 and the two highest in 1913. It is hard to believe that the monetary base is not endogenous in those two countries, being driven by the demand for money, which itself is driven by the growth of real income. For the table, in order to facilitate comparison between the log-level figures for the two periods, we have put an asterisk in the bottom part of the table next to those correlation coefficients that are higher when comparing the two periods. There are ten such cases, eight of which involve Italy and the United States. The Italian result is somewhat curious, since they were not on the gold standard for much of the period. Readers should recall the statement by Fratianni and Spinelli (1984), reported above, which noted that during this period Italy was guided by the norm of the gold standard.

Looking at the results for growth rates, however, one is impressed by the fact that there are very few large positive correlations (and these involve only Germany and the Scandinavian countries). These results are not strong enough, though, to warrant any further discussion. Note that we have looked at growth rates here primarily because these data are non-stationary in levels (and stationary in growth rates); non-stationary data are generally dominated by trend in such a way that tests of the level figures can be seriously misleading. In first difference form, there is no appreciable connection among the monetary bases of these countries. Under the gold standard – operating by means of the traditional specie-flow mechanism – gold production should have led to a high correlation among the monetary bases (and, as we shall see in Chapter 6, money growth rates also do not show much correlation across countries in this period).

We begin our formal testing with a discussion of the stationarity of the monetary base data. We have already indicated, in Chapter 3, that non-stationary data – which is very common with macroeconomic series such as the monetary base – must be handled carefully in many of the standard time series tests. In fact, usually one has to difference the data in order to induce stationarity before conducting certain tests. The details of this are spelled out in the Technical Appendix. The way we proceed, then, is to determine if the data contain unit roots by applying the Augmented Dickey–Fuller test; the test procedure is explained further in the footnote and in the Technical Appendix.[21]

The results of testing for unit roots in the logarithms of gold and the six monetary bases are given in Table 5.3. The entries in the table are the values of the Dickey–Fuller test statistic; if they are greater than the critical value of the test statistic (–3.52), then one cannot reject the hypothesis that the data contain a unit root (at a level of significance of 5 per cent); this explains column 1, where all series are shown to have unit roots (even at the 1 per cent

Table 5.3 Unit root tests, monetary bases, 1871–1913

	Levels	Growth rates
Gold	–2.78	–5.00
Germany	–1.59	–6.96
Italy	–2.43	–7.03
Norway	–1.19	–5.51
Sweden	–1.32	–4.62
United Kingdom	–1.54	–5.44
United States	–2.07	–3.23*

Note: *No unit root at 10% level. The value of the test statistic (5% level) is –3.52.

level, for that matter). In column 2, none of the series have unit roots at the 10 per cent level, although the United States does at the 5 per cent level;[22] the other series do not show a unit root at the 5 per cent level.

If the unit roots of the data are of order 1, as seems to be the case since the growth rates of the same variables do not contain unit roots (except, possibly, for the United States), then we can also describe the variables as *integrated of order 1*. If two variables are affected by trend, the possibility exists that they *share* a common stochastic trend; if so, they are *cointegrated*. In particular, if a time series variable achieves stationarity after differencing, and if a linear combination of the original series is stationary, then the series are cointegrated. The test procedure to determine stationarity, both of the individual variables and of their linear combination, is again the Augmented Dickey–Fuller test.

Above, we showed that each of the monetary base and gold series at which we look show a trend; these trends appear very similar (in Figure 5.1). What we now wish to test is whether the patterns in trends are consistent with cointegration. The economic significance of finding cointegration among gold and the monetary bases of these countries is quite straightforward. Under the gold standard, countries that play by the rules would tend to have monetary bases that are driven (to a large extent) by changes in world supplies of gold. The reason is that as gold flows in or out of the domestic financial system it should produce automatic responses in the monetary base, whatever the cause of the situation; presumably the main influences would be differences in interest rates and/or rates of inflation across these countries. In other words, if all countries on the gold standard played by the rules and operated by the specie-flow mechanism, then equilibria would be obtained among the monetary bases of those countries; indeed, the constraints imposed by the rules of the game would also cause inflation rates and money growth rates to show a similar pattern.

The cointegration test could fail if there is no common stochastic trend or, of course, if countries do not play by the rules of the game. It could also fail if the gold standard failed in some fundamental way which differed from adherence to the rules and, of course, if it operated in some other way than through the specie-flow mechanism. Quite simply, when we performed the cointegration test for the six monetary bases and the world gold stock, there was absolutely no sign of cointegration. The residuals from each regression failed to achieve stationarity. In fact, these results were decisive. While it might be argued that this result is a consequence of an inadequate number of observations, we need to point out that later in this study, when we come to study real variables and the price levels of these same countries over approximately the same time period, substantial cointegration is revealed.[23]

This finding is, therefore, a very strong rejection of one of the pillars of the conventional story of how the gold standard works, which is that changes in the world supply of gold would in someway provide a common stochastic trend to the monetary bases, money supplies and price levels of the countries on (or allied to) the system. We have yet to present our evidence on prices and money stocks, and we need to discuss the behaviour of the demand for money and of real commodity flows, so there is a long way to go before we can close this particular discussion. We do think, however, that the gold standard did function successfully in this period, as we have already indicated.

We have already described the Granger-causal procedure, in Chapter 4, so we can proceed, with a modicum of discussion, to our reasons for employing the procedure here. What we are most interested in, in fact, is the possibility that movements in world gold do have an influence on current monetary bases, but that there are significant lags in the process. The Granger-causal procedure basically establishes a temporal ordering of the data, with the dependent variable (the 'causee') being explained by its own lags and the lags in some other variable (or variables). In this case, degrees of freedom could easily become a problem, since the usual procedure is to add two right-hand variables at a time (one lagged dependent and one lagged independent variable each time). Even so, it is important to try to see whether the system contained a long-run anchor in the form of the gold standard, even if short-

Table 5.4 Granger-causal tests of gold and the monetary base, 1871–1913

	\multicolumn{5}{c}{p–values for lags of}
	1	2	3	4	5
Gold independent					
Germany					
Italy					
Norway					
Sweden				.02	.05
United Kingdom	.08				
Gold dependent					
Germany	.01				
Italy	.04				
Norway					
Sweden					
United Kingdom		.06	.03	.07	

run deviations proved to be substantial (as they have). After all, the gold standard would break down if it did not work in the long run – that is, if it did not provide the much acclaimed anchor – and history tells us that it did not break down in this period.

Table 5.4, then, illustrates the results of applying the Granger-causal model (given in Equation 4.1 or the Technical Appendix) to the growth rates of the monetary bases of these six countries. The independent variables are lagged growth rates of world gold production. We are employing growth rates here because the log-level figures are non-stationary; the Granger procedure uses an F-test that requires a finite variance to be valid. Series that contain unit roots cannot be shown to have finite variances. Since the growth rates of the variables do not contain unit roots, we are able to conduct our tests here in growth rates. Table 5.4 shows the results of applying the Granger-causality model. Here we list the dependent variable on the left and the results for five different regressions on the right. From left to right the table shows a one-lag to a five-lag model. Note that what appears is the 'p-value' associated with the F-test. If this value is .05 or less, we have established Granger-causality at the 5 per cent (or better) level; we are including p-values up to .10 (the 10 per cent level) in the table. In the tests, we excluded the United States, since the growth rate for its monetary base was non-stationary at the 5 per cent level. For the remaining countries, there is no broad pattern. For two countries, gold Granger-causes the monetary base with a lag; the lag is four and five years for Sweden. We anticipated that this might show up and would interpret it as consistent with the long-run operation of the gold standard. The lags for Sweden do appear to be a little on the long side, however.

The results in the bottom of the table, where gold appears to be 'driven' by domestic monetary bases, is a little more problematical. We have already alluded to the possibility that the international payments system – under the gold standard – operated as if what is known as the 'monetary approach to the balance of payments' rather than the 'specie-flow approach' is correct for this period. We shall explain this more fully in Chapter 6, but a preliminary discussion is in order. Under the monetary approach, domestic prices are driven by international prices and it is not necessary, to clear commodity markets, for gold to move; commodities can move instead. A country with relatively low prices would have its economy expand under this process; this implies that the demand for money in that economy would expand. If the money stock expands with its demand, and by this point it is reasonable to argue that there is a lag in the process, then the monetary authorities, by statute, would need to increase the monetary base. In the short run they could buy securities, but in the long run they would add to their gold stocks. In this case there would be an intertemporal link between the monetary base and gold running from the former to the latter. The authorities could purchase gold directly, of course, but this would imply a more direct relationship between gold and the base than appears to be the case in this period.

5.5 CONCLUSIONS

In this chapter we reviewed the history of central banking in Europe. We saw that, with the Bank of England as a model, one country after another created a central bank that handled the state's accounts, in most cases possessed a note-issuing monopoly and (often later) served as a lender of last resort. By the end of the period only Spain, Portugal and Austria-Hungary had central banks that did not perform all these duties to some degree. We believe that this convergence of activities performed by these central banks is another form of economic convergence that has often gone unnoticed in the literature.

The empirical evidence presented in this chapter resolves some issues, but leaves a critical issue unresolved: what, exactly, is the best way to describe how the international payments system operated during the high water mark of the gold standard? We have shown how countries committed to the gold standard, and described their experiences; with the exception of Portugal and Spain in our sample, the system was maintained at relatively unchanged exchange rates. Never before or since has this occurred. In this chapter we showed that monetary bases (for five countries) were also highly correlated. Even Italy, a country that was not on the gold standard for the whole period, followed this pattern.

We have also outlined a model of the determination of domestic price levels under a gold standard. The principal influences on price levels are gold, the values of domestic money multipliers and the domestic demand for money. We considered the smaller literature on multipliers; by and large, the domestic money supply was influenced by all three components of the multiplier. These are the currency/deposit ratio, the reserve/deposit ratio, and the monetary base. The latter effect was never shown to be as large as one might anticipate under a gold-standard regime; the most usual explanation of this in the literature is that these countries did not play by the rules of the system (and sterilized their money bases from outside influences).

To study this phenomenon further, we conducted a correlation, cointegration and Granger-causality analysis of the relationship between monetary bases and the world gold supply. Correlations, as noted, were high, but there were no cointegration results between monetary bases and the gold supply. What should have happened is that the base should have been driven by gold (either cointegration or Granger-causality) but the base, in turn, should not have driven the money stock. In fact, the Granger-causality tests show that a more likely scenario is that the base drove the gold supply, a result we are able to interpret under the alternative scenario (from the specie-flow approach) of the monetary approach to the balance of payments.

We realize, at this point, that this is not much evidence on which to base these conjectures. We need to look at the details of money and price interaction; we need to study the demand for money in each case; and we need to document interaction at the real product level. Each of these is done in succeeding chapters. The monetary approach continues to offer an effective way to explain these results.

6 Money and Prices, 1850–1913

6.1 INTRODUCTION

In Chapter 5 we reviewed the mechanics of the international gold standard as it operated in the period 1873–1913. After considering an extensive literature on the subject, we considered the operation of the classical gold standard in terms of the behaviour of high-powered money across the various European countries and the United States. A gold standard operating by the classical rules would be expected to show closely matched high-powered money stocks. This result follows because gold and convertible currencies move to equate price levels internationally. While the levels of the high-powered money stocks were in fact highly correlated in this period, we generally were unable to establish an interconnection in the growth rates of high-powered money, and cointegration and Granger-causality tests also failed to indicate integration, even among the major economies that were supposedly supporting the system. In that discussion we did not conclude that the system was not working properly, but clearly something needs to be explained.

In the present chapter, to push the matter further, we extend the search for financial integration to the price levels and monetary stocks of the individual countries. We shall take the same approach, employing correlation, cointegration and Granger-causality methods on these variables. The most important variable one could look at, to see whether the system worked, is the price level. That is, a prediction of the gold standard is that price *levels* (and inflation rates) will be closely integrated across countries, with the system providing discipline both for those with overly rapid inflation and for those with price levels that grow more slowly than their competitors. The fact is, the price levels are closely related across countries, as demonstrated in this chapter by the three tests just mentioned.

If price levels behave as if the system is working, then one might naturally expect that money stocks (and money growth rates) would follow suit. In fact, while money stocks (and money growth rates) show increasing correlation over the period – and correlations across countries are impressively high – we are unable, for a large set of countries, to establish either cointegration of the money stocks or Granger-causality for the growth rates of the money stocks. This result therefore corresponds with that obtained for high-powered money, and clearly requires some explanation.

The first thought one might have is that the monetary data are defective. We do not think this is the case, in view of our examination of ten different monetary series. Instead, we suggest that our finding can be explained by the 'monetary approach' to the balance of payments, under a gold-standard regime, rather than the traditional specie-flow mechanism (in the same context). We believe that the monetary approach, which emphasizes goods flows and a stable demand for money, predicts that the law of one price will hold (as demonstrated in the cointegration of price levels), but that money stocks need not show the same behaviour. This theory contrasts with the specie-flow theory in that the latter is driven by movements in money stocks. Several other facts, discussed elsewhere, support the monetary approach. These include the probable stability of the demand for money for these countries (discussed in Chapter 7), the increasingly close integration of the real sectors of these economies (discussed in Chapter 8) and the closer coincidence of business cycle turning points as we approach the twentieth century (discussed in Chapter 9).

The plan of this chapter is as follows. We begin in Section 6.2 with a discussion of the data for money and prices. We present several tables and graphs illustrating the behaviour of the average growth rate and its variance for each of the series we have. For all three price indices inflation rates are, as one might expect, lower in the gold-standard period (1873-1913) than over the entire run of data, which in some cases begins in 1850. Similarly, their variances are lower from 1873 to 1913 and, more tellingly, these inflation rates are more highly correlated across countries in the 1873-1913 period than over the entire period. While this result is certainly generally known, we offer here the most complete tabulation in the literature of this phenomenon.[1] One expects such a finding from a successful gold standard. The money growth rates also appear in this section, but here some anomalies show up, the most noticeable being a lower correlation across countries during the later period.

Next, we put the same data through a series of cointegration and Granger-causality tests. We begin with the results of unit root tests for all series: Section 6.3 contains this material. The results confirm the presence of unit roots in the log-level figures, while the growth rates of most of these variables are stationary, as expected. Section 6.4 considers the results of cointegration tests across these series; these are tests of wholesale prices, money, consumer prices, and national income deflators. As noted, the money stocks are not cointegrated. We then discuss the 'monetary approach' to the balance of payments in some detail, since it offers a solution to the different results for money than for prices.

In Section 6.5 we summarize the results of Granger-causality tests for the same set of series. Most of the series show some such 'causality' during this period, although it is stronger over the entire period than during the gold-standard period alone. We have no reason to interpret any pattern of Granger-causality test as damning (since it could fail if the 'causation' comes from different places at different times), so we think of these results as those from a diagnostic test that confirms the results for money growth and inflation interactions of this period rather than casting any further doubts on the role of money.

In Section 6.6 we look further into the law of one price and into the behaviour of inflation rates over time; here we apply the results of two recent tests to the price data. To test to see if prices adjusted as the law of one price level implies, we employ a test of Hatton's (1992) that concentrates on the autocorrelations of relative price levels (one country relative to another). This test shows that these autocorrelations are significant and that the lags in adjustment implied are reasonably short. The second test, of the mean reversion of price levels, is less successful; our provisional conclusion is that such tests would be difficult to implement (and interpret) on these particular data. The last section of the chapter offers some conclusions as well as some important *caveats* about the effectiveness of both the data and our methods of analysis.

6.2 EUROPEAN MONETARY GROWTH AND INFLATION: AN OVERVIEW

In this section we describe briefly the nature and extent of the money and price data, and locate any underlying trends. Of course, each country has a unique historical record, but even at the level of comparison offered here, it is evident that strong industrial and financial growth and the transformation of the European economy into a predominately industrial one generally moved quite rapidly across most of these countries, particularly as the nineteenth century waned. Table 6.1 compares the rates of change of money and price series used in this chapter for the various European countries and the United States. Here we see inflation rates that are lower for all countries except the United States (for the income deflator) when the gold-standard period is compared to the entire period.[2] Money growth rates also behave in

Money and Prices, 1850–1913

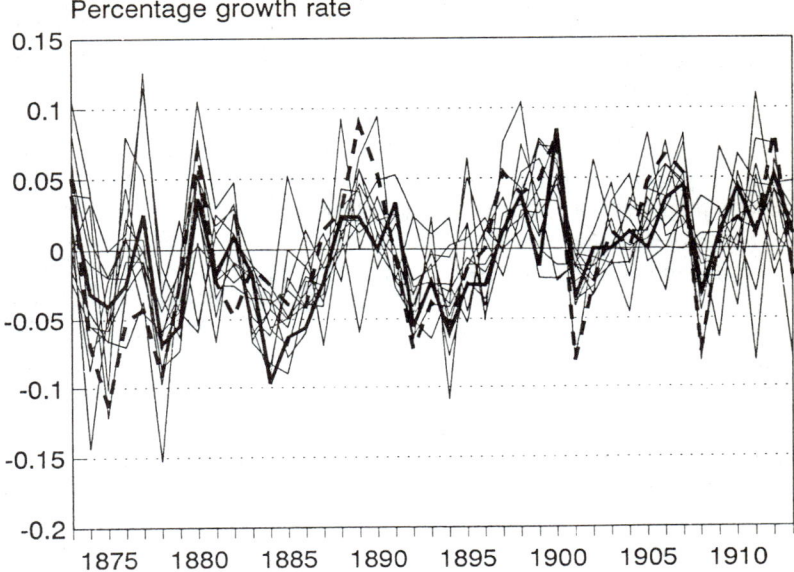

Figure 6.1(a) Wholesale price inflation, 1873–1913

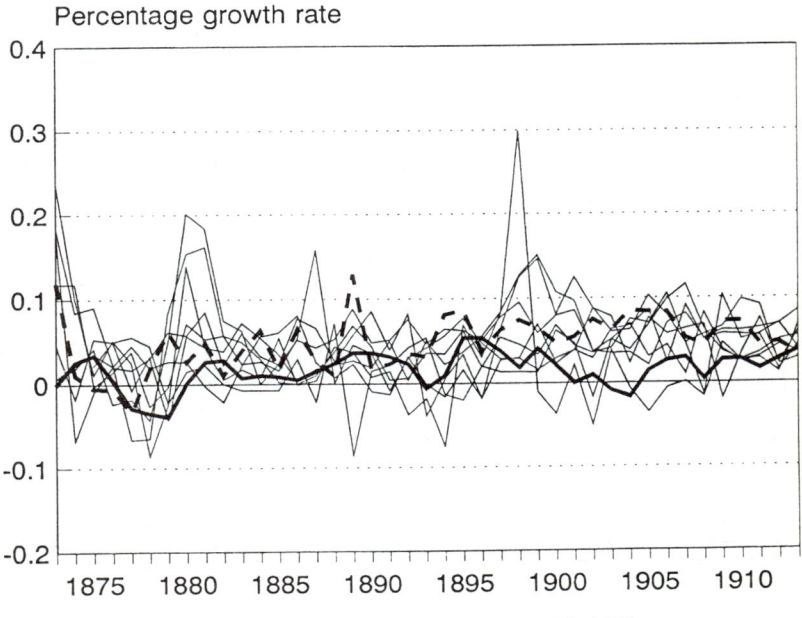

Figure 6.1(b) Money growth rates, 1873–1913

this way, although it is noticeable that money growth rates are rather more rapid than inflation rates. We attribute this result to changes in velocity (as described in Chapter 4) and the related fact that the income elasticity of the demand for money is greater than unity for all these countries except the United Kingdom (see Chapter 7). In any event, the bottom line here is that the gold-standard period produced lower rates of money growth and inflation. This result is certainly not inevitable, since fluctuations in gold production and real (domestic) growth rates can also differ across regimes, but it appears to be true in this case.

Even though the inflation and money growth series do not all refer to the same countries, it is possible to look at all of them together in order to see if the differences narrow over time, as the operation of the classical (post-1870) gold standard suggests might be the case. This plot appears in Figure 6.1, where the wholesale price inflation rates summarized in Table 6.1 are graphed, along with the money growth rates.[3] Note that the series plotted exclude Italy, Spain and the United States. The first two were not on the gold standard for the entire period, while the latter shows less integration with the European countries.

What the pictures do is to illustrate three points very clearly. One of these is that both series have upward trends. Under the gold standard, then, there is a slight upward drift in both inflation rates and money growth rates. The second point is that the inflation rates are much more coincident across series than are the money growth rates. Indeed, the latter look quite disparate, country to country. This illustrates, in another way, the rather unexpected behaviour of the money series. Finally, there does not appear to be any substantial change over the period in the correlation of the series (within each category). This finding suggests that, to a certain extent, financial integration was achieved in Europe before 1873. Others have argued, as we have noted elsewhere, that a much earlier date than this is in fact correct. Note, finally, that the other two measures of prices show the same pattern as the wholesale prices. We selected wholesale prices because of our feeling that they are likely to be the most reliable series available for this period.

We next look at the correlations across borders for both money and prices. For these series, this is easy to do for the 1873–1913 period, but for the earlier years the uneven lengths of the series confuse the comparisons somewhat.[4] The entries in Table 6.2 refer to the growth rates of the variables, with the higher correlations (comparing periods) marked with an asterisk. These results illustrate no real differences across the two periods for consumer price and national product deflator inflation (in parts C and D) since the number of asterisks is about the same on the two sides of the table. On the other hand,

Table 6.1 Money growth and inflation, 1850–1913

	Overall	1873–1913	Data period
A Money growth			
Austria-Hungary	5.68	4.79*	1867–1913
Denmark	5.33	4.75*	1870–1913
France	2.47	2.21*	1850–1913
Germany	5.01	4.62*	1850–1913
Italy	4.44	3.17*	1861–1913
Norway	5.49	4.56*	1850–1913
Spain	1.98	1.98	1874–1913
Sweden	5.89	5.03*	1850–1913
United Kingdom	1.71	1.59*	1871–1913
United States	5.45*	5.68	1867–1913
B Wholesale price inflation			
Austria-Hungary	−0.23	−0.26*	1867–1909
Belgium	0.30	−0.07*	1850–1913
France	0.07	−0.54*	1850–1913
Germany	0.54	−0.46*	1850–1913
Italy	0.05	−0.12*	1861–1913
Netherlands	0.06	−0.66*	1850–1913
Spain	0.63	0.58*	1850–1913
Sweden	0.02	−0.30*	1860–1913
Switzerland	0.25	−0.65*	1850–1913
United Kingdom	0.11	−0.66*	1851–1913
United States	0.30	−0.68*	1850–1913
C Consumer price inflation			
Austria	−0.05*	−0.04	1867–1913
Belgium	0.20	−0.34*	1850–1913
Denmark	0.11	−0.32*	1850–1913
France	0.61	−0.02*	1850–1913
Germany	1.45	0.56*	1850–1913
Italy	0.38	−0.10*	1861–1913
Netherlands	−0.23	−0.38*	1871–1913
Norway	0.63	−0.27*	1870–1913
Portugal	0.22	0.03*	1850–1913
Sweden	0.63	0.16*	1850–1913
United Kingdom	0.00	−0.45*	1850–1913
United States	0.42	−0.38*	1850–1913
D Income deflator inflation			
Denmark	0.80	0.01*	1850–1913
France	0.45	0.08*	1850–1913
Germany	0.82	0.15*	1850–1913
Italy	0.58	0.03*	1861–1913
Norway	0.72	0.27*	1865–1913
Portugal	0.18	0.14*	1850–1913
Sweden	0.38	0.24*	1861–1913
United Kingdom	0.10	−0.22*	1870–1913
United States	−0.50*	−0.31	1869–1913

Note: *Lowest value comparing the two periods.

Table 6.2 Correlations among inflation rates and money growth, 1851–1913 compared to 1873–1913

A Money growth

1851–1913

	Denmark	France	Germany	Italy	Norway	Spain	Sweden	UK	USA
Austria-Hungary	.113*	.184*	.052	.021	.059	-.109	.146*	-.254	.050
Denmark	–	-.185*	.407*	.090*	.315*	-.068	.479*	.238*	.344
France		–	-.059*	.260*	-.047*	-.046	.226*	-.189*	-.090*
Germany			–	.215	.237	.020	.359*	-.376*	.202
Italy				–	.104*	-.028	.111	.113*	.199*
Norway					–	.357	.461	.412	.294
Spain						–	.266	.204	.201
Sweden							–	.420*	.194
United Kingdom								–	.228*
United States									–

1873–1913

	Denmark	France	Germany	Italy	Norway	Spain	Sweden	UK	USA
Austria-Hungary			.593*	.106*	-.032	-.109	-.053	-.002	.324*
Denmark		.035	.176	-.045	.159	-.068	.221	.190	.451*
France		-.272	-.376	.184	-.085	-.046	.015	-.214	-.130
Germany				.256*	.242*	.020	.156	.172	.314*
Italy					-.012	-.028	.175*	-.205	.140
Norway						.357	.722*	-.445*	.326*
Spain							.266	.204	.201
Sweden								.359	.463*
United Kingdom									.220
United States									–

B Wholesale price growth

1851–1913

	Belgium	France	Germany	Italy	Netherlands	Spain	Sweden	Switzerland	UK	USA
Austria-Hungary	.596	.699	.631	.345	.705	.614	.601		.685	.561
Belgium	–	.646	.601	.293*	.581*	.646	.404*		.661	.317
France		–	.778*	.509	.770*	.734	.716*		.787*	.407
Germany			–	.345*	.709*	.756	.653*		.694	.346
Italy				–	.458	.445	.340		.469	.015
Netherlands					–	.679*	.692*		.824*	.333*
Spain						–	.254*		.318	.509*
Sweden							–		.776*	.498
Switzerland								–	.706	.565
UK									–	
USA										–

1873–1913

	Belgium	France	Germany	Italy	Netherlands	Spain	Sweden	Switzerland	UK	USA
Austria-Hungary	.598*	.748*	.733*	.460*	.784*	.389*	.701*	.645*		.762*
Belgium		.661*	.675*	.261	.517	.122*	.751*	.385		.677*
France		–	.772	.526*	.696	.356*	.803*	.715		.682*
Germany			–	.500	.694	.290*	.811*	.610		.556*
Italy				–	.472*	.429*	.516*	.345*		.775*
Netherlands					–	.209*	.659	.512		.590*
Spain						–	.299*	.190		.723*
Sweden							–	.595		.504*
Switzerland								–		.668
UK									–	.456*
USA										–

Table 6.2 (continued)

C Consumer price growth

	Belgium	Denmark	France	Germany	Italy	1851–1913 Netherlands	Norway	Portugal	Sweden	UK	USA	Belgium	Denmark	France	Germany	Italy	1873–1913 Netherlands	Norway	Portugal	Sweden	UK	USA
Austria	.285*																					
Belgium		.149	.351	.319		.249	.417	.090*	.250	.443	.239	.284	.232*	.420*	.376*	.354*	.254*	.444*	.083	.385*	.466*	.339*
Denmark		.539*	.462*	.507*	.344*	.202*	.400*	.436	.506*	.386	.076		.393	.322	.312	.242	.181	.334	.391	.365	.424*	.355*
France			.472*	.531*	.362	.266	.600	.378*	.696*	.583*	.158			.098	.126	.266	.609*	.004	.554	.426	.326
Germany				.630*	.491*	.176	.227	.352*	.481*	.488*	.024				.285	.669*	.227*	.364*	.308	.252	.302	.189
Italy						.344	.536	.350*	.523	.361	−.090					.393	.484*	.402*	.327	.530*	.519*	.322*
Netherlands					.338	.275*	.495*	.196	.387*	.306	−.132							.240	.377	.275	.338*	.212*
Norway							.408*	.005	.436*	.651	.180								.392	.433	.287	.210*
Portugal								.197	.837*	.292*	.221									.007*	.824	.680*	.362*
Sweden									.378*	.445*	.095*									.214*	.282	.372	−.039
United Kingdom										.515	.016											.554*	.292*
United States											.309												.624*

D Deflator growth

	France	Germany	Italy	1851–1913 Norway	Portugal	Sweden	UK	USA	France	Germany	Italy	1873–1913 Norway	Portugal	Sweden	UK	USA
Denmark	.561*	.556	.344*	.731	.329*	.617	.557*	.513	.451	.654*	.232	.754	.022	.746*	.554	.607*
France		.557*	.362	.344	.442*	.317	.416	.435		.484	.419*	.353*	.133	.340*	.498*	.498*
Germany			.491*	.692*	.301*	.670*	.708*	.344			.339	.685	.133	.636	.612	.523*
Italy				.445*	.233	.423*	.505*	.257				.330	.292*	.215	.368	.350*
Norway					.202	.824*	.633*	.489*					.230*	.812	.551	.637*
Portugal						.205	.114	−.005*						.229*	.458	−.084
Sweden							.567*	.395								.492*
UK								.425								.607*
USA																

Note: The higher correlation of the two periods is denoted by *.

wholesale price growth rates show higher correlations (on average) in the period of the gold standard. Since these are the goods most likely to be traded internationally, this is not really an unexpected result. Furthermore, the correlations for inflation rates are often surprisingly high (and marginally higher for wholesale prices than the other measures).[5] Even more interesting are the very low correlations for money growth rates. This result is quite decisive and somewhat unexpected in view of the close correlations among inflation rates. There are also more asterisks (23) in the overall period than in the 1873–1913 period (13). This unusual result for money growth rates continues in all the remaining tests in this chapter. We offer an explanation below.

Looking at the standard deviations of the data provides yet another way to illustrate the operation of the gold standard. In Table 6.3 we illustrate the standard deviations of the first differences (of the logs) of the data, following the format laid down in Table 6.1. This set of results presents overwhelming evidence in favour of something widely thought to be true about the operation of the gold standard: the variation of inflation rates is lower under such a regime. The lower standard deviations, comparing the overall period with the 1873–1913 period, are marked with an asterisk in the table. Whether or not such an outcome derived inevitably from the gold standard, it certainly happened during the period in which the system was widely in operation. We found similar results for the money growth rates as well, except for the United States and the United Kingdom. This result, too, is not unexpected and is not inconsistent with the other results we have for money, since it is the lack of correlation of money stocks, rather than variation *per se*, that is what makes money different from prices.

From this inspection of the data, it appears that there is strong *prima facie* evidence supporting the effectiveness of the classical gold standard, provided that one can explain why money stocks are not correlated across countries. We have done so, provisionally, but now need to investigate the interactions among these variables using cointegration and Granger-causality procedures in order to present yet more of this sort of diagnostic material.

6.3 THE STATIONARITY OF THE DATA

We begin with a discussion of the monetary and price level data.[6] We have several reasons for needing to look at this before proceeding. For one thing, if the data contain unit roots in the level form, then, as an

Table 6.3 Standard deviations of money growth and inflation, 1850–1913

	Overall	1873–1913	Data period
A Money growth			
Austria-Hungary	.049	.031*	1867–1913
Denmark	.054	.048*	1870–1913
France	.038	.034*	1850–1913
Germany	.038	.032*	1850–1913
Italy	.054	.029*	1861–1913
Norway	.039	.032*	1850–1913
Spain	.058	.058	1874–1913
Sweden	.086	.045*	1850–1913
United Kingdom	.017*	.021	1871–1913
United States	.053*	.054	1867–1913
B Wholesale price inflation			
Austria-Hungary	.039	.039	1867–1909
Belgium	.043	.038*	1850–1913
France	.047	.045*	1850–1913
Germany	.056	.052*	1850–1913
Italy	.050	.050	1861–1913
Netherlands	.045	.042*	1850–1913
Spain	.065	.046*	1850–1913
Sweden	.043	.042*	1860–1913
Switzerland	.053	.044*	1850–1913
United Kingdom	.048	.039*	1851–1913
United States	.085	.058*	1850–1913
C Consumer price inflation			
Austria	.030	.029*	1867–1913
Belgium	.052	.048*	1850–1913
Denmark	.035	.027*	1850–1913
France	.049	.035*	1850–1913
Germany	.066	.036*	1850–1913
Italy	.037	.035*	1861–1913
Netherlands	.053	.054*	1871–1913
Norway	.038	.036*	1870–1913
Portugal	.087	.076*	1850–1913
Sweden	.042	.034*	1850–1913
United Kingdom	.032	.027*	1850–1913
United States	.048	.019*	1850–1913
D Income deflator inflation			
Denmark	.042	.030*	1850–1913
France	.043	.032*	1850–1913
Germany	.036	.028*	1850–1913
Italy	.051	.049*	1861–1913
Norway	.038	.037*	1865–1913
Portugal	.059	.039*	1850–1913
Sweden	.037	.034*	1861–1913
United Kingdom	.022	.019*	1870–1913
United States	.026*	.027	1869–1913

Note: Lowest value comparing the two periods is denoted by *.

implication of having non-finite variances, certain test procedures would be invalid; the Granger-causality procedure, which uses an F-test, is one. Since almost all the series contain unit roots, we must test for this sort of 'causality' in first difference form. Indeed, one of the reasons for looking at growth rates and not levels of the data in Section (6.1) was our knowledge that levels of the data generally contain unit roots, while growth rates generally do not.

We also search for unit roots in the data because if the data contain unit roots, then the data might be cointegrated. By this we mean that two (or possibly more) of the series share a common stochastic trend – that is, around whatever common trend can be established, year-to-year deviations from the trend are purely random and have an expected value of zero. In other words, if the price levels in, say, Germany and the United Kingdom both had some long-run (slightly) upward trend, if this trend could be described by a linear combination of the two and if the expected value of any deviation from the combination of the two in a given year would be zero, then we would have established the existence of a common stochastic trend. One might expect such a finding for the gold-standard period, at least when money demand is stable and the trend is provided by the world production of gold. The test procedure is the Dickey–Fuller test (both for establishing a unit root in the unit root test and for establishing the absence of a unit root for the cointegration test).[7]

Table 6.4 contains the results of the unit root tests for the level and growth rates for the two subperiods of the data we are examining. In the table we compare the overall period with the 1873–1913 period that we are identifying with the full operation of the gold standard. The result given is the value of the Dickey–Fuller test statistic, and the value of p indicates the number of lags in the Augmented Dickey–Fuller test. Almost all the results that show a unit root have a zero for the value of p; this indicates that the unit root could be established with the basic Dickey–Fuller test. All unit roots indicated are at the 5 per cent level. When there is no unit root, which is the case for most series when growth rates are examined (on the right side of the table), we indicate this with a 'No'. The following tests of cointegration and Granger-causality take account of the exceptions noted in Table 6.4.

These results present a clear picture for only one of the sets of price data, those for wholesale prices. In this case, all the log-level figures show unit roots at the 5 per cent level of significance, while the growth rates do not. This finding means that cointegration tests can be performed for all of the series in the log-levels, while the Granger-causality tests in Section 6.4 must be performed on the first differences. For the money stocks, the level figures

Money and Prices, 1850–1913

Table 6.4 Unit root tests for money and prices, 1850–1913

	Overall	(p)	Log levels 1873–1913	(p)	Overall	(p)	Growth rates 1873–1913	(p)
A Money								
Austria-Hungary	−1.99	0	−3.15	0	No		No	
Denmark	−2.60	4	−2.63	0	No		No	
France	−1.56	0	−0.37	0	No		No	
Germany	−1.40	0	−2.82	4	No		−2.14	4
Italy	−2.01	0	−0.02	0	−2.17	3	No	
Norway	−2.85	0	−1.20	0	No		No	
Spain	−2.34	0	−2.34	0	No		No	
Sweden	−1.77	0	−1.75	0	No		No	
United Kingdom	−1.79	0	−2.19	0	−3.15	0	−3.28	0
United States	−1.91	0	−2.12	0	No		No	
B Wholesale prices								
Austria-Hungary	−0.10	0	−0.77	0	No		No	
Belgium	−2.13	0	−0.84	0	No		No	
France	−1.84	0	−0.75	0	No		No	
Germany	−2.17	0	−3.03	0	No		No	
Italy	−1.55	0	−1.76	0	No		No	
Netherlands	−2.48	0	−1.65	0	No		No	
Spain	−2.15	0	−2.04	0	No		No	
Sweden	−0.55	0	−1.52	0	No		No	
Switzerland	−2.24	0	−1.06	0	No		No	
United Kingdom	−2.57	0	−0.51	0	No		No	
United States	−1.94	0	−1.64	0	No		No	
C Consumer prices								
Austria	0.23	0	−0.83	0	No		No	
Belgium	−2.50	0	−1.18	0	No		No	
Denmark	−3.00	0	−1.22	0	No		No	
France	No		−1.37	0	No		−1.83	3
Germany	No		−2.24	0	No		No	
Italy	−2.03	0	−3.22	0	No		No	
Netherlands	−1.50	0	−1.58	0	No		No	
Norway	−0.53	0	−1.27	0	No		No	
Portugal	No		−3.21	0	No		No	
Sweden	−2.46	0	−1.32	0	No		No	
United Kingdom	−1.84	0	−0.85	0	No		No	
United States	−1.85	0	0.34	0	−2.54	0	−2.60	2
D Income deflators								
Denmark	−3.23	0	−1.02	0	No		No	
France	−2.84	0	−0.79	0	No		No	
Germany	−2.85	0	−2.49	0	No		No	
Italy	−2.49	0	−2.93	0	No		No	
Norway	−0.98	0	−1.43	0	No		No	
Portugal	No		−2.22	0	No		No	
Sweden	−1.33	0	−1.65	0	No		No	
United Kingdom	−0.99	0	−3.07	0	No		No	
United States	−0.73	0	−1.42	0	No		No	

142   *The Financial System*

all contain unit roots, but in several cases there are also unit roots in the growth rates. This result would stack the odds against cointegration in those four cases, while those data would have to be differenced again for valid inferences to be drawn from the Granger tests. We note that consumer prices have some of the same problems as well as three cases in which the level figures do not contain unit roots.

6.4 COINTEGRATION TESTS FOR MONEY AND PRICES

We have already pointed out that if a vector of time series contains a unit root which vanishes after differencing, and if a linear combination of the series is stationary, then the series are cointegrated. What we now wish to test is whether the patterns in the trends are consistent with cointegration. Recall from the discussion in Chapter 5 that what we are testing for is an equilibrium relationship between the money stocks and price levels among a number of European countries and the United States. The hypothesis is that domestic adherence to the gold standard and the price-specie-flow mechanism drove prices and money to (and maintained) equilibria in the face of supply and demand shocks.

The economic significance of finding cointegration among economic time series should be apparent by now. Under the gold standard, countries that play by the rules would tend to have price level and monetary data that are driven (to a large extent) by world supplies of gold. In this case we do not necessarily have to establish causation running from country to country, since the common trend would be shared by all countries, whatever the origin of the disturbance. That is to say, if all countries on the gold standard played by the rules, then equilibria would be obtained among the prices and money stocks of those countries, and the constraints imposed by the rules of the game would drive prices and money back to their initial equilibria following any shocks to the system. Note that this scenario describes a common stochastic trend. The cointegration test could fail if there is no common trend or, of course, if countries do not play by the rules of the game. It could also fail if the gold standard failed in some fundamental way, although that does not appear to have been the case in this period. Note from our discussion about economic growth in Chapter 3, and from Table 6.1 above, that all these countries had rapidly-growing money supplies relative to the growth of their aggregate output and (especially) their price levels.

Table 6.5 contains the results from tests of the cointegration of the monetary quantities. For the Italian and British cases, as Table 6.4 suggests, we would expect failures of cointegration for the overall period, because there may well be unit roots in the growth rates of the data. We would expect failures for Germany and the United Kingdom for the gold-standard subperiod, for the same reason. Note that the dependent variable is listed on the left-hand side of each table and that cases of 0.05(**) and 0.10(*) significance are indicated. Further, note that in this table we have excluded the French, German and Portuguese results for consumer prices, and the Portuguese result for the gross domestic product GDP deflator, since cointegration cannot be established for series that are not integrated in the first place.[8]

Part A of Table 6.5 shows quite strikingly that the cointegration tests undertaken for the monetary quantities allow us to reject the cointegration hypothesis, both for the entire period and for the gold-standard subperiod. While several of the series contain a second unit root and so would not be expected to show cointegration (look back to Table 6.4), the table still presents a pretty convincing demonstration of a general absence of cointegration among the money stocks, since only one case in each period shows any cointegration at either the 5 per cent or 10 per cent levels; they both involve Germany, incidentally. Of course, the monetary data are suspect in some cases and probably not as reliable as the wholesale or consumer price data, but this result is such a general one that it is unlikely to be the result of a data problem.

One of the reasons the results just stated are remarkable is that the price series, no matter which collection or which period we look at, do show considerable cointegration.[9] It is, of course, possible that the price series are measured more consistently than are money stocks, particularly across countries. But the results in Table 6.5 are quite decisive, showing the opposite of what was found for money, with considerable cointegration shown for both wholesale and cost-of-living indices. Furthermore, the cointegration appears a bit stronger for the gold-standard period. Such a finding would be in line with the operation of the law of one price (level) under the gold standard. Table 6.6 shows the number of cases in which significant cointegration is revealed at the 10 per cent level or lower.

Looking further into the details, we see that the United States is almost never involved in the cointegration story, and neither is Spain (we only have data for wholesale prices for Spain). For the former we shall argue that, since the mechanism that made the gold standard work is the transfer of commodities across borders, the geographic separability between Europe and the United States may well have been decisive. In other words, because of the distances involved, deviations of US price levels from purchasing power

Table 6.5 Cointegration of money stocks and price levels, 1851–1913 compared to 1873–1913

A Money stocks

1851–1913

	Austria-Hungary	Denmark	France	Germany	Italy	Norway	Spain	Sweden	UK	US
Austria-Hungary	–	No	No	No	No	No	No	No	No	No
Denmark	No	–	No	No	No	No	No	No	No	No
France	No	No	–	No	No	No	No	No	No	No
Germany	No	No	No	–	No	No	No	No	No	No
Italy	No	No	No	No	–	No	No	No	No	No
Norway	No	No	No	Yes*	No	–	No	No	No	No
Spain	No	No	No	No	No	No	–	No	No	No
Sweden	No	No	No	No	No	No	No	–	No	No
United Kingdom	No	No	No	No	No	No	No	No	–	No
United States	No	No	No	No	No	No	No	No	No	–

1873–1913

	Austria-Hungary	Denmark	France	Germany	Italy	Norway	Spain	Sweden	UK	US
Austria-Hungary	–	No	No	No	No	No	No	No	No	No
Denmark	No	–	No	No	No	No	No	No	No	No
France	No	No	–	Yes*	No	No	No	No	No	No
Germany	No	No	No	–	No	No	No	No	No	No
Italy	No	No	No	No	–	No	No	No	No	No
Norway	No	No	No	No	No	–	No	No	No	No
Spain	No	No	No	No	No	No	–	No	No	No
Sweden	No	No	No	No	No	No	No	–	No	No
United Kingdom	No	No	No	No	No	No	No	No	–	No
United States	No	No	No	No	No	No	No	No	No	–

B Wholesale prices

1851–1913

	Austria-Hungary	Belgium	France	Germany	Italy	Netherlands	Spain	Sweden	Switzerland	UK	US
Austria-Hungary	–	No	No	No	No	No	No	No	No	No	No
Belgium	No	–	Yes**	Yes**	No	Yes**	No	Yes*	No	Yes**	No
France	Yes**	–	–	No	No	No	Yes*	No	No	No	No
Germany	No	No	No	–	No	No	Yes*	No	No	No	No
Italy	Yes*	No	No	No	–	No	No	Yes**	No	No	No
Netherlands	Yes**	Yes*	No	No	No	–	Yes**	No	No	No	No
Spain	No	No	No	No	No	No	–	No	No	No	No
Sweden	No	No	No	No	No	Yes**	No	–	Yes**	No	No
Switzerland	Yes**	Yes*	No	No	No	No	Yes**	No	–	Yes**	No
United Kingdom	No	Yes**	No	No	No	No	No	No	No	–	No
United States	No	No	No	No	No	No	No	No	Yes**	No	–

1873–1913

	Austria-Hungary	Belgium	France	Germany	Italy	Netherlands	Spain	Sweden	Switzerland	UK	US
Austria-Hungary	–	No	No	No	No	No	No	No	No	No	No
Belgium	No	–	No	No	No	No	No	No	No	Yes**	Yes*
France	No	–	–	No	Yes**	Yes**	Yes*	Yes*	Yes*	Yes**	No
Germany	No	No	No	–	Nu	No	No	Yca*	No	No	No
Italy	No	Yes*	Yes*	No	–	Yes*	No	Yes**	Yes**	Yes**	Yes*
Netherlands	No	Yes**	No	No	No	–	No	No	No	No	No
Spain	No	Yes*	No	Yes**	No	–	–	Yes**	No	No	No
Sweden	No	Yes*	No	Yes**	Yes**	No	–	–	No	Yes**	No
Switzerland	No	No	No	Yes*	No	No	Yes**	–	–	No	No
United Kingdom	No	Yes**	Yes*	No	No	No	No	Yes*	No	–	No
United States	No	No	No	No	No	No	No	No	No	No	–

Table 6.5 (continued)

	1851–1913										1873–1913									
	Austria	Belgium	Denmark	Italy	Netherlands	Norway	Sweden	United Kingdom	United States		Austria	Belgium	Denmark	Italy	Netherlands	Norway	Sweden	United Kingdom	United States
C Consumer prices																			
Austria	–	No	No	No	No	No	No	No	No		–	No	No	No	No	No	No	No	No
Belgium		–	Yes**	No	Yes*	Yes**	Yes*	Yes*	No			–	Yes*	No	Yes*	Yes**	No	Yes*	No
Denmark	Yes**		–	No	Yes*	Yes*	No	No	No		No	Yes**	–	–	Yes**	No	Yes*	Yes**	Yes**
Italy	No	Yes**	No	–	No	Yes*	No	No	No		Yes**	Yes**	Yes*	–	No	Yes*	Yes**	Yes*	No
Netherlands	No	Yes*	No	No	–	–	No	Yes**	No		No	Yes**	Yes*	No	–	No	No	Yes*	No
Norway	No	Yes*	No	No	No	–	No	No	No		No	No	No	No	No	–	No	No	No
Sweden	No	No	No	No	Yes**	No	–	No	No		No	Yes*	Yes*	No	No	No	–	No	No
United Kingdom	No	No	No	No	No	No	No	–	–		No	No	No	No	No	No	No	–	No
United States	Yes**	No	No	No	No	No	No	No	–		No	No	No	No	No	No	No	No	–

	1851–1913								1873–1913							
	Denmark	France	Germany	Italy	Norway	Sweden	United Kingdom	United States	Denmark	France	Germany	Italy	Norway	Sweden	United Kingdom	United States
D Deflators																
Denmark	–	No	Yes**	No	No	No	No	No	–	No	No	No	No	No	No	No
France	No	–	No	No	No	No	Yes*	No	Yes**	–	No	Yes**	No	No	No	No
Germany	Yes*	No	–	No	No	No	No	No	Yes**	Yes*	–	No	No	No	No	No
Italy	Yes**	Yes*	Yes*	–	Yes*	No	No	Yes**	No	Yes**	Yes**	–	No	No	No	Yes**
Norway	No	No	No	No	–	No	No	No	No	No	No	No	–	No	No	No
Sweden	No	No	No	No	No	–	No	No	No	No	No	No	No	–	No	No
United Kingdom	No	No	No	No	No	No	–	No	No	No	No	No	No	No	–	Yes*
United States	No	No	No	No	No	No	No	–	No	No	No	No	No	No	No	–

Note: The probability of obtaining a test statistic as large as was obtained in this case when the null hypothesis is true is 0.10 for * and 0.05 for **.

Table 6.6 Tabulation of cointegration results for Table 6.5

	Overall	1873–1913
Money	1	1
Wholesale	26	30
Consumer	16	23
Deflator	8	7

parity were not eliminated prior to the system receiving a fresh shock; thus the United States may well not have been cointegrated because the form of the test (as performed here) requires a completed reaction within a calendar year. Spain, on the other hand, was not on the gold standard and so nothing much was expected in that case.

For the countries that displayed cointegration, looking at the result for wholesale prices, we notice that interaction is very strong across the board for European countries, with the exception of Germany. Since Germany shows up well on consumer prices, we conjecture that this could well be a data problem with the calculation of the German wholesale price index.[10] These patterns are encouraging, since cointegration of price levels is the expected result for a functioning gold standard, as this one was (in the sense that most countries did not need to devalue in this period).

To explain our results, we now have recourse to the 'monetary approach' theory of the balance of payments. Suppose that the balance of payments of a country is defined in terms of the following *flow* constraint, where X denotes exports and M imports of goods (g), capital (c), and money (m).

$$(X_g - M_g) + (X_c - M_c) + (X_m - M_m) = 0 \qquad (6.1)$$

Then, ignoring capital flows, if domestic prices are lower than international prices, so that X_g is greater than M_g, equilibrium in the balance of payments requires that M_m be greater than X_m – that is, that there be a money inflow. This is the usual explanation of the specie-flow mechanism. In the domestic country, however, the *stock* of money must also be in equilibrium, and nothing we have said so far implies that this result will hold. A standard form of the stock demand for nominal money balances is the following where y denotes real income, and i is a nominal interest rate:

$$M^d = f(y, i, P) \qquad (6.2)$$

If this function is a stable function of its arguments, and ignoring changes in real income for the moment, then with the price level (P) and the interest rate determined exogenously, P and i would drive money demand. For stock equilibrium to hold under these conditions, money supply would have to accommodate itself to money demand (that is, to the exogenously determined price level and interest rate).[11]

The world price level and level of interest rates, then, would be determined by arbitrage in world commodity and capital markets, which would tend to create uniform price levels and interest rates across countries. Frequently, one hears of the 'law of one price' in this context. Usually, this phrase refers to, and is tested by, the cross-country behaviour of individual commodity prices, such as those that largely make up the wholesale price indices with which we have been working. The theories we are considering – both the monetary approach and the specie-flow mechanism – refer to broader measures of prices, although in principle one could sort through the individual product price linkages to arrive at a useful generalization. We are operating at a macroeconomic level of analysis and so we shall forbear. Thus our interest is in whether price levels are stitched together: (a) as if the primary agent were commodity price arbitrage; or (b) as if domestic prices were driven by world gold flows (via domestic money stocks).

We have used the word 'arbitrage' to describe the process that links prices across countries. Necessarily, arbitrage exists in single product lines rather than in price indices and, equally necessarily, it is weakened by transactions and transportation costs, by tariffs and by the state of information available to individuals. Nevertheless, the process of arbitrage, product-by-product, will go into action as soon as the average of prices (or the interest rate) in one country is out of line with that of its trading competitors, and will continue until the difference is eliminated. It is important to emphasize that we are speaking here of arbitrage in the relative *money* prices of commodities, not relative prices *per se*, because what drives both the monetary approach and the specie-flow approach is the quantity theory of money. When the price levels are in line there will be no further changes in the price levels although further arbitrage opportunities may be possible in individual commodities. The former process might be complete, while the latter continues. This observation should help explain why failure to achieve perfect arbitrage in single commodity markets, often found to be the case, is irrelevant to the question of 'arbitrage' across currencies, unless aggregation concerns are dealt with fully.

To see the role of information in the process we have been describing, consider the following offering from McCloskey and Zecher (1981, p. 189):

A flow of gold is by no means a necessary part of this process of arbitrage. In fact, the mere *threat* of arbitrage may be sufficient to bring a nation's prices and interest rates into line with the world's, without flows of anything.

This view is somewhat extreme, but it does underscore the role of information. That is, economic agents in one country, upon receiving information that their money prices are out of line, and knowing that exchange rates will not adjust to validate their prices, will quickly react to adjust their prices. In so doing, they alter the domestic price level, which, in turn, induces a change in the domestic demand for money. This change is either accommodated by the monetary authorities or supplied from the world's stock of money (see also McCloskey and Zecher, 1984).

One thing that is different about this explanation, compared to the usual specie-flow mechanism, is that it argues that international prices drive domestic prices directly and, through money demand, domestic money stocks. In the usual specie-flow theory, it is money entering the monetary base that drives the domestic monetary base, the domestic money stock, and, ultimately, the domestic price level (provided the demand for money is stable and homogeneous). For another, and here we return to our seemingly anomalous results for money and prices, it implies that the domestic demand for money operates as a filter for this effect, transmitting a different effect to the domestic money supply depending on the nature of money demand. For the specie-flow mechanism, the money-demand function filters money stock changes on their way to changes in the price level. In either case, the demand for money has a role to play.

The demand for money is also a function of real income, and a combination of differences in the income elasticity of money demand and different variances and rates of growth of income would cause the money-demand filter to produce a lack of correlation among money stocks, especially in the short run (the context of the correlation and cointegration tests reported to this point). Price levels would be correlated, of course, since that result is achieved by direct arbitrage in international commodity markets. In the long run we would expect the money stock to show a closer relationship across countries, at least if there are infrequent shocks to the system (such as those coming from new gold discoveries). Indeed, we see something like this in the next section, where we look at the intertemporal ordering – at the lags of these relationships – by means of the Granger-causality tests. These results show considerably more monetary interaction, especially for the full run of data (as opposed to only 1873–1913), where the number of cases of such interactions for money is both large and comparable to that for prices.

Most of the studies we shall refer to are 'within country' and, as such, merely try to establish a link between money (or prices) and (usually) the monetary base or high-powered money (currency plus the reserves of the banking system). Jonung (1976), for example, shows that for much of the 1871–1913 period, the high-powered money stock of Sweden was not a particularly effective proximate determinant of the money stock. This finding could be interpreted as a failure to play by the rules of the gold standard, but Sweden in fact stayed on the system throughout the period, so they must have been doing something right. Furthermore, a direct link between Swedish and foreign prices, as argued by the monetary approach to the balance of payments, would not require anything more than an accommodating adjustment of the monetary base.[12] We feel that much of the 'rules of the game' literature can be so interpreted (see the discussion in Chapter 5).

6.5 GRANGER-CAUSALITY TESTS

Another way to proceed to explore the interaction of money and price levels is to employ the test of Granger-causality to search for signs of one-way or bi-directional 'causation' among the nominal variables being considered. We have already described this test in Chapter 4; we now proceed directly to the results. As we pointed out above, since most of these series show unit roots, it is necessary to run the test in first difference form (for those cases). While several of the series do not have unit roots, we believe that for the sake of consistency, all should be handled in first differences.

In Table 6.7 we indicate with a 'yes' the cases in which Granger-causality is established at a 5 per cent level of significance. Note that the causal (independent) variables are listed in the left-hand column and the dependent variables are listed across the table. The data are tested for lags out to five years. The results are summarized rather severely here, thus suppressing some potentially interesting information (such as cases in which bi-directional causation is at different lag lengths, as it usually is), because the amount of material thus generated was just too large.

The Granger-causality tests show considerable interaction among these economies, pretty much across the board except for the United States and Spain. Since the United States is geographically isolated, and Spain is not a member of the gold standard club, this is, again, not surprising. It is noticeable that there is considerably more Granger-causality for money growth than there is cointegration for the same variable. As noted above,

150

Table 6.7 Granger-causality tests for inflation and money growth, 1851–1913 compared to 1873–1913

1851–1913

	Austria-Hungary	Denmark	France	Germany	Italy	Norway	Spain	Sweden	UK	USA
A Money growth										
Austria-Hungary	–									
Denmark	Yes	–							Yes	
France		–	–							
Germany	Yes	Yes		–		Yes		Yes	Yes	
Italy	Yes	Yes	Yes	–	–				Yes	
Norway	Yes			Yes	–	–		Yes	Yes	
Spain							–			
Sweden	Yes				Yes	Yes		–		
United Kingdom	Yes	Yes			Yes	Yes		Yes	–	Yes
United States					–				–	–

1873–1913

	Austria-Hungary	Denmark	France	Germany	Italy	Norway	Spain	Sweden	UK	USA
Austria-Hungary	–									
Denmark	Yes	–								
France		–	–	Yes				Yes	Yes	
Germany			Yes	–	Yes			Yes		
Italy				–	–					
Norway					Yes	–				
Spain					–		–	Yes		
Sweden								–	Yes	
United Kingdom									–	–
United States									–	–

1851–1913

	Austria-Hungary	Belgium	France	Germany	Italy	Netherlands	Spain	Sweden	Switzerland	UK	USA
B Wholesale prices											
Austria-Hungary	–										
Belgium	Yes	–			Yes	Yes				Yes	Yes
France	Yes	Yes	–		Yes	Yes			Yes	Yes	Yes
Germany	Yes	Yes		–	Yes	Yes				Yes	Yes
Italy	Yes		Yes		–	–		Yes			
Netherlands		Yes					–			Yes	Yes
Spain								–			
Sweden		Yes			Yes	Yes		–		Yes	Yes
Switzerland		Yes			Yes	Yes		Yes	–	Yes	Yes
United Kingdom	Yes	Yes	Yes		Yes	Yes	Yes	Yes		–	–
United States							Yes				–

1873–1913

	Austria-Hungary	Belgium	France	Germany	Italy	Netherlands	Spain	Sweden	Switzerland	UK	USA
Austria-Hungary	–	–		Yes	Yes						Yes
Belgium	Yes	–		Yes	Yes					Yes	Yes
France	Yes	Yes	–							Yes	Yes
Germany	Yes	Yes		–							Yes
Italy	Yes	Yes	Yes		–	Yes				Yes	
Netherlands	Yes	Yes	Yes		Yes	–	Yes			Yes	
Spain				Yes			–	Yes			
Sweden								–			
Switzerland									–		
United Kingdom										–	–
United States										–	–

Table 6.7 (continued)

C Consumer prices

1851–1913

	Austria	Belgium	Denmark	France	Germany	Italy	Netherlands	Norway	Portugal	Sweden	UK	US
Austria	–	Yes	–	Yes	Yes	Yes	Yes		Yes	Yes	Yes	–
Belgium	–	–	–	Yes	Yes		Yes		Yes	Yes		
Denmark	Yes	–	–	–	Yes	Yes	Yes		Yes	Yes		Yes
France			–		–	Yes	Yes					
Germany	Yes	Yes	Yes	Yes		–	Yes		Yes	Yes	Yes	Yes
Italy			Yes	Yes	Yes		–		Yes	Yes	Yes	Yes
Netherlands	Yes	Yes			Yes				–			Yes
Norway	Yes			Yes	Yes	Yes	Yes		Yes	–	Yes	Yes
Portugal				Yes	Yes	Yes	Yes			–		
Sweden	Yes	Yes	Yes	Yes	Yes	Yes	Yes	Yes	Yes	–	Yes	Yes
United Kingdom											–	
United States	Yes						Yes		Yes	–	Yes	–

1873–1913

	Denmark	France	Germany	Italy	Norway	Portugal	Sweden	UK	US
Austria	Yes	Yes		Yes		Yes	Yes		Yes
Belgium	–					Yes			
Denmark			Yes	–		Yes	Yes	Yes	
France			–	Yes	Yes	Yes	Yes	Yes	
Germany	Yes	–		Yes	–				Yes
Italy	Yes	Yes	Yes		Yes	Yes			Yes
Netherlands				–		Yes			
Norway	Yes	Yes	Yes	Yes		Yes	–	–	
Portugal	Yes	Yes	Yes	Yes					
Sweden								–	
United Kingdom	Yes	Yes	Yes	Yes	Yes	Yes	Yes		–
United States								Yes	–

D Deflators

1851–1913

	Denmark	France	Germany	Italy	Norway	Portugal	Sweden	UK	US
Denmark	–		Yes	Yes		Yes	Yes	Yes	
France	Yes	–	–	Yes		Yes	Yes		
Germany	Yes	Yes		Yes	–	Yes	Yes		
Italy				–		Yes	Yes		
Norway						Yes	–		Yes
Portugal							Yes		
Sweden	Yes	Yes	Yes	Yes		Yes		–	
United Kingdom	Yes	Yes	Yes	–	Yes				
United States							–		–

1873–1913

	Denmark	France	Germany	Italy	Norway	Portugal	Sweden	UK	US
Denmark	–	Yes		Yes		Yes	Yes	Yes	
France	–	–		Yes		Yes			
Germany	Yes			Yes			Yes		
Italy	Yes		Yes		–	Yes	Yes		
Norway	Yes					Yes	–		Yes
Portugal							Yes	Yes	
Sweden	Yes					Yes			
United Kingdom						–	Yes	–	
United States									–

Note: Yes = The probability of obtaining a test statistic as large as was obtained in this case when the null hypothesis is true is 0.05.

since we expect some such interaction but are agnostic as to the lag length, this is interesting. On the other hand, for the gold-standard period, monetary interaction is considerably less than inflation interaction, a result that is consistent with what we have found before. Note that for the gold-standard period there is less Granger-causality shown than there is for the entire period. We cannot say whether this is the result of smaller samples for the gold-standard period, whether it reflects a failure of the gold standard or, even, whether it reflects the inability of the Granger-causal model to pick up the influences in the later period because the shocks to the system are administered at different geographical locations. But there is certainly a lot of interaction revealed, whatever the time period, and that is the basic finding.

Table 6.8 represents an attempt to organize the results given in Table 6.7 to locate interesting historical regularities. In Table 6.8 we list the total number of interactions in the 'Overall' column, while in the 'Causal' column we indicate the number of times the country on the left-hand side Granger-caused another country. We think of this as establishing its leadership in the sense revealed by the Granger-causal test. Note that we have attempted to identify the leaders in this process with asterisks. These indicate a significantly above average number of interactions or 'leaderships' in the table. We have also totalled the number of interactions here, although the totals have already been referred to in our discussion.

Germany and the United Kingdom are consistently in the lead in all categories, while Italy is, too, for the various measures of prices. France and Austria-Hungary are the two other major economic powers in Europe, at least

Table 6.8 Summary results: Granger causality test

	Overall		1873–1913	
	Total	Causal	Total	Causal
A Money				
Austria-Hungary	12*	6*	3	3*
Denmark	7*	4*	3	1
France	3	1	3	1
Germany	8*	4*	6*	5*
Italy	9*	5*	3	1
Norway	8*	3	4*	2
Spain	1	1	1	1
Sweden	4	3	3	0
United Kingdom	9*	4*	4*	1
United States	1	0	0	0
Total	62		30	

Table 6.8 (continued)

	Overall		1873–1913	
	Total	Causal	Total	Causal
B Wholesale prices				
Austria-Hungary	5	1	8*	3*
Belgium	10*	4*	7*	3*
France	8*	6*	7*	5*
Germany	5	5*	5	3*
Italy	8*	2	4	0
Netherlands	7*	2	6*	2
Spain	1	0	1	0
Sweden	7*	4*	7*	5*
Switzerland	7*	6*	8*	8*
United Kingdom	10*	4*	8*	2
United States	2	1	1	0
Total	70		62	
C Consumer prices				
Austria-Hungary	8	7*	8*	6
Belgium	11*	6*	2	0
Denmark	8	4	6	1
France	7	2	5	3
Germany	16*	9*	11*	6*
Italy	10*	6*	9*	6*
Netherlands	11*	2	10*	2
Norway	7	3	7	2
Portugal	11*	6*	3	3
Sweden	10*	3	5	2
United Kingdom	13*	7*	8*	3
United States	4	3	10*	8*
Total	116		84	
D Income deflators				
Denmark	3	1	9*	4*
France	5*	4*	4	3*
Germany	6*	3*	4	3*
Italy	4	1	7*	5*
Norway	3	2	3	2
Portugal	5*	1	5*	1
Sweden	6*	2	5*	1
United Kingdom	7*	6*	4	2
United States	1	0	1	0
Total	40		42	

Note: Cases in which the number of causal relationships exceed the mean are denoted by an asterisk.

as measured by the size of their economies. France is also above average in price interactions, but not in money; as conjectured above, this might be a data problem (for the estimates of the French money stock). There is no usable Austria-Hungarian price data for such comparisons, but money growth for that country is well above average in its Granger-causal interaction. While Granger-causality is important primarily for establishing the nominal links across countries – and such there clearly were – it is also an important finding that the major economies usually lead the way. That is, because the monetary approach to the balance of payments suggests that commodity flows 'arbitrage' the price level differences among nations, and since the causation generally runs from large (and large exporting) countries to smaller, the result is certainly consistent with the theory. Almost any pattern would be consistent, of course, but one would view with suspicion any revealed mechanism that did not involve the major economies as leaders in some sense. Further, as we shall argue in Chapters 8 and 9, real export flows and real business cycle interactions continue to support the theory in the same way. Finally, except, for consumer prices, the United States is not involved in the Granger-causal interactions. We might expect this result in so far as the mechanism is commodity rather than money flows. We have no explanation of why US consumer prices behave in the way they do, but conjecture that the answer probably lies in the particular make-up of the US consumer price index.

6.6 THE LAW OF ONE PRICE AND MEAN REVERSION

We have shown that the gold-standard period featured high correlations among national price levels (and inflation rates), and strong evidence of cointegration, at least compared to money growth rates. Although these results are consistent enough to establish a case, there are other ways to ascertain if national price levels conformed to the predictions of the law of one price in this period. One such measure is employed by Hatton (1992) who estimates autocorrelation coefficients for UK prices relative to foreign prices. His model is of the form

$$\log\left(\frac{P_k}{P_i}\right)_t = \beta_0 + \beta_1 T + \beta_2 \left(\frac{P_k}{P_i}\right)_{t-1} \tag{6.3}$$

where P_k is the UK price level; P_i is the world price level; and the variable T identifies a time trend. The values of β_2 in his tests are uniformly high, as the theory predicts; in addition, the value $\beta_2 (1 - \beta_2)$ yields an estimate of the length of the lag (the 'mean lag' of the relative domestic price adjustment), which he found to be 1.8 years (on average) for wholesale prices and

Table 6.9 Estimates of autoregressive coefficient relative wholesale prices, 1873–1913

Numerator	Austria-Hungary	Belgium	France	Germany	Italy	Netherlands	Spain	Sweden	Switzerland	United Kingdom	United States
Austria-Hungary	–	.637	.526	.785	.614	.542	.839	.491	.267	.570	.770
Belgium	.619	–	.705	.800	.539	.539	.797	.777	.627	.575	.784
France	.498	.713	–	.822	.650	.609	.902	.582	.545	.475	.684
Germany	.817	.797	.821	–	.687	.716	.813	.636	.660	.797	.817
Italy	.594	.538	.658	.684	–	.428	.860	.642	.485	.610	.735
Netherlands	.580	.501	.611	.724	.426	–	.791	.415	.232	.454	.739
Spain	.781	.806	.913	.814	.869	.800	–	.865	.826	.952	.895
Sweden	.585	.779	.580	.637	.642	.410	.856	–	.358	.675	.718
Switzerland	.353	.592	.551	.668	.482	.233	.808	.352	–	.418	.714
United Kingdom	.514	.619	.476	.801	.613	.467	.938	.678	.421	–	.725
United States	.745	.743	.683	.814	.731	.733	.883	.710	.710	.725	–
Averages:											
Overall	.609	.672	.652	.755	.625	.548	.849	.615	.513	.625	.758
w/o US, SP	.570	.647	.616	.740	.582	.493	–	.572	.449	.572	–

155

3.4 years for GDP deflators. These he judged to be a little on the long side for comfort.

In Table 6.9 we reproduce this test for the period 1873–1913 for all the wholesale price indices we have available. What is in the table are the values of the coefficient β_2 for all possible combinations of relative price levels; all were significant at the 5 per cent level, which confirms Hatton's results in this respect. We have averaged the columns of the table to produce some country-specific results. These coefficients can be used to calculate the 'mean lag' as just described; this is the average lag, in years, implied by the autoregression coefficient β_2.

In more recent years, the lag between money and prices is on the order of 6–18 months (that is, 0.5 to 1.5 in annual terms). If money has to move in order to bring national price levels into line, then it would be reasonable to expect at least that long a lag in this period, and thus Hatton's overall result of a lag of 1.8 years, or ours, calculated from the table (overall) of 1.91 years, are not really in conflict with the predictions of the system.[13] But the figures in the table are biased upwards by the inclusion of Spain (which was not on the gold standard) and the United States (which was somewhat remote from Europe, considering the transportation and communications networks of the time). Dropping these two countries yields a mean lag of 1.39 years for the table, which is shorter than Hatton's result and, in any case, short enough to be in the range predicted by the theory just discussed. The results thus confirm the existence of a law of one price for price levels across countries.

Another thing one might verify is whether domestic (wholesale) inflation rates in this period exhibit 'mean reversion', as one might expect from the stabilizing influence of the gold standard. There is a test of this phenomenon by Meltzer and Robinson (1989) for the period of the gold standard. Their procedure is to look at the first-order autocorrelation of inflation rates within countries, either in raw form (which shows mean reversion only for Italy, a country that was not on the gold standard for the whole period), or filtered. For the filtering (by the Kalman filter), Meltzer and Robinson separate anticipated from unanticipated price level changes and then compare forecasts from the former. They were interested in comparisons between the gold-standard period and the two post-Second World War periods of (relatively) fixed and fluctuating exchange rates. The gold-standard period turned out to have more variable inflation anticipations in many cases, but this result could be (as they note) the result of other factors, notably that national outputs in the earlier period were more variable in the much more agricultural economies of the nineteenth century (see our discussion in Chapter 9 and in Fisher (1992)). We do not find this result implausible, but, at any rate, will not replicate that test here.

For the mean reversion test, we note that the model fitted by Meltzer and Robinson, an ARIMA (1,1,0) may not, in fact, correctly describe the process that generates the price levels in our data period. In Table 6.10, to illustrate the point, we show the result of comparing three reasonable model specifications for the eleven countries for which we have wholesale price data. The specifications are ARIMA (1,1,1), (1,1,0) and (0,1,1), although second lags on both the autoregressive and moving average components were also tried (unsuccessfully). The ARIMA model is described in the Technical Appendix.

We have designated the models selected (by the data, in effect) in the last column of the table. While we did not use a formal criterion such as the

Table 6.10 Model specifications for mean reversion test (t-values in parentheses)

Country	Models				Conclusion
	(1, 1, 1)		(1, 1, 0)	(0, 1, 1)	
	AR(1)	MA(1)	AR(1)	MA(1)	
Austria-Hungary	−0.737	0.880	0.101	0.152	ARIMA (1,1,1)
	(4.20)	(8.81)	(0.16)	(0.92)	
Belgium	0.073	0.270	0.333	0.303	ARIMA (1,1,0)
	(0.19)	(0.78)	(2.30)	(2.03)	or (0,1,1)
France	−0.104	0.518	0.328	0.437	ARIMA (0,1,1)
	(0.57)	(3.02)	(2.24)	(3.07)	or (1,1,0)
Germany	−0.126	0.718	0.407	0.594	ARIMA (0,1,1)
	(0.87)	(6.46)	(2.94)	(4.78)	
Italy	−0.758	1.012	0.122	0.300	ARIMA (1,1,1)
	(5.15)	(119.3)	(0.15)	(2.01)	
Netherlands	0.215	−0.111	0.121	0.130	No model
	(0.26)	(0.13)	(0.75)	(0.80)	
Spain	0.056	−0.115	−0.026	−0.061	No model
	(0.23)	(0.40)	(0.19)	(0.39)	
Sweden	0.023	0.409	0.369	0.427	ARIMA (0,1,1)
	(0.12)	(2.10)	(2.56)	(3.08)	or (1,1,0)
Switzerland	0.452	−0.392	0.136	0.189	No model
	(1.29)	(1.14)	(0.90)	(1.24)	
United Kingdom	0.140	0.092	0.227	0.213	No model
	(0.29)	(0.19)	(1.49)	(1.41)	
United States	−0.255	0.432	0.169	0.182	No model
	(0.98)	(1.81)	(1.10)	(1.19)	

'Akaike' (Akaike, 1970), we could argue that such a procedure would have made the selections noted. Five countries did not produce any model, suggesting that the first differencing was rejected in these cases; we did not pursue these cases further in view of our interest in the mean-reversion hypothesis. Of the six remaining, four show some signs of mean reversion, while two (Austria-Hungary and Italy) show significant mean reversion. This is the same result, essentially, as Meltzer and Robinson report, since they did not include Austria-Hungary. But, again, we must emphasize that their model (ARIMA (1,1,0)) is rejected in seven cases, and in the four cases in which it figures it is preferred (over the ARIMA (0,1,1) model) in only one case. Belgium, France and Sweden thus stand as rejections of the theory, since the AR coefficients are significantly positive (not negative, as the theory implies), but only in Belgium is the AR(1) the superior specification and in this case it is marginally so. We regard this test – and the similar test by Meltzer and Robinson, as inconclusive, on these data.

6.7 CONCLUSIONS

Quite possibly the most important thing we can do at this point is to underscore the limitations of our results. Aside from the usual *caveats* concerning the methods employed – and they are all known to have low power statistically – we must call attention especially to the nature of the data employed. The most important drawback is the shortness of the samples. We have at most 63 observations for each country, and only 40 for what we are calling arbitrarily the 'gold standard period'. That is not enough to appeal to asymptotic results for our statistical methods, so we must be prepared to find different results for different ways of looking at the data. Another problem is that all the data, but especially the monetary data and the national income deflators, could be far off the mark, in view of the difficulty of reconstructing such economy-wide aggregates after the lapse of so many years. For another, annual data such as these are not really the best vehicle for conveying information about financial events that may well have been shorter than a year in duration during this period. We are not, however, in a position to test for the proper frequency of these data.[14]

A further problem, also alluded to in the above discussion, is the concern that individual events could easily run one way and then another – causally speaking – so that general tests such as the Granger-causal test, examining the hypothesis that causation ran one way over the entire period, could easily be confounded. Certainly, the literature makes much of specific well-publicized events, such as the Crash of 1873 and the Baring Crisis of the early 1890s, which originated in different spots.

A related concern is that the period of the gold standard is really two periods, one of falling or level prices (1873–86) and one of rising prices (1897 onwards). We think this observation is not necessarily a concern for correlations, since these should work equally for rising or falling prices and money stocks, but cointegration tests (because of different stochastic trends) and Granger-causality tests (because of different locations of the shocks and long lags) could be compromised. We think this is not a serious problem with our overall results, but in view of the short periods that would be produced by further dividing the 1873–1913 period, are not in a position to evaluate this concern.

We return, then, to the question of how the gold standard worked in this period. First, in terms of the contemporary issue of the inflationary tendencies of fiat currency regimes, the late nineteenth century was a period of relative calm in inflation rates. The fact that the system had a long-run anchor that the monetary authorities could not avoid indefinitely did produce an era relatively free from inflation. In this respect, the gold standard did provide one of the benefits its supporters claim for it.

Concerning the extent to which the prices in gold-standard countries were tied together, resulting in one price level, the results again support the working of the gold standard. Inflation rates were more closely correlated across countries during the gold-standard period and, marginally, there were also more cases of cointegration. In any case, the correlations were surprisingly high for inflation rates, especially when they are compared with money growth rate correlations across these same countries. For money stocks and money growth rates, on the other hand, there are many signs of anomaly, at least if one tries to interpret the results from the point of view of the specie-flow mechanism. Money growth rates were rapid compared to inflation rates, and there were very low correlations of money growth rates across nations. Even more seriously, in this period there was essentially no cointegration of money stocks across borders. Only the Granger-causality tests, which further support the notion of price level interaction, provided any evidence of monetary interaction at this time. Since this is a lagged effect (by the definition of Granger-causality) we conjecture that it is the result of the long-run tendencies of the system to produce money stocks consistent with the successful operation of a gold standard. Throughout all this we have employed the monetary approach to the balance of payments, which emphasizes the arbitrage and threat of arbitrage in goods rather than gold, following the lead of McCloskey and Zecher (1981, 1984), as more consistent with our findings than the alternative specie-flow mechanism.

7 The Demand for Money

7.1 INTRODUCTION

The literature on the demand for money in the late nineteenth century features quite a few results, but they focus typically on individual countries and there are few firmly supported generalizations available. The central questions concern the existence, and stability, of this function but, beyond that, at least for the period we are considering, there are important questions concerning how the demand for money functions of the various European countries interacted with the gold standard. We raised this issue in earlier chapters; now we want to present the results that, we feel, show how this function was important in this period.

In the empirical work reported in this chapter, we locate a stable demand for money in a majority of the nine countries studied, for the gold-standard period (again, arbitrarily 1873–1913). We have usable monetary (and income) data for Austria-Hungary, Denmark, France, Germany, Italy, Norway, Sweden, the United Kingdom and the United States (which we are including partly as a benchmark). In our tests, we employ a model of the demand for money that is very similar across countries, both in form and with respect to the variables employed. This approach, we feel, is consistent with much of the literature on this topic, although there are some important qualifications with regard to the list of countries for which a stable demand could be found, to the literature, and to how our results might be interpreted.

In Section 7.2 we explain a standard econometric model of money demand. The main purposes are to explain the general form of the money demand function and the reasons for choosing the particular function employed. For the gold-standard period, the model often stands by itself, but for the longer period it is often necessary to augment it with structural variables in order to produce better estimates. We explain all this in Section 7.2, before undertaking the empirical work. Section 7.3 contains a summary of the results for all countries, both for the overall period and for the period of the gold standard. We find stable money-demand functions in both periods, but there is a difference: the functions reported for the period of the gold standard generally do not require arbitrary structural variables to render them stable.

The bulk of the chapter undertakes a case-by-case study of each country: this material appears in Section 7.4. We shall survey the existing literature in each case, before turning to the new empirical work. Section 7.5 singles out one coefficient – the income elasticity of the demand for money – and considers what might explain the patterns observed in that parameter, both across countries and over time. This variable appears to interact with structural change in interesting ways in this period, and partly explains how differences in the demand for money might have obscured the workings of the gold standard. Finally, Section 7.6 contains some concluding remarks and some important qualifications.

7.1 ECONOMETRIC SPECIFICATION OF MONEY DEMAND

The model used in this study features partial adjustment in money holding and smoothing in the computation of permanent income. Let the long-run demand for money in per capita real terms be given by

$$m_t^d = \alpha_1 + \alpha_2 y_t^e + \alpha_3 i_t + u_{it} \tag{7.1}$$

where y_t^e is expected (permanent) per capita real income, and the adjustment in money demand is given by the following equation:[1]

$$m_t - m_{t-1} = \beta(m_t^d - m_{t-1}) + u_{2t}. \tag{7.2}$$

Here, β would be less than unity if adjustment were achieved in more than one year. Finally, let expected (permanent) income be defined by the following conventional partial adjustment equation:

$$y_t^e = (1 - \gamma)(y_t + \gamma y_{t-1} + \gamma^2 y_{t-2} + \ldots). \tag{7.3}$$

Here γ is less than unity. If $\gamma = 0$, then expected income would be equal to actual income in period t.

The solution to this model of money demand is given by substituting Equations (7.1) and (7.3) into Equation (7.2) and then performing the Koyck transformation (subtracting γm_{t-1} from each side of the resulting equation). The result yields a 'reduced form' of:

$$m_t = (1-\gamma)\beta\alpha_1 + (1 - \beta + \gamma)m_{t-1} - \gamma(1-\beta)m_{t-2} \\ + \beta\alpha_2(1-\gamma)y_t + \beta\alpha_3 i_t - \gamma\beta\alpha_3 i_{t-1} + w_t - \gamma w_{t-1} \tag{7.4}$$

where w_t is a combination of the (presumed to be independent) errors of Equations (7.1) and (7.2). This equation has five parameters and five variables and is non-linear in the parameters. It is a reduced form – hence the quotation marks – only to the extent that y_t and i_t are exogenous to the money-holding decision. For the countries in our sample, this model is initially tested as the following equation:

$$m_t = \alpha_1 + \gamma m_{t-1} + \alpha_2 i_t + \alpha_3 y_t + e_t. \tag{7.5}$$

Note that this formulation treats the quantity of money as being endogenous (see below).[2]

In Equation (7.4), we have both partial adjustment (β) and income smoothing (γ) and could, in principle, estimate each of these, but we prefer to combine these two elements, in effect, by assuming $\beta = 1$; this produces Equation (7.5). This assumption is simply for convenience, but it would be formally correct if money markets do not take more than a year (our data period) to clear. In effect, then, we are retaining the assumption of the permanent income hypothesis, but not that of partial adjustment. The permanent income assumption in Equation (7.3) is in fact itself a joint hypothesis, with the general notion of forming an expectation about income being coupled with a specific functional form. The specific functional form used here has a geometrically declining set of weights attached to past values of the observed scale variable, as laid out in Equation (7.3). In Equation (7.5), then, α_1, α_2 and α_3 are the values of the parameters of the demand for money. Special interest lies in the value of α_3, the income elasticity of the demand for money when m and y are measured in the logarithms, since, compared to other periods values in this period tend to be high (even above two in some cases, as we shall see). Such a result is consistent with the hypothesis that economic agents placed special emphasis on the services provided by money (and by banks) in this period of rapid growth.[3] This is evaluated by dividing the estimated coefficient on y_t in Equation (7.5) by $(1 - \gamma)$ under the assumption that β is equal to unity.

Note that in Equation (7.5) we are treating the money stock as being endogenous. The reason is that under a fixed exchange rate regime (and a gold-backed fixed exchange rate regime) the monetary authorities must line up domestic prices and interest rates with those of their major trading partners, or risk losing their exchange rate peg. They do this, in effect, by providing money-demand with whatever balances it requires, within the range permitted in the exchange-rate stabilization scheme. What determines the demand for money, then, depends on the exogenously determined interest rate(s) and real income. The former is largely determined in international markets in this period, in effect, while the latter is determined in the domestic economy (see Friedman and Schwartz (1982), and Capie and Wood (1994)). This framework is consistent with our explanation – in Chapter 6 – of why inflation rates but not money stocks are integrated across the European economies. In a nutshell, it is the (dominant) effect of real income on the demand for money that breaks the international link of money supplies.

The way we search for stability with this model is to estimate Equation (7.5) with an appropriate interest rate. Should this function appear to be stable over the period studied – as judged by the tests indicated later in this section – that is the end of the search. If not, the next thing we do is consider two interest rate proxies proposed by Friedman and Schwartz (1982), one measuring the yield on physical assets (a 'proxy yield') and the other measuring liquidity. We shall explain these variables in due course. While this approach generally is the end of the search for the gold-standard period, for the longer period there are still quite a few cases left for which a stable demand for money function cannot be found. What we do then, as suggested by Friedman and Schwartz (1982) and Bordo and Jonung (1987), is to include one or more variables designed to pick up the influence of structural change. What we are after is the effect of urbanization and industrialization on money holding, and our proxies, which are often successful, involve variables such as the ratio of agricultural production (or spending, or income) to industrial production in the economy. This approach was generally successful in improving the fit of the model, but produced only marginally better results for our stability tests.

In our empirical tests, the interest rates employed cover a wide range, with sometimes long rates appearing and sometimes short, and with foreign interest rates performing better than domestic in some cases. We used foreign interest rates because of the possibility that European capital markets were sufficiently well-integrated in this period to qualify these rates as measures of the opportunity cost of holding money (in the absence of better domestic data). Furthermore, in many cases, we use more than one interest rate. This procedure is certainly not inconsistent with the underlying theory of the demand for money. For one thing, one rate could be proxying the direct yield of money (with a positive sign) and the other an opportunity cost (with a negative sign). For another, many of these interest rates are probably poor proxies, being overly smoothed or even largely based on relatively inflexible official rates. Thus two rates might simply pick up different characteristics of the opportunity cost of holding money. This observation could account for the cases when we report two or more interest rates with significantly negative signs.

One of the interest rate variables we use is something Friedman and Schwartz (1982) call a 'proxy yield on physical assets'. In fact, money plays dual roles in the economy, as both an instrument for conducting transactions and as a vehicle for storing wealth. In its second role, money, as any asset, is sensitive to the returns paid on alternative assets, financial or physical. One such easily measured opportunity cost is the growth rate of nominal income. Friedman and Schwartz (1982) use this growth rate as a proxy for the nominal return on physical assets. The justification for this begins with the fact that the rate of growth of nominal income is composed of both the rate of inflation and the rate of growth of real income. The inflation rate captures the expected devaluation over time of a given nominal stock of money compared to commodities, while the growth rate of real income provides a measure of the real growth rate of physical assets. This measure is relevant as an alternative since it proxies the rate of return on real assets (on, in effect, all the real assets in the economy). Both as a hedge against inflation and as a real opportunity for money holders, real assets represent a substitute for money. Accordingly, the expected sign for the variable is negative.

We also employed another transformation of interest rates that appears in Friedman and Schwartz (1982) – the spread between long- and short-term rates. Such a measure captures the direct value of the liquidity provided by money. That is, the difference between long-term and short-term rates could represent the liquidity premium attached to short-term securities. Money is a close substitute for the short-term assets whose yield is measured by the short rate, and so the premium attached to those assets could also apply to money. Thus, as this premium grows – as long-term rates diverge from short – the *ex post* liquidity premium attached to money grows. The rational investor would hold more money, *ceteris paribus*. It is important, in thinking about this variable, to realize that the direct opportunity cost for holding assets of any maturity is likely to be in the same equation, in the form of the percentage change in nominal net national product (NNP) or some other interest rate. Thus the interest rate differential measures the effect of a change in the liquidity premium on money demand. This premium, as noted, is an aspect of the 'own rate' of return on money.

We realize that because we 'fish' in the data pool in the way we do, we cannot claim that these demand-for-money functions are stable; rather, we shall make the claim that a stable money-demand function can be found in many cases, and that it is a stable function of a few key variables. We believe this finding is sufficiently interesting to warrant some attention. In fact, during this period, the countries we are examining experienced quite a few events that could have interfered with the location of a stable demand for money, even assuming that such a thing exists. These include bouts of inflation (and deflation), periods off and then on the gold standard, political upheavals, and wars. Growth rates in domestic product are not steady, either, and there are certainly changes in the way money is produced. Under these conditions, even if one had not read the literature on the individual countries, one has to take very seriously the proposition that money demand is unstable in some of these countries, at least some of the time.

The way this stability is judged is to test for stability using all five of the following tests in each case:[4]

- Recursive residuals
- CUSUM
- CUSUM-squared
- 1-step forecast F-test
- n-step forecast F-test.

In the recursive residuals test, the residuals are added to each other, beginning with the first observation and continuing to the end of the series. If this series wanders outside a band set at plus or minus two standard errors, a violation of stability is indicated. The CUSUM test is based on the cumulative sum of residuals divided by the standard error of the regression, again calculated by adding in one observation at a time. The CUSUM-squared test compares the squared residuals, formed cumulatively, to total residuals, with a ± 5 per cent confidence interval assumed. The 1-step forecast test uses the recursive residuals as one-step-ahead forecasts. This forecast is compared with its standard error to see if it provides a significant deviation of the fit of the model. This version of the Chow Test is calculated cumulatively. The n-step forecast test performs a sequence of Chow tests, computing cumulatively (adding an observation at a time) all feasible breaks in the data. These tests are further explained in the Technical Appendix at the end of the book.

7.3 TESTS OF MONEY DEMAND IN NINE COUNTRIES: SUMMARY

Full data period

In this section, we present a summary of the tests just described for all the countries in our sample. To economize on space, we shall begin with summary tables and illustrative figures to which the reader should refer as the individual countries' stories are related (in Sections 7.4 and 7.5). In Table 7.1 we present the basic estimates of Equation 7.5 achieved by trying different interest rates (or the 'proxy yield'); this is a reasonably strict test of Equation 7.5 as it is written above. We judge a test to be 'successful' when it produces the best goodness-of-fit parameters (R-bar square, *t*-values, and BG *p*-values).[5] These results are, as we have already emphasized, not *the* demand for money in each case, but *a* demand for money.

Table 7.1 Demand for money, 1850–1913, basic model, one interest rate

Country and period	Constant	Lagged money	Income	Long rate	Short rate	Adjust R^2	BG p-value
Austria-Hungary[a]	−1.216	0.876	0.337	−0.311		0.995	0.022*
1867–1913	(2.77)	(27.85)	(3.26)	(3.11)			
AR(1)	−0.661	0.927	0.193	−0.215		0.996	0.095
	(2.21)	(41.45)	(2.68)	(2.70)			
Denmark[b]	−0.530	0.738	0.402	−0.162		0.992	0.101
1870–1913	(1.20)	(10.52)	(3.00)	(3.06)			
France[c]	−1.324	0.778	0.403	−0.449		0.990	0.316
1850–1913	(5.07)	(18.40)	(5.45)	(4.25)			
Germany[d]	−1.302	0.833	0.362	−0.264		0.997	0.060
1850–1913	(3.56)	(17.11)	(3.60)	(3.11)			
Italy[e]	0.260	0.905	0.373		−0.507	0.985	0.989
1861–1913	(2.99)	(39.32)	(3.65)		(4.47)		
Norway[f]	−0.674	0.960	0.150	−0.290		0.998	0.310
1865–1913	(1.65)	(33.05)	(1.66)	(3.86)			
Sweden[g]	−0.974	0.885	0.284		−0.026	0.994	0.005*
1861–1913	(1.61)	(16.56)	(1.93)		(1.86)		
AR(1)	−1.692	0.800	0.477		−0.031	0.995	0.980
	(1.94)	(9.87)	(2.26)		(1.99)		
United Kingdom[h]	−0.255	0.546	0.458		−0.017	0.973	0.017*
1871–1913	(2.49)	(6.71)	(5.47)		(4.48)		
AR(3)	−0.279	0.589	0.425		−0.011	0.980	0.646
	(1.95)	(4.95)	(3.71)		(2.93)		
United States[i]	0.581	0.736	0.575		−0.012	0.996	0.045*
1869–1913	(6.73)	(17.18)	(5.70)		(2.85)		
AR(1)	0.697	0.691	0.668		−0.019	0.996	0.153
	(5.92)	(12.29)	(5.20)		(3.94)		

Notes: Figures in parentheses are *t*-statistics.
Variables used : [a] Proxy yield, GNP; [b] German long-term rate, GDP; [c] Proxy yield, GDP; [d] Proxy yield, NNP; [e] Proxy yield, GNP; [f] Norwegian long-term rate (spliced to British Consol rate, GDP; [g] Bank of Sweden discount rate, GDP; [h] Open market discount rate, GDP; and [i] Commercial paper rate, GNP. All money stocks are measures of broad money. The AR process is described in the Technical Appendix.
Sources: See Data Appendix.

The fits of these equations are good in terms of t-values and R^2 statistics, but four of the nine tests fail the serial-correlation check (indicating possible misspecification). When we use an autoregressive correction (usually an AR(1)), the serial correlation problem disappears. These results are included in the table and marked AR(n) immediately after each of the unsuccessful tests. The parameters of the nine correctly specified equations indicate significantly negative interest rate coefficients lying between 0 and −0.5; these are consistent with theoretical expectations. The income coefficients are, similarly, highly significant. They are, though, short-run estimates; we have included long-run estimates for these equations in Table 7.4 on page 183, using only the results that show no significant serial correlation. These present a plausible set of coefficients even though all but the UK result yield long-run elasticities significantly greater than unity. We believe this aspect of the demand for money is characteristic of this period of relatively rapid monetization, as was the case in all these countries except the United Kingdom. This topic is considered further in Section 7.5.

When we apply the stability tests referred to in Section 7.2, however, we encounter further problems. For the four cases where serial correlation required an AR term, we are unable to perform the stability checks. Of the five remaining cases, four show significant failures of the stability checks. In Figure 7.1 we report the worst-case result for these five countries, with the pictures shown being the Recursive Residuals test and the CUSUM of Squares test. For all but Denmark, whether it is $+/-$ 5 per cent significance or $+/-$ two standard errors around the estimates, there are isolated spikes that penetrate the boundaries. Germany is a particularly interesting case, with the spikes in 1864 and in the early 1870s. Whether it is a serial correlation problem or a failure of the stability check, these tests of the basic model – using just one interest rate – are clearly not successful over the entire set of data available.

We can see why, at least in an approximate sense, by introducing structural variables into the same testing format. In Table 7.2 the same equation is tested for the entire period, but this time with the addition of arbitrary structural variables and with the admission of more than one interest rate. In all but the stable Danish case, which was not retested since it passed in the first round, this produces a better fit by one criterion or another.

The purpose of this exercise is to see what it costs – and what variables are involved – to stabilize the money-demand function. Note that we intend to explain the specific structural variables in the detailed discussion of each country. The general idea, though, is to try to pick up the effect of changes in

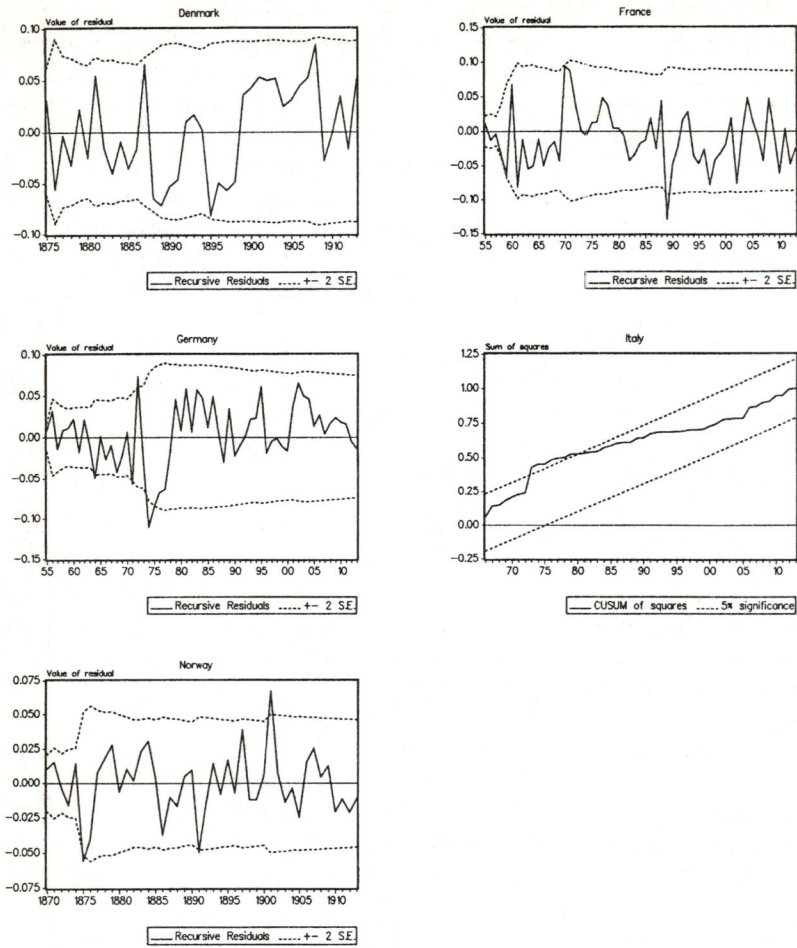

Figure 7.1 Residuals tests for Table 7.1

the financial community that were induced by the transformation of these countries from an agricultural base to an industrial/commercial base. Increasing urbanization is an aspect of this transformation as well, although we do not have annual indices to measure this influence directly. In any case, the multiple interest rate, structural variable format does produce sensible results, on the whole, with significant (and positive) income coefficients and

Table 7.2 Demand for money, 1850–1913, basic model with structural variables

Country and period	Constant	Lagged money	Income	Long rate	Short rate	Structural variable	Adjust R^2	BG p-value
Austria-Hungary[a] 1870–1909	−0.277 (0.48)	0.693 (8.39)	0.284 (2.98)	−0.260 (2.89)	0.005 (1.53)	−0.0005 (2.50)	0.996	0.039*
AR(1)	−0.828 (3.13)	0.932 (47.88)	0.212 (3.38)	−0.207 (2.94)	0.006 (3.29)		0.997	0.057
Denmark[b] 1870–1913	−0.530 (1.20)	0.738 (10.52)	0.402 (3.00)	−0.162 (3.06)		0.992	0.101	
France[c] 1850–1913	−1.368 (5.14)	0.881 (18.22)	0.290 (3.80)		−0.008 (1.20)	0.210 (4.19)	0.989	0.384
Germany[d] 1850–1913	−1.328 (3.15)	0.722 (12.70)	0.416 (3.34)	−0.275 (3.23)	−0.124 (3.14)	0.151 (3.05)	0.997	0.131
Italy[e] 1861–1913	−0.100 (0.80)	0.639 (8.49)	0.603 (5.46)	−0.502 (4.96)		0.265 (3.67)	0.988	0.235
Norway[f] 1865–1913	−0.420 (0.99)	0.887 (17.59)	0.156 (1.76)	−0.214 (2.52)		0.014 (1.75)	0.998	0.315
Sweden[g] 1861–1913	−0.602 (0.99)	0.873 (17.37)	0.212 (1.70)		0.009 (2.51)	−0.019 (0.96)	0.995	0.164
United Kingdom[h] 1871–1913	−1.392 (4.14)	0.604 (7.91)	0.706 (7.33)	−0.031 (2.06)	−0.015 (4.15)	0.091 (3.79)	0.979	0.641
United States[i] 1869–1913	0.989 (8.64)	0.673 (18.74)	0.501 (6.28)	0.030 (2.70)	−0.025 (4.96)	−0.037 (5.27)	0.998	0.509

Notes: Figures in parentheses are *t*-statistics.
Interest rate and proxy variables used by row: [a] Proxy yield, US call money rate, coal production (Austria-Hungary) per capita; [b] German long-term rate; [c] French short-term rate (LLB), ratio of agricultural to non-agricultural production (nominal); [d] Proxy yield, per capita coal production, per capita railroad track open; [e] Proxy yield, per capita track open; [f] Proxy yield, currency–deposit ratio; [g] US call money rate, ratio of agricultural to industrial production in GDP; [h] Open market discount rate, Consol rate, ratio of agricultural production to industrial production; and [i] Commercial paper rate, commercial bond rate, ratio of agricultural production to pig iron production. All money stocks are measures of broad money.
Sources: See Data Appendix.

significant (and generally negative) interest rate coefficients.[6] Note that there is now only one case – Austria-Hungary – that shows significant serial correlation. The discussion of these results on an individual country basis continues in Section 7.4.

In Figure 7.2, we show results for all cases in which the stability checks, discussed above, failed to hold. Indeed, there are five cases in which this could be claimed, putting aside the Austria-Hungary case as possibly misspecified. We shall argue below that the French result is because of the way the monetary data are prepared, and could be taken as suggestive of stability. But Italy, Germany, Norway and Sweden stubbornly remain unstable for this period. Thus only three of the nine countries showed fully satisfactory results, although the failures in France and Norway at only one point in each case are certainly encouraging, and this result is an improvement (over Table 7.1), but still leaves quite a few unsatisfactory money-demand functions. Again, we remind readers that in this chapter we

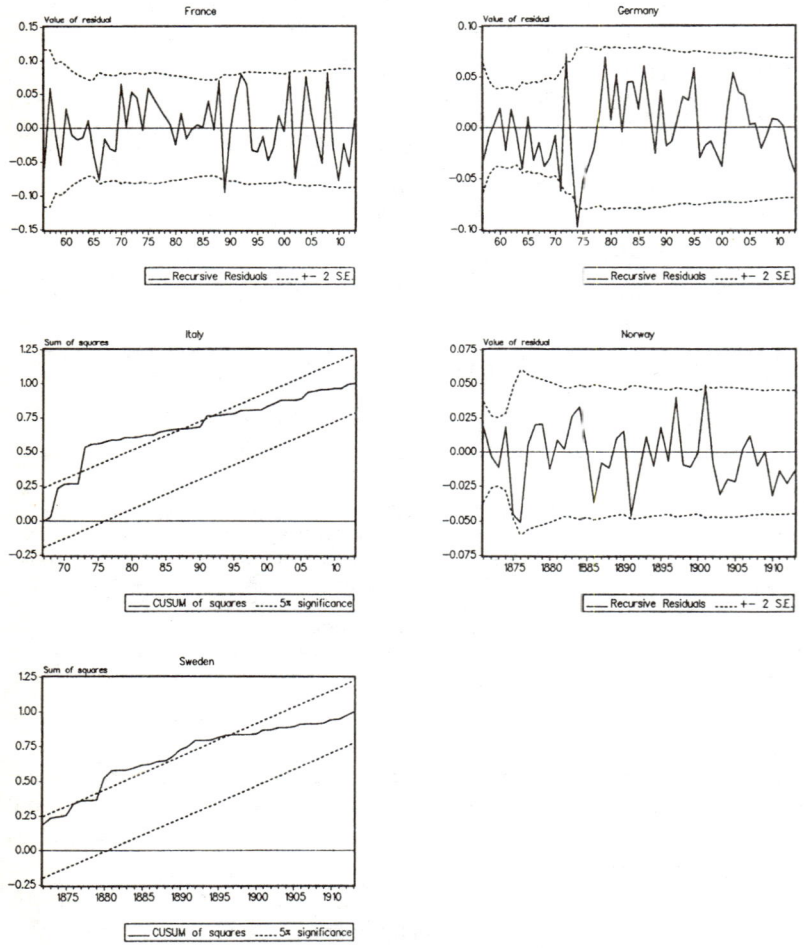

Figure 7.2 Residuals tests for Table 7.2

are trying to locate a stable demand for money function. It is readily apparent that there does not exist a simple notion of the demand for money that is stable for the entire period studied in this section for all countries, at least for the data we were able to muster.

1873–1913

Table 7.3 contains the results for the tests of Equation (7.5) for the 1873–1913 period – that is, the period that we have identified arbitrarily as that of the gold standard. Most of these countries spent some time on the gold standard during this period, although Italy and Austria-Hungary were off the gold standard more than they were on over the forty years, and France was de facto on the system from 1878 through the end of the period in question.

These equations appear to work very well in terms of coefficients of determination; BG serial correlation p-values; and the signs, values and t-values of the coefficients for most of these countries, although there are still a few problems. The income coefficients are always significantly positive and the interest rate coefficients negative when only one interest rate is used. The interest rate coefficients (which are approximately short-run elasticities) have the values one typically finds in such studies. The two exceptions are for the German short-term rate, which is the interest rate differential (and has the expected positive sign), and the Swedish long-term rate. Since there are two rates in the latter case, one (the long-term rate) may be proxying the 'own' rate of interest on money (which would be expected to have a positive sign). We shall have more to say about this and all other cases in Section 7.4, on a country-by-country basis, and in Section 7.5, when we look at the behaviour of income elasticities.

When we look at the residual tests for stability for these equations, for the non-AR versions, only Austria-Hungary and France show violations. We shall not produce these two results, but note that the Austria-Hungary result shows a violation for the 'recursive residuals' test at only one data point (1906), while the French test (caused, we believe, by the interpolation procedure adopted by Saint Marc (1983)) continues to show an anomaly at 1889. Of the remaining seven cases, two show significant serial correlation (Denmark and the United Kingdom); while they are treated successfully by an AR correction (as shown in the table) they can no longer be tested for stability. Thus five cases show completely satisfactory results and stability, which compare favourably with the three cases in Table 7.2 and the one in Table 7.1. Note, also, that the cases treated with an AR correction could be stable for all we know, while the unstable cases might be exhibiting data

Table 7.3 Demand for money for nine countries, 1873–1913 (t-values in parentheses)

Country	Constant	Lagged money	Income	Long rate	Short rate	Proxy yield	Adjust. R^2	BG p-value
Austria-Hungary[a]	−0.859	0.930	0.223			−0.237	0.998	0.841
	(3.11)	(43.76)	(3.37)			(3.91)		
Denmark[b]	−0.561	0.730	0.364	−0.068			0.989	0.028*
	(1.10)	(8.13)	(2.40)	(2.64)				
AR(1)	−1.387	0.546	0.673	−0.113			0.990	0.864
	(1.47)	(3.22)	(2.31)	(2.41)				
France[c]	−0.956	0.711	0.411			−0.554	0.967	0.711
	(3.18)	(10.28)	(4.43)			(4.28)		
Germany[d]	−1.122	0.767	0.428	−0.053	0.013	−0.328	0.996	0.768
	(2.42)	(12.26)	(3.53)	(3.54)	(2.10)	(2.79)		
Italy[e]	1.838	0.653	0.510	−0.075		−0.529	0.985	0.475
	(5.21)	(10.85)	(6.02)	(4.42)		(6.46)		
Norway[f]	−1.169	0.547	0.612	−0.049	−0.042	−0.242	0.998	0.475
	(2.59)	(5.54)	(4.29)	(3.34)	(2.36)	(2.60)		
Sweden[g]	−1.180	0.814	0.377	−0.030		0.247	0.997	0.057
	(2.46)	(12.96)	(2.84)	(2.84)		(1.90)		
United Kingdom[h]	−0.208	0.571	0.423	−0.015			0.971	0.000*
	(1.87)	(7.12)	(4.98)	(3.44)				
AR(1)	−0.279	0.589	0.425	−0.011			0.980	0.646
	(1.95)	(4.95)	(3.71)	(2.93)				
United States[i]	0.618	0.739	0.585	−0.026			0.997	0.174
	(7.47)	(18.88)	(6.38)	(4.27)				

Notes: Figures in parentheses are t-statistics.
Interest rate data by rows: [b] US corporate bond rate; [d] Italian long-term rate and difference between German long and short rates; [e] Italian long-term rate; [f] Norwegian long-term rate and Italian long-term rate; [g] US corporate bond rate; [h] UK open market discount rate and [i] US commercial paper rate.
(*) This equation also has the deposit currency ratio (coefficient = .036 (t = 3.60)).

problems at isolated points. Thus we tentatively conclude that the gold standard (period) brought more stability to the demand for money of these countries (although it also, no doubt, brought better data as well). We remind readers that we searched for these stable functions by adding variables to the basic model, so this only establishes the *existence* of a stable function when

The Demand for Money

this could be demonstrated. Whether a stable function exists for the other countries is an open question that could be affirmed with better data or for different formulations of the model.

7.4 DISCUSSION OF INDIVIDUAL COUNTRIES

The data for *Austria and Hungary*, thanks to the work of Komlos (1981, 1983, 1987, 1990), appear to be adequate for the task at hand. Part of the problem is that these were two distinct economies in many respects – although they had a close relationship politically – and so it is not clear that an aggregation across borders makes complete economic sense; see our discussion in Chapters 1 and 2 on this matter. In particular, Austria in this period was more industrial than Hungary and, concomitantly, had a more-developed financial system. Hungary, in turn, had a stronger growth rate in its industrial sector in this period, from a smaller base.

Komlos (1987) has published a demand for money paper that is very similar to our approach and, in particular, includes recursive residual tests to check for stability. Komlos reports:

> The recursive residuals test, described below, detected instability in the functional relationship of a standard money-demand equation: the coefficients of the independent variables varied systematically over time. The tests indicated a marked departure from stability in the late 1880s. (p. 588)

This result is produced by a precipitous decline in the income velocity of money at that point. He attributes this decline to a new postal savings system (in 1883), a decrease in the required reserves of the central bank (in 1887), the adoption of the gold standard (in 1892), an increase in high-powered money caused by a government fiscal transfer, and to a government-led switch to deposit banking.

In Table 7.1 we show two estimates of Equation 7.5, one with an evident serial correlation problem and one with an AR(1) correction. Note that while we did have interest rates for Austria-Hungary, they did not work as well as foreign rates in any of the tests reported in this chapter. Instead, the best-performing 'interest rate' in our collection, in terms of its t-statistic, proved to be the proxy yield (the growth rate of nominal GNP in Austria).[7] A stability test on the misspecified first result is irrelevant; the same test cannot be performed for the specification with the AR(1) correction. Thus we cannot address the stability question for Austria-Hungary for this period, although the second estimate does appear to be well-determined (with statistically significant and sensible coefficient values). In Table 7.2, for the same period, in the first row we show a reasonably well-fitting equation, using the per capita volume of coal output as a structural proxy, but again, it has serially-correlated errors. It took an AR(2) correction to eliminate the serial correlation in this case, but the resulting coefficients made no sense. We report, therefore, a result that has no serial correlation after correction, but equally has no structural proxy. Again, we are unable to address the stability question when an AR term is present.

In Table 7.3 we show our estimate of Equation (7.5) for Austria-Hungary for the 1873–1913 period (of the gold standard). Here, again, we use the proxy yield as the sole interest rate. This approach works well, with the expected sign. In this case, the serial correlation test succeeds, but the formulation nevertheless fails the recursive residuals test at one point (1906).[8] While we are, in this instance, able to confirm Komlos's finding of instability for the demand for money in Austria-Hungary, our shift is not at one of the points he identifies. We think, in any case, that further improvements in the data are especially likely to clarify the situation for Austria and Hungary.

Continuing with our alphabetical tour of Europe, we next look at the demand for money in *Denmark*. There is no literature here, in any of its guises, and so the following results stand on their own. The Danish data, particularly those for national income, appear to be adequate for the task. In Table 7.1 we record a satisfactory result for the basic test of Equation (7.5), The various stability checks, further, show no instability; this result is, indeed, the only completely successful one in Table 7.1, showing no obvious anomalies at all (this is not shown in Figure 7.1, which merely records the failures). Note that the successful interest rate in this case is a German one, in view of our inability to locate any Danish interest rates in the literature. Since this case produces stability, we have carried the same results over into Table 7.2.

The equation reported in Table 7.3 for 1873–1913 is not satisfactory, however, in view of the presence of serial correlation (the interest rate in this case is the US commercial paper rate). An AR(1) correction cleared up the serial correlation problem, as reported in the table, but, again, no stability checks were possible. This case could be judged stable (since the uncorrected result in Table 7.3 is stable) but we have not shown that.

The only previous study of the *French* demand for money appears in Fisher (1992). Fisher found French money demand to be unstable and only estimated it satisfactorily for two arbitrarily separated subperiods: 1850–70 and 1880–1910. Indeed, other investigations in that study found quite a few anomalies in the relationship between money and prices in France, with only a simple test of the Fisher-effect (between inflation and nominal interest rate) confirming monetarist predictions.

Table 7.1 has an estimate of Equation (7.5) for the French data for the entire period. This result appears to fit well, with sensible coefficients and no serial correlation. The interest rate used is the proxy yield on physical assets as described above. With respect to the stability check, as Figure 7.1 indicates, there appears to be a shift of the function in 1889. This version of the model also produces failures of the stability check for the 1-step and n-step Chow tests. There was only one data point, however, that produced the failure in all cases. Inspection of the underlying data suggests very strongly that the interpolation procedure used by Saint Marc (1983) is to blame and that the French demand for money may well, in fact, have been stable.[9]

In Table 7.2 we show a result for the French data using a structural proxy (and a different interest rate). The proxy is the ratio of agricultural to non-agricultural production, measured in nominal terms. This model also fails the stability check, as indicated in Figure 7.2; again, it is the 1889 observation that lies outside the boundary. Table 7.3 has the estimate of Equation (7.5) for the French data for the 1873–1913 period; this again appears to fit quite well, with reasonable signs, values and significance for the various coefficients. The interest rate is the proxy yield on physical assets in this case. Again, there appears to be a shift of the function in 1889 (not shown). This version of the test also produces failures of the stability check for the 1-step and n-step Chow tests at the same point. We continue to believe that it is the method of preparing the monetary data that produces this result. We cannot claim stability here, of course, but we do suggest that the French function is stable, if only because any effort to smooth out that spike in the data would likely produce stability.

For *Germany*, estimates of the demand for money appear in Fisher (1992). Fisher finds, using money demand functions with AR corrections, that the function is unstable, centred around 1882. He produces CUSUM and CUSUM-Square tests to support this conclusion. Our result for Germany for the 1850–1913 period appears in Table 7.1. The equation fits well, employing the proxy yield on physical assets as the opportunity cost; this variable has the expected negative sign. The serial correlation p-value is marginally satisfactory (at 0.06), but, even so, the equation tested is unstable, as Figure 7.1 illustrates, with the 'recursive residuals' shooting outside the boundaries twice in the early 1870s. We tried quite a few structural proxies in the German case, ending up with two (probably interacting) ones, the per capita logs of coal production, and railway track open. These appear in the estimate reported in Table 7.2. Separately, these would indicate the influence of industrialization (and even urbanization) on money demand, but it is impossible to rationalize their offsetting signs, unless they are performing in separate periods (possibly railways early and coal later, during the dramatic increase in steel production towards the end of the century). Since the model remains unstable, as illustrated in Figure 7.2, the point is moot. Note that the proxy yield continues to serve as the interest rate, with the expected sign.

For Germany, estimates of the demand for money for 1873–1913 appear in Table 7.3. The equation fits well, with the proxy yield on physical assets (with the expected sign), the Italian long-term interest rate, and the difference between the German long-term and short-term rates. In this test, the sign of the interest rate differential is the anticipated positive one, as described above. This function passes the stability tests in this form and also exhibits no serial correlation. A stable money-demand function can thus be located for Germany for the period of the gold standard.

The demand for money in *Italy* has received some attention in the literature, with the original and still-prevailing position being that of Spinelli (1980, p. 83), as follows:

> The central result is that there exists a stable demand for money for Italy during this period. This function is homogeneous in prices and yields parameter estimates close to those found previously for other countries.

Spinelli's study covers the very long period 1867–1965, on annual data. A later paper (Calliari, Spinelli and Verga, 1984) acknowledges that there was an error in the money stock series and that the interest rate employed was an official discount rate and therefore not a market rate. The later paper also deflates by the cost of living index rather than the GNP deflator. While the new results appear to be consistent with the earlier work, and there is an estimate over a period of time comparable to that used in this study, there are no formal tests of stability offered. In a study by Fisher (1992), which is the only other result in the literature, the stability of the demand for money is not confirmed. The main result is that there appears to be a sharp contrast in the way the model fits over two subperiods, with a relatively well-defined function appearing for the period 1880–1910, while the same function fitted over an earlier (and overlapping) period does not fit very well at all (in terms of producing no significant independent variables).

When we put the Italian data through our tests for the entire data period, we are again unable to confirm its stability. In Table 7.1, we show the estimate of Equation (7.5). This equation is well-determined and shows no serial correlation, but proves to be unstable, as indicated in Figure 7.1, where the CUSUM-square calculations wander outside the significance bounds for much of the 1870s. In Table 7.2 a structural proxy, the per capita logs of railway track open, improves the fit of the equation marginally, but, as revealed by Figure 7.2, produces an even less impressive graph for the CUSUM-square test. These results are the best-determined of quite a large number of passes at the data, using a full battery of interest rate and structural proxy variables. All results that were at all well-determined proved to be unstable, and so this result has to stand for the Italian case for the entire period.

When we test the Italian data over the period 1873–1913 we obtain a comparatively good fit, with no sign of serial correlation; the result appears in Table 7.3. These results were achieved with the Italian long-term interest rate and the proxy yield on equities. Note that these variables have the expected (negative) signs. The stability checks are also satisfied for this formulation (not shown). So, in this case, we side with the literature in locating a stable money-demand function for Italy in the gold standard period.

Norway was part of the successful Scandinavian monetary union in this period, and so it might be expected that we would obtain similar results to those for Denmark and Sweden. In a 1983 paper, Klovland tests a variety of money-demand functions for Norway, for the 1867–1980 period. His specification includes permanent income, a three-year moving average of the ratio of deposits to currency, a long-term interest rate, and a measure of expected inflation.[10] His measure of money is broad money (M2). The results indicate a stable demand for money over the entire period. One of the successful tests reported employed a Chow test at a break in 1913 (comparing 1867–1913 with 1914–39). This seems quite promising.

There are some slight differences in the data used in our version of the Norwegian test. The results of testing Equation (7.5) appear in Table 7.1. We are modelling the permanent income hypothesis implicitly in this study, and not separately measuring inflationary expectations, (though they appear in the nominal interest rate, of course). Furthermore, the interest rate is the proxy yield on physical assets in our tests. Here we show a reasonably close fit with no serial correlation, although the income parameter is just significant at the 10 per cent level. Even so, as indicated in Figure 7.1, the equation produced fails the 'recursive residuals' test.

Table 7.2 reports a second result for Norway, employing the deposit-currency ratio as an additional variable; this is Klovland's procedure. We conjecture that this variable picks up the effect of the increasing financial sophistication of the Norwegian economy on the decision to hold deposits rather than currency. That is, a positive sign is consistent with the increasing (per capita) use of the financial services provided by banks in this period. The fit is not as good as one might wish (the two marginal coefficients are significant only at the 10 per cent level), and there is a marginal rejection of stability (in 1901). This result appears in Figure 7.2. A three-year moving average of the deposit-currency ratio is actually employed successfully by Klovland in his study. We tried this adjustment, and several other proxies, but the deposit-currency ratio, unsmoothed, worked the best. We think this is a marginal case – possibly stable – but cannot make that claim on the evidence given here, for this period.

For the period 1873–1913, we report in Table 7.3 what proves to be a stable money-demand function for Norway. It is important to note, however, that this result differs from the other ones reported there, in that we continue to employ the deposit-currency ratio. In fact, it proved to be impossible to achieve stability without this variable; in using this we are basically following Klovland's procedure and departing somewhat from our own. Nevertheless, as noted above, the currency–deposit ratio is determined by the users (demanders) of monetary services, and so an influence here is not necessarily that of a structural change but rather of a variable reflecting a change of preferences in financial transaction. Since we have added a variable to the model, this result is not on a par with the others reported in Table 7.3. In any case, this formulation shows no serial correlation and is stable by all the recursive residual tests; it is also well-determined, although the presence of three statistically significant interest rate terms, all with negative signs, is unique among the results reported in this chapter. We believe our finding of stability for Norway should be set down as only a tentative finding, in the sense that we had to go outside our framework to obtain stability.

Unlike many of our countries there is an explicit literature on the *Swedish* demand for money. In a paper addressed to the topic of the demand for money, Jonung (1978) comments on work on the velocity function for Sweden. He is interested in the decline in velocity in Sweden and discusses the country's increasing financial sophistication (as we have, in Chapter 4). Explicit estimates of the Swedish demand for money exist in studies by Fisher and Thurman (1989), and Fisher (1992). These works do not address the stability question directly, although there are very satisfactory estimates of that function – including some work with the money supply – in both these studies.

In fact, Sweden turns out to show quite a few problems in terms of the testing of Equation (7.5). For one thing, there is a serious serial correlation problem indicated in the result in Table 7.1. Furthermore, the model does not show significance at the 5 per cent level for the interest rate and income coefficients (they are significant at the 7 per cent and 6 per cent level, respectively). In Table 7.2, with the aid of the US corporate bond rate and the ratio of agricultural to industrial production (as components of GDP), we were able to provide a better result (in that there was no serial correlation) but the income coefficient is only marginally significant. The signs of the significant variables are as expected, but, in any case, the function proves to be unstable, as indicated in Figure 7.2, with the CUSUM of Squares plot wandering outside its bounds through much of the 1880s and 1890s.

In Table 7.3, the Swedish money-demand function is shown to be stabilized with the US corporate bond rate and the proxy yield on Swedish physical assets over the 1873–1913 period. The signs are those expected, and the resulting function passes all the stability checks. The serial correlation test just passes (at 0.057), but, in any case, this result establishes the existence of a stable function for Sweden for the period of the gold standard. Thus, of the three Scandinavian countries, Sweden and Norway (possibly) provide stable functions during the gold standard era, while Denmark's case is indeterminate.

In the literature on the demand for money in the *United Kingdom* over this period, the results run generally towards satisfactory estimates, although there are also some hotly contested econometric issues that have surfaced. The dominant work in the literature is that of Friedman and Schwartz (1982) who build up their money demand model from a velocity equation. Putting aside their many experiments, the final result for the United Kingdom for a period much longer than ours includes real per capita income, the differential yield on money, a proxy yield on physical assets that is not significant, and several structural variables. They do not test this particular version of the model for subperiods (although many of the earlier experiments do). They observe the following for the United Kingdom and the United States (Friedman and Schwartz, 1982, p. 283):

> The implication is that money demand is stable over time – in the sense of a demand function – as well as between countries.

The stability between the two countries is not tested in our work.

There have been several other studies of the UK demand for money and, by and large, they agree with Friedman and Schwartz and with our own work, below. An earlier test of the function we use in this chapter is by Huffman and Lothian (1980). Their model has real per capita *high-powered* money as the dependent variable and per capita real income and an interest rate as independent variables; the period covered is 1833–80. While they do not test for stability, they claim it (on the basis of the behaviour of the model's coefficients over time); their estimates of the income elasticity of money demand lie between 0.863 and 1.118. Mills and Wood (1982) enter the fray with yet another dependent variable, bank deposits; they cover the period 1880–1913. They do considerable work with the dynamic specification, following the suggestions of Hendry (1979). This produces estimates of the real income elasticity of unity, but there were no explicit tests of stability offered.

The two studies just mentioned were hampered by the apparently inadequate monetary data; this was not the case for Capie and Rodrik-Bali (1985) who had the new Capie and Webber (1985) money stock estimates with which to work. Their money-demand function is $M/P = f(y^e, i^L, i^s)$ where y^e is expected income, and they, too, do considerable work with the dynamic specification. They found the long-run income elasticity to be unity; they also reported the results of several diagnostic tests, two of which tested successfully for the stability of their formulation. Finally, Klovland (1987) uses the Friedman and Schwartz (1982) framework, with a number of lags on their independent variables; he compares the Friedman and Schwartz data with the new Capie and Webber data and finds that the basic results for income elasticities and stability in the literature are confirmed on both sets of data.[11]

Turning to our own work, for the entire period for the United Kingdom, a test of Equation (7.5) produces the estimates given in Table 7.1. This simple formulation appears to fit quite well, in terms of its coefficients, but there is a serial correlation problem. An AR(3) correction is necessary to eliminate the serial correlation; this result also appears in Table 7.1. We are, then, unable to test for stability, although we should note that the coefficients of this function make sense. In this connection, note that the long-run income elasticity here is not significantly different from unity (and is the lowest of all the countries tested). This result and further discussion appear in Section 7.5. In Table 7.2, the UK money demand function is estimated with two interest rate terms and a structural proxy (the ratio of agricultural production to industrial production); this result is, again, for the entire period. The interest rates here are the open market discount rate (short) and the Consol rate (long). In this case, there is no serial correlation and the model in fact passes all the stability tests. This, essentially, confirms the results in the literature on the UK demand for money.

The UK result for the 1873–1913 period is reported in Table 7.3. This test is relatively successful in terms of fit, with an open market discount rate as the only interest rate, but there is again a dramatic failure of the serial correlation test.[12] Again, an AR(3) correction is necessary to remove the serial correlation problem. This result is similar to that reported in Table 7.1, because there are only two fewer observations in this case. Thus we are, as before, unable to report on the stability of the model.

Obviously, the *United States* is not physically part of the growing European community of this time, but it clearly is in an economic sense. When we discussed financial institutions and background material in earlier chapters, we generally omitted the United States, except for its role in the international financial community. Indeed, when it comes to discussing interaction – both nominal and real – the United States is very much a part of the European story. The main reason, of course, is that the United States was an important member of the group of gold-standard countries (after 1878). Furthermore, we have found that US interest rates sometimes provide effective interest rates in some European money-demand functions. This finding attests to the integration of capital markets and will be studied further in Chapter 8. Finally, and more provocatively, Friedman and Schwartz (1982) have estimated successfully a common demand for money for the United Kingdom and the United States; common, that is to say, except for a different pace of financial development. This is as far as we have gone with the US literature on money demand, since our interest in this study is in European integration.

In Table 7.1, we show the result of applying Equation (7.5) to the US data. This function, indeed, fits well over the period, but shows serial correlation (with a p-value of 0.045); the AR(1) result added to the table is satisfactory, but this formulation cannot be tested for stability. For Table 7.2 we added a long-term interest rate to our test and formed a proxy from an agricultural production index and a series on pig iron production (which was turned into an index number). The ratio of the two indices provides a measure of the influence of structural change, as similar measures have for other countries. With these adjustments, we produce the nicely fitting result given in Table 7.2. This formulation shows no serial correlation and proves to be stable by all the recursive residual tests. Accordingly, our results agree with those of Friedman and Schwartz for both the United States and the United Kingdom, although we do not attempt to locate a common demand.

For the 1873–1913 period, as reported in Table 7.3, the basic demand function again fits well and produces a stable money–demand function, with the US commercial paper rate appearing as the only interest rate. The serial correlation statistic is also satisfactory. This result contrasts with those of Friedman and Schwartz, then, for both the United Kingdom and the United States, although only in the sense that stability is achieved with a simpler function. For the longer run of data they study, where there are different trends in velocity and, certainly, more significant institutional changes, our formulation would most probably not work, as, indeed, it does not for the slightly longer periods reported in Tables 7.1 and 7.2.

In this section, then, we have demonstrated that a stable demand for money function can be located for most countries, but only for the period 1873–1913. Since this is the period in which many of these same countries managed successfully to stay on the gold standard, a connection is likely. It is surely reasonable to argue that a system that reduces inflation rates as well as the variation in inflation rates could encourage individuals and businesses to hold more money, and to hold it for longer periods. There are other factors at work in this period because, as we discussed in Chapter 5, this is also the period in which European banks, by and large, acquired and used the 'lender of last resort' function. This would have stabilized financial markets – and there are signs of this (see Chapter 9) – and would have, in all likelihood, helped to stabilize the demand for financial assets such as money.[13]

7.5 THE INCOME ELASTICITY OF MONEY DEMAND

Special interest attaches to the income elasticity of the demand for money in this period. In particular, we expect this elasticity to be higher than twentieth-century estimates, mainly because the money services industry was gaining acceptance during the late nineteenth century. Indeed, the pattern we expect is for a declining income elasticity of money demand, without any clear feeling for where it might end in 1913, although estimates ought to be higher than those at the end of the twentieth century. In this section we shall look at both long-run income elasticities and recursively generated short-run elasticities, after considering some of the important theoretical issues.

We can establish the general hypothesis as follows. Friedman and Schwartz note that the income elasticity of money demand was considerably higher in the United States than in the United Kingdom (where it was around unity), and associate this with a lack of relative 'financial sophistication' in the United States. By this they mean that the general lack of financial services made those that did exist (in banks) relatively valuable to Americans. What Friedman and Schwartz say about the United States in the 1870s (compared with the United Kingdom) is (1982, p. 146):

> The United States, by contrast, though wealthier and more populous, was still financially backward, conducting its international trade largely in sterling. Nearly three-quarters of the population was classified as residing in rural areas, and half of the working force (male and female) was still in agriculture ... These differences meant a much higher

demand for money relative to income by United Kingdom than by United States residents.

Indeed, say Friedman and Schwartz, much of the change to a sophisticated economy occurred between 1870 and 1906. The term 'sophistication' may be misunderstood, as it was just used, but it should be noted that we are merely comparing a characteristic of money holding in the two cases. In the United States, the marginal dollar appears to be worth more in income to the user, reflecting, it can be argued, a relative scarcity of such forms of payment (and certainly of the accompanying banking services).

In Table 7.4, we show the estimates of the long-run income elasticities calculated from the short-run estimates reported in Tables 7.1 and 7.3. We have used results, in both cases, that show no serial correlation, so quite a few are reported from equations with AR corrections. Of course, most of the other results in column 1 are from unstable functions, but in any case, the pattern is clearly sensible for most countries. The United Kingdom, for example, is the lowest, while the largely agricultural countries of Italy and Norway are the highest. France and Germany are possibly higher than one might expect, and Denmark lower, but otherwise we would look for values over 2.0 for countries with substantial agricultural sectors and rapidly growing money stocks. In the 1873–1913 period, the results follow the same pattern, but the coefficients are generally lower (6 of 9) than for the whole period. Note that the United Kingdom still has the lowest value, and that it is not statistically different from unity.

Table 7.4 Income elasticities of money demand, 1850–1913

Country	1850–1913 Table 7.1	1873–1913 Table 7.3
Austria-Hungary	2.629	3.208
Denmark	1.534	1.481
France	1.815	1.422
Germany	2.168	1.837
Italy	3.926	1.470
Norway	3.750	1.351
Sweden	2.377	2.027
United Kingdom	1.008	1.034
United States	2.166	2.241

A second look at the income elasticity can be obtained with reference to a recursive residuals test that we have not so far employed; this is a plot of recursively-generated income coefficients. Taking the four completely satisfactory results from Table 7.3, and calculating the model at each point, a time series of each coefficient and its associated standard errors can be generated, at least for the four cases that are stable (we cannot perform the procedure on results with an AR correction). Note that what is shown here is the recursively-generated coefficient, along with a band around the coefficient that marks plus-and-minus two standard errors. Also notice that these are short-run elasticities.

In Figure 7.3 we show the recursively-generated income coefficients for the four cases – Germany, Italy, Sweden and the United States – that showed no instability and no serial correlation. These figures show a decline over the period, although, because the early numbers are imprecisely estimated, it may not be a statistically significant decline. The figures shown in Figure 7.3, however, are short-run elasticities, while it is the long-run elasticities we are interested in. These can be computed from the numbers used to generate

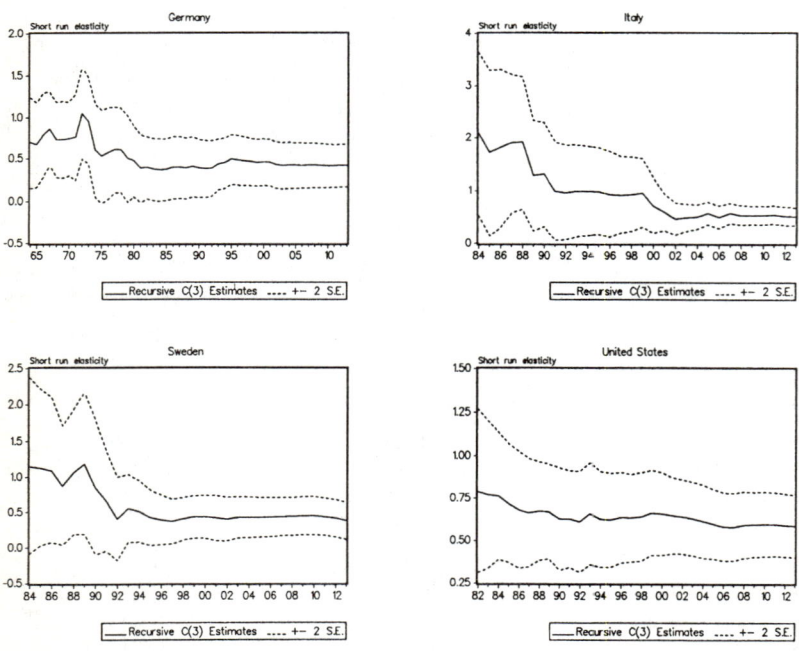

Figure 7.3 Recursive short-run income elasticities

Figure 7.3 (using, also, recursively-generated coefficients on the lagged dependent variables). This produces results for the 1913 observation for Germany (1.841), Italy (1.471), Sweden (2.019) and the United States (2.246). These are so like the estimates for the entire period (in Table 7.4) that it seems likely that there is no statistically significant change in these elasticities over the 1873–1913 period. The unusually strong demand for monetary services we have noticed seems to have carried right through to the end of the period, at least for these countries.

7.6 CONCLUSIONS

In this chapter we have searched for the conditions under which there exists a stable demand function for money for the nine countries we analyzed, for the period 1873–1913. Generally, some form of the basic model was successful for these countries. Indeed, a very simple functional form, based on partial adjustment and estimated in real, per capita terms, works well in most cases.

We need to sound a warning here, however, as we have elsewhere in this survey, about the adequacy of the data. In one case, the French monetary data, we believe we have located a serious problem with the way the data were constructed. In several cases, the presence of AR corrections to functions on annual data that already have a lagged dependent variable, might suggest that the monetary data have been oversmoothed. This was especially noticeable for the UK data, but AR corrections were also needed for Austrian-Hungarian, Danish, Swedish and US data. Income data, too, might not be as good as needed. We believe the Swedish income data are causing problems (recall the poor determination of the income coefficient); for a discussion, see Sheffrin (1988). The income data for Austria and Hungary also seem to us to be provisional; we note, especially, the absence of nominal figures in this literature. There are numerous interest rates in the literature, but some are clearly not market rates, and the exact periods to which they refer differ a good deal across our sample. It is no comfort to us, although we think it is interesting, that we find foreign interest rates working in domestic money-demand functions, even when domestic rates are available. Overall, we think that some caution is warranted about any claims for or against stability of the demand for money in any of these countries. We say this even though we have come down, in effect, on the side of stability under some conditions in most cases.

There are a number of important implications of our findings. For one thing, taking a nationalistic point of view, a stable demand for money is an important fulcrum for monetary policy. For another, this establishes yet another way that Europe was integrated financially in this period, since the similar demand for money results – all based on broad money – suggest that there was a widely parallel development of the financial sector that was shared by each of these countries. We did not pool the data for these countries, as Friedman and Schwartz did for the United States and the United Kingdom, but we suspect that such an undertaking would be at least partly successful for these and still more countries in Europe. In this connection, we do need to point out that our use of interest rates in this chapter, borrowing from one country to feed the demand for money of another, is explicit evidence of financial integration.

One final matter concerns the connection of our results with the results we have obtained for money and prices – and the gold standard. The model of price level determination by Barro (1979) that was discussed in Chapter 5 points out that under the gold standard, domestic prices and money stocks would be *dominated* by world gold production but influenced, as well, by domestic financial institutions and by (differences in) the domestic demand for money. What we found earlier was that while price levels appeared to be integrated closely, neither money stocks nor high-powered money were. This result is hard to rationalize within the specie-flow mechanism of the gold standard, but can be explained with reference to the monetary approach to the balance of payments.

If the demand for money were *unstable* within each country, this would provide an independent reason why prices and money follow different patterns across nations. This argument applies to both the specie-flow and monetary approach. Since this is apparently not the case – and these functions appear to be stable – this need not be considered further. Changes in velocity, which we attribute either to structural change or to the unusual attractiveness of monetary services to users, do play a role here. In the specie-flow mechanism, since the money stock is driven by the world money stock, in effect, money demand accommodates itself to the situation. In this case, the money demand function filters the influence of the world stock of money on domestic prices. In the monetary approach, the money demand function filters the influence of world prices on the domestic money stock. Since it is domestic money stocks (and monetary bases) that are not well correlated or cointegrated, one could argue that structural changes and changes in the attractiveness of money are driving a wedge between the prices and money stocks of countries for which money demand is (otherwise) stable. These findings are consistent with the monetary approach.

Part III

Growth and Cycles: Toward an Integrated Economy

8 The Integration of Product and Capital Markets

8.1 INTRODUCTION

As we pointed out in Chapter 3, European commodity and capital markets were on their way to an effective integration centuries before 1850, and we believe that we can show that, by the beginning of the twentieth century, Europe was for many purposes a truly integrated economy, possessing the characteristics which a century later are often associated with the word 'global'. In a way, this theme has marked our study throughout, and this chapter contains some of the most important evidence in support of this view. We have pursued this topic in earlier chapters, having already discussed the real growth of these economies as well as the growing integration of their financial sectors during this period. In this chapter we add an analysis of the integration of exports and imports, investment expenditures and, finally, nominal and real interest rates. Real integration involves more than these topics, to be sure, and so we shall add a discussion of the integrated business cycle in Chapter 9, as well as a general summary, in Chapter 10, to complete the story.

With respect to exports and imports, we show that the real value of these items generally grew more rapidly than the overall economies of these countries (judged, of course, by the growth of real product). This observation is worth emphasizing, if only because some of the literature on trade tends to take a mercantilist line, at least in some respects. For example, under the heading of 'free trade', Mathias considers the possibility that if British overseas investment 'had been invested in home industry it would have expanded British exports and made them more competitive' (Mathias, 1983, p. 303). He goes on to ask: 'Did the cushion of income from foreign investment, which was masking certain industrial problems and hiding the absence of new export sectors by increasing rentier-status in the world, encourage the breeding of rentier attitudes?' (p. 304). By phrasing the question in this way, the interactive nature of both trade and capital flows is ignored – an interactive nature from which *all* nations could profit. In particular, the operation of the principle of comparative advantage and the increasing mobility of capital, fed on and encouraged the European economies that we observe in this period. We argue that the effect of this growth in trade was strong enough to have provided more jobs for the domestic economy than could have been achieved by a regime that restricted foreign investment or raised protective tariffs. In all this, as we shall see, the growth rate of trade was above the growth rates of national output of the various economies throughout the period.

With respect to investment and international capital flows there are not many time-series available, but we are able to explore the links between the investment sectors of the most important European economies in this period. This material documents one aspect of capital market links, although not as clearly as one might have wished. We also examine interest rates across countries, which offers another way to get at some of the same issues. Here we consider both nominal and real rates. We expect nominal rates to be tied together, since they are composed of real rates plus expected inflation rates and the latter have already been shown (in Chapter 6) to be closely related – to be co integrated, in fact. The evidence presented here supports these contentions. For real rates, we shall make an effort to see if the rate that concerned investors – the *ex ante* real rate – was integrated across nations in this period. To get an *ex ante* rate we need to model inflationary expectations, and we do so by using a distributed lag of past inflation rates. While this is a relatively naïve approximation, the results obtained seem reasonable to us. In fact, we find substantial evidence of the integration of real interest rates in this period.

We are going to begin, however, with a brief discussion of the transmission (or diffusion) of goods, capital, people and ideas across Europe in this period. What we shall do is to collect the general material in Section 8.2 and then include brief discussions of specific ideas in each of the later sections of the chapter containing the empirical work. Readers should note that there is much more to come in later chapters. It is also worth remarking that our material in this chapter only skims the surface of the subject and is included here mainly to suggest how our empirical work might be interpreted.

8.2 EUROPEAN INTEGRATION: SOME GENERAL ISSUES

By 1850, economic agents in most sectors of most countries in Europe were well aware of at least some of their international competition. While exposure to other countries varied considerably from country to country in 1850, by 1913 data on real trade and on capital flows across borders suggests, since these variables were growing more rapidly than national product in real terms, that this exposure had increased substantially. We shall discuss the particular phenomena in our separate sections on exports and imports, investment and interest rates, but for now, taking a broad perpective, we attempt to explain what caused this situation.

The first thing one notices is that the political and institutional climate of the period was conducive to growth, by and large. By 1850, many European governments were wedded to a policy of promoting the growth of their economies by building infrastructure (roads, docks and railways, for example); by promoting economic activity in numerous ways; but *not* by adopting mercantilist notions of economic management. Even so, one finds relatively low levels of government expenditure for most of these countries (compared to modern times), coupled with a relatively low level of tariffs and other impediments to trade. Over the period, while transportation and communications facilities improved dramatically (and costs fell substantially), some of it by government design but much of it at the behest of private economic agents, tariffs declined under the climate of *laissez-faire*, at least until the 1880s. Indeed, the prosperity between 1850 and 1873 featured the dramatic growth of railways (and capital markets) and the accompanying decline of tariffs rates over a broad front, while the general stagnation from 1873 to around 1879 for most countries and (especially) the agricultural stagnation of the 1880s onwards was associated with higher tariffs. After 1895 or so, tariffs eased somewhat. But throughout the period trade grew faster than national product for most of these countries for most of the time, and much of the swinging back and forth on tariffs was the result of nations trying to soften the impact of foreign competition in specific (usually agricultural) markets.

Rosenberg and Birdsall (1985) argue that the West grew rich in this period because of its conducive political structure and its flexible and innovative institutions. Indeed, it was a combination of these factors and the relentless drive of profit-seeking private economic agents, with or without government assistance, that pushed aside political and institutional barriers. Furthermore, even the institutions themselves were adjusted as the need arose. Whether or not one can defend these views, what does seem clear is that in this period there were institutional changes that had a profound effect on events. Perhaps foremost of these is the growth of the joint-stock company, which considerably reduced the risk to entrepreneurs and thereby aided materially in the raising of capital and in the internationalization of the capital markets. In this period, this form of business organization, known but not widespread anywhere before, became the general practice. Indeed, in countries where the joint-stock company was not widespread (for example, Portugal and Spain), there was little growth.

Perhaps of comparable importance in this period, and certainly tied to the joint-stock principle, is the development of modern banking, often as a tool to aid in domestic economic development. As we have already seen, the governments of many of the countries that perceived themselves to be behind the British in this period, promoted Credit-Mobilier-style investment banks, to lend to themselves, to railways, to industry and even, in some cases, to agriculture. The more successful of these ventures evolved into or were absorbed by modern mixed banks as governments on the one hand monopolized the profitable currency issues and on the other permitted a wide variety of activities in the burgeoning financial sector. The banking industry, indeed, provides a perfect example of how ideas and practices swiftly crossed borders, and how domestic governments and financial institutions adjusted rapidly to the new financial climate. In many countries, as we have seen, this development seemed to be especially rapid, as discussed in Chapters 4 and 5.

A piece of the puzzle, an important part really, is the international gold standard. In 1850, countries attempted, as they long had, to maintain the integrity of their currencies *vis-à-vis* the precious metals (or the British pound), but by the end of the century central banks had been instructed to maintain this link utilizing their control over the monetary base. Where central banks did not exist, or where their legal mandate was less than this, they were often empowered to dominate, if not to monopolize, in this sphere. What emerged was a partly co-operative, credible, international payments system that produced a good record of exchange rate and domestic price stability compared, we think, to what might have occurred without it. This financial integration must have aided integration in product and factor markets considerably, although empirical verification of this possibility is generally only on a 'regime' basis that is contaminated by all the other differences that the gold standard period has when compared with periods earlier (as we are doing) and later (as in much of the literature).

All this harmony is, of course, exaggerated in the foregoing and we have to pay more than lip-service to the dissonance. History teaches us that the political disharmony among the European nations is the chief factor to consider, and we would be remiss if we did not underscore the many wars that occurred in Europe and elsewhere over the centuries, which left substantial political debts unpaid by 1913. In addition (Morris and Adelman, 1988), there are many other factors that differ materially across these countries that attest to an unfinished economic agenda. For example, Spain, Italy and parts of Austria-Hungary, among the countries we have been considering, had considerably more poverty than the other nations, while those three countries and France, Denmark, the Netherlands and Norway still had relatively large agricultural sectors in 1913. Social legislation also differed considerably across countries, with the beginnings of modern welfare systems emerging in some cases but not in others. And there are many demographic factors (for example, birth, death and marriage rates) that differ across countries as well. While we do not think these factors necessarily dominate in any general discussion of growth and integration in Europe, one would be unwise to ignore them in any appraisal of the paths individual nations were taking toward a modern, economically-integrated, Europe in the 1850–1913 period.

8.3 THE FOREIGN SECTOR: EXPORTS AND IMPORTS

It is hard to exaggerate the importance of trade flows in the development and integration of Europe during our 63-year period. In 1850, the British dominated trade (and much of production) overwhelmingly in Europe, but by 1913, the British were being challenged on all fronts and no longer had the lead in some sectors. We have remarked that trade (as measured either by exports or imports) grew faster than did national product, generally, for these nations, and we shall document this claim in a moment. For now, we need to emphasize that trade flows of finished and (especially) unfinished goods and materials, inspired both capital and labour flows and encouraged the diffusion of the ever-changing modern technology. While this is often discussed in the literature, we also want to emphasize two characteristics of the increasing foreign trade of the nations that are of interest in our study. The first of these is that trade provided an important – and documentable – link between the business cycles of these countries. The second is (as we have argued in earlier chapters) that trade flows rather than gold flows provided the mechanism that underlay the successful functioning of the international gold standard. Thus we expect to see considerable, and possibly increasing, correlation, cointegration and Granger-causality for exports (and imports) during this period.

We shall begin the empirical work in this chapter by introducing the basic data for exports and imports. We are interested in the volume of exports and imports, since this would provide evidence of the basic linkages of commodities across nations. Table 8.1 contains the growth rates of real exports and imports for twelve European countries and the Unites States.[1] The figures in the table illustrate in the broadest terms an early growth and then a slowing of foreign trade during the later part of the period. For imports, only four countries experienced more rapid growth in 1873–1913 than for the whole period considered (1850–1913), and for exports there were only two such cases. These are indicated by asterisks in the table. These exceptions to

Table 8.1 Compound growth rates of real exports and imports, 1850–1913

Country	Date	Imports		Exports		National Product Growth	
		Overall	1873–1913	Overall	1873–1913	Overall	1873–1913
Austria-Hungary	1867	2.82	2.51	2.92	2.37	2.17	2.26*
Belgium	1850	4.32	3.54	4.10	3.41	–	–
Denmark	1869	3.81	3.89*	3.86	4.06*	3.12	3.19*
France	1850	3.20	1.87	2.85	2.42	1.45	1.49*
Germany	1880	–	3.48	–	2.85	2.68	2.71*
Italy	1861	2.47	2.75*	2.33	2.16	1.16	1.40*
Netherlands	1850	5.10	4.64	5.21	4.96	1.86	1.97*
Norway	1865	2.87	2.84	2.61	2.64*	1.87	1.89*
Portugal	1865	2.05	2.11*	0.95	0.82	1.95	1.45
Spain	1850	2.16	0.80	2.57	0.97	–	–
Sweden	1850	4.05	2.76	3.72	2.88	2.57	2.57
United Kingdom	1850	2.96	2.09	2.74	2.25	2.07	1.94
United States	1850	3.60	3.14	4.23	3.74	3.82	3.78

Notes: The date column refers to the starting point of the trade figures. Austria-Hungary figures run 1867–1909. These figures are computed from regressions of log x on trend except for the Netherlands, for which end points were used. The asterisk indicates a higher growth rate for the later period.

the general rule are for peripheral countries (except Italy); all the other major countries saw slower growth in these figures.

As noted, Table 8.1 shows that the growth of the whole system (both exports and imports) seemed to slow down somewhat during the later period, although whether the causes are related to the patterns of trade, the result of country-specific tariff (and other) policies, or a general slowdown of economic activity is not clear at this level of generality. With respect to the latter point we have included the real national product figures in Table 8.1 mainly to show how growth and trade may be related. For Sweden, the United Kingdom and the United States, slower real output growth may have contributed to slower real export and import growth, comparing the two periods in the table. This result would surely not be surprising.[2] Finally, we should also emphasize that the general result is for both export and import growth to exceed national product growth; trade, in a sense, is leading the way upwards, at least in this simple sense.

Moving on to the statistical tests, the first thing we need to do is to search for unit roots in the data because of the strong trends in both exports and

Table 8.2 Unit root tests, exports and imports, 1850–1913

Country	Exports		Imports	
	1850–1913	1873–1913	1850–1913	1873–1913
Austria-Hungary	−1.42	−3.94*	−3.17	−2.62
Belgium	−3.71*	−3.46	−2.84	−2.19
Denmark	−2.14	−2.74	−3.52*	−3.81*
France	−2.76	−2.18	−2.70	−2.20
Germany	−0.75	−0.75	−3.38	−3.38
Italy	−3.22	−2.99	−2.19	−2.03
Netherlands	−2.70	−1.87	−2.89	−3.02
Norway	−2.65	−2.53	−3.12	−2.38
Portugal	−4.01*	−4.55*	−3.36	−3.10
Spain	−2.48	−2.11	−3.31	−2.82
Sweden	−3.44*	−2.75	−2.79	−3.78 (3)
United Kingdom	−2.49	−2.10	−2.15	−4.23*
United States	−2.59	−3.45	−2.71	−2.39

An asterisk indicates no unit root is indicated at the 5 per cent level. The figure in parentheses is the number of lags in the Augmented Dickey–Fuller test.

imports. The tests, we have in mind in this section are correlations across countries, Granger-causality tests, and cointegration tests for real exports and imports. Table 8.2 contains the results for the unit root tests. There are 52 cases reported in the table, with 44 of them showing unit roots by the Dickey–Fuller (or Augmented Dickey–Fuller) test.[3]

In the remainder of this section we shall be comparing the entire period with the gold-standard subperiod. We shall do this for three reasons. First, because most of the tests we are employing are known to be sensitive to lag length, we include the entire period to obtain the maximum possible degrees of freedom. Second, and more importantly, we are trying to measure increasing integration in this period; if it exists, then this breakdown gives us some leverage on that topic, although a better comparison would be one that made a simple break at, say, 1873. We cannot do this, however, because the pre-1873 time series are too short for our statistical procedures. Finally, we want to test for the possible effect of the gold standard on trade. We saw in Chapter 6 that one of the arguments in support of the international gold standard claims that a fixed exchange rate regime would facilitate the expansion of international trade, because such a regime eliminates the risk associated with trading under flexible exchange rates. Thus, comparing the

Table 8.3 Correlations of log-level exports and imports, 1850–1913

	Belgium	Denmark	France	Germany	Italy	Netherlands	Norway	Portugal	Spain	Sweden	United Kingdom	United States
A Exports 1850–1913:												
Austria-Hungary	.921*	.835	.904*	.867	.779*	.950*	.873*	.574*	.780*	.916*	.860*	.955*
Belgium	–	.970	.984*	.957	.950*	.980*	.973*	.794*	.906*	.982*	.986*	.930*
Denmark		–	.972	.948	.925*	.933*	.980*	.665*	.581*	.953*	.962*	.912*
France			–	.968	.934*	.964*	.972*	.744*	.862*	.968*	.990*	.889
Germany				–	.949	.891*	.954*	.697	.080	.903*	.956*	.855
Italy					–	.902*	.927*	.779*	.741*	.919*	.939*	.891*
Netherlands						–	.950*	.757*	.898*	.974*	.964*	.954*
Norway							–	.764*	.741*	.972*	.979*	.915*
Portugal								–	.727*	.786*	.787*	.733*
Spain									–	.930*	.892*	.884*
Sweden										–	.978*	.925*
United Kingdom											–	.902*
United States												–
B Exports, 1873–1913:												
Austria-Hungary	.890	.852*	.863	.867	.750	.941	.846	.512	.581	.896	.826	.933
Belgium	–	.975*	.976	.957	.915	.952	.970	.708	.564	.947	.960	.935
Denmark		–	.979*	.948	.923	.930	.979	.651	.465	.951	.956	.929
France			–	.968	.908	.936	.974*	.707	.524	.949	.978	.908*
Germany				–	.949	.891	.954	.697	.080	.903	.956	.855
Italy					–	.827	.898	.681	.326	.832	.879	.834
Netherlands						–	.929	.683	.646	.957	.912	.962*
Norway							–	.682	.558	.969	.968	.898
Portugal								–	.477	.677	.701	.575
Spain									–	.648	.576	.543
Sweden										–	.946	.921
United Kingdom											–	.876
United States												–

Table 8.3 (continued)

	Austria-Hungary	Belgium	Denmark	France	Germany	Italy	Netherlands	Norway	Portugal	Spain	Sweden	United Kingdom	United States
C Imports, 1850–1913:													
Austria-Hungary	–	.974*	.976*	.899*	.975	.880*	.961*	.959*	.865*	.704*	.956*	.974*	.935*
Belgium		–	.978*	.973	.971	.931*	.975*	.960*	.930*	.894*	.979*	.991*	.919*
Denmark			–	.897*	.876	.915*	.972	.978*	.917*	.631*	.965	.982*	.936*
France				–	.991	.865*	.946*	.892*	.871*	.936*	.969*	.984*	.891
Germany					–	.892	.985	.972	.855	.020	.975	.988	.923
Italy						–	.900*	.888*	.940*	.671*	.881	.899*	.829*
Netherlands							–	.957*	.921*	.888*	.975*	.974	.961*
Norway								–	.897*	.665*	.950	.971*	.914*
Portugal									–	.696*	.913*	.922*	.864*
Spain										–	.917*	.916*	.878*
Sweden											–	.986*	.939*
United Kingdom												–	.919
United States													–
D Imports, 1873–1913:													
Austria-Hungary	–	.969	.976	.839*	.975	.855	.958	.944	.828	.398	.932	.966	.884
Belgium		–	.973	.894*	.971	.928	.946	.948	.904	.455	.946	.971	.898
Denmark			–	.878	.991*	.899	.973*	.976	.897	.502	.981*	.989*	.925*
France				–	.876	.840	.908	.822	.823	.666	.864	.912	.904*
Germany					–	.892	.985	.972	.855	.020	.975	.988	.923
Italy						–	.864	.844	.919*	.459	.888*	.884	.810
Netherlands							–	.935	.893	.582	.968	.982*	.954
Norway								–	.842	.418	.951	.964	.899
Portugal									–	.558	.912	.901	.837
Spain										–	.571	.542	.688
Sweden											–	.974	.930
United Kingdom												–	.942*
United States													–

* Higher correlation of the two periods compared.

gold-standard period with the entire period allows us to explore this effect, although there is certainly not much fluctuation of exchange rates at any time after 1850 (until 1914), except for a few wartime situations before 1873.

We now look at correlations among the real exports and imports of these countries. While we expect the level figures to be highly correlated, since they are driven by such strong trends, we have no particular view about the first differences (or the cointegration results, for that matter) because, while the discounted value of each country's future trade flows should balance – that is, imports less exports and 'invisibles' should equal specie flows – they need not do so between any two countries in any particular year or subset of years. Indeed, commodity trade between any two countries could easily grow out of 'balance' because, while countries often traded the same products (textiles, iron, agricultural products,) they did not do so necessarily with each other, and the operation of comparative advantage does not imply a simple relation for these variables. Indeed, they often did not trade the same products at all, probably again guided by comparative advantage.

In Table 8.3 we begin with the correlations for the log-levels of the data; the first differences would have provided a preferable comparison in view of the unit roots in the data, but basically these showed no correlations across countries. As anticipated, the levels show very high correlations across countries in general, and they are higher for the entire period, for both exports and imports, than they are for the period 1873 to 1913. A simple tabulation shows that sixty correlations for exports are higher in the overall period (and six lower), while fifty-six of the import correlations are higher in the overall period (and ten lower).[4] This result is quite strong and would seem to contradict the predicted effect of the adoption of the gold standard, but it could be that other factors – such as the increase in tariff barriers in this period – were responsible for the lower correlations. This situation would materialize to the extent that tariffs were designed to affect specific industries (in specific countries). In any case, the pattern is consistent, with very few series not conforming, although sometimes the differences across periods are not very large. It is worth remarking that the United States has generally high correlations with the other countries, and that Spain and Portugal have much lower correlations. Neither of these last two countries could be said to be participating in the industrialization of Europe along the lines of the rest of the countries in this sample, and that is probably the main reason for this result.

We now turn to the cointegration tests for these variables to measure the extent of common integration. We do this on a pair-wise basis. What we expect here is little or no cointegration of imports and exports, for reasons basically related to the fact that countries are competing with each other in these markets. That is, countries will specialize in the products for which they have a comparative advantage, and the increasing similarity of the European economies and lower transportation costs imply that more and more countries would be dominated by a particular country's comparative advantage in particular products. Indeed, one would certainly expect one country's exports to be cointegrated with another's imports, but the exploration of such a relationship would be obscured seriously by the complicated – and changing – patterns of trade across these countries.

In fact, we were able to establish very little cointegration among these data for the 1873–1913 period, as the summary in Table 8.4 makes clear. While the longer period does have more instances of statistically significant (at the 5 per cent level) cointegration, this is still a very low incidence overall, especially in the 1873–1914 period. Since the test is vulnerable to sample size, and the longer sample has as many as twenty-three more observations than the shorter, we do not care to claim any difference here. But what is certainly most obvious is the low incidence of cointegration, in comparison to results for other variables (in other chapters or, below, for interest rates).

Finally, we report the results for Granger-causality tests of these variables. We do expect to find Granger-causality, even with the first differences of the variables, since we would expect some delayed responses to expansions and contractions across countries. For example, if Germany were to experience a recession, then its imports would decline, causing the cycle to be exported to other countries. These other countries, in turn, would experience a contraction in their imports as their economies decline. Thus both exports and imports would be expected to be affected with a lag, but less so later in the period, when the same year co-ordination of business cycles is likely to have been greater (see Chapter 9 for a more complete discussion of business cycles across countries). These comments apply to expansions as well as contractions, of course.

We have described the Granger-causality test in earlier chapters. We need to reissue the warning, however, that this test is diagnostic in its intent and identifies not causation in the sense that the word is typically used, but rather

Table 8.4 Cointegration results: frequency

	1850–1913	*1873–1913*
Exports	7	6
Imports	14	4

Table 8.5 Granger-causality of exports and imports, 1850–1913

	Austria-Hungary	Belgium	Denmark	France	Germany	Italy	Netherlands	Norway	Portugal	Spain	Sweden	United Kingdom	United States
A Exports, 1850–1913:													
Austria-Hungary													
Belgium			Yes	Yes				Yes		Yes	Yes	Yes	
Denmark							Yes				Yes	Yes	
France					Yes								
Germany		Yes											
Italy	Yes			Yes								Yes	Yes
Netherlands		Yes	Yes	Yes									Yes
Norway											Yes		
Portugal						Yes		Yes		Yes	Yes		
Spain				Yes				Yes					
Sweden				Yes									Yes
United Kingdom									Yes				
United States	Yes												
B Exports, 1873–1913:													
Austria-Hungary			Yes	Yes									
Belgium				Yes			Yes			Yes	Yes	Yes	Yes
Denmark	Yes	Yes									Yes		
France	Yes	Yes									Yes		
Germany						Yes					Yes		Yes
Italy					Yes								
Netherlands	Yes												
Norway			Yes							Yes	Yes		
Portugal								Yes					
Spain		Yes				Yes							
Sweden													
United Kingdom				Yes		Yes							
United States				Yes									

Table 8.5 (continued)

	Austria-Hungary	Belgium	Denmark	France	Germany	Italy	Netherlands	Norway	Portugal	Spain	Sweden	United Kingdom	United States
C Imports, 1850–1913:													
Austria-Hungary			Yes										
Belgium			Yes				Yes					Yes	
Denmark												Yes	
France			Yes				Yes						
Germany	Yes		Yes					Yes					
Italy				Yes	Yes			Yes		Yes			
Netherlands									Yes	Yes			
Norway										Yes			
Portugal										Yes		Yes	
Spain								Yes			Yes		
Sweden	Yes									Yes		Yes	
United Kingdom	Yes										Yes		
United States													Yes
D Imports, 1873–1913:													
Austria-Hungary		Yes	Yes										
Belgium			Yes				Yes						
Denmark													
France			Yes										
Germany	Yes							Yes			Yes		
Italy					Yes								
Netherlands													
Norway													
Portugal													
Spain										Yes	Yes	Yes	
Sweden	Yes												
United Kingdom											Yes	Yes	
United States		Yes											

intertemporal ordering. That the proposed 'causes' include shocks and cycles penetrating national borders after a lapse of some time is merely a conjecture, although we feel it is a reasonable one. Table 8.5 offers a summary of the Granger results, with the statistically significant cases marked 'Yes'; a 5 per cent level of significance is adopted. As parts A and C of the table indicate, there is indeed considerable Granger-causal co-ordination of exports and imports over the entire 1850–1913 period. There are 33 such episodes for exports and 28 for imports. For the 1873 to 1913 period, on the other hand, the numbers drop to 24 for exports and 16 for imports, as anticipated. We cannot assert a major difference here, again, because of having fewer degrees of freedom for the later period, but these results are suggestive, nevertheless.

We believe that the successful use of lags in the Granger test implies considerable interaction after all among exports (especially) in this period. It appears that contemporaneous tests (of correlations of the first differences and cointegration) simply do not pick this up. We shall offer further discussion of this in our conclusion to this chapter, after the rest of our evidence on real interaction is assembled.

The results to this point in the chapter are a little puzzling, on the whole. While the main point – that trade flows increased faster than national economies in this period – is maintained, all our tests indicate more interaction in the overall period than in the 1873–1913 period. Here we should point out that the increasing integration hypothesis does not require that the diagnostic tests show any particular result, simply because the increasing and shifting complexity of trade flows could make such (single-direction) test procedures produce non-significant results. In fact, increasing integration is indicated by the faster growth of trade *per se* since the percentage of each country's domestic product that was involved in foreign trade grew in this period.

8.4 THE INTERACTION OF CAPITAL MARKETS

During this period, financial capital expanded across borders in increasing volume, although certainly not in anything like a regular pattern. Perhaps the most widely discussed aspect of this on a general level is the expansion of lending internationally, led by the United Kingdom, but all the major countries were involved in both absorbing and exporting financial capital in this period, as their individual investors seized on either local or international opportunities as they arose. The main characteristics of these capital flows (Ashworth, 1987) were (a) that the largest volume of capital tended to flow to already-mature economies (and sectors) rather than to relatively capital-poor countries (such as Spain and Portugal); and (b) that all countries relied on their own savings pools for most of their capital needs. Even so, the pool of international lending was led by the United Kingdom, France and Germany in this period, and its expansion was augmented by the arrival of US capital exports after 1890.[5] Similarly, the destinations of these funds were other European countries (and the United States) until after 1870, when India and the areas of white settlement around the world began to attract significantly more capital. Finally, we note that a sizeable portion of the capital involved went to governments rather than to the private sector, although there are so many differences across countries and over time that generalizations beyond this are hard to produce.

What would be best for an analysis of European capital markets would be actual capital flow data, but this is simply unavailable on an annual basis, except in a few instances, and never for the entire period. Stock price data are also available in some cases, but these, too, are insufficient in number to provide any significant leverage on our pan-European themes. We do have interest rates, of course, and those will be studied in Section 8.5. For now, we will look at some data on investment, for which we can offer some cross-country comparisons of the level of investment and its ratio to income. The number of countries involved (seven) is not sufficient to draw a full picture, but because we do have the major economies represented, the results are certainly suggestive of the more important relationships in Europe at this time.

We need to be clear, at this point, about what we are looking for. In Europe, at this time, successful capital formation played a decisive role in helping to determine the rate of absorption of the industrial revolution among countries. As we have observed, this process was essentially a domestic matter, but the international pool of capital provided substantial assistance and was part of the conduit, as it were, that also moved labour, products and technical ideas across borders. Perhaps the best way to begin our empirical investigation of their issues is to introduce the sample of investment figures by looking at real growth rates and rates of domestic capital formation. We do this, in Table 8.6, utilizing the periods 1850–1913 (designated 'overall') and 1873–1913.[6]

Table 8.6 lists the point at which the data series begins in each case; this starting date affects the overall period but not the period 1873–1913, for which the data are complete. In the table we list real growth rates and growth rates of investment (both calculated by regression), and the ratio of investment to national product. Beginning with the growth rates of real product, we note, as in Table 8.1, that these are often higher (marginally) in the later period than in the first. The second column in the table shows that

Table 8.6 Growth rates and investment in Europe, 1850–1913

Country	Date	Overall			1873–1913		
		National product (%)	Investment (%)	I/Y (level)	National product (%)	Investment (%)	I/Y (level)
Denmark	1870	3.12	3.72	10.74	3.19*	3.91*	10.74*
France	1850	1.45	1.31	6.62	1.49*	1.62*	6.71*
Germany	1850	2.68	3.87	11.88	2.71*	3.62	13.30*
Italy	1861	1.16	2.54	10.45	1.40*	3.18*	11.13*
Norway	1865	1.87	2.67	15.85	1.89*	2.55	16.45*
Sweden	1861	2.57	3.78	9.71	2.57*	3.27	10.58*
United Kingdom	1850	2.07	2.44	6.89	1.94	1.63	7.32*

Notes: The date column reflects the start of the investment series in each case. The first two columns in each period are growth rates generated by regression of log *x* on trend. The third column in each period is the average value of investment to national product over the period. The asterisk indicates faster growth (or a higher level) in the 1873–1913 period than overall. The data are real except for French investment; the French ratio is of nominal values. See the Data Appendix for further discussion of the data.

except for France, investment in these countries grew faster than real product. This result is expected, but the relationship shown in the third column for the ratio of investment to income is in fact more interesting. In particular, growth theory argues that (*ceteris paribus*) countries will grow faster if I/Y rises; that is exactly what is shown in the table for all countries except the United Kingdom.[7] Thus, the key role of investment in the accelerating growth of these countries in the nineteenth century is clearly indicated here. Note, also, the support of the convergence hypothesis in that the two most advanced countries in 1850 also have the lowest investment ratios in the table.

The next thing to do is to investigate the time-series properties of the data. As it happens all the investment series except the level and ratio figures for Germany contain unit roots (by the basic Dickey–Fuller test for all cases except Italy). The results are shown in Table 8.7. Furthermore, the first differences of all of these series do not contain unit roots. This result is very straightforward and implies that cointegration tests (except for Germany) might provide interesting evidence of interaction, taking us beyond the simple correlations. The Granger-causality tests reported below, because of the presence of unit roots in the level figures (but not in the differences) are performed on the differenced data.

Table 8.7 Investment and investment ratios, unit root tests

	Levels	Differences	Ratios	Differences
Denmark	−2.047	−4.388*	−1.769	−4.725*
France	−2.610	−6.140*	−2.880	−5.354*
Germany	−3.831*	−9.090*	−4.324*	−9.269*
Italy	−2.195 (1)	−12.456*	−2.117 (1)	−12.783*
Norway	−1.497	−4.772*	−2.123	−5.145*
Sweden	−2.411	−5.754*	−2.551	−5.649*
United Kingdom	−1.352	−3.298**	−1.213	−3.030

Notes: Figures in parentheses are numbers of lags in Augmented Dickey–Fuller test.
* No unit root identified at 5 per cent level of significance.
**No unit root identified at 10 per cent level of significance.

We shall not produce correlation coefficients for either of the investment series, partly because the unit roots in the data make such calculations suspect. We do think, however, that a picture of the two series we shall use – real investment expenditures and the investment ratio – for all the countries in our sample will be useful. These appear in the two graphs of Figure 8.1. The increasing integration of capital markets in the sense of having parallel experiences is not that obvious in the investment ratios, as shown in Figure 8.1(b); on the other hand, the expected trend is there. But the investment figures themselves (Figure 8.1(a)) – which we saw were relatively highly correlated across countries – do show a close relationship, with the sharply increasing trend of the period after the 1890s being especially marked. Note that we are presenting the investment figures in normalized form (each series being divided by its mean) in order to facilitate comparisons.

Moving on to our statistical tests, we begin with a series of cointegration tests for both investment levels and ratios. In these tests, we use the longest runs of data available (see Table 8.6). For the ratios, there is absolutely no pair-wise cointegration evident for any of these cases (excluding Germany, of course, and testing Italy at one lag). For the level figures there are signs of Norwegian and Swedish investment affecting German; and French, Norwegian and Swedish investment affecting Italian. But the converse does not hold in any of these cases. These tests suggest that there is essentially no cointegration for either investment or its ratio to income for these countries.[8]

206 *Towards an Integrated Economy*

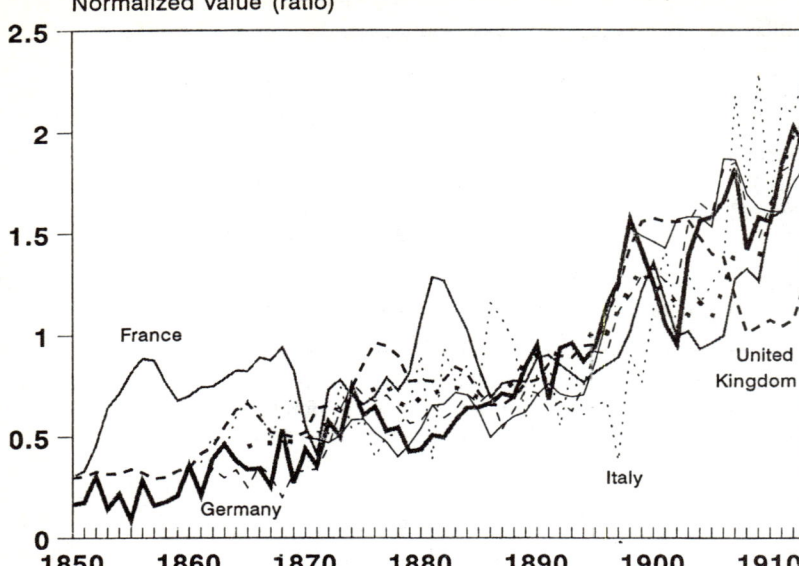

Figure 8.1(a) Investment levels – normalized, 1850–1913

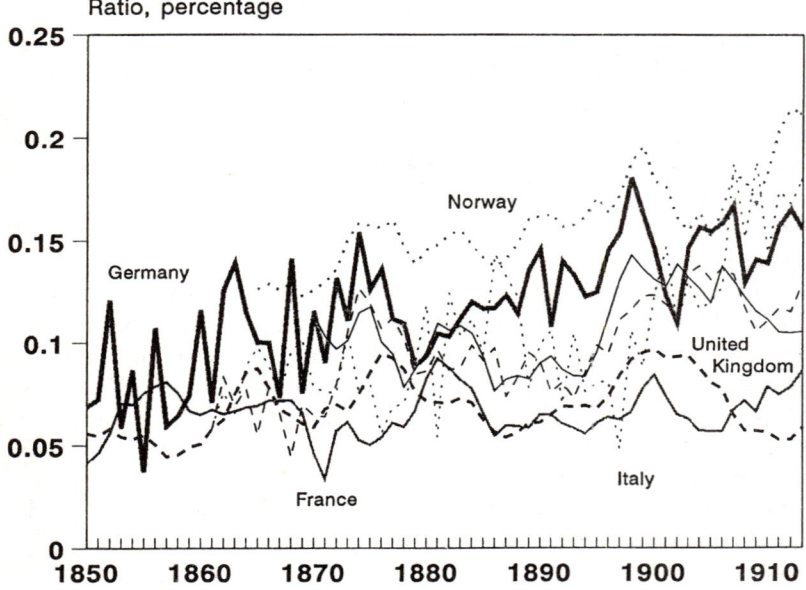

Figure 8.1(b) Ratio of investment to national product, 1850–1913

The Granger-causality tests were again conducted on the entire sample, since we wished to investigate our results with relatively long lags and needed the extra observations. We also employ first differences of the data, as discussed above. These do show considerably more interaction, although the incidence for real investment is much less than it was for exports and imports. For the investment figures, ignoring the nominal French data, there is certainly some evidence of Granger-causality, as the following summary shows, with the causal variable listed on the left.

Denmark → Germany, Italy, Norway, Sweden
UK → Germany, Norway, Sweden
Italy → Germany
Germany → Norway
Norway → UK
Sweden → Germany.

There is a consistent Granger-causation running from Denmark to four other countries, while German investment is Granger-caused by the investment of four different countries. For the investment ratio figures, the links are as follows:

Denmark → Germany, Italy, UK
UK → Germany, Norway, Sweden
Sweden → Germany, UK
Italy → Germany.

The German investment figures are again subject to temporal predetermination by the investment figures of four other countries. We are not surprised to see UK investment Granger-cause investment in other countries, in view of the size, success and visibility of the UK economy. On net, then, we can certainly see some interaction at this time, involving all the major economies in Europe. Indeed, one reason the Granger-causality tests are successful is that they exploit the lags in these relationships. Accounting for lags is especially important when we are considering how the investment climate in one country might influence that in another because of the long time it takes for actual investment spending to occur after a change in the underlying economic situation. We are referring to gestation and construction lags, in the first instance.

This section, then, contains much the same results for investment that we found for exports and imports. That is, first differences of the data show low or zero correlations, while the non-stationary level figures are usually highly correlated. The cointegration tests for either investment or the investment ratio are totally unsuccessful, showing little or no cointegration, as judged by the Dickey–Fuller tests. On the other hand, there is substantial evidence of lagged relationships across these countries; this evidence is revealed by the Granger-causality tests.

We conjecture that investment – and technology transfers – were indeed increasingly integrated across the European landscape at this time, but we admit we are unable to show this except with the rather low-power Granger-causality tests (and only for the entire period). This lack of decisiveness is hardly surprising, we think, in view of the fact that our only adequate general data are domestic investment expenditures. Actual investment is subject to long and variable lags and is, perhaps more importantly, very volatile over time. This latter point is discussed further in Chapter 9. The fact that we have a relatively small sample of countries on which to base our generalizations is not a problem, we feel, since these are the major economies, and the interactions that occurred primarily involved this set of countries in any case. Furthermore, as we shall see in the next section, our parallel work on interest rates supports our few generalizations in this section.

8.5 INTEREST RATES

In this section we shall look at results for both nominal and real interest rates. The linkage of *nominal interest rates* across these countries is of importance in the interaction story, for quite a few reasons. For one thing, attempts to control nominal rates through monetary policy were certainly part of the foreign exchange control procedures of the gold-standard countries. These policies would tend to bring some coincidence of nominal interest rates. Another thing nominal rates might show is the interaction of capital markets. Here we are thinking, in particular, of bond market interaction; that is, the nominal interest rate is the appropriate rate to use for (nominal) bonds. Finally, and to confuse the issue somewhat, by means of the Fisher Effect $(i = r + \pi_e)$ nominal interest rates would reflect the different (expected) inflation experiences of the various countries. We have found inflation rates to be interrelated across countries, and so would anticipate that nominal interest rates would tend to show somewhat the same pattern, country by country.

Real interest rates would tend to be tied together internationally to the extent that (real) capital markets are. We have looked at the real investment figures themselves, finding only Granger-causal interaction. At the very least, we would expect real interest rates to show the same thing for the same countries. We also might pick up some other effects with real rates, however, since we have a larger sample of these, because real rates are almost certainly measured more accurately than investment, and because interest rates would be expected to respond faster than investment spending (which generally responds to interest rate changes with a lag).

We begin with a discussion of the correlations tests among these interest rates, both long and short. In the top part of Table 8.8 we exhibit the results of the correlations for nominal and real long-term rates. Note that in this section we shall not be generating results for separate periods, but using the maximum amount of data available; we gain degrees of freedom in this way. In any case, we did not locate any interesting differences for those tests that involved the usual subperiods of the data. The correlations for the nominal long-term rates are quite high in the table, a result not unexpected, since inflation rates are fairly highly correlated between countries, as shown in Chapter 6. Here we note that the United States is very involved in the nominal interaction, with four cases showing correlation coefficients over 0.9. We also note that the countries with the highest correlations are also, on the whole, the most rapidly-growing countries. In particular, Germany, Sweden, the Netherlands and the United States all show quite a few high correlations, and three of these countries (excluding the Netherlands) have the highest three growth rates in the sample for this period (see Table 8.1). The nominal short-term rates are not as highly correlated, as shown in the lower half of the table, but still exhibit strong positive correlations.

To calculate real rates for Table 8.8, we generated an expected inflation rate with an arbitrary distributed lag of actual inflation rates, and then deducted this from the nominal long-term rate. The weights for the distributed lag were 0.4, 0.3, 0.2 and 0.1, beginning with the currently observed inflation rate. While the resulting correlations among the real rates are lower than those for nominal rates, obviously because of the deduction of the highly correlated expected inflation rates, the correlations for real rates are still quite high. Interaction among interest rates seems well-established, on these numbers alone. Interestingly, the United States shows the lowest correlations among the real rates, especially long-term real rates. This finding, that the United States is involved more in nominal than real interaction with Europe, echoes a finding in Friedman and Schwartz (1982) for the pair-wise comparison between the United Kingdom and the United States.

Graphs of the series we are considering enable us to pinpoint several characteristics of these data that are both peculiar to this time period and not possible to discern from the summary numbers just given for the entire period. In Figure 8.2 we graph long-term rates; the nominal rates appear in

Table 8.8 Correlations among interest rates, 1850–1913

	Belgium	France	Germany	Italy	Netherlands	Norway	Sweden	United Kingdom	United States	Date
A Nominal long-term interest rates										
Belgium	–	.834	.857	.793	.850	.860	.906	.808	.878	1850
France		–	.830	.840	.842	.580	.899	.735	.932	1850
Germany			–	.823	.940	.885	.909	.866	.936	1850
Italy				–	.819	.593	.810	.622	.897	1861
Netherlands					–	.836	.902	.830	.921	1850
Norway						–	.756	.750	.726	1870
Sweden							–	.729	.915	1870
United Kingdom								–	.725	1850
United States									–	1867
Real Long-term Interest Rates										
Belgium	–	.777	.691	.635	.710	.589	.680	.698	.463	
France		–	.804	.715	.883	.564	.652	.861	.656	
Germany			–	.622	.833	.728	.685	.774	.482	
Italy				–	.698	.496	.550	.519	.485	
Netherlands					–	.685	.706	.904	.678	
Norway						–	.835	.643	.407	
Sweden							–	.713	.554	
United Kingdom								–	.712	
United States									–	

Table 8.8 (continued)

	France	Germany	Netherlands	United Kingdom	United States	Date
B Nominal short-term rates						
France	–	.624	.743	.587	.704	1850
Germany		–	.847	.613	.417	1850
Netherlands			–	.802	.590	1873
United Kingdom				–	.545	1871
United States					–	1867
Real short-term interest rates						
France	–	.745	.814	.741	.549	
Germany		–	.784	.545	.359	
Netherlands			–	.763	.638	
United Kingdom				–	.638	
United States					–	

Notes: The long-term rates are as follows: Belgium, 2.5% Rentes; France, long rate on Paris; Germany, long; Italy, long; Netherlands, 2.5% Perpetual Governments; Norway, long; Sweden, long; United Kingdom, Consol; and United States, corporate Bond Rate. The short-term rates are as follows: France, short-term rate for Paris; Germany, open market discount rate; Netherlands, open market discount rate; United Kingdom, call money; and the United States, commercial paper.

Towards an Integrated Economy

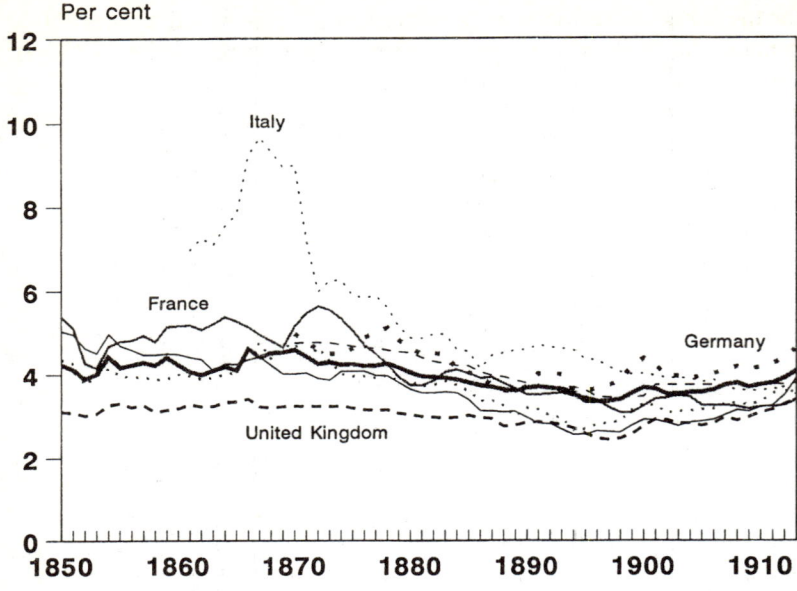

Figure 8.2(a)   Nominal long-term rates, 1850–1913

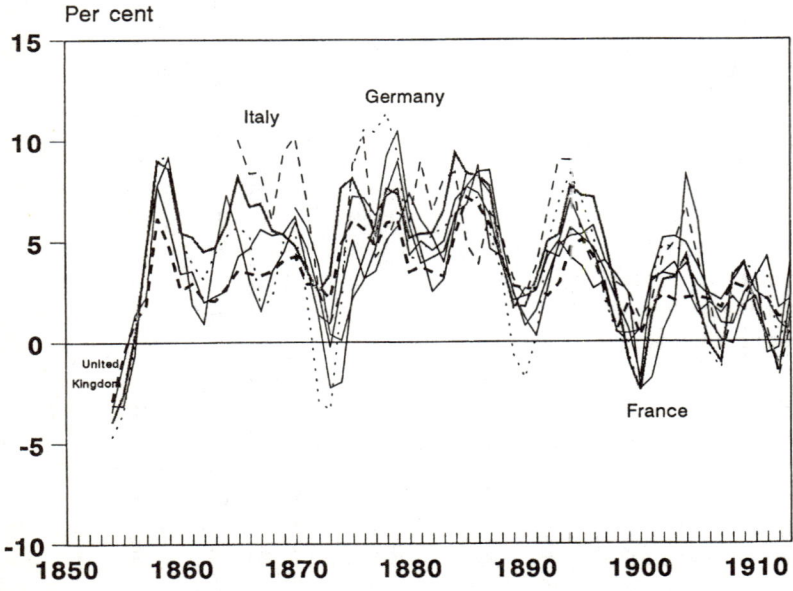

Figure 8.2(b)   Real long-term rates, 1850–1913

the top panel and real rates in the bottom; Figure 8.3, which follows below, contains the short-term rate graphs. Note that both series are for the longest runs of data available, and that the rates for the United States have been excluded since we are, after all, primarily interested in the European situation (and the US rates, both nominal and real, appear to be outliers).

For both nominal series there is a slight downward drift over most of the period, with a slight upward drift beginning around the turn of the century. Again, for both nominal series, these rates move closer together as time passes, although this closure is more obvious for real rates than it is for nominal. The bottom long-term rate, towards which the others gravitate, is in fact the British Consol rate. None of this is very surprising; the closeness of these rates (Italy aside) over the entire period is the main result. It is consistent with the close integration of capital markets, influenced to an extent for the nominal rates by the operation of the gold standard.

For real rates, even though the correlations are not as close as they were for nominal rates, there is a remarkable coincidence throughout the period. Again, the Italian long-term rate is out of line (especially early on), but nowhere near as much as it was for nominal rates. Real rates are basically trendless (after the 1850s) until the mid-1880s, at which point they begin to drift down for both long and short rates. We believe this attests very strongly to the close integration of capital markets in this period. This integration is stronger at the end, but strong throughout the period, at least as judged visually. Finally, notice that in both nominal and real rates that volatilities seem smaller at the end of the period than at the beginning. This finding is especially noticeable in the real rates.

The next thing to do is to study the time series properties of these rates. We begin with the results of unit root tests for both the nominal and real short- and long-term rates. Table 8.9 shows a summary of the results, taking 1870–1913 as the sample period. We use this time period because that is the longest period for which we have data across all countries; we are also interested in focusing on the gold-standard period, of course, and we note that Figures 8.1–8.3 show a quite close correspondence of all these rates during this period. The nominal rates all show unit roots, using the Dickey–Fuller test or (for Italy) the Augmented Dickey–Fuller test, apart from the short-term rate for the United States. This result no doubt follows primarily from there being a unit root in (expected) inflation. The real rates show three cases where there are no unit roots: for Italian long-term rates, and Dutch and UK short-term rates. In all cases, the first differences show no unit roots, as judged by the Augmented Dickey–Fuller test, carried out to five lags in each case; certainly, the Belgian data might have a unit root (one was identified at the 10 per cent level of significance). It follows, then,

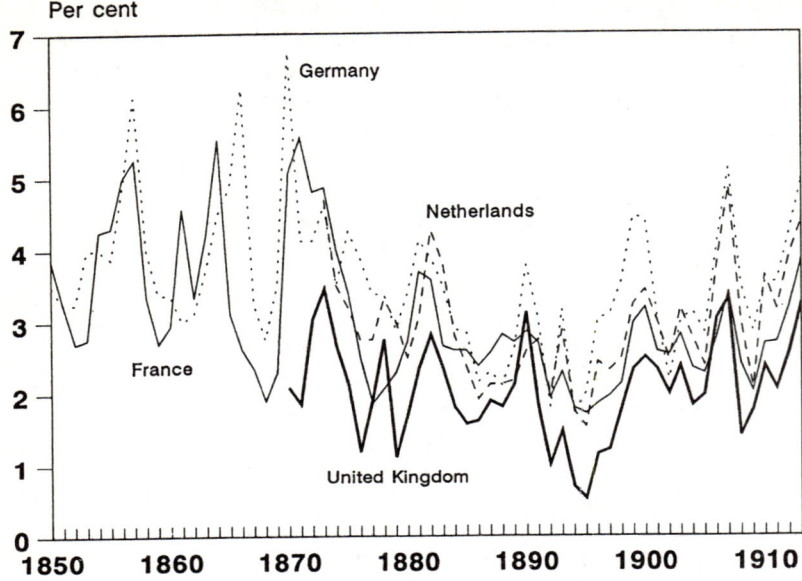

Figure 8.3(a)   Nominal short-term rates, 1850–1913

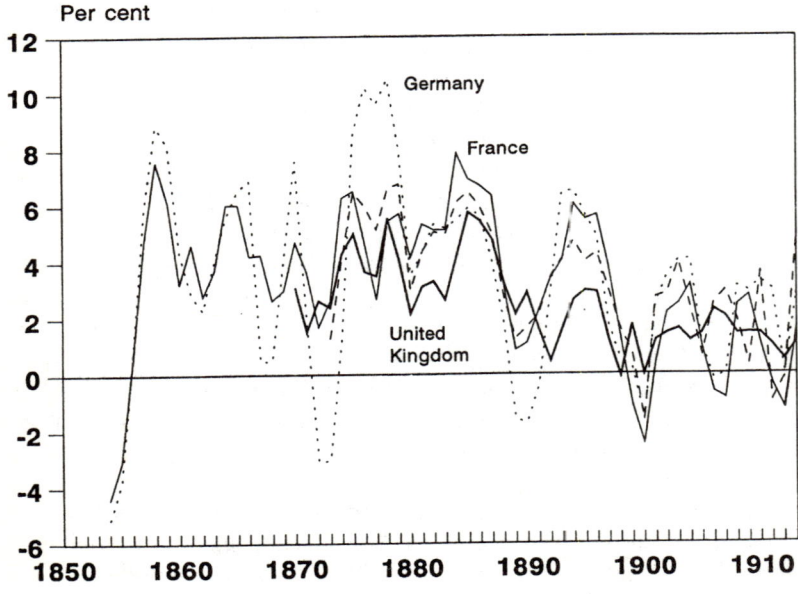

Figure 8.3(b)   Real short-term rates, 1850–1913

Table 8.9 Unit root tests for interest rates, 1870–1913

	Nominal levels	Real levels	Nominal differences	Real differences
A Long-term rates:				
Belgium	2.012	−3.241	−3.370**	No
France	−1.335	−3.070	No	No
Germany	0.256	−2.619	No	No
Italy	−2.218(2)	−3.546*	No	No
Netherlands	−1.060	−3.329	No	No
Norway	−0.805	−2.299	No	No
Sweden	−0.060	−2.509	No	No
United Kingdom	0.562	−3.156	No	No
United States	−1.218	−3.020	No	No
B Short-term rates:				
France	−2.872	−3.056	No	No
Germany	−3.055	−2.581	No	No
Netherlands	−3.435	−4.256*	No	No
United Kingdom	−3.461	−3.896*	No	No
United States	−4.444*	−2.889	No	No

Notes: The number in parentheses is the number of lags in the Augmented Dickey–Fuller test.
*No unit root identified.
** No unit root at 10 per cent level.

that we can test for the cointegration of both nominal and real rates but not, because of the lack of unit roots, for the four cases where we have placed asterisks. We can also do Granger-causality tests for each set of numbers, but these must be on the first differences. In our experience, finding unit roots in interest rate series is not all that uncommon; we think possibly it is caused by a combination of the strong trends in the use of money, in growth rates, and in the increasing integration of European capital markets in this period.

Beginning with cointegration tests for long-term nominal rates, we note first that we do expect to find cointegration, in view of the presence of expected inflation (at least if we continue to interpret nominal interest rates by the Fisher Equation). Of course, we showed cointegration with *actual* inflation rates and not *expected* inflation rates, but this is still a reasonable expectation. In fact, for the 1870–1913 period we are looking at, there is absolutely no cointegration of these series. These were the results of pair-wise tests of cointegration, but tests of three or more countries showed no cointegration.[9] Whatever caused nominal long-term interest rates to march together in this period, it was not the result of capital markets being influenced by common stochastic trends.

When we remove the troublesome inflation expectations from the long-term data, there is much stronger evidence of cointegration. That is, long-term *real* rates of interest show cointegration for thirteen cases, as follows:

Belgium	→ Netherlands
France	→ Belgium, Netherlands
Germany	→ Netherlands
Italy	→ Belgium
Netherlands	→ Belgium, France, UK
Norway	→ Netherlands
Sweden	→ Belgium, Netherlands, UK
UK	→ Netherlands

This represents a fairly high incidence, suggestive of interaction (there are fifty-six total possible cases). Even so, we note that many results do not run both ways (there are four countries to the right of the arrow and eight on the left). Furthermore, we do not show cointegration among the three largest economies at this time (the United Kingdom, France and Germany). But there certainly is substantial cointegration among real interest rates in this period, even though it mostly involves the second echelon of economic powers.

For short-term rates, there is in fact considerable nominal (but not real) interaction revealed by the cointegration tests. The cases of nominal interaction number eight (of sixteen); for short-term real rates there was only one case of cointegration. The cases for nominal rates are the following:

France	→ Netherlands, UK
Germany	→ Netherlands
Netherlands	→ Germany, UK
UK	→ France, Netherlands
US	→ France, UK

These involve all the major industrial economies as well as the United States. We believe that what we are picking up here, in the short-term nominal rates, is an important characteristic of the operation of the gold standard in this period. In particular, the gold standard would force countries to keep their short-term nominal rates in line with those in other countries, with the (expected) inflation rate being the dominant factor in this determination. For example, if a country has a relatively rapid rise in its inflation rate, this would produce a balance of trade deficit directly and, because its short-term rates would rise, a partially-offsetting short-term capital inflow. It is clear, then, that in their efforts to avoid trade deficits under the gold standard, countries would also tend to keep their nominal interest rates in line, which, we believe, is a major reason for the cointegration of nominal short-term interest rates. Long-term rates, probably, are not as involved in these necessary arbitrage operations. Note that the cointegration of inflation rates already established in Chapter 6 is another way one might explain directly the result noted here. In this case, we would just be making an appeal to the Fisher effect without necessarily making reference to the gold standard.

For short-term real rates, which were not cointegrated, we have no particular explanation. It is certainly not unreasonable for short-term real rates to be correlated, but we must admit that our method of calculating expected inflation, using a four-period distributed lag of inflation rates, might have left us with a real rate that is seriously off the mark. We do not think so, however, if only because a simple model such as this would have sufficed to predict the modest inflation observed in this period. If this is so, then our result says that short-term borrowing, which for these rates mostly involves governments (with their differing agendas in this period), is not cointegrated across nations. Recall, in this connection, that long-term real rates were more often cointegrated. At any rate, we again note the interesting result that the United States is involved in the nominal interaction reported here, but not in the real interaction; this is also what Friedman and Schwartz (1982) found.

We are performing Granger-causality tests in this chapter primarily as a diagnostic device. While interaction could occur – even lagged interaction – the Granger test will not necessarily show this, since it requires consistent and generally one-way intertemporal relationships (at a given lag). On the other hand, a successful Granger test is interesting, under the limitations, of course, of this sort of low-power test. Somewhat surprisingly, then, as the following tabulation makes clear, the Granger test does provide considerable interaction, for both nominal and real long-term interest rates. For nominal long-term rates there are twenty-two cases of Granger-causality significant at the 5 per cent level, as follows:

Belgium	→ Germany, Norway, Sweden, UK
France	→ Netherlands, Norway, US
Germany	→ Sweden, UK
Italy	→ Netherlands, US
Netherlands	→ Germany, Italy
Norway	→ Germany, Netherlands, Sweden, UK
UK	→ Sweden
US	→ Italy, Sweden

Every country is involved in this interaction, with the major countries interacting among themselves as well as with the 'second-tier' industrial nations in the sample. We suspect that what we are picking up here are financial capital market effects, probably involving both the underlying real rate and the expected (long-term) rate of inflation; these capital market effects would be expected to lag considerably, as we have argued above.

Although the incidence is certainly not the same country by country, the results of our tests of Granger-causality for long-term real rates, which follow, produce something like the same overall incidence (nineteen cases), again involving a wide selection of countries:

Belgium	→ Italy
France	→ Belgium, Italy, Netherlands, Norway, UK
Germany	→ Belgium, Norway, Sweden, US
Italy	→ Belgium, France, Norway
Netherlands	→ Belgium, Norway, Sweden
Sweden	→ Germany, Norway
US	→ Norway

Here, however, the relationships are often different from those revealed for nominal rates. We argued that there might be *both* inflation and real rate effects mixed together in the nominal rate Granger-causality results just discussed. In any event, there is still considerable interaction among the major industrial economies shown in this test. We must again warn, however, that this test is not a very sensitive indicator of cross-country influences, which in fact might have strong cyclical effects that may not be consistent over time. As usual, we should like to suggest that the existence of Granger-causality tells us something about interaction, without measuring magnitude in any way. Indeed, there are no really good ways of measuring such real magnitudes involving prices or interest rates in the macroeconomic literature, where the data are so sketchy.

For short-term rates, for the five countries for which we have data, there are eight cases of Granger-causality for nominal rates. This result is not unexpected, and is again, we believe, the result of the close integration of short-term capital markets that is required by the successful operation of the gold standard. The cases are as follows:

France	→ US
Germany	→ France, Netherlands, UK, US
Netherlands	→ France
UK	→ France, Netherlands

Here, German short-term rates Granger-cause the rates of all the other countries and, once again, we see general interaction (of the lagged variety) among the leading industrial countries in Europe. For real rates, the only cases of Granger-causality that could be established were for:

Germany → UK
US → France

This finding is essentially uninteresting, except that it repeats the results for our cointegration tests, which reported strong nominal links for short-term rates, and basically no real links. Our explanation for the Granger tests is, accordingly, the same as for the cointegration tests.

8.6 CONCLUSIONS

What this chapter has sought to do is to look for product and capital market interaction, using the appropriate components of national income and long- and short-term interest rates, in the general spirit of a macroeconomic approach to the problem. In some cases, our search was inhibited by the length or number of data series, but in the main we were able to establish considerable interaction. We are not able to compare periods here, for the most part, and thus we can hardly claim that there was more integration than earlier periods or less than later, but we think, nevertheless, that both statements hold. We also think that the considerable amount of interaction found suggests a full integration of the major economies in Europe and, even, for the countries normally taken to be peripheral to the main economic powers of the time.

For exports and imports we found, somewhat to our surprise, that there is some decline in the growth rates of these over the period; this finding is less surprising, though, when one considers that not only were overall growth rates sometimes lower at the end of the period than before 1870, but also tariffs were often higher, and higher for many important products (Kenwood and Lougheed, 1983, pp. 86–89). Turning to the statistical tests, our results indicate very high correlations of exports and imports across countries, although these results are suspect because of the existence of unit roots in the data. Of course, having unit roots enables one to test for cointegration. However, little of this could be established. We conjecture that it was the existence of lags in the linkage of export and import markets that produced this failure (the cointegration tests were conducted at zero lags). As partial evidence of this, our Granger-causality tests showed considerable interaction for both exports and imports. Our conclusion, then, is that export and import markets are closely related in this period, with correlations and Granger-causality tests providing the strongest evidence for this integration.

It would be nice to have better data for capital markets than we do, and so we must regard our results for the seven series on real investment as, at best, suggestive. We have no real doubts about our interaction hypothesis, but here we are restricted to making claims on the basis of our macroeconomic evidence. As with exports and imports, the investment figures are highly correlated across countries, again because of the trends in the data; here we also looked at investment ratios (I/Y) since such a concept tells us something about the causes of growth. Indeed, there is clearly some indication that the faster-growing countries had higher investment ratios, as the Harrod–Domar growth model predicts. Since most of these series contain unit roots, it is possible to test for cointegration; again, there was no evidence of this, and again the Granger-causality tests provided the main evidence of interaction. Indeed, the interaction involved the major countries in Europe and not the United States. In this case, a lagged relationship rather than a contemporaneous one is the most obvious result, since the lags between stimulus and response in aggregate investment are known to be relatively long.

The interest rates we have available are more numerous, especially for long-term rates, and they are likely to be reasonably accurate. We can, accordingly, have greater faith in these results. Of course, the general idea is that capital–market integration can be revealed by looking at interest-rate interaction, although we explore only the 1870–1913 period, primarily for data reasons. Nominal and real interest rates are generally pretty strongly correlated (with nominal being more so than real); again, however, many of these series contain unit roots, rendering the correlations of levels suspect. Note that real rates were computed using a distributed lag of past inflation rates, since it is *expected* real rates that we are interested in. In any case, graphs show a remarkable coincidence of real rates, for both long and short rates. This is exactly what we expected to find.

For the cointegration tests that are possible for the series containing unit roots, there is no cointegration for long-term nominal rates, but there is for short-term rates. We attribute the latter to the operation of the gold standard, since the short-term nominal interest rate is the key capital-market rate (partly because it contains expected inflation) for the managers of this system. The results of cointegration tests for long-term real rates do show cointegration; on the other hand, and consistently, the short-term real rates do not show cointegration. For the Granger tests, there are signs of Granger-causality for nominal long-term rates; we believe these are the results both of the lagged real relationship that is contained in the nominal rate (by means of the

Fisher effect), and by real rate interaction. Of course, we have no strong evidence of this, but we do note that the real rates show about the same incidence of Granger-causal interaction as do the nominal rates.

Our conclusions? We feel that considerable interaction is established here, with suitable lags, for both product markets (exports and imports) and capital markets. The real interactions are dominated by market-driven interaction, on the whole, while the nominal results, for short-term interest rates at least, are driven, at least to some extent, by the requirements of the gold standard. While there is considerably more evidence to assemble, mainly involving industrial production and business cycles, we think the results of this chapter are about what one might have anticipated for countries that are sharing product and capital markets, and for which a common financial bond was firmly established.

9 The European Trade Cycle: 1850–1913

9.1 INTRODUCTION

There appears to be a strong tradition in the literature on European business cycles that by the beginning of the twentieth century these events are correlated quite closely across countries. The most prominent lines of influence mentioned in the literature are either real (with either foreign trade or capital flows serving as the transmission mechanism) or nominal (with the gold standard serving in the same capacity). Most studies deal with a particular country, the result being that what we could call the 'pan-European cycle' is hard to pin down, even though many of the parts to the puzzle exist. Broadly, then, we propose to search the empirical record, with the object being a closer identification of the common cyclical influences in this period.

The next section of this chapter considers where we stand on the question of a pan-European cycle, including a summary of the literature on this topic as well as a summary of the information from our earlier chapters that has a bearing on the question. That done, we shall present new results for real GNP for twelve countries (including the United States); these results will provide what we think is an effective quantitative picture of the magnitude and timing of these events in Europe. Since business cycles are more than just fluctuations in real GNP – and because the national product data for these countries are often suspect, we need to do quite a bit more work to pin down the cycles (and hence the cyclical interaction). First, we shall examine the cyclical behaviour of what are usually pro-cyclical and coincident indicators of the cycle. What we have identified as being useful are series on industrial production, imports, and real investment. We also have scattered information on unemployment (often either a coincident or a lagging indicator). Finally, we shall examine the record generated by the dozens of economists and historians who have written on this topic about the countries we are studying. With this material, then, the last section of the chapter will provide our best guesses as to the cross-country co-ordination of the major cycles of this period.

9.2 PREVIOUS WORK ON THE PAN-EUROPEAN CYCLE

Beginning with the financial variables discussed in Chapters 4 to 7, we first note that there is a strong tradition in the literature that financial crises in one European economy spread to others, producing roughly simultaneous financial and real contractions for a number of countries. What is curious about this conjecture is the finding in the formal causality literature that, with only a few exceptions, monetary influences on real events generally cannot be demonstrated within countries; the international evidence has rarely been put forward. This material was discussed in Chapter 4. What we argued in Chapter 6 is that while inflation rates are closely related across countries – through correlation, cointegration and Granger-causality tests – money growth rates are not. Our explanation of the failure of money to fit into the pattern – as predicted by the 'specie-flow mechanism' of the gold standard – is that adjustment was in fact by means of a mechanism described in the 'monetary approach' to the balance of payments, so that international financial equilibrium was achieved through trade and capital flows rather than via direct monetary adjustment. This result implies that in all likelihood the money stock would not serve in its traditional role as a leading indicator, while price levels and interest rates, being determined internationally, would offer little assistance in identifying cycles *within* each country.

With respect to other variables, Chapter 8 investigated exports and imports, investment, and nominal and real interest rates. The evidence of interaction here is strongest for both exports and imports, with Granger-causality tests (and simple correlations) providing clear evidence of interaction. We also noted a tendency for this interaction to decline over the period (in contrast to what we found for inflation rates in Chapter 6). For investment, the paucity of data precludes any firm conclusions; in any case, all that emerges are some signs of Granger-causality across countries. Finally, for long-term interest rates, we found strong evidence of correlation, for both real and nominal rates (using a distributed lag to identify inflationary expectations). Cointegration tests show that this is not the result of sharing a common stochastic trend; in contrast, there is considerable evidence of Granger-causal links among these countries. Some evidence for short-term interest rates, on a smaller sample, confirms these results, on the whole. What these results imply to us, taken together, is that there is sufficient real interaction among the major European economies for both financial and real interaction to have produced a pan-European cycle in this period.

Turning to the literature on the international cycle, then, our point of departure is the Friedman–Schwartz study (1982). What they found is that there is cyclical interaction between the United States and the

United Kingdom, but that it is primarily monetary in nature. Even so, they note real effects running from the United States to the United Kingdom. Later, when we review the literature, for individual countries, we shall note that both real and monetary shocks emanating from the United States are mentioned frequently as proximate causes of European cycles.

A test procedure that is similar to our Granger-causality tests is by Huffman and Lothian (1984) also on US and UK cycles; they refer to the period 1834–1914. The hypothesis of their study is that monetary shocks in one country induce real reactions in the other – and it is the operation of the specie-flow mechanism of the international gold standard that makes this possible. In their view, money is non-neutral in each country, and money supplies are linked by the gold standard. As discussed in Chapter 6, we are not able to locate the cross-country money effects. As we shall see in our survey of particular countries, financial shocks frequently are thought to be important in generating downturns in this period, but if we understand Huffman and Lothian correctly, the mechanism by which one country's real product is contaminated by shocks in another is very complicated. This conclusion leaves room for our results and theirs to coexist. Note, however, that our work is on a much larger sample of countries than theirs.

There is a Granger-causality study by Easton (1984) of real interactions among the European countries in this period, which focuses on changes in real national income for somewhat different data than we employ below. Easton's results, for the countries at which we are looking, for the period 1881–1913, show Granger-causality (with a probability of 0.05 or less) as follows:

Denmark	→	Italy
Germany	→	United States
Sweden	→	Italy
Sweden	→	Denmark
United Kingdom	→	Norway
United States	→	Denmark

This test certainly uncovers a substantial amount of interaction, although it does not cover as wide a group of countries as we were able to study, and is for a different time period. Also, it does not include the major countries of France and Austria-Hungary (for which the data were unavailable when Easton did his work). Here it is also worth underscoring Wood's (1984) concern that the Granger test, by mixing together positive and negative influences (for example, demand or supply shocks) could, indeed, fail to record a cyclical interaction on net. Easton deals with this problem by testing the absolute values of the changes in real national income, also to no avail. We shall conduct our own tests, on a broader sample, in Section 9.3.

In a recent study, Craig and Fisher (1992) analyzed five European countries – France, Germany, Italy, Sweden and the United Kingdom – and the United States, employing Granger-causality and cointegration tests. The period covered was 1871 to 1910, and both money stocks and real national product were included in the tests. In the Granger tests, there were signs of interaction among the monetary quantities, involving the major European economies in particular; the tests for real interaction were unsuccessful. For the cointegration tests, exactly the opposite obtained: real quantities showed cointegration, while monetary quantities did not. Even though the present study obtains results similar to this for a similar time period, the present study also covers different periods and includes many more countries, and so we shall reserve our comments on this work until we have presented the detailed results.

For the United Kingdom, a survey by Ford (1981) contains the international themes in which we are interested. Ford discusses the causes of business cycles in this period – although his methods are not formally causal. He notes that Matthews (1959) and Coppock (1972) had previously argued for real interactions – overseas investment for Matthews and exports for Coppock – as well as for specific internal shocks. In these Keynesian-orientated studies, investment (usually domestic) or residential construction and exports dominate; both are taken as exogenous variables capable of unleashing multiplier effects. In any case, Ford also conducts empirical tests, using both regressions and cyclical phases across France, Germany and Britain, and notes (Ford, 1981, p. 38):

> Particular international shocks could help to explain one major feature of the business cycle – the marked parallelism between Britain, France, and Germany, who were in the same phase of their reference cycles in 83 per cent of all months between 1879 and 1914.

Ford also runs separate regressions comparing the influence of money and exports on UK *nominal* national income; the value of exports wins hands down. Ford's work says little directly about the business cycle, however, since that topic normally refers to fluctuations in *real* national product. The difference between real and nominal cycles would be especially troublesome if it were shown that nominal factors do not themselves influence real factors. Incidentally, our results, described above, generally agree in that money is not cointegrated across the European countries while real exports and imports are.

9.3 INTERACTION AMONG REAL NATIONAL PRODUCTS[1]

Obviously, the main way we would want to identify the cycle for each country is by means of the behaviour of real national product. We have data for eleven countries (one of which is the United States), although the data for the Netherlands only begin on an annual basis from 1900. We immediately have a problem with these numbers, however, because for most countries, they appear to contain unit roots; Table 9.1 shows this, and serves to introduce the data. Here we find three countries not showing unit roots in the level figures, while for the first differences, three countries do. This implies that cointegration tests must be performed with only seven countries (the Dutch sample is not long enough), while Granger-causality tests can be conducted in first differences (again omitting the Netherlands), omitting the fifth lag case for France and Norway.

Because of the non-stationarity of the log-level figures, a comparison of correlation coefficients across countries would be less interesting; on the other hand, correlations of the first differences of these series rarely turn up anything: most such correlations across countries are not very large in absolute terms. While this is not especially favourable for the hypothesis of

Table 9.1 Unit root tests and data description measures of real national product or income

Country	Level	Different	Series	Period
Austria-Hungary	No	No	GNP	1867–1913
Belgium	No	No	GDP	1860–1913
Denmark	Yes	No	GNP	1850–1913
France	Yes(5)	Yes(5)	GDP	1850–1913
Germany	No	No	NNP	1850–1913
Italy	Yes	No	GNP	1861–1913
Netherlands	Yes	Yes	NI	1900–1913
Norway	Yes	Yes(5)	GDP	1865–1913
Portugal	Yes	No	GDP	1850–1913
Sweden	Yes	No	GDP	1861–1913
United Kingdom	Yes	No	GNP	1850–1913
United States	Yes	No	GNP	1869–1913

Notes: The numbers in parentheses indicate the number of lags in the Augmented Dickey–Fuller test. All 'Yes' results not so qualified were achieved at zero lags (in effect by the standard Dickey–Fuller test). The data are described in the Data Appendix.

the pan-European cycle, we do have an alternative, as employed both by Friedman and Schwartz (1982), and Ford (1981). This alternative involves counting the percentage of the years in which these economies were in the same phase of the business cycle (expansion or contraction), where the phases are identified by the sign of the changes in the level figures. What is useful about this technique, which ignores magnitudes, of course, is that expansion years are treated as being equal with contraction years. It is the fashion, in the literature, to look mainly at the timing of contractions, as if all we cared about with respect to cycles were the downturns. We believe the phase-coincidence approach provides a useful alternative. Most importantly, in this section and when we look at industrial production figures in the next, this measure seems to overcome the impression one gets from looking at correlations of the first differences, that these aggregates are not related.

Table 9.2 contains the results of calculating the percentage of the years when these economies were in the same cyclical phase. We look at the entire period (which is defined for each country in Table 9.1) at the top of the table, and the subperiod 1890–1913, at the bottom. If one merely tries to line up the years of downturns, one gets the impression that these countries are not especially in phase; when the good years are included, however, since they are so numerous, the results are stronger. For the entire period, the average of these figures (unweighted) is .669, indicating coincident phases in two out of every three years. For the 1890–1913 period, the average of the figures (in Part B of Table 9.2) is higher, at .709. For the major industrial economies (Belgium, France, Germany, Sweden, the United Kingdom and the United States), the comparable numbers are .705 for the overall period and .746 for the 1890–1913 period; these are noticeably higher and indicate that the correspondence of cyclical phases for these countries had reached three out of every four years by the end of the period. We conjecture that the widening of international product and capital markets and the shrinking of the volatile (and often out of phase) agricultural sectors of these countries are the principal factors involved here. Notice, in this connection, that Italy and Portugal, two economies for which the agricultural cycle dominates to the end of the period, are at the low end of these comparisons; indeed, Portugal shows decreasing phase coincidence over the period. These numbers, at any rate, provide evidence of considerable *and increasing* coincidence throughout the period.

Phase-coincidence is one way to think about integration, but certainly cointegration and Granger-causality tests could provide others. Unfortunately, cointegration tests of real national product are not really possible on enough of these countries because of the problems revealed (in Table 9.1) by the unit root tests. In particular, three countries do not have unit roots in their

Table 9.2 Integration of business cycles: frequencies

	Austria-Hungary	Belgium	Denmark	France	Germany	Italy	Norway	Portugal	Sweden	United Kingdom	United States
A 1850–1913											
Austria-Hungary	–										
Belgium	.630	–									
Denmark	.696	.887	–								
France	.609	.623	.540	–							
Germany	.565	.774	.603	.651	–						
Italy	.674	.654	.654	.596	.577	–					
Norway	.609	.854	.792	.604	.667	.625	–				
Portugal	.609	.717	.651	.540	.603	.596	.625	–			
Sweden	.522	.904	.827	.635	.769	.558	.833	.692	–		
United Kingdom	.674	.774	.682	.635	.635	.635	.667	.619	.654	–	
United States	.609	.818	.795	.523	.636	.682	.727	.659	.727	.682	–
B 1890–1913											
Austria-Hungary	–										
Belgium	.708	–									
Denmark	.750	.958	–								
France	.708	.667	.708	–							
Germany	.583	.792	.750	.708	–						
Italy	.667*	.708	.750	.708	.667	–					
Norway	.750	.958	.917	.625	.750	.667	–				
Portugal	.625	.583*	.542*	.500*	.542*	.542*	.625	–			
Sweden	.667	.958	.917	.750	.833	.667	.917	.625*	–		
United Kingdom	.708*	.750*	.792	.667	.625*	.708	.792	.500*	.708	–	
United States	.667	.792*	.833	.583	.667*	.667*	.750	.542*	.750	.708	–

Note: *: indicates that total period has a larger frequency of similar phases than 1890–1913.

figures (as revealed by the Adjusted Dickey–Fuller test), while three others would continue to show unit roots in the residuals of the level figures because they exhibit unit roots in the first differences. Omitting these countries leaves six countries – but only one major country (the United Kingdom) left to study. We forbear.

On the other hand, Granger-causality tests of the first differences of the data are possible (although the Netherlands at all lags and France at five lags cannot be tested). We drop Norway, as well, for lack of sufficient observations (see Table 9.1). Still, we have enough data to analyze for an interesting test. The hypothesis, of course, is that economic activity in one country systematically leads it in another – and *may*, indeed, Granger-cause that in the other. The results, for the entire sample of data in this exercise, indicate a fairly widespread pattern of Granger-causality (at the 5 per cent level), as follows (numbers of interactions are shown in the left-hand column):

3 Austria-Hungary	→	Belgium, Denmark
7 Belgium	→	Sweden, UK, US
5 Denmark	→	France, Germany, Italy
3 France	→	Belgium, Germany
5 Germany	→	Belgium
3 Italy	→	Belgium, Germany
2 Norway	→	Portugal
4 Portugal	→	Austria-Hungary, Denmark, Norway
4 Sweden	→	Germany, UK
3 UK	→	Sweden

Here, all countries except the peripheral one of Norway have three or more interactions. The geographically-distant United States figures in only one significant Granger-causal result. These results are suggestive of considerable real interaction in Europe – especially, we believe, in comparison with the results for money growth given in Chapter 6. We turn, now, to comparisons of pro-cyclical variables, beginning with an analysis of the important industrial production figures.

9.4 THE BEHAVIOUR OF THE PRO-CYCLICAL VARIABLES

We have a set of *industrial production* indices for eight countries for this period, with the US series, which begins in 1884, being the only short one. Industrial production is an important part of GNP, of course, but it is generally more volatile than GNP.[2] We have already argued that the increasing coincidence of business cycles across countries is partly the result of industrial activity replacing agricultural, as the main component of national product, towards the of the period. The reasons for this are that the industrial sectors of these nations are knitted more closely together to begin with and that, as time passed, this integration increased more than did the agricultural. This situation is a result of what is traded internationally, in the first instance.

In present-day studies, typically one finds that industrial production is a coincident and procyclical variable. It is certainly a procyclical variable in this period, with very high correlations with GNP; we are not in a position to test for its coincidence here, because we are going to assume that it is, and use it as a further indicator of the business cycle in each country. Looking across countries, first, we see that as with many other real variables, the levels of the production indices are very highly correlated, while their first differences are not. We shall not present these results here, since they would add little to what we have already seen.

The industrial production indices, as anticipated, show unit roots in the level figures (except for France and the United States); the first differences appear to be stationary. For the six series that could be so tested, the only cointegration results were for the Spanish data. We argue that this is merely an artifact of the data/test and not an example of cointegration. If that is correct, there is no cointegration in the industrial production data for this period. We found essentially the same result with the real national product figures. On the other hand, we found considerable Granger-causality with the national product figures, but this is not as apparent with industrial production, with only six (instead of twenty) cases uncovered. These were as follows.

France	→	Sweden
Spain	→	Germany
Sweden	→	Austria-Hungary
UK	→	Spain
US	→	France, Sweden

We think these unimportant, on the whole, in view of the lack of linkages between the major European industrial countries (France and Sweden being the only such interaction). Furthermore, we think that the volatility and narrowness of the index, and the different patterns of industrial specialization among these countries, inhibits the success of this particular diagnostic test.

On the other hand, a phase-coincidence tabulation, done in the same way as Table 9.2, reveals a pattern remarkably similar to that for real national product. The results, which are the relative incidence of first differences of the data showing the same sign, are shown in Table 9.3. These numbers are lower than the real national product numbers, we believe, because of the narrower base of the industrial production index (and, of course, because they are more volatile). Even so, only four of the relationships show lower coincidence of phases in the 1890–1913 period than overall. This result is similar to the real national product calculations. Similar, too, is the difference in the averages, with the entire period showing an average of .660, while the 1890–1913 period, omitting the United States for consistency across the two parts of the table, shows an average coincidence of 0.700. This finding supports our argument that increasing industrialization is one major reason why cycles grew together during this period.

Another coincident variable in modern studies of the business cycle is the level of real *investment*. We do not have as many of these series as we have for GNP and industrial production – and the French data are nominal – but the results still fit the pattern already revealed. First of all, recall that unit root, cointegration and Granger-causality tests are reported in Chapter 8, where we were looking for the extent of the integration of

Table 9.3 Industrial production: phase coincidence

	Austria-Hungary	France	Germany	Italy	Spain	Sweden	United Kingdom	United States
A 1850–1913								
Austria-Hungary	–	.635	.651	.558	.571	.538	.541	–
France		–	.619	.635	.587	.731	.619	–
Germany			–	.788	.698	.769	.712	–
Italy				–	.615	.750	.692	–
Spain					–	.750	.651	–
Sweden						–	.712	–
United Kingdom							–	–
United States								–
B 1890–1913								
Austria-Hungary	–	.750	.667	.583	.708	.667	.667	.750
France		–	.708	.583*	.625	.750	.667	.750
Germany			–	.750*	.625*	.833	.833	.667
Italy				–	.625	.750	.750	.500
Spain					–	.792	.625*	.458
Sweden						–	.750	.583
United Kingdom							–	.625
United States								–

Note: *indicates more frequent coincidence in the entire period than in the 1890–1913 period.

Table 9.4 Investment: phase coincidence

	Denmark	France	Germany	Italy	Norway	Sweden	United Kingdom
A Overall							
Denmark	–	.605	.535	.488	.674	.581	.674
France		–	.555	.577	.625	.596	.571
Germany			–	.481	.500	.558	.524
Italy				–	.396	.442	.404
Norway					–	.646	.604
Sweden						–	.577
United Kingdom							–
B 1890–1913							
Denmark	–	.625	.625	.500	.625*	.625	.667*
France		–	.583	.667	.667	.667	.625
Germany			–	.667	.500	.583	.458*
Italy				–	.500	.417*	.458
Norway					–	.667	.458*
Sweden						–	.625
United Kingdom							–

capital markets. There we also studied investment in the form of the investment ratio. Unit roots were revealed in the level figures but not the first differences. Cointegration tests failed, though, while considerable interaction was revealed using the Granger-causality procedure. We believe that further testing of the series themselves (not in ratio form) would not provide any further information, so we now move on to the frequency results; these are reported in Table 9.4.

In Table 9.4 we see a similar pattern to that we saw for real product and industrial production. Here, the average phase coincidence of the 1890–1913 period is 0.581, while that for the overall period is 0.553. Looking at it another way, for most cases (sixteen of twenty-one), the phases were more coincident in the 1890–1913 period than they were overall. The numbers in the table are not as high as those for real product (as discussed above), but this difference is not really surprising, since investment is considerably more volatile than national product. On net, then, this indicator – quite probably a coincident one – shows the same increasing integration that the other measures show.

Table 9.5 Real imports: phase coincidence

	Austria-Hungary	Belgium	Denmark	France	Germany	Italy	Netherlands	Norway	Portugal	Spain	Sweden	United Kingdom	United States
A Entire period													
Austria-Hungary	–	.690	.750	.667	.667	.524	.571	.643	.522	.619	.595	.595	.548
Belgium		–	.659	.682	.444	.577	.641	.614	.438	.619	.571	.682	.508
Denmark			–	.614	.889	.614	.659	.841	.591	.636	.795	.750	.591
France				–	.556	.461	.635	.604	.375	.714	.635	.587	.508
Germany					–	.556	.556	.728	.728	.556	.778	.556	.889
Italy						–	.596	.542	.625	.385	.635	.654	.538
Netherlands							–	.614	.562	.619	.651	.635	.538
Norway								–	.500	.583	.646	.667	.583
Portugal									–	.500	.521	.604	.625
Spain										–	.476	.492	.603
Sweden											–	.746	.556
United Kingdom												–	.619
United States													–
B 1890–1913													
Austria-Hungary	–	.850	.800	.750	.800	.650	.650	.750	.300*	.600*	.650	.600	.450*
Belgium		–	.917	.750	.833	.667	.833	.875	.458*	.542*	.708	.792*	.500*
Denmark			–	.750	.917	.667	.750	.875	.458*	.542*	.792*	.708*	.500*
France				–	.667	.417*	.667	.792	.208*	.625*	.708	.625	.500*
Germany					–	.750	.750	.792	.458	.458	.708	.792	.583
Italy						–	.667	.542	.708	.292*	.625*	.708	.583
Netherlands							–	.708	.542*	.667	.667	.708	.500*
Norway								–	.333*	.667	.417*	.667	.542*
Portugal									–	.500	.500	.583*	.625
Spain										–		.500	.625
Sweden											–	.792	.458*
United Kingdom												–	.583
United States													–

Notes: * indicates cases in which the overall period has the higher coincidence. See Chapter 8 and the Data Appendix for sources and dates.

The last coincident indicator studied here is the volume of *real imports*. We prefer imports to exports in this role because we are trying to measure cycles within each country, and imports are a component of national demand that would be driven by domestic real incomes (among other things, of course). In Chapter 8 we established that imports generally have unit roots in this period; we also found some cointegration of imports across countries and even more incidence of Granger causality. Granger causality is less frequent in the later data than in the earlier. What remains, then, is to study the pattern of phase coincidence, as we have already defined this, for imports. The results appear in Table 9.5; they are achieved by comparing the signs of changes in real imports across countries (as a percentage of the total possible in each case). Again, the coincidence is higher in the second period than in the whole period. This is especially noticeable among the major European economies, since 20 of the 25 exceptions (marked with an asterisk in the table) involve the United States, Portugal and Spain (there are 78 cases in all). Dropping these three countries, we get an overall average of 0.714 for the 1890–1913 period; this compares with 0.640 for the whole period. If we also dropped the agricultural economies (notably Italy), we would find coincidence to be near 80 per cent for the major European industrial economies in the 1890–1913 period. This is a new result, but it is not an unexpected one.

We conclude, then, that contemporaneous, real variables appear to draw together over this period, with rather high associations (and correlations of the level figures, of course) occurring for all variables and most countries in the 1890–1913 period. Of course, there is more integration to occur in Europe, and the process will certainly go on indefinitely, but we believe that we are looking at an especially important period here, since it is the rapid growth (and rapid relative growth) of the industrial sector that seems 'proximately' responsible for much of the interaction we have observed. We also note that since these are contemporaneous variables in a cyclical sense, we have a strong indication, on net, that cycles are becoming more closely integrated by the end of the period. We shall continue to look at this matter in the next section, where we use the variables just identified to try to pin down the cyclical turning points within countries.

9.5 COUNTRY STUDIES: FIVE MAJOR ECONOMIES

United Kingdom

We begin with the real GNP data of Mitchell (1978) for the United Kingdom. These appear in the first column of Table 9.6. Negative changes of one

Table 9.6 Growth rates of various indicators in the United Kingdom, 1855–1913

	GNP	Unemployment	Industrial Production	Imports	Investment	Exports
1855	2.64	3.70	3.08	−4.58	6.36	−0.21
1856	3.85	3.20	−16.07	18.35	−4.83	18.92
1857	2.13	4.20	3.50	5.87	−10.69	2.59
1858	0.66	7.30	−2.08	−3.76	2.67	5.10
1859	2.07	2.60	5.13	6.39	10.01	8.78
1860	1.52	1.80	5.51	12.19	4.65	0.26
1861	4.93	3.70	0.00	3.64	18.61	−7.60
1862	0.00	6.00	2.18	2.78	7.28	−1.64
1863	0.96	4.70	0.31	8.48	19.11	15.36
1864	1.53	1.90	7.41	9.93	14.79	8.47
1865	2.89	1.80	6.36	0.19	4.88	5.33
1866	−0.11	2.60	3.68	7.66	−11.33	12.15
1867	1.36	6.30	−6.13	−7.02	−12.78	−4.32
1868	3.43	6.70	0.00	7.85	−1.53	0.28
1869	3.00	5.90	−1.66	1.68	−3.12	7.09
1870	7.52	3.70	11.59	3.53	4.65	5.98
1871	6.24	1.60	7.89	6.31	20.48	8.35
1872	−0.67	0.90	2.94	7.00	2.44	13.80
1873	0.00	1.10	1.11	2.76	−4.94	−2.04
1874	5.83	1.60	2.40	5.64	17.38	−0.15
1875	1.43	2.20	0.64	4.62	14.81	−3.80
1876	1.10	3.40	1.70	1.17	11.27	−9.48
1877	0.85	4.40	−0.21	4.94	−1.65	−1.00
1878	0.69	6.20	−0.21	−0.94	−5.13	2.55
1879	−1.86	10.70	−3.66	1.29	−15.12	2.41
1880	7.37	5.20	9.81	8.54	1.02	11.08
1881	−0.14	3.50	6.17	−1.54	−1.02	6.74
1882	1.66	2.30	4.03	4.93	1.02	3.92
1883	4.26	2.60	1.43	3.33	7.77	−0.42
1884	−0.62	8.10	−3.79	−4.04	−3.81	2.07
1885	−0.21	9.30	−4.32	1.39	−12.39	−2.59
1886	1.10	10.20	−2.13	−3.60	−9.20	2.22
1887	4.73	7.60	7.73	4.50	0.00	5.27
1888	1.61	4.90	5.64	6.94	5.85	5.69
1889	1.97	2.10	6.80	8.68	9.74	4.66
1890	1.43	2.10	1.43	−1.65	2.04	5.85

Table 9.6 (continued)

	GNP	Unemployment	Industrial Production	Imports	Investment	Exports
1891	3.35	3.50	1.26	3.27	9.62	−6.66
1892	−1.51	6.30	−4.96	−3.68	4.48	−9.56
1893	−0.49	7.50	−1.65	−3.47	−0.88	−2.93
1894	5.18	6.90	5.67	5.34	6.01	3.68
1895	2.97	5.80	4.62	4.56	0.83	6.91
1896	4.46	3.30	7.11	5.82	12.42	6.01
1897	0.27	3.30	2.76	−0.37	13.63	−4.91
1898	5.43	2.80	4.79	0.87	14.22	−3.90
1899	5.11	2.00	3.95	5.23	8.47	11.32
1900	0.73	2.50	0.00	1.89	1.01	7.55
1901	3.40	3.30	0.25	0.91	−1.01	−2.75
1902	−0.71	4.00	1.73	1.14	0.00	1.07
1903	−0.05	4.70	−2.10	1.70	0.51	1.68
1904	0.90	6.00	1.24	0.37	−5.72	2.28
1905	2.50	5.00	5.64	2.51	−5.50	9.20
1906	2.98	3.60	4.11	6.25	−1.14	11.97
1907	2.29	3.70	1.88	3.93	−15.42	10.36
1908	−3.09	7.80	8.36	−6.43	−15.86	−10.09
1909	3.13	7.70	.71	4.19	3.08	−0.80
1910	4.34	4.70	1.41	6.03	2.98	10.78
1911	3.68	3.00	6.78	−0.74	−2.98	4.39
1912	2.85	3.30	2.59	6.08	2.98	3.97
1913	5.76	2.10	6.29	1.19	16.25	5.53

percent or more in this aggregate occur in 1879, 1892 and 1908 and, as we shall see in what follows, the literature concurs in the view that these are years of recession. Lesser downturns occur in the table in 1866, 1872, 1881, 1884–5, 1893 and 1902–3, so these years, too, could be added to the list of primary suspects as recession years for this period. Over the entire sample, then, there are 11 years of GNP-recession out of the 58 possible between 1855 and 1913; this yields, on average, four years of upturn for each year of downturn in this period. Cycles (say, peak to peak) presumably are slightly over five years in duration.

The literature for UK cycles is too large for us to condense it to fit the small space we have available, but we can certainly attempt to characterize it. One

Table 9.7 Reference cycle turning points in the United Kingdom, 1854–1913

| Rostow (1948) | | Friedman/Schwartz (1982) | | Capie/Mills (1991) | |
Peak	Trough	Peak	Trough	Peak	Trough
1854					
	1855 (1)				
1857					
	1858 (1)				
1860					
	1862 (2)				
1866					
	1868 (2)		1868		
1873		1874		1871	
	1879 (5)		1879 (5)		1879 (8)
1883		1883		1882	
	1886 (3)		1886 (3)		1886 (4)
1890		1890		1889	
	1894 (4)		1893 (3)		1893 (4)
1900		1900		1899	
	1904 (4)		1904 (4)		1904 (5)
1907		1907		1907	
	1908 (1)		1908 (1)		1908 (1)
1913		1913			

Notes: Numbers in brackets are years of recession.

thing that struck us, in comparison with the other countries we shall discuss (and with the United States, which we shall not), is that cycles are relatively long *in the literature* on the United Kingdom. To convey this information, we have compiled a subset in Table 9.7 of the cyclical datings from some of the better-known sources in the literature. While the methodology differs across these efforts, as we shall indicate, a somewhat longer cycle seems pretty well entrenched in this literature, with many downturns of three or more years indicated (in parentheses) in the table.

In the first two columns of the table we list the cycle dates established by Rostow in 1948; this employs the 'reference cycle' approach of the National Bureau of Economic Research (NBER) in the United States. Friedman and Schwartz (1982) also use the NBER methodology in their dating of a somewhat shorter period; these numbers appear in the next two columns of the table. Even so, we find these two datings remarkably similar. Not quite the same is an attempt to establish an alternative reference cycle dating, using time series methods, by Capie and Mills (1991). They find even longer cycles, with a different (earlier) date for the peak in four of the five cycles they identify in the 1871–1913 period.

One thing that strikes us immediately about these particular statistical attempts to characterize the British cycle is that the level of real GNP in a trough of the cycle is frequently higher than it was in the previous peak. Now this can happen because the table identifies 'turning points' rather than years of recession (so that the later year is typically a year of growth), but we think this does not resolve the problem, since there are years of substantial growth *within* most of the recessions identified in Table 9.7. For the recession in the 1870s, for example, real output in 1879 was 8.4 per cent higher than it was in either 1873 or 1874; furthermore (see Table 9.6), the economy grew substantially, at modest unemployment, in 1874, 1875 and 1876. While the 1883–6 downturn seems reasonable (in the reference cycles of Rostow, or Friedman and Schwartz), the Capie and Mills determination, covering 1882–6, is for a period showing some growth (at 4.6 per cent). The depression from 1890 to 1894 also shows substantial growth in real GNP (of 6.7 per cent), as does the alternative dating of 1889–93 (of 2.8 per cent). The problem, again, is that 1891 was a year of rapid growth. Moving the dates to 1889–93 eliminates some of the problem, at least statistically. The identified recession from either 1899 or 1900 to 1904 has to deal with the problem that the only years of declining GNP in this period are 1902 and 1903 (so that, at most, by this simple accounting, the recession went from some time in 1901 to some time in 1904). In sum, while the turning points in the literature seem well established, we believe there are both contractions and expansions within these depressions (at least in the sense that we would use the term today). Below we shall offer our own, admittedly preliminary, alternative dating for the UK recessions in this period.

The major debate in the British literature, at least if one agrees that the dating of the long cycles is accurate, concerns the causes of these events. In most of the other countries we look at, writers on cycles tend to emphasize shocks to the system emanating from the collapse of investment, financial (stock markets and/or banks) or export markets, and there is a strong international flavour to these discussions. There were financial collapses in the United Kingdom (in 1857 and 1866, as discussed in Chapter 4), which are associated with a clear recession (see Table 9.7). Thus a vigorous debate has emerged about what did cause the events we have already described.

One possibility, which we are not in a position to evaluate, we might term the 'trend-tectonics' theory. The view here is that recessions occur at the junctures of long (or very long) waves in economic activity, much as earthquakes occur at the junctures of the earth's plates. While the metaphor is ours, the work on long waves in the British economy is both extensive and challenging (see, for example, Solomou, 1987); it also deals with the problem of finding causes for the events we have been discussing, since trends in such things as population, world agricultural markets, urban construction and the like, with their differently-timed phases, could produce our data. Our particular period of time is too short for such models, but we note that 1873 and somewhere in the mid-1890s are popular trend intersections, and there are more dates in the literature.

We wish to note here, as we shall in later sections, the idea of a Great Depression in Europe between 1873 and 1896. If by 'depression' is meant 'stagnation', then this does occur in some countries, but not in the United Kingdom, although this was once thought to be the case. (See Saul (1985), and Capie, Mills and Wood (1991) for recent discussions.) The problem is, basically, that output figures do not show such a result, as already discussed here. Similarly, the popular idea of a Great Victorian Boom, extending from 1850 to 1873, has run into difficulties, as explained in general terms by Church (1975), and in terms of a new industrial production index by Crafts, Leybourne and Mills (1989). In both cases, the problem is the failure to find a metric that makes this period look very different from either an immediately earlier or an immediately later period (the so-called Great Depression is, in fact, the later period!). We believe these episodes require further study, since all these studies have been working on a narrow base.

Turning to the theories of causation for the period 1850–1913, we find (again, curiously in our opinion), a tendency for writers to advance dominant-causation theories, often on mainly statistical grounds. Fluctuations in investment spending have been on the agenda since Keynes (see Aldcroft and Fearon, 1972), and a glance at Table 9.6 shows instances when there was a substantial decline in investment spending either during, or even before, a recession starts (let us say, as identified by Rostow as shown in Table 9.7 (1948)). We identify such cases in 1856–7, 1866–7, 1873 (and 1877–9), 1884–6 and 1907–8. It did not happen in the other recessions, though, and, in any case, it is nearly impossible, in the absence of detailed historical evidence, to ascertain whether the connection noted between investment and GNP is cause or effect. One reason this is so is that there are often long (and variable!) gestation lags between investment decisions and investment expenditures. Indeed, in recent years, investment is generally considered to be an effective *coincident* indicator of the business cycle, and that is how we will generally treat it in this study.

Another theory frequently put forward concerning this period involves the behaviour of UK exports. A sudden and substantial decline in exports would produce both a cause (exports are up to 20 per cent of GNP) and a way to link the United Kingdom with the widely-accepted international cycle of this period (see Ford, 1981). We have included changes in real exports in Table 9.6, not as an indicator, although that is how the table is labelled, but as a potential causal variable. Again using Rostow's cycles as our benchmark, we see significant declines in exports in 1854 (the year of the peak), in 1861 (the first full year of the downturn), in 1867 (again, one year into the downturn), in 1873–7 (at the peak and in many of the following years of depression), in 1885 (near the end of the downturn), in 1891–3 (again, during the downturn), in 1897–8 (a false signal!), in 1901 (a modest decline) and in 1908 (the year of the trough). On net there are fifteen years (not counting 1884) in which exports decline by one per cent or more, of the fifty-eight possible years. These data track the cycles very well (more as a coincident rather than a leading indicator), but are clearly suggestive of shorter cycles than appear in the literature or are shown in Table 9.7; they also suggest an important international dimension to the UK cycle. This summary, we believe, is reasonably close to Ford's position.

Our last candidate as a primary causal agent is a monetary one. We have already argued that for countries on the gold standard, the money stock is endogenous, but for the United Kingdom at least, since it may well have had the role of being the primary reserve-creating country in this period, this may not be accurate. In addition, there is at least some evidence for the short-run non-neutrality of money for the United Kingdom, as discussed in Chapter 4. Looking at the timing of changes in high-powered money (H) and the reference cycle for the period 1830–1914, Huffman and Lothian (1984) find H leading the cycle in all such episodes except for the 1862–8 cycle. Their Granger-causality tests for this period show significant causation for 1830–70, but only what they call 'weak causation' thereafter. But the primary supporter of the monetary explanation is Eichengreen (1983), who uses a vector autoregression technique to demonstrate that in the 1869–1901 period, fluctuations in the monetary base were the single most important determinant of the business cycle. This finding is somewhat surprising in view of the absence of widespread financial panics in this period, and is not supported, as noted, by the earlier Huffman and Lothian study. In any event, using a different detrending procedure (and vector auto-regression), Capie and Mills (1991) find only a weak (at most) relationship running from money to real output, and Capie (1992) further explores the possible ways money might be involved, to no effect.

At this point, rather than merely reporting what the literature has to say about UK cycles, we thought we would explore a different methodology in order to establish the dimensions of what we think were a series of shorter cycles. What we will do is to use a series of *indicators* (drawn from Table 9.6), based loosely on what we might expect to find in more modern data, in an attempt to establish which years were recession years in the United Kingdom. This approach is not as precise a way of dating cycles as the 'turning point' method, but it is basically all we can do if we stick to annual data. Our approach does, however, have the advantage that it can be used for all the countries in this study, so that we can work on the topic of 'the integration of the European business cycle' for this period. This concept is convenient because there is no reference cycle dating for any of the other countries.

There are some unemployment figures for the 1855–1910 period in the United Kingdom, as produced by Feinstein (1972). In Figure 9.1 we reproduce these numbers, along with the changes in real GNP, that (also) appear in Table 9.6 on page 235. We have marked some potential recession years in Figure 9.1, using a 5 per cent unemployment rate, arbitrarily, as our guide for that series. Whatever the labels, there appears to be a remarkable coincidence of these series, although for some of the unemployment cycles, the real GNP series does not always show a decline. The most noticeable difference, apart from the lack of negative correlation over much of the

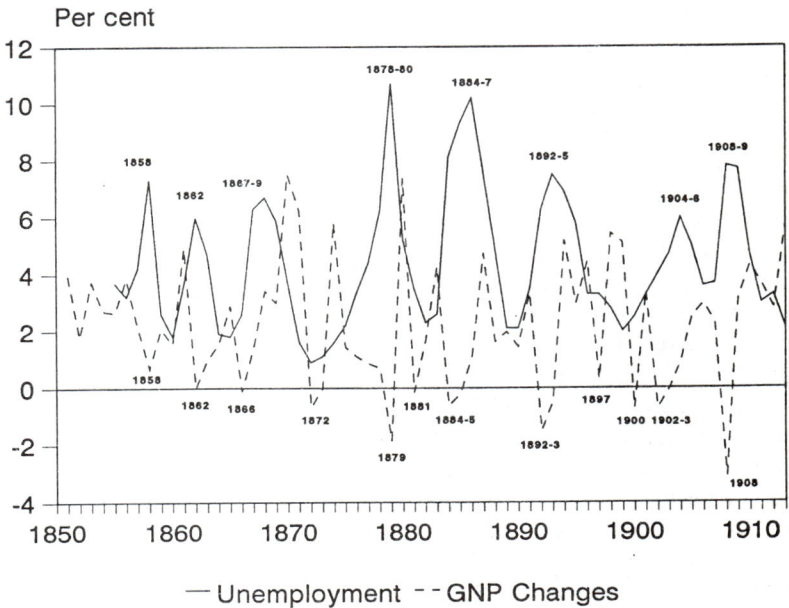

Figure 9.1 United Kingdom unemployment and changes in GNP, 1851–1913

1870s, is that while unemployment often rises above 5 per cent in the same year that GNP growth dips significantly, the unemployment downturns often outlast the GNP downturns. This very modern phenomenon is especially noticeable for those times when GNP growth is in fact negative (1872 and 1900 being exceptions). So, apart from the 1870s, the unemployment datings confirm the GNP datings pretty well on the whole.

We have been analyzing five sets of data for the United Kingdom, four of them coincident indicators of the UK cycle, and one (unemployment) sometimes a coincident and sometimes a lagging indicator. This analysis gives us a fair macroeconomic picture of the annual cycle, although it is far short of what the National Bureau of Economic Research does to date American cycles. What we now propose to do is to put these data together and attempt a cycle dating mainly on these five series. We believe these are likely to be the major items in any compilation that is attempted, so this exercise should produce a reasonable cycle dating, accepting, of course, that the data are sufficiently reliable.[3]

The years we shall designate as downturns are:

1858
1866, 1867
1873, 1878, 1879
1884, 1885, 1886
1892, 1893
1902, 1903
1908

This determination has been made on the basis of the five series other than exports in the table, as well as by a cross reference with the longer cycles listed in Table 9.7.

The year 1858 was selected because of slow growth, a decline in industrial production, and imports and unemployment each over 7 per cent; in this case, unemployment was treated as a coincident indicator, which it sometimes appears to be. As we noted in Chapter 4, there was a financial panic at this time (in October 1857) that began in the United States. There was also a financial panic in May 1866, and in 1866 real GNP declined, and so did investment, rather dramatically. We are designating this a recession year, in rough agreement with the literature on the foregoing numbers and on the behaviour of unemployment (in 1867); this is an example of using unemployment as a lagging indicator. The year 1867 gave us a problem, since GNP grew that year (1.37 per cent), but the lagging unemployment indicator and all the other contemporaneous indicators clearly signalled a recession. Again, this conclusion is in agreement with the literature. These

European Trade Cycle, 1850–1913

two events, though, mark the end of the 'financial panic–recession' syndrome that occurs much more frequently in the explanations of cycles in other countries at this time.

In 1872 and 1873 there were signs of recession in the GNP figures, especially with zero growth in 1873. Only investment, of the other indicators, showed recession, although industrial production also grew rather slowly that year. In any case, difficulties were reported in most of the other countries in our study, including the United States, which suffered a financial panic along with the collapse of its railway boom at this time. Indeed, indicating the international dimensions of this event, the real export figures decline at this time (in 1873). The year 1874, however, is too good to indicate as one of recession, and we believe the same can be said for 1875 and 1876. Possibly the next downturn started in 1877, but the evidence for designating that year a recession year from the coincident indicators was not convincing. The year 1878, at least, had significant unemployment and a drop in all the other indicators (except GNP). There was a financial panic in the countryside in 1878, and a much publicized failure of the City of Glasgow Bank that same year, but there was no general panic (and none in London). The year 1879, however, was also a clear case. Unemployment continued to be high after this event, as it frequently does in this period, fulfilling its role as a lagging indicator.

At least some of the reference cycle literature finds a turning point for the next recession in 1883, and we think this is a likely date. We have designated 1884, 1885 and 1886 as recession years, and, from the data, this appears to be the most serious and longest-lived event in this period. While GNP growth was stagnant at this time, taking the three years as a whole, we note that unemployment was high for four years (again showing a lagging pattern in 1889). The other indicators also offered considerable support for this choice. This recession was arguably the worst of the period, but it has no strongly certified causes other than the collapse of an investment boom.

In 1892 and 1893 there are very strong signs of recession from all the indicators (except investment in 1892). The year 1894 is such a strong year in all but the lagging indicator that it is clearly not a year of recession, although part of it could have been, which is how one might interpret the designation in the reference cycle literature. There were financial panics in other countries at this time (including the United States), and most countries had recessions at this time; signs of this occur in the export figures for the United Kingdom, which are very bad for the three-year period from 1891–3. This downturn is the clearest example of an export-led recession in the period, especially in view of the failure of other indicators to provide any assistance in explaining the event.

The years 1902 and 1903 were more weak growth years than clear cases of recession; here we have used the fall in GNP and the lagging indicator, as well as the weak performance of the coincident indicators for our designation. The year 1904 could also have been included, but we feel GNP growth is just too rapid for a recession. Clearly, the lower turning point of the 1902/03 downturn is at some time in 1904, while the previous upper turning point may well have been in 1901, as at least some of the literature suggests. International events are again suggested for this episode, although the end of the Boer War (in 1902) is sometimes mentioned. Exports declined in 1901, but it is a modest decline; more convincing, for the international explanation, is simply the fact that many other countries had recessions at this point. Finally, 1908 is a clear case in all respects, with unemployment performing clearly as a lagging indicator.

The upshot of all this is that the shocks appear to come from three sources: international, where the contact is both through the financial markets and the commodities markets; domestic financial disruptions (at least early on); and special cases (for example, war or its abrupt end). All this suggests that a single-theory methodology (for example, a Granger-causality test of exports) would not work particularly well in the British case, at least not over the entire period.

France

For the French economy there exists a real gross domestic product series that was compiled by Toutain (1987). We show a graph of the growth rates of these data in Figure 9.2; Germany is included there also, partly to establish certain comparisons. The French figures are remarkable, to put it mildly, with the series being very choppy, showing extreme fluctuations in the period up to the mid-1880s, at which point the cycles in real GDP become generally milder and somewhat less frequent. The German figures, which appear well co-ordinated with the French, also show milder cycles at the end of the period. The finding that the severity of the cycle moderated considerably in the 1850–1913 period for these two countries (but not for the United Kingdom) fits well into our general theme that this is the critical period during which these countries came to look alike (and have comparable cyclical experiences). They do so because the UK cycle, as we have seen, was much milder than either French or the German cycles before 1880.

On the basis of changes in real GDP alone, as indicated in the first column of Table 9.8, there were substantial declines in the French output in 1853, 1859, 1867, 1870–1, 1873, 1876, 1879 and 1910; these cannot be ignored. In addition, there were declines of one per cent or more in GDP in 1851, 1855,

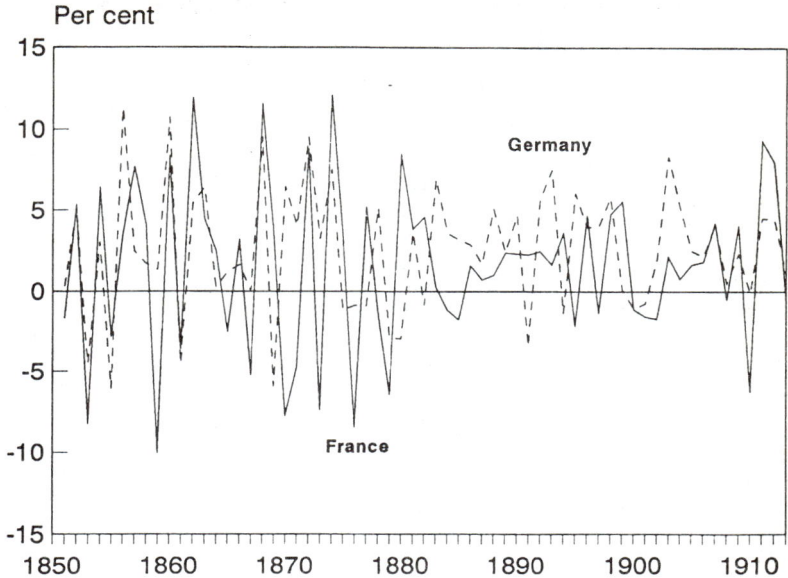

Figure 9.2 Changes in real product in France and Germany, 1851–1913

1861, 1865, 1878, 1884–5, 1895, 1897 and 1900–2. Two other years showed even smaller declines. For the sixty-three years in the table, there were twenty-three years of decline.

There is a literature on the Great Depression in France for this period. Price (1981, p. 225) takes this view, as represented in the following: 'Along with other industrialising countries, France experienced a long period of economic depression and crisis. The period c.1880 – c.1914 is characterised by this'. The view probably accounts for the absence of any detailed cyclical discussion in this particular work. Note that this is not the same timing as in other countries (it is usually 1873–96). Also note that in 1913, real GDP was 75 per cent higher than it was in 1880. Cameron (1961) also refers to a 'Great Depression' in France, but his runs from the peak in 1882 to the recovery in 1897–8. He allows that there was a temporary recovery in 1887–9, but that financial disruption, industrial stagnation and stagnant international trade were the principal agents of this depression. Even so, we note that GDP in the recession year of 1897 was 18 per cent above GDP in 1882 (and 21.5 per cent above 1885, a recession year in our tabulation below). Again, we would argue that these long periods are punctuated by shorter cycles.

Table 9.8 Business cycle indicators for France – growth rates

	GDP	Industrial Production	Imports	Investment
1851	−1.67	−1.23	−2.44	9.07
1852	5.34	9.04	17.82	31.95
1853	−8.25	7.60	3.47	33.70
1854	6.42	−0.35	1.45	10.78
1855	−2.80	7.08	17.03	13.26
1856	3.49	1.62	20.90	8.16
1857	7.70	−2.93	−2.80	−0.91
1858	4.15	−2.00	−8.36	−14.02
1859	−10.04	−2.73	4.87	−11.78
1860	8.40	9.88	9.51	3.47
1861	−3.58	10.13	26.65	5.94
1862	11.90	−3.17	−10.48	0.49
1863	4.46	8.94	9.12	5.12
1864	2.51	4.70	5.53	4.79
1865	−2.51	−0.51	11.01	−0.30
1866	3.22	11.84	4.09	7.67
1867	−5.24	1.58	10.27	−1.39
1868	11.55	8.38	8.00	6.89
1869	3.57	1.64	−3.15	−13.25
1870	−7.79	−17.22	−11.79	−40.10
1871	−4.77	−6.98	18.16	−28.99
1872	8.82	16.41	−4.17	57.48
1873	−7.39	−1.10	−0.42	6.48
1874	12.07	2.19	7.37	−10.94
1875	3.26	6.30	3.12	−6.32
1876	−8.45	0.81	11.25	6.06
1877	5.19	4.35	−8.83	12.60
1878	−1.27	−0.58	21.41	−8.64
1879	−6.44	0.58	12.09	11.54
1880	8.50	9.23	6.57	27.33
1881	3.84	6.65	−0.90	17.77
1882	4.57	4.83	1.75	−1.35
1883	0.29	−0.79	3.20	−10.64
1884	−1.16	−3.38	−1.55	−10.52
1885	−1.76	−3.84	−4.05	−19.40
1886	1.61	5.63	7.02	−19.57
1887	0.72	0.32	−1.21	9.46
1888	1.01	2.06	−2.26	1.92
1889	2.40	4.61	0.90	−0.79
1890	2.35	0.75	2.74	14.03

Table 9.8 (continued)

	GDP	Industrial Production	Imports	Investment
1891	2.29	6.63	9.22	1.92
1892	2.50	2.07	−9.86	−5.52
1893	1.68	−0.55	−7.25	−5.23
1894	3.64	3.38	7.63	−5.36
1895	−2.12	−1.74	−1.11	6.34
1896	4.67	6.41	5.69	4.32
1897	−1.33	4.94	2.84	4.28
1898	4.76	1.79	8.71	12.70
1899	5.53	5.76	−6.80	18.01
1900	−1.10	−8.40	−2.34	11.14
1901	−1.57	1.44	−3.14	−15.05
1902	−1.71	−0.84	1.63	−16.23
1903	2.16	3.80	6.77	2.56
1904	0.78	−2.95	−4.35	−8.68
1905	1.66	3.07	1.80	2.98
1906	1.85	5.21	10.39	3.51
1907	4.22	2.51	5.37	24.62
1908	−0.51	−1.30	−2.21	3.87
1909	4.06	7.25	10.20	−4.84
1910	−6.26	−2.88	7.15	22.00
1911	9.31	10.87	7.19	1.93
1912	7.98	10.90	−2.30	14.88
1913	−0.63	−0.42	3.99	10.57

The data in Table 9.8 indicate, that French cycles are dominated by the volatile agricultural sector, which, in fact, was larger than the industrial sector until the twentieth century. To see this, consider Table 9.9. We can think of these entries as being subindices of real GDP; the asterisks in the table indicate the cases in which the marked subindex contributed to the decline in the overall index (GDP), in the sense of declining further than the average. Note that there are other sectors in the economy (for example, services) that often act to smooth the cycle. In the main, it is agriculture that earns the asterisks, with all but the 1870–1 downturn made worse by the decline in agricultural production. Generally, in turn, the industrial sector tends to smooth the cycle, at least until the 1880–1913 period. The 1870–1 decline is exceptional, so a pretty convincing case for the general dominance of agriculture in French cycles can certainly be made. But we must also

Table 9.9 The role of agriculture and industrial production in the major declines in French real GDP

Date	Overall	Agricultural Production	Ind. Prod.
1853	−8.2	−17.6*	+7.6
1859	−10.0	−14.4*	−2.7
1861	−3.6	−12.1*	+10.1
1867	−5.2	−12.4*	+1.6
1870–1	−11.8	−10.4	−21.5*
1873	−7.4	−13.1*	−1.1
1876	−8.4	−17.1*	+.8
1878–9	−7.4	−17.6*	0.0
1884–5	−1.2	−3.8*	−7.0*
1900–2	−4.3	−10.0*	−7.5*
1910	−6.3	−15.5*	−2.9

emphasize (see Price, 1981) that the influence of the agricultural cycle diminishes over the period as, indeed, the relative importance of agriculture in the economy declines.

The literature on French cycles makes much of the financial crises that sometimes accompanied these events, and these have a partly international flavour. Looking at the basic figures, we note that the contractions of the 1850s and 1860s all show very sharp agricultural declines, and two of these years (1853 and 1861) in fact exhibit perversely strong gains in the industrial sector. Henderson (1961) locates a recession in 1863–4, perhaps related to difficulties brought on by the American Civil War; below, we shall argue that 1865 is a better choice for this event, at least in the annual data. The decline in 1867 was coincident with the collapse of the Crédit Mobilier, and Henderson refers to this as a commercial crisis that severely affected railway construction, but there was also a harvest failure at this time. According to Price (1981), this is the last of the general agriculturally-induced downturns in this period.

International events are more important – and agricultural events less so – as we consider the last forty years of the data. The military disaster in 1870 produced considerable financial pressure (including a sizeable indemnity), and thus the industrial collapse of 1870–1 hardly needs further explanation. The international financial crisis of 1873 does not seem to have been as important in France as the agricultural decline of that year (of 13.1 per cent); nevertheless, this was a year of recession in France. The sharp downturns in 1876 and 1878–9 seem primarily to have been agricultural, although Levy-Leboyer and Bourguignon (1990) note that the investment market 'toppled' in 1876, suggesting that they believe a financial event might have precipitated the first of these events. Henderson (1961) notes that there were railway failures in 1878 as well as a failure of the grain harvest (and an outbreak of the dreaded phylloxera!). From 1878, there was apparently a financial and speculative boom – as well as a rather steady industrial expansion. Another financial collapse began with bank failure in January 1882; this distress is associated with a recession in 1883–5 that probably began in 1882. The expansion itself might have got out of hand (in the traditional over-investment sense); evidence for this exists in the rise of investment as a percentage of nominal GDP to 9.1 per cent in 1882, and then an abrupt decline to 6.3 per cent thereafter.[4] In fact, these events occurred alongside an international financial crisis that 'lastingly weakened the Banque de France and brought about the collapse of the main banks in the Lyons market in January 1882' (Levy-Leboyer and Bourguignon, 1990, p. 83, and Henderson, 1961). As if this were not enough to think about, Caron (1979) and Marczewski (1988) argue that sharpened international competition in the agricultural markets (especially floods of American and Russian wheat) also undermined the French agricultural sector. That is, 1884 provides a peak in agricultural output so that the decline of agricultural production in 1885 helped to prolong that particular recession.

The international financial crises of the 1890s seem to have bypassed France, and French downturns in the period (in 1893 and 1895) were relatively mild ones. An industrial decline in 1900 did contribute to a general decline (the agricultural contribution here was also considerable), but we note that quite a few other economies were recessed at this time. Recessions in 1904 and 1908 are also echoed around the world, but 1910 is specific to the French economy: this was a full-blown agricultural event, however, the last of its kind in modern French history.

We have four indicators of French cycles available, but lack unemployment data. Unfortunately, also, the French data on investment growth are nominal, which makes them considerably less useful, depending on what is happening to the prices of investment goods; Table 9.8 contains these data. What we have done, bearing in mind that the agricultural contribution is already embedded in the real GNP figures, is to use industrial production, real imports and real investment as indicators of the cycle. The years with substantial declines in GDP cannot be ignored, of course, and many of the years with declines in at least three of the four indicators, similarly, would seem to be clear cases. The latter are 1851, 1865, 1878, 1893, 1895, 1901, 1902, 1904 and 1908. In 1893 and 1904, in this set, real

GDP in fact increased, so this is far from a certain designation. Finally, 1855, 1861 and 1897 remain undecided in our view, although we are inclined to treat the first two, at least, as years of recession, on the basis of the GDP figures alone. These considerations yield the following set of years for recessions in France, combining our statistical work with our earlier review of the literature:

1851, 1853, 1855, 1859
1861, 1865, 1867
1870, 1871, 1873, 1876, 1878, 1879
1883, 1884, 1885, 1886
1893, 1895, (1897?)
1900, 1901, 1902, 1904, 1908, 1910

This approach yields twenty-three (or twenty-four) recession years in total.

It is worth noting that the years 1873, 1878–9, 1883–6, 1893, 1901–2 and 1908 also occur in the United Kingdom, even though we have given a rather different historical explanation of what went on in France. We conclude that while the detailed evidence suggests that the French shared in world cycles for many of these events – and the industrial sector exhibits an increasing influence – the agricultural cycle was still a major part of the French cyclical experience, even at the end of the period. War was also important in the French case, and mention is often made of the influence of foreign competition, especially in the 1880s. Domestic financial crises are not frequent, however, with the experience in the early 1880s being the only good example of the traditional cycle. As we shall see later in this section, the French are a lot like the Italians in having their cycles so related to agricultural events.

Germany

German business cycle data are also a little on the sparse side, so the following discussion relies rather heavily on the real net national product data of Hoffmann (1965). We have already plotted German growth rates in this period, taken from the Hoffmann data, in Figure 9.2. Here, as in the French case, the cycles appear to be slightly less numerous, and they show smaller amplitude in the second half of the period. Looking at the first column of Table 9.10, then, we see that the dates of a significant decline in real NNP are in 1853, 1855, 1861, 1869, 1879–80, 1882, 1891, 1894 and 1900–1. These provide our primary suspects for the German case.

Before considering the German numbers further, though, we shall review some of the German literature. We begin with the detailed survey of the

Table 9.10 Business cycle indicators for Germany, growth rates of the data, 1851–1913

	GNP	Industrial Production	Imports	Investment
1851	0.32	3.11	–	5.56
1852	5.10	2.02	–	56.35
1853	−4.51	−1.01	–	−77.32
1854	3.06	−2.04	–	42.74
1855	−6.06	3.05	–	−91.09
1856	11.33	9.53	–	117.66
1857	2.50	8.70	–	−56.80
1858	1.74	0.00	–	9.80
1859	1.36	0.00	–	15.98
1860	10.74	8.00	–	55.31
1861	−4.52	0.00	–	−54.18
1862	5.45	0.00	–	62.94
1863	6.40	14.31	–	16.52
1864	0.26	0.00	–	−18.94
1865	1.22	6.45	–	−12.39
1866	1.66	6.06	–	1.38
1867	0.01	0.00	–	−31.08
1868	9.54	5.72	–	75.21
1869	−5.95	5.41	–	−68.88
1870	6.46	0.00	–	49.49
1871	4.04	10.01	–	−20.72
1872	9.52	13.35	–	47.33
1873	3.26	8.00	–	−14.06
1874	7.54	3.77	–	40.55
1875	−1.16	0.00	–	−21.30
1876	−0.86	3.64	–	6.77
1877	−0.89	−3.64	–	−20.51
1878	5.17	3.64	–	3.08
1879	−2.84	−3.64	–	−23.84
1880	−2.95	−3.77	–	2.17
1881	3.67	3.77	7.45	14.95
1882	−0.84	0.00	9.34	−2.34
1883	6.92	7.14	5.10	15.35
1884	3.60	3.39	3.00	10.41
1885	3.21	3.28	−6.25	0.37
1886	2.90	0.00	2.39	3.23
1887	1.71	6.25	6.48	6.83
1888	5.09	5.88	1.82	−2.34
1889	2.44	10.82	12.12	19.57
1890	4.71	2.53	−1.75	11.78

Table 9.10 (continued)

	GNP	Industrial Production	Imports	Investment
1891	−3.42	2.47	0.32	−33.40
1892	5.68	2.41	3.78	31.66
1893	7.52	2.35	2.62	2.48
1894	−1.35	4.55	4.83	−9.51
1895	6.05	8.52	5.77	7.78
1896	3.97	2.02	4.46	19.22
1897	4.00	5.83	2.92	9.79
1898	5.80	5.51	4.23	21.57
1899	0.13	3.51	2.41	−10.12
1900	−1.07	5.04	−2.65	−12.01
1901	−0.74	−3.33	1.88	−17.60
1902	1.97	1.68	6.24	−9.62
1903	8.35	8.00	5.17	37.21
1904	5.17	4.51	5.68	11.83
1905	2.53	2.90	6.75	1.20
1906	2.17	4.20	5.04	4.80
1907	4.16	7.90	3.35	9.48
1908	0.49	−1.27	−5.72	−25.13
1909	2.35	3.77	9.48	10.70
1910	0.12	5.99	2.50	−1.35
1911	4.51	5.65	7.06	16.94
1912	4.46	6.38	1.58	9.26
1913	1.01	3.05	2.70	−5.01

German economy in this period by Kitchen (1978). Kitchen identifies the period 1857–61 as a depression and emphasizes that it was international in scope, having begun (possibly) in the American agricultural sector, where a production boom in 1857 produced falling prices world-wide. He argues that domestic (German) over-investment in the boom from 1850 to 1857 produced an overheated (p. 96), undercapitalized economy that was vulnerable to shocks. Henderson (1975, p. 117) makes a more modest claim, arguing:

> Germany's industrial expansion was briefly halted in 1857 by an economic depression that began in the United States and had world-wide repercussions ... Some German manufacturers and bankers received a salutary lesson in the folly of over-expansion.

The cause, he says, was a bumper wheat crop. In Germany, then, it was the export–import firms and their banks that were hardest hit. But Kitchen's claim for a four-year recession seems wrong, on the evidence, because the only year in which real net national product declined in the 'depression' was in 1861; indeed, real net national product was 9.8 per cent *higher* in 1861 than it was in 1857. But it is certainly true that real investment fell sharply in 1857, more than recovered by 1860, and then fell sharply again in 1861. We suspect this is really two events, with the more serious recession occurring in 1861.

Kitchen notes that there was a financial panic in 1866, partly caused by unease concerning the war between Prussia and Austria. There was, in fact, a stock market crash in that year, and there were falling prices in some sectors, but in 1866 and 1867, real NNP rose. Indeed, a failure of the harvest was the principal reason for the very slow growth of the German economy at this time, although the war (and what Henderson (1975) describes as a civil war in June 1867) certainly took a toll. Henderson does not mention a recession here, however.

Between 1870 and 1873, Kitchen argues, another investment boom occurred, with an accompanying expansion of the banking sector (Borchardt (1976), says roughly the same thing). The crash in 1873, to Kitchen, ushers in the Great Depression, the first signs of which were price declines and the collapse of the stock market in Vienna in May 1873. Henderson argues that the collapse was of a 'speculative mania' that was partly based on the easy finance resulting from large French indemnity payments. He calls it (Henderson, 1975, p. 164) 'a wild orgy of speculation'. By the end of 1874, the iron trade was in trouble, and the difficulties for the German economy continued even through 1880, says Kitchen, who goes on to note (1978, p. 150):

> Yet in spite of an over-all improvement in the economy it was clear that Germany was still in the midst of a depression, and although there was a general expression of relief the business world knew that it was far too soon to speak of a recovery.

Here it is worth noting, again referring to Table 9.10, that NNP in that year was 4.1 per cent higher than it was in 1873 (the peak). But it is certainly likely that 1875, 1877, 1879 and 1880 were years of recession (in terms of declines in real NNP). We could possibly agree on the proposition that the period from 1873 to 1880 was one of stagnation for Germany, as it was for quite a few countries world-wide in this period. But contrary to Kitchen's (1978) implication, and Borchardt's (1976) explicit claim to the contrary, the stagnation was over after 1880, with only mild downturns in 1891 and 1894.[5]

Finally, Kitchen describes a recession that ran from 1901 to 1903/4. He appears to attribute this event to financial market difficulties. We note, yet again, that the real NNP of Germany (as measured by Hoffmann, of course) was 11 per cent higher in 1903 than it was in 1901. Indeed, based solely on real NNP, the period 1898–1902 was more a period of stagnation, although we shall argue below that 1900 and 1901 were the true recession years in this period.

There are some employment and unemployment figures available for Germany in this period. These are probably most accurate for the short span between 1900 and 1913, but there is some information in a slightly longer set going back to 1880. Table 9.11 lists the growth rates of real NNP taken from Table 9.10 and two new series, one on total employment obtained from Hoffmann (1965), and one on unemployment from Pierenkemper (1987).[6] The other data given in Table 9.10 add only a little to the dating established by the GNP figures themselves. Part of the reason is the state of the data. In particular, the production figures are heavily rounded, the real import series only begins in 1881, and, finally, the real investment figures seem to be unusually volatile.

It is easy to see recessions in 1853 and 1855 solely on the basis of the NNP growth rates. In 1853, both industrial production and investment, our coincident indicators, declined sharply; in 1855, though, industrial production in fact increased; the culprit in that recession, as far as our data take us, was an agricultural collapse (agricultural income and employment both fell sharply that year) – and they also fell in 1853, for that matter.[7] We believe that the literature has established the existence of a recession in 1857, as well, although it may have lasted less than a year. The next significant decline in GNP was in 1861; during that year investment also fell sharply, while industrial production remained level; agriculture was also important in this event, with agricultural income falling 6.74 per cent (agricultural employment in that year was slightly up, though). GNP growth was slow in 1864 and industrial production was stagnant (and industrial employment fell slightly); agriculture expanded in 1864, however. The conclusion we draw about these early cycles is that they appear to be dominated by events in the agricultural sector, whether because of domestic scarcity or foreign abundance.

In the 1870s, most countries experienced slow growth, especially after 1873, and some accounts for some countries show an extremely long contraction running from 1873/4 to 1878/9. This is also discernible in the German NNP data, with 1875, 1876, 1877 and 1879 all showing declines. None of this shows up in the employment figures, however, and the first three years show an average yearly decline of NNP of only around 1 per cent. This

Table 9.11 NNP, unemployment and employment cycles in Germany, 1880–1913

Date	NNP growth	Employment growth	Unemployment
1880	−2.95	0.43*	
1881	3.66	0.54*	
1882	−0.83	1.07	
1883	6.92	1.14	
1884	3.60	1.19	
1885	3.21	0.71*	
1886	2.90	1.91	
1887	1.71	1.38	0.60
1888	5.09	1.59	4.15*
1889	2.44	2.22	0.60
1890	4.71	1.27	2.40
1891	−3.42	0.50*	4.20*
1892	5.68	0.46*	6.15*
1893	7.52	0.66*	3.15*
1894	−1.35	1.44	3.30*
1895	6.05	1.44	3.15*
1896	3.97	2.06	0.80
1897	4.00	1.66	1.35
1898	5.80	1.75	0.70
1899	0.13	1.46	1.35
1900	−1.07	1.84	2.25
1901	−0.74	0.27*	6.95*
1902	1.97	0.98*	3.05*
1903	8.35	1.84	2.70
1904	5.17	1.82	2.10
1905	2.53	1.43	1.60
1906	2.17	1.87	1.20
1907	4.16	1.54	1.60
1908	0.49	0.65*	2.90
1909	2.35	1.44	2.80
1910	−0.11	2.26	1.90
1911	4.51	2.07	1.90
1912	4.46	1.70	2.00
1913	1.01	1.36	2.90

Note: *Employment growth under 1 per cent, unemployment 3.00 and over.

seems more like stagnation. Industrial production shows somewhat the same pattern, with significant declines in 1877 and 1879. In fact, both series declined sharply in 1879 and 1880. Agricultural incomes fell in 1876, and again fell sharply in 1879; generally, however, agricultural employment also rose in this period. The investment figures provided in Table 9.10 show sharp declines in 1873, 1875, 1877 and 1879. The year 1879 clearly was a difficult one by any standard. Note, again, that one can see a dampening of the amplitude of German cycles in this period.

There appears to have been a mild downturn in NNP in Germany in 1882; this downturn is echoed in the production and investment figures in Table 9.10 as well. We can now consult Table 9.11 for employment factors to corroborate the event, but with a growth of employment of 1.07 per cent during that year, we are clearly looking at what is at most a mild downturn; agricultural income and employment were up for that year as well. In 1885 there was a sharp drop in imports, but all the other figures were up strongly that year, and the next downturn was not until 1891. For 1888, Table 9.11 reports unemployment of 4.15 per cent, but all the other numbers show strong growth (including agricultural income) that year. In 1891, when NNP fell by 3.41 per cent, we see a rise in industrial production, but a sharp decline in investment and, as shown in Table 9.11, slow growth in employment and a rise in unemployment to 4.20 per cent. The proximate cause here is once again agricultural, although the investment swing is also important; in this year, agricultural incomes fell by 6.01 per cent. Notice that NNP growth and industrial production growth were quite strong for the following two years, but unemployment continued high; in fact, it was not until 1896 that it dropped below 3 per cent. This pattern has a very modern sound to it, since we have often observed such behaviour in the late twentieth century (and we saw this also in the UK data already discussed). The year 1894 also shows a recession rather clearly, using unemployment, investment and NNP data as the basis for this judgement; agricultural incomes also fell that year (by 1.35 per cent).

NNP declined in 1900 and 1901, while unemployment exceeded 3 per cent in 1901 and 1902; if unemployment is playing the role of a lagging indicator, then this suggests that 1900 and 1901 are recession years. In 1900, industrial production was up sharply, while investment and imports were down; since agricultural incomes were also up, it is not obvious which sector led the way in this particular event. It is, however, a sharp enough decline to be recorded as a recession. The year 1901 shows a general decline, as indicated in Tables 9.10 and 9.11; agricultural figures (for employment and income) also fell sharply that year. There was a slight decline in 1910, probably emanating from the agricultural sector, but it is too small to record as a downturn; the year 1908, when NNP in fact rose a little, seems a better bet for a short recession, since unemployment was up significantly over the previous year, and employment growth was slow. The year 1908 also showed declines in all the other figures that appear in Table 9.10. We are listing it, somewhat tentatively as a recession year in spite of the slight growth in GNP.

On the basis of these considerations, and with the help of the literature discussed above, it seems likely that the recessions in the German economy occurred in the following years:

1853, 1855, 1857
1861, 1867, 1869
1873, 1875, 1876, 1877, 1879
1880, 1882
1891, 1894
1900, 1901, 1908

This review yields eighteen years of decline out of the sixty-three possible, which is fewer recessions than shown in the French case. Note that we list 1908 as a year of recession, on the basis of what happened to the indicators other than real NNP, and we list 1867 and 1873 on the basis of our review of the literature. Finally, we note that agriculture is in fact more dominant in the German case than might have been expected, in view of the strength of industrial growth in Germany throughout the period. That is, the downturns in 1855, 1861, 1869 and 1891 were all fairly severe, and in all but one of these, industrial activity in fact expanded rapidly, as revealed by the percentage changes in the industrial production index, while agricultural production invariably declined in these recession years.

Italy

To begin, as with the other countries, we shall look at the cycles in the Italian GNP data of this period. There are, indeed, numerous downturns in these data, with 17 of the 52 possible years showing recessions in GNP – meaning that the typical pattern was roughly for one lean year to be followed by two years of growth. This pattern appears in the first column of Table 9.12. While the more severe downturns were scattered over the entire period, as the top line in Figure 9.3 suggests, there is a slight tendency for the Italian business cycles in fact to get worse over the period. This is a pattern unlike that in the two other European countries we have looked at or, for that matter, for the Swedish real domestic product data that we have included in Figure 9.3.

An early and influential discussion of Italian downturns is by Clough (1964). He identifies an agricultural crisis in 1853–4 and what he calls 'deep

Table 9.12 Business cycle indicators for Italy, growth rates of the data, 1851–1913

	GNP	Industrial Production	Imports	Investment
1862	2.52	0.00	7.86	28.35
1863	−1.86	0.00	12.83	−16.99
1864	4.28	0.00	8.70	35.16
1865	3.12	−2.74	−0.37	12.71
1866	2.03	2.74	−14.96	−7.40
1867	−8.45	5.26	1.21	−27.16
1868	2.12	0.00	−4.76	28.40
1869	3.17	2.53	11.38	8.14
1870	−0.58	4.88	−3.55	−26.10
1871	0.38	0.00	4.06	−1.79
1872	−0.58	2.35	12.52	−1.89
1873	4.67	4.55	0.57	37.90
1874	−0.82	2.20	2.92	−33.64
1875	2.45	2.15	5.01	8.02
1876	−0.89	0.00	11.10	−37.08
1877	1.28	2.10	−26.08	22.14
1878	0.06	0.00	−4.02	2.55
1879	0.71	0.00	22.75	24.68
1880	3.34	9.91	−5.85	31.61
1881	−5.66	7.28	11.06	−84.32
1882	5.15	6.78	−3.66	88.33
1883	−0.93	6.35	11.37	−19.69
1884	1.82	3.03	6.70	9.95
1885	2.54	7.20	4.93	−14.39
1886	2.91	5.41	−0.70	44.86
1887	1.09	14.66	16.58	−7.19
1888	−3.39	0.00	−32.86	−10.94
1889	−3.57	−2.30	11.23	−49.10
1890	6.68	−4.76	−7.86	31.33
1891	0.91	−11.62	−12.97	7.48
1892	−4.84	−5.64	9.08	−46.07
1893	3.14	4.26	7.98	43.18
1894	−0.79	5.41	−5.45	−32.88
1895	1.82	2.60	2.99	7.49
1896	1.73	1.27	−1.32	2.90
1897	−3.93	3.73	2.99	−56.58
1898	7.33	7.06	14.29	86.38
1899	1.27	9.74	3.92	−17.29
1900	5.05	3.06	7.51	38.78

Table 9.12 (continued)

	GNP	Industrial Production	Imports	Investment
1901	6.36	0.99	1.53	24.00
1902	−2.13	2.93	3.68	−32.86
1903	4.54	8.30	5.96	22.94
1904	−0.34	5.17	8.09	−11.51
1905	4.44	11.12	2.89	7.57
1906	1.72	13.35	18.41	7.46
1907	9.34	12.36	6.11	48.07
1908	−2.11	13.06	3.81	−23.43
1909	6.73	3.51	5.81	28.45
1910	−7.37	3.86	4.10	−34.08
1911	7.54	3.26	−3.43	26.45
1912	2.29	1.82	1.45	−1.40
1913	2.19	−0.90	1.04	9.51

depressions' in 1865–6, 1874–9, 1888–93 and 1906–8.[8] The 1865–6 event he regards as having originated in America. He mentions the recovery of the cotton industry and the fall of American demand because of demobilization from the Civil War; this scenario, he says, coincided with a peak in railway construction in Italy and with a widespread over-extension of credit there. In fact, there was a banking panic in 1866, and we can see the outlines of a recession in the data for 1867 (preceded by a sharp decline of imports in 1866). Thus it is likely that the event began in 1866 and that 1867 is the year of recession; it is also likely that the causes mentioned by Clough were an important part of the story. Clough refers, next, to a 'Western Civilization-wide economic crisis which began in 1873' that hit Italy in 1874. This event, too, was international in scope (originating, possibly, in US railways), although Toniolo (1990) suggests that it started with a financial crisis in Berlin. While Clough has the depression lasting the entire period, we feel that the time is really one of stagnation (since real GNP declined in only two of the five years). Indeed, real GNP in 1879, in the trough, was 1 per cent higher than in 1874, the peak!

Clough refers to another deep depression (or crisis) from 1888 to 1893 that he believes originated in the tariff war with France that ran from 1888 to 1898. Cafagna (1976, p. 294) says 'The years between 1889 and 1896 were the darkest years of the great depression in the international sphere and bore

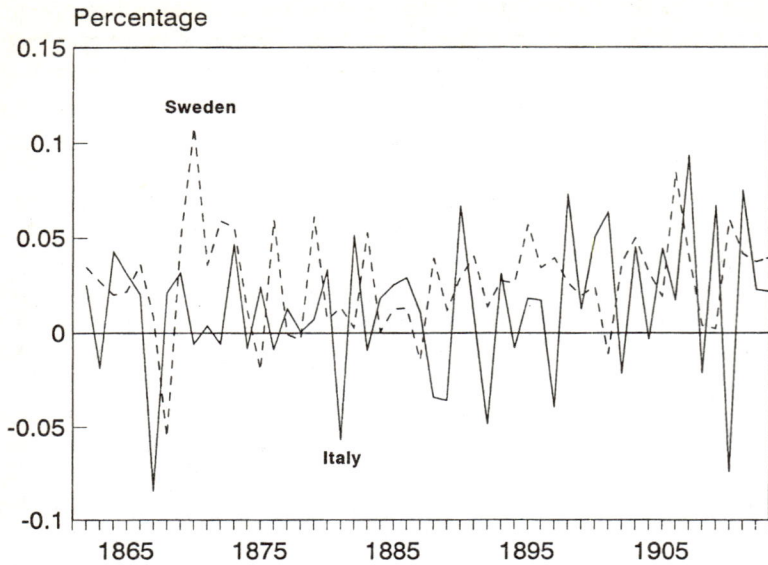

Figure 9.3   Italian and Swedish national product, 1861–1913, growth rates

especially heavily on the Italian economy.' He also discusses the banking crisis, which, he says, began in 1889. Indeed, the loss of both exports and imports (look at the disastrous import figures for 1888 in Table 9.12) appear to have undermined the Italian banking structure and may have produced, as a result, the 1893–4 crisis in banking that resulted in a major overhaul of the banking system (see Chapters 4 and 5). Again, Clough mentions the overextension of credit and investment in non-profitable enterprises by the banks, and there was (Zamagni, 1993) a withdrawal of foreign capital that led to a drain of gold reserves. In fact, the numbers in Table 9.12 support the idea of recessions in 1888–9, 1892 and 1894, and growth was quite modest in 1891. But we again must caution that real GNP in 1894 (the trough) was larger than in 1887 (the peak). Luzzato (1963), as described by Toniolo (1990), refers to the period 1884–94 as the 'blackest' for the new Italian Kingdom, but Toniolo's discussion of the numbers follows ours, essentially: he says (p. 87), 'if we accept the existing estimates, it is likely that the "blackest years" were not seen as such by the great mass of Italians'. Toniolo also notes, correctly we feel, that the entire period from 1861 to 1896 shows no appreciable growth in per capita GDP in Italy. Thus one might refer to this period as the Great Stagnation, to coin a phrase. The stagnation, then, appears to have lasted longer in Italy than in the other countries we have examined. Quite possibly this is because the Italian economy was more agricultural than the others discussed for this particular period; in general, these were not good years for European agriculture.

Clough finally identifies 1907 and 1908 as a depression, although he does not indicate what the causes might be. Toniolo (1990), though, mentions an investment boom that had a temporary interruption in those years; cotton, machine tools and machinery stand out in his summary. He also mentions a stock market collapse in 1906 and a general financial crisis in 1907. Clough, in turn, regards the declines in real national income in 1897, 1902, 1908 and 1910 as being slight. These are also years we shall indicate as being recessed below (with real GNP declining by more than 2 per cent in each case). It seems, then, that Clough is emphasizing downturns that were international in scope, as well as ones that featured a domestic financial aspect. This approach somewhat exaggerates Italy's place in the international cycle, in our opinion; we also think that it overly emphasizes the influence of financial problems. But we do not disagree in substance with Clough's determination of the dates of Italian cycles, putting aside his belief in longer cycles than we observe.

We have remarked in previous subsections on theories of long waves and of a Great Depression in the last quarter of the nineteenth century, and now it is time to do the same for Italy. Gerschenkron (1962), basing his work mainly on industrial figures, feels that long cycles dominated short ones in this period. For the period 1881–1913, he identifies only one cycle, with 1881–8 and 1896–1913 being periods of growth, and the downturn being 1888–96 (he in fact calls it a period of stagnation). He does, however, identify mild downturns (and upturns) in several years within his long wave. Another writer favouring a long cycle (a 'Kuznets cycle') in construction, migration and capital flows at least, is Fenoaltea (1988). In his view, this cycle had peaks in the 1870s, late 1880s and just before the First World War. While his explanation favours international factors (resource flows), it is worth noting that neither Gerschenkron nor Fenoaltea refer precisely to the overall business cycle. Yet Fenoaltea (p. 606), for one, claims that those who dismiss the long cycle as 'happenstance' represent a minority view, although the majority view is not, apparently, that the Kuznets cycle is a 'true self-perpetuating cycle'. This point narrows the area of disagreement somewhat.

In Table 9.12 we list four cyclical indicators for Italy for the 1861 to 1913 period, although the obvious smoothing of the production index and the rather large fluctuations of the real investment figures suggest that there might be problems with the data. There are, as in the table just shown, quite a few downturns in the annual real GNP figures, but not all of these are echoed in the other indicators. Using the GNP figures mainly, there appear to be major downturns in 1867, 1881, 1888–9, 1892, 1897 and 1910. On the basis of some separate figures (not shown) provided by ISTAT (1957), there were substantial agricultural declines in 1881 (20 per cent), 1888–9 (11 per cent), 1892 (10 per cent), 1897 (14 per cent) and 1910 (17 per cent). Some of these were related to the tariff war with France (1888–98), but in any case, the agricultural nature of most of these severe declines seems to be well established. There are also recession-level declines of GNP in 1863 (1.86 per cent), 1902 (2.13 per cent) and 1908 (2.11 per cent), and there is some support from the investment figures for these events; again, agricultural production declined in each of these years (by 4 per cent, 10 per cent and 7 per cent, respectively). We can add 1870 and 1894 to the list, since three of the four indicators are down in these years (and agricultural production declined as well). We also note that 1872, 1874, 1876, 1878, 1883 and 1904 may well represent milder recessions.

The years of recession thus revealed from both the literature and the data can be arranged as follows:

1853, 1854
1863, 1867
1870, 1872, 1874, 1876, 1878
1881, 1883, 1888, 1889
1892, 1894, 1897
1902, 1904, 1908, 1910

If we count all these years after 1861, there were eighteen years of recession from a possible total of fifty-two; this is an economy in recession 35 per cent of the time, which is roughly one out of every three years. Note, about these figures, that even though agriculture is a prime suspect in quite a few downturns, Italy shows recessions in many of the same years we have already seen for other countries. In addition, Italy seems to have experienced the same long 'stagnation' of the 1870s, with possibly five years of recession during the 1870s.

Italy, then, does show an international dimension to its cycles, but this dimension differs from the countries we have been studying up to this point in being tied somewhat more to international agricultural events. Furthermore, Italy does not appear to show either fewer or less severe cycles over the period and this, too, we attribute to the stronger influence of the agricultural sector. There are occasional problems in the financial sector, as our review of the literature suggests, and some of this may be related to Italy's part-time participation in the gold standard in the period. But, for the most part, in Italy it seems that financial collapse followed agricultural disarray, rather than the reverse.

Sweden

The last of the major economies that we plan to treat as a separate case is Sweden. Sweden is unusual in having the most rapid per capita growth of any of these countries in the late nineteenth and early twentieth centuries. Sweden in 1850 was dominated by its agricultural sector, but by 1910 the industrial sector had passed it (as a percentage of GDP), and was moving very rapidly in terms of its relative contribution to national product. Sweden does not show the cyclical patterns of other countries in its real GDP series, partly because of the rapid growth rate, and perhaps partly because of the smoothing of the data (see Sheffrin, 1988). In any case, we exhibit Swedish indicators in Table 9.13 and changes in Swedish real domestic product in Figure 9.3, along with the Italian figures.

The literature on the Swedish cycle tends to concentrate on the role of export fluctuations in temporarily undermining the Swedish economy; it also

Table 9.13 Business cycle indicators for Sweden, growth rates of the data, 1851–1913

	GNP	Industrial Production	Imports	Investment
1862	3.46	6.45	–13.36	39.89
1863	2.71	6.06	4.95	–15.63
1864	2.01	0.00	2.73	12.97
1865	2.18	11.12	10.01	–31.51
1866	3.62	–5.41	3.92	38.05
1867	0.79	0.00	11.12	–16.48
1868	–5.55	10.54	–2.72	–44.35
1869	4.86	18.23	4.34	50.15
1870	10.85	4.08	9.56	2.78
1871	3.57	–27.44	12.74	2.70
1872	5.89	5.13	20.30	27.76
1873	5.57	0.00	15.27	33.94
1874	1.14	13.98	9.71	18.95
1875	–1.98	4.26	–11.86	8.05
1876	5.97	4.08	7.03	–4.62
1877	–0.07	0.00	6.89	4.62
1878	–0.36	–4.08	–19.11	–10.18
1879	6.14	4.08	–2.69	–12.14
1880	0.68	0.00	19.38	2.39

Table 9.13 (continued)

	GNP	Industrial Production	Imports	Investment
1881	1.35	14.84	1.71	12.56
1882	0.27	3.39	6.10	−10.23
1883	5.28	−3.39	12.44	6.69
1884	0.06	9.84	1.08	11.54
1885	1.26	6.06	10.12	−6.62
1886	1.31	−6.06	−7.78	7.90
1887	−1.43	6.06	2.38	−29.19
1888	3.93	5.72	6.35	15.66
1889	1.20	2.74	10.20	14.79
1890	2.93	7.80	−1.46	−1.89
1891	4.02	7.23	−5.83	−13.63
1892	1.38	4.55	−0.04	7.72
1893	2.76	6.45	−4.04	−7.72
1894	2.63	8.00	9.11	19.20
1895	5.70	−1.94	−1.92	19.63
1896	3.42	11.12	4.00	−1.00
1897	3.95	1.74	8.49	20.29
1898	2.65	6.67	6.07	6.71
1899	1.98	6.25	8.39	7.71
1900	2.45	2.99	3.29	2.79
1901	−1.11	2.90	−11.03	−4.93
1902	3.71	4.20	7.54	−0.72
1903	5.00	5.33	4.24	21.51
1904	3.17	3.82	8.81	5.98
1905	1.92	1.24	−2.00	−3.08
1906	8.49	9.42	8.27	12.82
1907	4.07	3.32	1.04	1.74
1908	0.39	−2.20	−14.11	−12.58
1909	0.22	−8.10	3.71	−10.29
1910	5.98	15.59	8.58	10.84
1911	4.17	2.04	4.17	9.53
1912	3.75	3.96	6.33	2.25
1913	3.97	−2.96	7.86	15.94

emphasizes the fact that Sweden's downturns throughout the period are tied to the international cycle. Heckscher (1963), for instance, says (p. 211):

> Beginning with the crisis of 1857, however, Sweden has regularly reflected the international business cycle. Even though sometimes the amplitudes of

the fluctuations have been a great deal smaller than in other countries, Sweden has hardly ever remained unaffected by such developments abroad.

He specifically mentions the collapse of export markets that deal in industrial materials (iron ore and timber, presumably). The banking system, he feels, weathered these storms very well, perhaps because the downturns were so mild.

Jorberg, in another study (Jorberg, 1961) compiles a set of reference cycles for Sweden based, he says, on the examination of between 96 and 180 individual series, some monthly. He establishes lower turning points in 1869, 1879, 1887, 1893, 1901 and 1909 but allows that the 1869 and 1893 dates could be set a year earlier on the basis of annual data alone. His reference cycles, then, are as shown in the table below:

Peak	Trough	Duration (years)	Change in GDP (peak to trough) (%)
1875	1879	4	+12.4
1884	1887	3	+1.1
1890	1893	3	+8.5
1900	1901	1	−1.1
1907	1909	2	+0.6

We have calculated the duration of the recessions in the tabulation, assuming that the downturn in the cycle runs from (for example) mid-1875 to mid-1879. While we have noted downturns in real domestic product in 1875 and 1878, 1887, 1901 and 1908, we think Jorberg's downturns are too long to fit the data we present. In particular, on the annual numbers, Swedish real domestic product was generally higher at the trough than at the peak, as noted in the last column of the tabulation; the only exception, of course, is the one-year recession at the turn of the century.

On the other hand, the emphasis of both Heckscher and Jorberg on the international origins of Sweden's downturns seems largely to be correct. For one thing, as we note below, the years of Sweden's cycles are the same as those of the majority of the major industrial economies in this period, with the exception of the downturn in 1868. For another, Sweden's real exports seem to be an unusually volatile coincident indicator of the cycle, as the following table suggests (just for the recession years already noted):[9]

Peak	Trough	Export decline (peak to trough) (%)
1855	1858	60.7
1867	1868	11.4
1874	1875	9.1
1877	1878	9.3
1885	1886	2.4
1900	1901	8.1
1907	1908	11.3

With the exception of 1885–6, these recession years are all years of substantial decline in real export volume. Note that iron ore exports (not shown) were particularly volatile in this period, declining by 40 per cent in 1867, 80 per cent in 1876, 37 per cent in 1886, and 14 per cent in 1909. This view follows approximately what the literature claims about the Swedish cycle.

The years of decline in real domestic product, in the fifty-three that are available, number only six, and of these, only 1868 represents anything like a major decline in real GDP. These declines appear in Table 9.13; of the six, only the declines in 1868 and 1875 are clearly recessions; In both of these events, agricultural production declined sharply (by 12.9 per cent and 5.6 per cent respectively); these figures do not appear in the table (see Krantz and Nilsson, 1975). In fact, the agricultural sector contributed to the overall cycle in five of six cases, while the industrial sector did so in only one, the very mild downturn in 1877.

As with Italy, the other indicators show considerable volatility as well as smoothing, as shown in Table 9.13. Looking for overwhelming evidence of recession, and recalling our discussion of the literature, we believe that the following were the years of downturn in this period:

1857, 1858
1868
1875, 1878
1887
1901
1908

We have selected most of these downturns as being obvious from the real GDP and indicator results, and have added 1908 because of the decisive declines of the three other indicators (and the very small growth in real GDP). Recall that these are annual numbers, and that they are far from definitive, so that there very well might have been a recession in GDP in 1908. There are also two years that are doubtful, in our opinion. These are 1877, where there was a very small decline in GDP (but imports and investment grew) and 1909, in this case a year of small GDP growth, but with sharp declines in industrial production and investment. Finally although we lack complete data, after reviewing the literature, we note that 1857–8 should be added to our list of downturns (Heckscher(1963)).

9.6 INTERNATIONAL DIMENSIONS OF CYCLES: FURTHER RESULTS

There are two remaining tasks in the analysis of the data bearing on the international cycle in this period. One of these is to draw together the cyclical results for the five countries we have studied in detail here, and the other is to extend the results to the other countries we have discussed in this study, in so far as the data can bear the load. We note that the latter task should not be expected to reveal much about the international cycle in this period, mainly because those other economies appear less integrated with the international economy than the ones just considered. In particular, while they could be expected to show some signs of the international cycle (as identified in the other results), they have their own cycles, more often tied to events in their agricultural sectors.

For the five major economies analyzed in detail, the data in Table 9.14 represent an attempt to line up the dates of downturn, as indicated by our earlier work. What we have done here is to attempt to locate periods in which most of these countries were in recession at approximately the same time. Within these periods, the years 1867–68, 1878–79, 1901–01 and 1908 stand out as representing the pan-European cycle, with five countries in recession in each cases. Of course, 1908 provides the best example, if the Swedish result is acceptable, since all five economies were in recession that year. In our compilation, in any event, a good case could be made for two international downturns in the 1850s, one in the 1860s, and three in the 1870s. In the 1880s only one recession stands out, and the same is true of the 1890s. There appear to be at least two international recessions in the first decade of the twentieth century.

Several notes need to be added to this compilation. First, the period of 'stagnation' in Europe, in the 1870s, stands out in this summary, with most

Table 9.14 The international business cycle among five major European economies, 1851–1913

Date	Number	Countries
1853–4	3	France, Germany, Italy
1857–9	4	France, Germany, Sweden, United Kingdom
1867–8	5	France, Germany, Italy, Sweden, United Kingdom
1873–4	4	France, Germany, Italy, United Kingdom
1875–6	4	France, Germany, Italy, Sweden
1878–9	5	France, Germany, Italy, Sweden, United Kingdom
1882–4	4	France, Germany, Italy, United Kingdom
1893–4	4	France, Germany, Italy, United Kingdom
1901–2	5	France, Germany, Italy, Sweden, United Kingdom
1903–4	3	France, Italy, United Kingdom
1908	5	France, Germany, Italy, Sweden, United Kingdom

countries in recession in each of the (arbitrary) two-year periods between 1873 and 1879. Indeed, only Sweden had as few as two bad years out of the seven, and Germany was in recession for five years. Second, judged somewhat casually, it is easy to see how a believer in the international cycle might notice something like a ten-year cycle in the data. This would show recessions in at least four countries in 1857–9, 1867–8, 1873–9, 1882–4, 1893–4, 1901–2, and 1908. Only the twentieth century shows more than one event in a decade, counting 1873–9 as a single recession, as the literature is prone to do. These dates encompass the downturns we feel were international in scope, but we must hasten to point out that individual countries experienced quite a few other downturns in the period that were not so well co-ordinated.

The way we are going to bring the other countries into our sample is to take those with real national product declines that match recession years for the countries we have studied in detail. We do not have the space to do more than this, and we believe that this deals with an interesting question: is it possible to show that the international cycles (just identified) also affected the other (peripheral) European countries? This exercise would establish, if this were true, an important way that they might have been integrated into the European economy in this period.

Table 9.15 The international business cycle among six other countries, 1851–1913 (growth rates of national product)

Year	Austria-Hungary	Belgium	Denmark	Netherlands	Norway	Portugal
1853			−0.12			−20.67
1854			−0.96			−16.39
1857			0.04			21.01
1858			−6.43			11.55
1859			6.00			−10.97
1867		0.52	2.33		2.42	−1.22
1868	2.80	3.57	1.06		−0.16	7.53
1873	−8.63	0.66	2.97		2.39	2.21
1874	6.40	3.24	2.37		3.68	2.70
1875	0.33	−0.21	0.80		2.77	6.36
1876	−2.60	1.27	1.58		2.95	0.66
1878	16.38	2.87	1.52		−3.57	0.36
1879	−15.56	1.00	3.86		0.90	1.80
1882	18.20	3.33	9.87		−0.12	0.97
1883	−0.74	1.44	5.56		−0.37	4.25
1884	4.10	0.89	1.14		1.72	10.80
1893	0.49	1.50	2.31		2.65	−0.50
1894	3.47	1.48	1.59		0.60	−0.25
1901	0.03	0.90	1.70	−4.65	2.49	−1.02
1902	6.82	2.02	2.59	6.06	1.51	3.89
1903	−0.05	2.23	4.00	2.61	−0.58	−0.11
1904	−7.98	2.54	3.65	−1.96	0.17	−3.33
1908	−0.23	1.00	−0.06	2.87	3.16	1.69

In Table 9.15 we list the log-changes in real national product for the six remaining countries in our sample. We do this only for the years we have already identified for the five major countries we have discussed in detail. The years listed on the left are groups of years in which the major countries generally showed some decline, as described in Table 9.14. While the table begins in 1853, we shall begin our discussion in 1867–8, when we have data for five of the six countries.

Counting the already-identified recessions in which these peripheral countries also show declines in their national products after 1870, we see that Austria-Hungary, with six such events of any magnitude, seems to have been most affected by the international cycle among these countries. Of the other countries, Portugal shows some reaction to international cycles, and so does the Netherlands, particularly in the twentieth century. On the other hand, Belgium does not.[10]

About these results, it should be emphasized that many of these countries have national products that are dominated by their agricultural sectors, and so they might be expected to be out of phase with the industrial countries. Were we to try to identify cycles purely from the industrial production figures, as our work on industrial production indices above suggests, we would show much more integration (of industrial cycles). This conclusion makes an important point: industrialization is one of the main mechanisms by which countries were brought into the European 'global' economy at this time (trade, capital flows and technology transfer are others). Countries on the periphery were being dragged into the European economy, but the signs of this in their overall product accounts are covered up by events in their large and relatively volatile agricultural sectors. We are not saying that there were not some integrating aspects to agricultural development, for there certainly were. We are merely concentrating on the main forces that produced something we think is dramatically different but unfinished in Europe in 1914.

9.7 CONCLUSIONS

There are at least four influences that we think lie behind the cyclical integration of the real sectors of the major economies in the late nineteenth century. First, technological change in the production of basic commodities and manufactured goods, and the growth of the transportation and communication networks provided the means of transporting the goods from one place to another; these factors are usually prerequisites for the growth of trade. Industrial production in all these countries grew rapidly in this period; indeed, among the industrial products involved, coal, iron (and iron ore), textiles and crude steel stand out. Agricultural products also benefited from the same sorts of improvement, and developments in international grain markets in particular are sometimes important in discussions of the business cycle in this period, as we have noted (especially in the 1880s).

Second, the growth in real incomes that was a result of the industrial revolution contributed to an increase in the demand for commodities, many of which were not domestically produced. Between 1870 and 1910, real output per capita grew rapidly in most of these countries, and with it domestic demand. Although estimates of aggregate output become less reliable the further back one goes, recent calculations of earlier numbers suggest that these growth rates are considerably above those produced earlier in the century. We have discussed this elsewhere in this study.

Third, increases in the rate of capital accumulation facilitated the growth of output and real incomes; this new capital spilled across national borders. Taking some figures from Mitchell (1978), we note that the investment/output ratio (in real terms) often grew in this period. For Germany, the ratio grew from 11.2 to 13.9 per cent; for Italy, from 7.8 to 14.4 per cent; and for Sweden, from 10.3 to 10.9 per cent. Only for the relatively mature economy of the United Kingdom did it decline (modestly). More directly to the point under consideration, there was an unprecedented increase in foreign investment in these countries. Between 1870 and 1914, foreign investment by the United Kingdom grew from 4 to 7 per cent of gross national income; indeed, the three major European economies (France, Germany and the United Kingdom) provided something like 75 per cent of the world's external investment over this period.

Finally, liberalization of the institutional arrangements for the exchange of goods and services was evident in the late nineteenth century. Average tariff rates in fact rose somewhat late in the century, and there were occasional tariff wars in the same period, tariffs were more normally employed as a means of raising government revenues rather than for protection. In fact, trade restrictions, quotas and tariffs as tools for the promotion of domestic industry were rare prior to the interwar years (see Kenwood and Lougheed, 1983) except for the protection of the agricultural sector from the 1880s. With respect to the growth of trade itself, the ratio of both imports and exports to total output grew for most of the countries in our sample during the period (as discussed in Chapter 8). Perhaps more importantly, the largest trading partners of each of these countries were other European economies.[11]

In summary, we argue that because the period we have studied was marked by an integration of the real economies of the major economic powers in Western Europe, business cycles were similarly integrated. While we have not offered evidence concerning the mechanism for the transmission of supply or demand shocks between these countries, we hypothesize, being very general about it, that when there was a downturn in one country, it was passed on to others through price and quantity changes that were stimulated by either positive or negative supply or demand shocks. In any case, there was a thriving international economy in this period, and there was also an international real business cycle, at least among the Great (economic) Powers, by the late nineteenth century.

10 The Integration of the European Economy by 1913

10.1 INTRODUCTION

At the outset of this study, we argued that, by 1913, Europe was so integrated in most important aspects of its economic life that it could be referred to as the major part of an international economy dealing in agricultural and manufacturing products, and experience movements of substantial capital and labour across borders. We used the term 'global economy' in this context, even though there is more to that concept than could possibly have applied to Europe at the end of the nineteenth century and the beginning of the twentieth, but we believe we have established that the modern European economy was largely in place by 1913, and that the later arrivals on the scene essentially attached themselves to the existing economic structure in ways dictated by their resources, energies and place in time. We shall now draw the threads of our study together around this theme, with respect to both the theoretical and empirical material that we have presented.

We used as much space as we did on the topic of the national political integration of the countries we have studied because many issues affecting economic integration are the result of political decisions. Our main observation, quite simply, is that every country (except Germany and Italy) that we have considered was essentially politically unified, within its modern borders, by 1850. Germany and Italy had somewhat unfinished agendas in this respect in 1850, but we believe this does not affect our conclusions in any major way. What unity brings, of course, is national economic policies of all sorts. We have concentrated on macroeconomic topics in our study, with banking regulations and (international) monetary policy at the head of the list. But we have also emphasized trade and capital flows that, after all, provide the major interconnections across nations. National policy enters here, as well, since by regulating, subsidizing, excising and tariffing, a nation can to some extent influence the direction and speed of economic growth. Of course, much of this has been implicit in our work, which has been deliberately macroeconomic in its tone.

Integration of European Economy by 1913 273

In this final chapter, we shall step back from our detailed and sometimes technical analysis to sketch out the information we have provided about growth and integration. In Section 10.2 we look at the time pattern of national incomes, and broad figures on exports and imports over the period. The general idea is to indicate the extent of the integration of these economies as induced by the global forces unleashed by industrialization and the growth of trade. Here, too, we discuss what we have learned about the integration of business cycles in this period. In Section 10.3 we consider financial topics, concentrating on the parallel growth of European financial systems and the remarkably similar behaviour of velocity and the demand for money across these countries. Furthermore, in this section, we re-enter the somewhat murky den of the international gold standard, with an eye to summarizing the many ways it interacted with the growing and integrated European economy. Our brief conclusions to this chapter appear in Section 10.4.

10.2 GROWTH AND TRADE: TWIN ENGINES OF INTEGRATION

In 1850, the economic development of Europe followed a roughly geographical line, with England at the top of the table, and the Balkans (and Spain and Portugal) at the bottom. Industrialization, urbanization, the expansion of the middle class, the volume of savings, the percentage of resources in the agricultural sector, and the development of the banking system pretty much followed a similar pattern, which flowed roughly from north-west to south-east. What happened over the next sixty-three years is quite remarkable: many of the other countries in Europe converged on the leader in one or more respects and all, even Spain, were experiencing a profound change in their economic structure by 1913. Let us look at some of the details.

During this era, the industrialization of Europe entered a new phase in which first iron, coal and railways joined textiles as the most important industries, later to be joined by steel, chemicals and electrical power. The growth of these new industries was accompanied by the proliferation of large-scale manufacturing operations in many sectors – large in both the size of their physical plant and the organizational structures by which they were managed. Technological change that increased the scale of iron and steel production and created whole new industries such as electrical power, played no small part in the process of modern economic growth. Foreign trade played a major role in the spreading of this process, but so too did integrated technological and financial systems that helped the latecomers to take advantage of the knowledge and savings accumulated at home and abroad.

As discussed in Chapter 3, *national income* grew rapidly in most of these countries in this period, even measured on a per capita scale. In Figure 10.1, we present per capita real national product statistics for the ten European countries for which such calculations could be made.[1] Note that these figures are normalized (that is, divided by their means) in order to facilitate comparisons. Thus, they essentially compare growth rates across countries.[2] There are a few outliers in the graph, certainly, but the overwhelming impression one gets is that there is a common growth path that these countries followed, with the German and Swedish growth rates converging from below, and Italy and Portugal (not marked) from above as 1913 approach. Interestingly, the United Kingdom, identified with a solid line in the graph, starts near the middle of the series, in 1868, but ends near the bottom in 1913.[3] This illustrates the notion of convergence as captured by these normalized data. From these data it seems clear that the common growth path was already established at the beginning of the period and, as argued earlier, nations grew along this path as their industrialization accelerated. Readers should again note that we are not showing equivalent levels or growth rates for these countries (see Chapter 3), but only how each country moves around the mean of its own national product in this period.

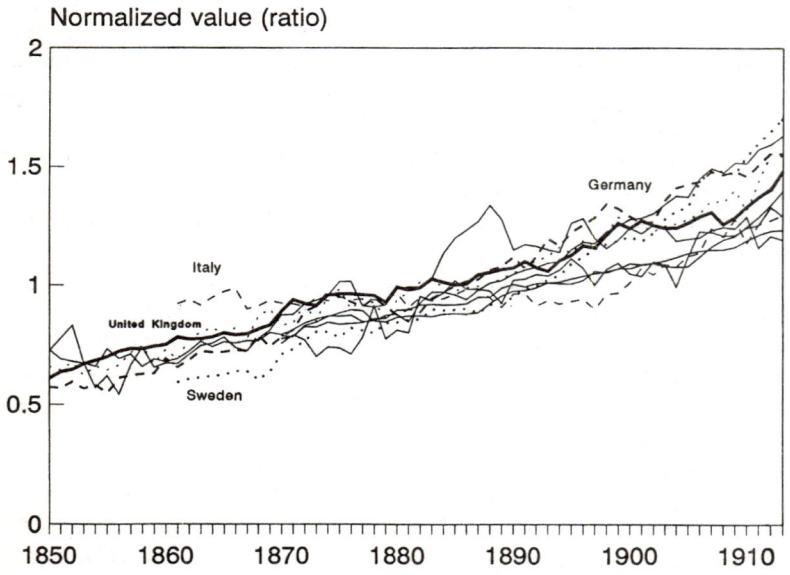

Figure 10.1   National products – normalized, 1850–1913, per capita

Integration of European Economy by 1913   275

A measure of growth that is not as broad as national product is *the industrial production index*; we have these for seven European countries. These data were studied in Chapters 3 and 9. In Chapter 3 we showed that industrial production outstripped overall output wherever we had comparable data; we also showed there that the industrial sector overtook the agricultural sector, in some cases at a remarkably rapid rate. In Chapter 9, then, we compared the 'phase coincidence' of the national product figures with that of the industrial production indices. These phases were very similar, at least in outline, and both series showed a large number of years in which the indices were in the same phase of the cycle, especially for the major industrial economies. Of course, one of the reasons for this phase coincidence is that it is the industrial cycle, rather than the agricultural, that these countries are likely to share. Furthermore, these countries, except for Spain, were in the process of becoming more industrial along parallel (and sometimes converging) paths.

Because the industrial production indices are not available as absolute numbers (although some can be reconstructed) their graphs can be a little misleading. Again, by normalizing each series, we can compare the resulting plots for signs of common growth rates. Figure 10.2 gives the results. Again,

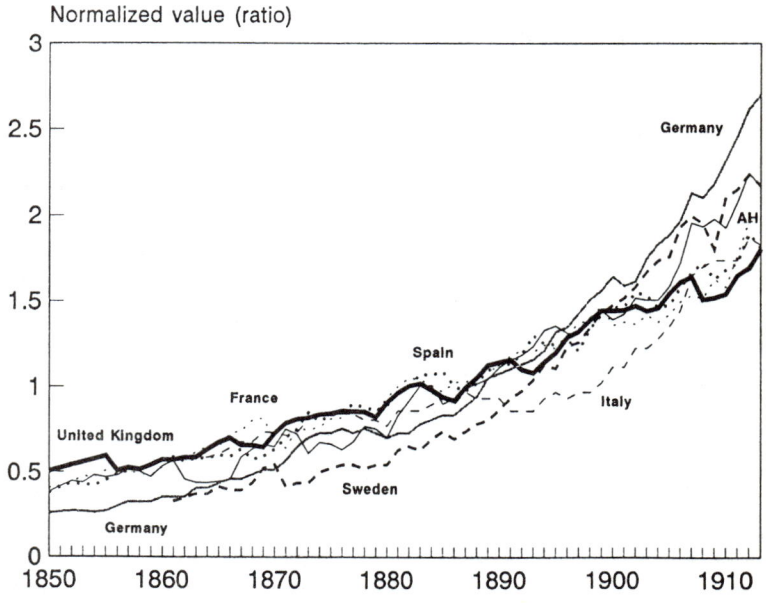

Figure 10.2   Industrial production indices – normalized, 1850–1913

we see the overwhelming evidence of a common growth path taken by these countries; in fact, generally speaking, even the curvature seems similar to that in Figure 10.1. Looking at the details, we see the United Kingdom, drawn as the thickest line, starting at the highest level and ending at the lowest; this comparison provides strong evidence of convergence, since each of the other countries, relative to its own mean, shows more rapidly-growing industrial output. Germany, the fastest-growing industrial economy, starts at the bottom and finishes at the top; Sweden shows a similar performance. So the industrial production indices reinforce the impression of convergence of growth paths already established by the national product figures.

We have argued that industrialization, as it spread across Europe, drew these countries together in the sense just described. If so, it is the behaviour of exports and imports that would show this, since it is by trade (and capital flows, of course) that the process would spread. For exports and imports we found, somewhat to our surprise, that there is some decline in the growth rates of these over the period in many countries; this is less surprising, though, when one considers that not only were overall growth rates sometimes lower at the end of the period than before 1870, but also that tariffs were higher.

Figure 10.3 shows a plot of the per capita *real exports* of eleven European countries; again, the figures are normalized in order to facilitate comparisons and to emphasize relative growth rates. The results here are very similar to those for real national product, but here Portugal does not seem to be trending upwards as the other countries are, but has normalized exports that fluctuate widely. While there was some acceleration in the national product and industrial production figures, this is more pronounced in the export figures. Recall, also, from Chapter 8, that both imports and exports generally grew faster than real national product in this period.[4]

Looking at the details, we see that the United Kingdom (the darkest solid line) grows relatively slowly compared to its mean, with only the much more agricultural countries of Austria-Hungary (the series that stops in 1909) and Portugal being lower at the end of the period. France is relatively high throughout the period, ending close to the Netherlands; this attests to rapid growth, of course, but note that the per capita calculation has a lot to do with this, since France's population grew very slowly in this period, while its industrial sector did quite well. Denmark, the Netherlands and Sweden all show rapid growth relative to their mean performance, and so does Germany, particularly at the end of the period. Finally, we again note that these countries do seem to be sharing a common growth path upwards, with the exception of the two agriculturally-dominated countries mentioned earlier.

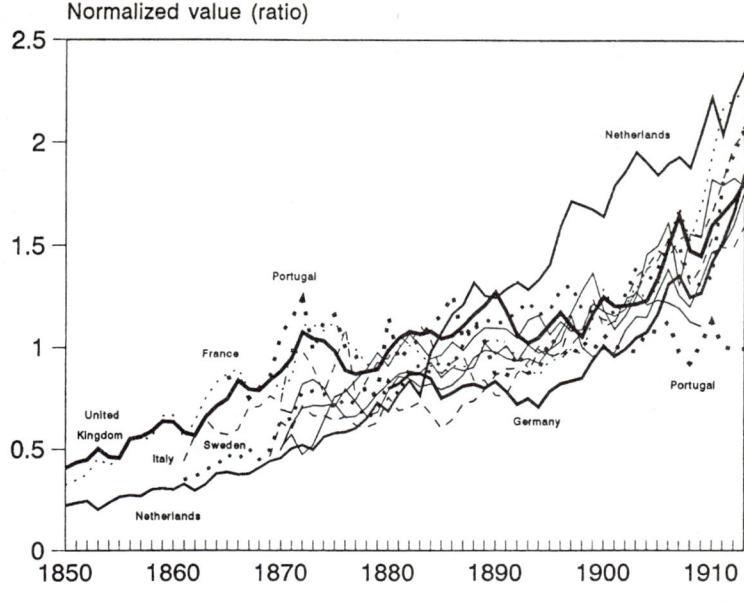

Figure 10.3   Real exports – normalized, 1850–1913

It would be nice to have better data for capital markets than we do, and so we must regard our results for the seven series on real investment (as described in Chapter 8) as being very provisional. As with exports and imports, the investment figures are highly correlated across countries in this period, again because of the trends in the data; here we also looked at investment ratios (I/Y) since such a measure provides information about the potential causes of growth. Indeed, there is clearly some indication that the faster-growing countries had higher investment ratios in this period, as the Harrod–Domar growth model predicts.

The interest rates we have available are more numerous, especially for long-term rates, and they are likely to be reasonably accurate. We can accordingly set greater store by these results. Of course, the general idea is that capital market integration can be revealed by looking at interest-rate interaction. Nominal and real interest rates are generally pretty strongly correlated (with nominal being more so than real). Note that real rates were computed using a distributed lag of past inflation rates, since it is *expected* real rates that interests us. In this case, graphs show a remarkable coincidence of real rates, for both long and short rates. We expected to find this result.

For the cointegration tests that are possible for the series that contain unit roots, there is no cointegration for long-term nominal rates, but there is for short-term rates. We attribute the latter partly to the operation of the gold standard, since the short term interest rate is the key capital market rate for the managers of this system. For real rates, the results of our cointegration tests for long-term real rates do show considerable interaction; on the other hand, the short-term real rates are not cointegrated. For the Granger-causality tests, there are signs of Granger-causality for nominal long-term rates; we believe these are the result of the lagged real relationship that is contained in the nominal rate, as well as by the influence of expected inflation. We did not attempt to measure the separate contributions of these two factors, but in our opinion it looks as if both matter.

In studying *business cycles*, we found increasing integration of these real events over this period, with a rather remarkable coincidence across countries by the early years of the twentieth century. We distinguished between the major industrializing economies and all others, with somewhat different patterns emerging for these two categories. The industrializing economies had more cyclical events in common, measured in various ways; when they did not, it was a financial shock (which was often damped by the actions of the central bank), a war or an agricultural disaster of some sort. The agricultural events are often limited to a single economy, at least in this period. Indeed, it is the locally-based agricultural cycle that seems partly to distinguish the two groups of countries already mentioned, with the less industrial countries being more dominated by agriculture cycles, and consequently being less tied into the general cyclical stories of the leaders. They are, though, often affected by the industrial-financial storms of the latter.

As a way of visualizing our results, we have compiled Figure 10.4, which shows the results of a simple enumeration of the countries in our sample in recession in each year from 1851 to 1913. For the five major industrial economies that we discussed separately, we used our evaluation of cycles, based on our empirical work and the literature. For the remaining five countries for which we had data (Austria-Hungary, Belgium, Denmark, Portugal and Norway) we simply recorded the years in which real national product declined. In this enumeration, 1908 stands out, with seven of the countries in recession at once. The years 1853, 1867, 1878 and 1901 are also good candidates for the class of international recessions, while there are eight more years when four of the ten countries are in recession at the same time.

When we look at Figure 10.4 more closely, several other conclusions emerge. While the recessions stand out, there are also many years (24 out of 63) when either only one or no countries were in recession. In Chapter 9,

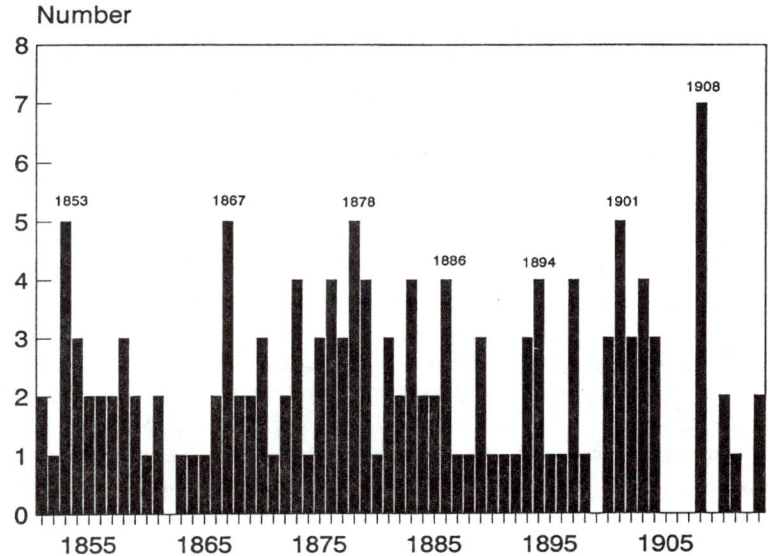

Figure 10.4 European business cycles, 1851–1913, number of countries in recession each year

we dramatized this result by looking at phase coincidence tables; the proposition is that, if we look at both downturns and upturns, a stronger case for closely-integrated cycles can be maintained for this period. Indeed, one notices immediately that six of the seven years when no countries were in recession came at the end of the period (1899 onward). This finding supports our conclusion of economic integration, by a method that is rarely discussed in the business cycle literature. Finally, we note that if one steps back from the graph, one can see times when the black lines appear to bunch up. These are 1853–9, 1866–70, 1875–9, 1881–6 and 1900–3. If one accepts that cyclical interaction can be delayed at least a year in its migration from one country to another, then these bunches (with the addition of 1893–7) give us one long *European* downturn in each of the six decades in the sample.[5] These are the ten-year cycles that are favoured in much of the literature.

A second way to visualize the cycles of the major industrializing countries is to plot the growth rates of their real national products. The countries involved in this exercise are Austria-Hungary, Belgium, France, Germany, Italy, Sweden and the United Kingdom, and the results appear in Figure 10.5. In the graph we have made no attempt to single out the individual economies, although we should note that the wider fluctuations there generally come from France and Austria-Hungary. The impression given by the graph is pretty strong that cycles measured only by national product fluctuations are much more closely integrated in the second thirty years of the sample than they are in the first. In fact, they are also milder in the later period, although one notices a slight increase in volatility at the end. In any case, the cycles are remarkably uniform as 1914 approaches, for these increasingly similar economies, and that is the main point of the exercise.

We have suggested that there are possibly four major real influences behind the increasing cyclical integration of these major industrial economies. First, an increasingly common technological change in the production of basic commodities and manufactured goods, and the growth of similar transportation and communication networks, caused these countries to expand their share in international markets for a wide variety of products. In sharing markets, they also shared cycles. Of course, agricultural output participated in many of the cycles, but we did not observe agricultural shocks, at least, drifting significantly across borders. Second, aggregate demand grew apace for each of these economies, with investment growing faster than the economy, in each case. Investment is the least stable of the

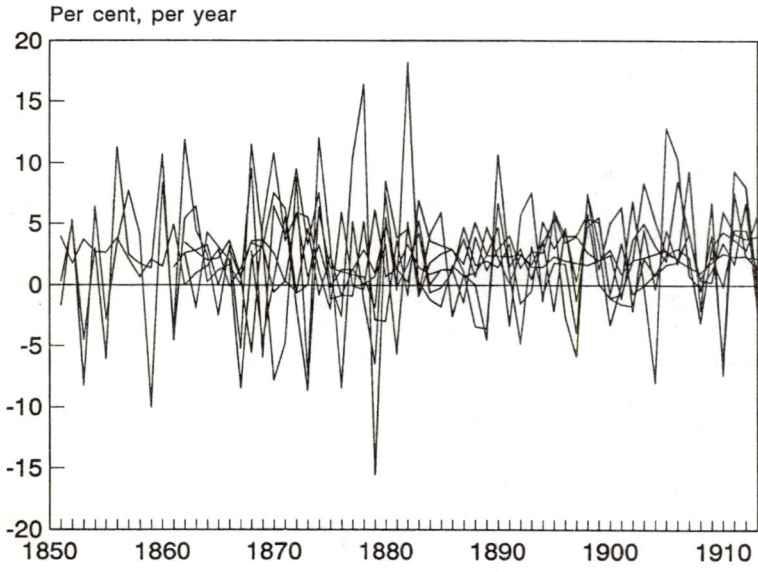

Figure 10.5 Fluctuations in national product, industrial economies, 1850–1913

major components of national spending, and this is another, related, way these economies came to interact more completely as the period wore on. Third, capital itself spilled increasingly across borders, so that capital markets became more 'global'; this produced linkages that we identified in terms of the behaviour of long-term interest rates. Finally, the increasing liberalization of the institutional arrangements for the exchange of goods and services was manifest in the late nineteenth century, although from time to time trade wars broke out after the mid-1880s, especially in the agricultural sector. With respect to the growth of trade itself, the ratio of both imports and exports to total output grew for all these countries, and each tended to find its largest trading partners among the set of seven countries used in the construction of Figure 10.5.

10.3 FINANCIAL INTEGRATION

In Chapter 4 we outlined the development of the banking systems of eleven European economies. What stood out most was the fact that, with very few exceptions, each of the countries that did not have a modern banking system went through the process of acquiring one during the period we have been examining. At the beginning of the period the United Kingdom was the financial leader, in the range and volume of its financial activities, but by the end of the period several countries had overtaken the United Kingdom, at least as measured by our 'financial sophistication' index. Convergence upon the leader was demonstrated very clearly, especially in Figure 4.1 (see page 70).

Another way we can see this, utilizing yet another set of data that are available, is to employ the data on bank assets that were collected by Mitchell (1992). We show these in Figure 10.6, on a per capita basis, normalized again, to facilitate comparisons. In the graph, we have detailed the plots for just a few countries, since the bulk of the countries seem quite tightly bunched together in terms of the growth of their per capita deposits compared to the mean (for each series). Germany, as discussed in Chapter 4, lies at the bottom of the graph until the 1880s, and then soars to the top; our explanation emphasizes the involvement of German banks in large-scale industrial development. Denmark had a similar experience.

The plot for the United Kingdom is quite flat in Figure 10.6, as one might expect for the most financially mature economy in Europe; this is shown by the solid line running through the middle of the graph. Note that the United Kingdom is above everybody else in 1870, and below everybody else in 1913. This figure illustrates perhaps the most impressive example of

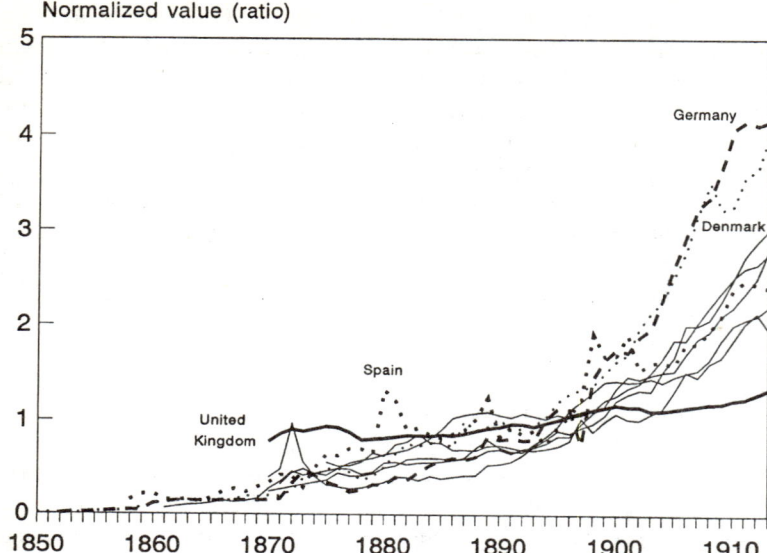

Figure 10.6   Normalized bank deposits, 1850–1913, per capita

convergence that we have presented, with all other countries growing much more rapidly (compared to their means), and hence converging on the United Kingdom. Note that even Spain stays in the pack here (although it does show some unusual spikes in the period); as we noted earlier, Spain was not formally on the gold standard and had some inflationary episodes uncharacteristic of the rest of Europe in this period.

We are interested in bank deposits because they are a proxy for all the services of the banking system. Money, of course, is a broader measure, but it is banks, above all, which led the way in financial development in this period. Of course, there are many other contributors to development, not themselves offering deposits, so we are merely employing this measure as an *indicator* of financial growth. Even so, the numbers here are so remarkable that we have performed some further calculations on them in order to illustrate the astonishing growth of this sector during the period. The numbers appear in Table 10.1.

The numbers in Table 10.1 confirm the catching up of all these countries compared to the United Kingdom, the strongest impression generated by the graph. In addition, these growth rates are very high (in per capita terms!) and, indeed, are the highest we have seen for any variables, nominal or real, in this

Table 10.1 Per capita bank deposits in Europe, growth rates, 1870–1913 (per cent)

Country	1870–1913	1890–1913
Austria	4.77	7.52
Belgium	3.33	4.21
Denmark	7.09	5.95
Germany	7.56	7.14
Italy	5.45	4.18
Norway	5.78	6.06
Spain	4.62	4.57
Sweden	4.65	4.84
United Kingdom	1.24	1.53

Sources: See Data Appendix. The Belgian data start in 1875 and the Swedish in 1871.

period. Finally, and this is not clear from the figure, the countries are evenly balanced over the whole table as to whether they grew faster overall or only in the 1890–1913 period. In that later period, again, the UK growth rate of per capita bank deposits was only slightly more than a third of the *lowest* of its emerging competitors. Of course, we realize that the development of other financial intermediaries was probably stronger in the United Kingdom, but even so, this comparison, too, provides a remarkably striking example of the (financial) convergence hypothesis.

One of the more detailed parts of our empirical work appears in Chapter 7, on the demand for money. There we tested a standard (monetarist-style) money demand function for the money and income data of each country, utilizing an international collection of interest rates to help locate a stable version of this function for each country. The use of interest rates in this way attests to the international dimensions of capital markets in this period: we have already made this point, of course. In addition, we find it remarkable that it was relatively easy to find stable, similar, demand functions for most countries. We believe this is yet another way that financial integration revealed itself in this period. We note, and this is surely a future research topic, that one could look for a common European money demand over at least the major industrial countries for this period, along the lines that Friedman and Schwartz did for the United States and the United Kingdom.

One of the reasons one might have found increasing financial integration in ways just mentioned is that the international gold standard might have brought increasing financial stability to Western Europe in this period. We found, in fact, that the variance of practically every series at which we looked, real or financial, declined over this period, and it is quite probable, although we are not in a position to defend our view, that the period of the gold standard (say, 1873–1913) saw the lowest variances of exchange rates, price levels, interest rates and money national income of any previous period of comparable length in recent history. If this observation is correct, the gold standard surely made some contribution to the integration of these economies.

We have not discussed, except in passing, a fairly substantial literature that has compared the gold standard period as a financial 'regime' with regimes that came later. In particular, scholars have questioned whether inflation rates were more stable during the gold-standard period than under the flexible exchange rates after 1971, whether business cycles were milder later than during the gold standard, and how a system with what we now know to have had serious flaws could have operated so effectively. For one thing, while the inflation rates were lower during the gold standard period than after 1971 (or, really, than any time after 1914), the unanticipated variances of inflation rates were, in fact, higher in the gold-standard period. This result is a little unexpected, but one should note that variances are relatively low for both periods, compared to the long run of history; put another way, the successful gold standard was probably a better system than anything that preceded it.

With respect to business cycles, we think that the increased financial stability that accompanied the gold standard must have helped to reduce the amplitude and possibly the frequency of these events, when compared with earlier periods. Cycles since 1950 have quite possibly been milder and less frequent, especially towards the end of the twentieth century, but in view of the significant differences in the institutional make-up of these economies (especially the relative importance of the agricultural sector) it is hard to pin down any particular effect for the gold standard itself, compared to modern monetary management. Finally we note (following Bordo and Schwartz, 1994) that the gold standard might have worked, in spite of its manifest shortcomings, because it was a credible system; the Bretton Woods system (the last gasp for fixed exchange rates) was not. A credible exchange rate system is one in which the member countries make believable commitments to the standard. To make their commitment believable, they have to be seen to support the system and each other in their stabilization efforts. It is not hard to document the failure of many countries to maintain their commitment to fixed exchange rates (and to domestic monetary stability) after 1918.

We did, looking further into our results, uncover a serious problem regarding financial harmony, as we found that neither high-powered money nor domestic money stocks were closely integrated across nations. Indeed, money stocks (and, for that matter, high-powered money stocks) grew quite rapidly in this period – more rapidly than national product, for example, while price levels hardly grew at all. As we have noted, a literature exists, which suggests that the gold standard really was not working, and that the increasing stability in financial variables we had observed might be caused by something else. For the gold standard part of this statement, we referred readers to the 'rules of the game' literature; central bank after central bank has been accused, on the basis of detailed examinations of their portfolio behaviour, of not playing by the rules (that is, of not importing and exporting inflation according to the requirements of the international system). In a sense, this conclusion is very obvious; the lack of correlation between money and price level behaviour is exactly what one would find if countries did not play by the rules. Central-bank balance sheets would, of course, reflect this behaviour.

There are three problems with this conclusion. One – and the most important – is that the international gold standard did work in this period. Most countries that belonged to the system managed to stay on the system at an unchanged parity. Indeed, other countries, completely or occasionally off the system, also did not see much fluctuation in their exchange rates. Italy is a case in point, for here, it is argued, the central bank was guided by the norm of the gold standard in one of the important periods after 1900 that it was not formally on the system. Of course, one can make up stories about how the system muddled through, but we think two other facts make this unlikely: (i) (our second point), that price levels were closely integrated across countries, as a functioning system would require; and (ii) (our third point) short-term interest rates showed a similar close integration, at least in the few cases where we could assemble such data. Both the second and third points can be attributed to the actions of central banks in stabilizing their currencies.

What we have done, then, is to offer an explanation of the paradox concerning the monetary quantities, as it exists in the literature, certainly, that invokes the monetary approach to the balance of payments. This theory argues that internationally-determined prices drive domestic price levels; what determines the international price level is, of course, the world stock of high-powered money, which, under the gold standard, is gold and convertible currencies. While each country is presented with an internationally-determined price level, it achieves a domestic money stock on the basis of its own rate of growth (which absorbs money), and its own money demand.

The demand for money enters the story in that the exogenously determined international price level, exogenously determined international interest rates, and the exogenously determined domestic real income determine the quantity of money demanded. This quantity is produced by money suppliers in the first instance. If the demand for money were unstable, then one would have an easy explanation for money stocks to be unrelated internationally; we do not find such a situation, however. Rather, we have argued, the demand for money (and the supply from the banking sector, for that matter) operates as a filter for international influences, with the income elasticity of money demand being the most important component of this filtering effect. In particular, in all these countries except the United Kingdom, the income elasticity of money demand was greater than unity – and it varied from country to country – so that fluctuations in income transmitted themselves to money demand (and the money stock) to produce rapidly-growing money stocks even though prices were not growing appreciably. They were uncorrelated, further, in view of the rather low correlations of money growth rates across countries. We believe this is a complete explanation that is, in addition, consistent with all the facts that we have assembled.

10.4 FINAL OBSERVATIONS

On net, we believe that considerable interaction has been established, with suitable lags, for both product markets (exports and imports) and capital markets. The real interactions are dominated by market-driven interaction, on the whole, while the nominal results, for short-term interest rates at least, are driven by the requirements of the gold standard. In summary, we argue that the period in question was marked by an integration of the real economies of the major economic powers in Western Europe. Although we have not offered evidence concerning the mechanism for the transmission of supply or demand shocks between these countries, we hypothesize that when there was a downturn in one country, it was passed on to others, either through higher input prices in the case of supply shocks, or lower output prices in the case of demand shocks. In any case, there was an international economy, and in that deviations from long-run trends in real output were cointegrated, there was an international real business cycle, at least among the largest players, during the late nineteenth century. In short the 'global economy' to which people often refer today has been around a long time.

Notes and References

1 Economic Integration in Theory and Practice

1. These works include those of Bonn, Hilgerdt, Ropke, von Mises, and Hayek. For a detailed discussion of the particular contribution of each of these writers, see Machlup (1977, pp. 4–9).
2. Abramovitz (1986) provides a recent summary of the arguments and Williamson (1992) has recently related convergence and catching up.
3. See the discussion in Sylla and Toniolo (1991).
4. We shall define the concepts mentioned in this section as we use them in later chapters. Readers wishing for a formal definition at this point should consult the Technical Appendix.
5. For a complete listing to the date, see Bordo (1986). We continue with examples that are relevant to this study.

2 The Political Integration of the European States

1. The revision of the traditional view of France as a backward country and late industrializer began with Roehl (1976) and Crafts (1977) and was expanded by O'Brien and Keyder (1978) though Landes (1994) has recently challenged these revisionist arguments.
2. Komlos writes (1983, p. 23), for example, that 'The people of the successor states (to the Hapsburg monarchy) ... need to know that, economically, that amorphous conglomerate of nationalities was viable indeed.' For supporting arguments and evidence, see Berend and Ranki (1974); Good (1974, 1978); Komlos (1987) and Trebilcock (1981, ch. 5).

3 The Nature and Causes of Economic Growth, 1850–1913

1. A summary of both the history and the current state of the standard of living debate can be found in Mokyr (1993).
2. For example, the growth rates of the real wages of agricultural labour and certain skilled (but outmoded) crafts slowed or even fell at times, while those participating in manufacturing, government, and the (other) professions typically rose (see Williamson, 1985).
3. Though we are primarily concerned with real output in this chapter, another example comes from the consideration of the banking systems and the central banks of the European countries, which emerged under quite different circumstances, and developed differently also (though with some similarities) across countries. Did the path of financial development affect the path of economic growth of these countries? Clearly, scholars such as Gerschenkron thought that it did. We explore these issues in Chapters 4 and 5.

4. For this to be a valid comparison across countries, we require that exchange rates reflect purchasing power parity. That is, rates of inflation should be the same across countries and, concomitantly, countries should maintain a fixed exchange rate with the pound. Obviously, the assumption of purchasing power parity going back to 1820 at 1913 exchange rates is a strong one. In fact, the extent to which the figures in the table deviated from the 'real' figures depended largely on the ability of countries to maintain convertibility. It was the countries at the lower end of the distribution that had the most difficult time maintaining convertibility. Thus the figures for countries such as Austria-Hungary, Italy and Spain may well be biased upwards in the table; these countries had the more rapid rates of inflation during the period, for the most part (see Chapter 6). The GNP figures for Austria-Hungary are for 1871 and 1912. The German GNP figures were calculated by estimating a capital consumption allowance and adding it to the NNP figures found in Hoffmann (1965). The 1870 and 1913 figures for Spain were calculated from the UK. GNP figures, using national income ratios found in Molinas and Prados de la Escosura (1989). The 1820 figures for each country were estimated using growth rates calculated from Maddison (1982), except for Italy, Portugal and Spain. For Italy and Spain, we used growth rates calculated from Molinas and Prados de la Escosura (1989) for the period 1830–60. For Portugal, we used the growth rate from 1850–70, which we calculated from Nunes *et al.* (1989).
5. Note, in particular, Spain's relative decline from the middle rung in 1820 to the bottom by 1913.
6. Recall from the discussion above concerning the purchasing power parity assumption that it was exactly these countries which had levels of output that were biased upwards, adding to the picture of continued relative backwardness.
7. The coefficient of variation is defined as the ratio of the standard deviation, σ, to the mean, μ (that is, $c.v. = \sigma/\mu$). The convergence hypothesis implies that, over time, the standard deviation of per capita output across countries would fall (or rise more slowly than the mean), while the mean rises; thus, a falling coefficient of variation supports the convergence hypothesis.
8. A standard explanation of this model appears in Phelps (1965).
9. In fact, in Table 3.3, there is a small positive correlation (of 0.25) between population and per capita output.
10. See the work of O'Rourke (1994) on the impact of Irish emigration on the subsequent level of Irish incomes. This study is an example of a negative influence. Sweden also lost farm population that Sandberg (1979) finds was near the top, in its level of human capital development, when it arrived in the United States. In Sweden, on the other hand, farm workers faced an agricultural sector that offered poor prospects for the future, partly on account of poor soil.

4 Money, Banking and Financial Sophistication

1. Velocity, V, is defined as the ratio of nominal output, Y, to the money stock, $M: V = Y/M$.

2. The Financial sophistication index, *FS*, is the product of the reciprocal of velocity, *V*, and the number of weeks in the year: $FS = (1/V) \times 52$.
3. We have omitted Austria-Hungary because we were unable to calculate nominal national income from the data available. An index based on real income and real money balances rose, as did most of the other indices reported in Figure 4.1 and Table 4.2, below.
4. The Bank of France replaced an earlier bank, the Caisse de Comptes Courants, founded in 1796.
5. See, for example, Rudolph (1972), Good (1974), Komlos (1983) and Trebilcock (1981).
6. The five were the Banca Nazionale del Regno, Banca Nazionale Toscana, Banca Toscana di Credito e d'Industria, Banco di Napoli, and Banco di Sicilia. In addition, the Banca Romana was the bank of issue in the Papal States.
7. The figures cited here are annual averages from Cohen (1972).
8. Not to create a mystery, we are referring to the possibility, as revealed by our work in these chapters, that the money stock may well have been determined endogenously in these countries, by the demand for money in each case. This creates a framework where strong results with money causing income would be unlikely. We do, though, find a few such cases.
9. In Norway, real income Granger-causes money at the 10 per cent level, so all is not lost, even in this case.
10. There are cases of prices significantly Granger-causing money in Norway and Sweden.

5 Central Banking before 1914

1. A central bank might be observed violating the rules if it displayed a lack of correlation between its assets and liabilities. For example, the bank might sell assets in response to an increase in deposits following an inflow of specie.
2. This section leans heavily on a survey by Dowd (1989).
3. One of the problems was the tendency to lend at bank rate, whatever the market rate. This practice was changed in 1878 to a policy of lending to its regular customers at market rate and to others at a penal rate (bank rate).
4. The crisis was precipitated by the failure of the City of Glasgow Bank on October 2, and it spread to other provincial banks, particularly those in depressed industrial regions. The London financial market remained relatively unaffected.
5. Of course, it also looks as if the bank was lending at temporarily high interest rates in order to enhance its profits.
6. Only in 1848–51, 1876–9 and 1884–5 did both prices and real income decline. In modern times, stagflation has been quite common, and the term is a modern one.
7. In addition to France, the original members of the Latin Monetary Union were Belgium, Italy and Switzerland, with Greece joining in 1867. The unit of account was the franc (in Italy the lira and Greece the drachma), which was coined in both silver (5 franc piece) and gold (5, 10, 20, 50 and 100

francs). The silver-to-gold ratio of the coins was 15.5 to 1. See Redish (1994) for the institutional details.

8. It has been alleged that the Prussian Bank's activities were (positively) causally linked to the growth of the financial sector as a whole, but this is hard to establish in view of the data, and, indeed, quite possibly not correct, at least up to 1870. See Tilly (1967) for a discussion.

9. Sommariva and Tullio argue that Reichsbank behaviour can be explained with reference to the monetary approach to the balance of payments, a theory that provides an alternative channel of influence to the better-known specie-flow mechanism. In particular, Sommariva and Tullio find that an increase in German output and prices induced a gold and silver inflow into Germany, while an increase in Reichsbank domestic assets induced an outflow. The negative correlation between the domestic and foreign assets of the Reichsbank (the violation of the rules of the game, as identified by Bloomfield) is attributed to bidirectional causation between the two accounts, and not to a policy of sterilization of gold flows.

10. The material in this section comes from Cameron (1967c) and Van der Wee and Goosens (1991).

11. Much of the material in this section comes from Jonung (1984), Egge (1983) and Hansen (1982).

12. As we noted above, Sommariva and Tullio (1987, 1988) made a similar claim for Germany; we have made this claim at several points and will explain it more fully in Chapter 6.

13. Even in the long run, however, prices could differ by the transaction costs of shipping gold between countries. See Officer (1986) for tests supporting the efficiency of the system based on violations of the 'gold points'. For a differing view, see Clark (1984), and for a longer-run perspective, Edison (1987).

14. The function is assumed to be linearly homogeneous in P and y, though the latter condition appears not to hold for this time period, as we discus in Chapter 7.

15. The Fisher equation for the nominal interest rate is $i = r + \pi$. If r, the real rate, is relatively constant, as is often argued, then either i or π is appropriate for Equation (5.3). We have data on i, of course, but have to assume some sort of model of expectations to study the *expected* rate of inflation.

16. Any country that over-values gold relative to the rest of the world will attract gold flows and suffer higher prices. This process continues until prices rise enough to restore equilibrium in the gold-importing country, or other countries adjust their gold prices upward. In either case, in the absence of changes in other variables, Equation 5.4 *eventually* holds for all countries on the standard.

17. Backus and Kehoe (1992) found considerable differences in both the means and standard deviations of real output during the gold-standard period among the countries in our sample.

18. Thus λ would have been a function of price expectations, a consideration omitted from our model.

19. Barro notes that when new countries on the standard started to acquire monetary gold, as did the United States after 1875, the depressing effect on

the world price level would begin. He also notes that Germany began purchases of gold in 1871.
20. The gold stock figures come from the *Report of the Director of the (US) Mint* (various years); it refers to world gold production. See the Data Appendix for the sources of the other data.
21. The Augmented Dickey–Fuller test involves testing the null hypothesis that $\theta = 0$ in the following equation:

$$\Delta x_t = \alpha + \theta x_{t-1} + \sum_{i=1}^{p} \beta_i \Delta x_{t-i} + \delta T + U_t$$

Here, p is the number of lagged dependent variables and T is a trend.
22. Note that these results all refer to the basic Dickey-Fuller test (unaugmented) under the rules laid out in the Technical Appendix to this study.
23. Note that we also tried all possible combinations of three countries (and gold), searching for cointegrating planes; this, too, proved to be unsuccessful, except in one case: Germany (as the dependent variable) with Sweden and Norway.

6 Money and Prices, 1850–1913

1. Hatton (1992), for example, surveys this literature (particularly that of the monetary approach) but his comparisons are only with the United Kingdom and his coverage of the price data is not as extensive as ours.
2. Note that the data in the two parts of the table do not refer to exactly the same set of countries. We have used all the available series in each of these categories, to the best of our knowledge. See the Data Appendix for a description of each of the series employed in this table.
3. For Denmark and Norway, we use the consumer price index, there being available no wholesale price index for either of these countries.
4. Table 6.1 lists the starting date for the correlations at the top of Table 6.2. The end date is 1880, so that there are very few observations for Spain (1874 onwards) and the United Kingdom (1871 onwards).
5. Hatton (1992) offers correlation coefficients for up to seven European countries and the United States for the 1880–1913 period for wholesale prices, GDP deflators and retail prices. The correlations are only with the United Kingdom, but his results certainly are similar to ours. He notes, as well, that the correlations are impressively high, and often higher for wholesale prices than for GDP deflators or retail prices.
6. For a definition of stationarity and a discussion of its importance, see the Technical Appendix.
7. These test procedures were explained in Chapter 5, when they were first employed. A more complete explanation, along with important *caveats*, is contained in the Technical Appendix.
8. The Danish money stock was tested at four lags, since that is the length of the series at which a unit root could be established.

9. Hatton (1992) presents cointegration results for the United Kingdom and eight other countries. He argues that the evidence for cointegration of price levels (wholesale, retail and GDP deflator) is quite weak for the 1880–1913 period. In our Table 6.5, the United Kingdom does show considerable cointegration with other European economies, especially for wholesale prices, but for different time periods. Hatton reports successful cointegration only for the United Kingdom with Belgium and France. The difference in results possibly reflects the low power of the test for such small samples (his is even smaller than ours). Of course, we are also emphasizing the striking difference between money and prices in the cointegration tests.
10. This is also quite possibly the case with the French consumer price index, as shown in Part C of the table.
11. Note that under a successful fixed exchange rate system, the domestic quantity of money would be determined endogenously, at least in the short run (Friedman and Schwartz, 1982). This topic is discussed and documented further in Chapter 7, where the demand for money function is interpreted and estimated for these same countries.
12. Jonung in fact finds a poor connection between the base and money in 1871–96, and a strong one in 1897–1913. We generally do not analyze such subperiods because, for our methods, the periods are too short, but this does raise an important question about the stability of such interaction over time.
13. If price levels are brought into line by international arbitrage in commodity prices, as the 'monetary approach' already discussed implies, then one might reasonably expect a shorter lag, although exactly what this might be would be impossible to say without detailed sectoral analysis.
14. See Chapter 7 for a further discussion of problems with the data.

7 The Demand for Money

1. Note that it is appropriate to measure income and money in real, per capita terms (see Fisher, 1989; and Barnett, Fisher and Serletis, 1992) and to work with the logarithms of money and income (but not the interest rate).
2. We take note here of an important recent discussion of the econometrics of money demand in the context of Friedman and Schwartz's study (1982). Our formulation hardly does justice to the complex issues raised, for example, by Hendry and Ericsson (1991).
3. This result, which is pretty general in the tests reported here, is also consistent with the finding that monetary velocity generally declined in this period. That is, velocity declined because economic agents were holding increasingly large money balances per dollar of income in order to benefit from the services associated with the growth of the 'money' (financial services) industry.
4. The tests were performed using the software package *Micro TSP*; the tests are explained there, as well, although we have included a brief description in our Technical Appendix.
5. The BG (Breusch–Godfrey) test is for serial correlation in the case when there is a lagged dependent variable. A *p*-value of 0.05 or less indicates

significant serial correlation at the 5 per cent level. See Johnston (1984) for a discussion of this test.
6. The long-run income coefficients for this table are not calculated, since there is generally too much interaction between the income coefficients and the structural variables.
7. Komlos does not provide a measure of nominal income in his study, so we created a synthetic measure by multiplying his real GNP measure by the consumer price index for Austria.
8. We also tried the currency–deposit ratio as an additional variable (indicating, possibly, changes in the public's preferences), but it did not improve the situation.
9. Saint Marc had data on gold stocks in private hands only at certain points. His interpolation procedure created big jumps in the monetary data where the forward and backward interpolations were linked: 1888 was one such point. Evidently, the 1889 estimate of the equation was (in all tests) unable to produce a tight fit with the 1888 value of the money stock as the lagged dependent variable.
10. Note that both permanent income and expected inflation were given explicit adjustment parameter values in these tests.
11. We note that Turner (1991) finds an income elasticity of 0.89 for the United Kingdom for the 1871–1913 period; it is significantly less than unity in his test.
12. We tried the currency–deposit ratio as an additional (demand) variable for this case, but it did not remove the significant serial correlation.
13. We also note that the data are generally better for the later period for most countries. If the demand for money were stable throughout the period, but the data differed in quality, a result like ours might well be obtained.

8 The Integration of Product and Capital Markets

1. While there were a few series for real exports and imports available, for most countries these data are nominal. For consistency, then, the real figures used in this chapter were created by dividing through by the wholesale price index for each country. Separately, we prepared a table of nominal data parallel to Table 8.1. The broad conclusions are the same as those described in this section for real exports and imports. This finding probably results from the fact that inflation rates were very low in this period.
2. France, with decisively lower exports and imports, has a slight increase in its estimated growth rate of national product. Note that Germany is not included in these comparisons because of the lack of early data.
3. For the nine cases in Table 8.3 that produced a Dickey–Fuller test statistic that was not significant at the 5 per cent level, eight of them continued to show no unit root with the Augmented Dickey–Fuller test (indicated by an asterisk in the table); the one that did was the Swedish result for imports (1873–1913) at three lags. The implications are that cointegration tests would have to exclude these eight cases – and so they do in what follows – and that Granger-causality and correlation tests should be performed in first differences. (See the discussion in the Technical Appendix for an explanation of the procedure employed here.)

4. Note also that import correlations are generally higher than export. This result could be caused by the import data being measured more accurately, as they almost surely are; that is, the difference is the result of the fact that the two series are not comparable. In any case, the import series is the appropriate benchmark here, we think.
5. Ashworth suggests that, even by 1914, British overseas lending was at least 50 per cent of the world total.
6. The growth rates are estimated by a regression of log x on trend. Note that the French investment data are nominal.
7. This occurs in the well-known Harrod–Domar growth model, for example; see the discussion in Fisher (1992).
8. Tests for cointegrating hyper-planes among these variables, involving three or more countries at once, were also unsuccessful.
9. Degrees of freedom problems, already severe, inhibit testing of this sort, in any case.

9 The European Trade Cycle, 1850–1913

1. The material in this section updates an earlier study by Craig and Fisher (1992).
2. Note that both industrial production and agricultural production, by themselves, show greater variances than national product in most countries. This situation results partly, from the shocks in these (individual) sectors having different timing. But more important, we think, is the stabilizing behaviour of the large service and 'other' sectors of these countries.
3. Note that we are omitting any reference to monetary factors. We believe that the relationship between money and the real economy is too weak in this period to provide any clear assistance to our task. There is some discussion of this relationship at various points in this study, notably in Chapters 6 and 7. Note that this is also the view of Capie and Mills (1991).
4. The particular domestic event here is the effect of the Freycinet construction plan (of 1878) for railways that might have set off an echoing boom in other kinds of construction, and in municipal schemes. Cancelled projects and vacancies appeared in the wake of the 1882 financial collapse. This, by itself, is not proof, since modern cycles typically exhibit such symptoms, but it is suggestive, none the less, of how complicated the situation becomes, once an economy modernizes.
5. Kitchen is aware that real indices do not support the idea of a Great Depression, as we have already noted. He prefers, though, to emphasize individual product prices and what he calls a 'psychological depression' (Kitchen, 1978, p. 161).
6. Note that the employment data go back to the beginning of the period but are very clearly interpolated over more than one year until the late 1870s. These employment data include at least some of the unemployed. The unemployment figures for 1887–1902 are averages of two figures provided.
7. We have obtained the agricultural statistics from Hoffmann (1965). They are not further described in the text.
8. The outlines of Clough's short cycles between 1873 and 1896 are hard to see because of his evident belief in the existence of a Great Depression over that

period. Like many early writers on the subject, he exhibits a tendency to confuse nominal with real events in this context.
9. There were also sharp declines in exports in 1860–1, 1880–1, 1893–4, 1897–8 and 1903–4. None of these appears to be associated with Swedish downturns, however.
10. The latter result is not really credible, but there is only one year of decline in the entire run of Belgian data (in 1875)!
11. For example, the United Kingdom and Germany were the two largest trading partners of France by 1910. The United Kingdom was the largest trading partner of Germany, and only Russia and the Austro-Hungarian empire had more trade with Germany than did France. After the United States, Germany and France were the largest trading partners of the United Kingdom.

10 The Integration of the European Economy by 1913

1. Note that we are using per capita data where possible, in order to neutralize the effects of population on our calculations.
2. The normalization converts each series into an index number, with unity at the point of the mean. For most of these countries this was in the decade of the 1880s.
3. All series are the same as were used in Chapter 9 and are described briefly there and in more detail in the Data Appendix. The following graphs for per capita real exports and imports are also based on the data used and described in Chapter 9.
4. We shall not look at imports here, since they show pretty much the same story (and were studied in detail in Chapter 8).
5. Recall that in Chapters 8 and 9 we conducted Granger-causality tests that demonstrated statistically significant lags in the Granger-effect of one country's real activity on another's.

Technical Appendix

Preliminary note This Appendix is arranged logically, beginning with time series methods, rather than alphabetically.

Stationarity and unit root tests

A major issue concerns whether or not the data are stationary. The concern is, in fact, whether the 'process' that drives the data is stationary (because, if not, it will tend to produce non-stationary patterns in the data) but the tests are, of course, on the data themselves. A *stationary* series of the variable x_t has a constant mean, finite variance and

$$COV(x_t, x_{t-k}) = \mu_k$$

for all k; this would be violated (be *non-stationary*) if

$$COV(x_t, x_{t-k}) = \mu_{k,t}.$$

In particular, dependence on 'time' of the autocorrelations in the series in question yields non-stationarity. Usually, trend in the basic series (or in its variance) is the probable direct cause of non-stationarity in economic time series (although seasonal factors are also relevant in this context). Since many macroeconomic time series exhibit trends, clearly we could prejudice a test involving several of these series if, at the same time, the trend were not an integral part of the hypothesis. Indeed, it is usually population growth that is the suspected cause of the dependence of macro variables on trend.

A widely-used test to detect stationarity is explained by Engle and Granger (1987); this is the Augmented Dickey–Fuller test. This involves testing the null hypothesis that $\theta = 0$ (that is, non-stationarity) in the following equation:

$$\Delta x_t = \alpha + \theta x_{t-1} + \sum_{i=1}^{p} \beta_i \Delta x_{t-i} + \delta T + U_t$$

Here, p is the number of lagged dependent variables and T is a trend. The general idea is that one must rule out firmly the possibility of a unit root (arbitrarily at a probability of 0.05 or better) to avoid compromising any tests (such as the F-test) that would be unreliable in the presence of unit roots; the basic statistical problem is inconsistency. Note that for $p = 0$ we have the Dickey–Fuller test.

The Augmented Dickey–Fuller test requires the a priori specification of the number of lags of the dependent variable on the right-hand side of the Dickey–Fuller equation just given. In order to determine the optimal number of lags, we employed a procedure suggested by Hall (1994), who shows that after specifying the initial lag length, the coefficient on the last lag should be tested for statistical significance. If one cannot reject the null hypothesis that the coefficient is zero, then that lag is dropped and the model estimated again. This procedure is repeated until either a statistically significant lagged coefficient is obtained, or the lags are exhausted. Unfortunately, neither statistics nor econometrics offers a guide for the initial specification of lag lengths; so economics must guide us. Because we use annual data exclusively in this volume, and because the real cycles typically do not last more than a few years, we used five years as the initial lag length.

Cointegration tests

The cointegration tests involve a two-stage process. First, the time series must be tested for unit roots. If the levels contain unit roots, then the first differences may be used, but these must be free of unit roots. The original series are said to be *integrated*. If the residuals from the regression of one unit-root process on another are stationary, then the original series are said to be *cointegrated*. It is important to note that the residuals from a regression involving the non-stationary series must be stationary; otherwise, the cointegration hypothesis is rejected. The specific procedure is to examine the errors of two non-stationary series by means of the Augmented Dickey–Fuller test. Should the residuals prove to be stationary, then cointegration is established. An excellent discussion of unit roots, cointegration and mean reversion appears in Dickey, Jansen and Thornton (1991).

Mean reversion

The following univariate time-series equation enables us to describe the concept of mean reversion:

$$y_t - \mu = \alpha(y_{t-1} - \mu) + e_t$$

Here, y_t is a univariate time series, μ is the series' mean, and e_t is a random error (with an expected value of zero and a finite variance). The coefficient α

measures the degree of persistence of deviations of y_t from μ. When $\alpha = 1$, the deviations are permanent, and y_t follows a random walk (that is, y_t can wander arbitrarily far from any given constant if enough time passes). In this case, the variance of y_t approaches infinity as t increases. When $|\alpha| < 1$, on the other hand, the series is 'mean reverting' and the variance of y_t is finite. Again, for readers interested in a detailed explanation we suggest Dickey, Jansen and Thornton (1991).

Autoregressive and moving average processes

If an economic time series can be represented by a moving average of order one (MA(1)), then it can be written as the following, where e_t is white noise:

$$y_t = e_t + \beta e_{t-1}$$

For a non-zero value of β, this successful estimation of a moving average parameter will smooth the original series. Indeed, according to Wold's Theorem, any stationary time series can be described by a deterministic part and by a moving average component (series) of possibly infinite order. Without the deterministic part, a moving average of order q is given by:

$$y_t = e_t + \beta_1 e_{t-1} + \beta_2 e_{t-2} + \ldots = \sum_{i=0}^{q} \beta_i e_{t-i}$$

This is a useful fact if the q required is quite small (since moving average processes are difficult to estimate) because it provides a possible decomposition of the data into a deterministic (permanent) and a stochastic (transitory) part.

If an economic time series depends on its own past values, as is frequently claimed to be the case for data generated under rational expectations, then it might be represented as an auto-regressive process of order one (AR(1)) as in:

$$y_t = \delta_1 y_{t-1} + e_t$$

Again, e_t is white noise. Many economic time series are at least AR(1) and, as we have seen, the estimates of the demand for money presented in this study had AR processes up to AR(3). The generalization of this equation is the following:

$$y_t = \delta_1 y_{t-1} + \delta_2 y_{t-2} + \ldots + e_t = \sum_{i=1}^{p} \delta_i y_{t-i} + e_t$$

where the AR process is of order p. Indeed, and even more generally, both processes can occur together, as in the ARMA(p, q) model of:

$$y_t = \sum_{i=1}^{p} \delta_i y_{t-i} + \sum_{j=0}^{q} \beta_j e_{t-j}$$

where, as before, e_t is white noise. Even more generally, it is possible to have an ARIMA process driving the data, where the differences of the data (of order n) are taken. This would be denoted as ARIMA (p, n, q) where n is the number of times the data are differenced. In the literature, n is also referred to as the 'degree of integration'.

In order to identify a model for a time series, one thing that can be done is to look at the autocorrelation and the partial autocorrelation functions. What we are looking for is explained in the following summary:

	MA(q)	AR(p)	ARMA(p, q)	White noise
Autocorrelation function	$D(q)$	T	T	0
Partial autocorrelation	T	$D(p)$	T	0

Here, for example, $D(q)$ means that the function drops off after lag q; T in the first column means that it tails off exponentially after a lag of q; and 0 in the last column means that the function is zero at all non-zero lags. The autocorrelation records the correlation between the error at t and $t-i$, while the partial autocorrelation is the correlation between successive error terms.

Granger-causality tests

A way to proceed to explore the interaction between two variables is to employ a test of Granger-causality to search for signs of one-way or bidirectional 'causation' among the nominal variables being considered. The test itself considers the distinct influence of lagged values of the independent variable (the proposed 'causal' variable) and so it is, strictly, a test of what is often called the 'temporal ordering' of the data. The procedure is to regress a variable in which we are interested – let us say the British money supply – on its own lags and on the lags of another potential causal variable – say, the

French money supply. If the lags of the other variable adds significantly to the explanation of the dependent variable, then it is said to Granger-cause that variable. The model used in this exercise is:

$$\ln y_t = \alpha + \sum_{i=1}^{p} \beta_i \ln y_{t-i} + \sum_{i=1}^{p} \delta i \ln x_{t-i}$$

where p is the arbitrary length of the lag. It is assumed to be the same for each variable in these tests, although procedures exist for searching for optimal lags (see Akaike (1970)). The statistical test, an F-test, is used to see whether the exclusion of all of the x terms in this equation would significantly reduce the explanatory power of the regression. Conventionally, we have argued in this study that Granger-causation is established if the probability that the proposed causal agent is not influential is 0.05 or less.

The use of the F-test requires that the residuals from each of the regressions be 'white noise'. Differencing, as discussed above, provides this in general for the variables we have studied, although we should emphasize that with as few as 43 observations, the asymptotic theory that supports such claims is not available. We should also note that the Granger test does not test for coincident causation (a serious concern for annual data such as these). In addition, a lagged variable may actually be responding to the expectations of economic agents concerning the future variable; in this case, the future variable is causing the lag, and not the reverse, although the test used here could (incorrectly) show significant Granger-causality. There are, of course, potential omitted variables in such tests.

Recursive residuals tests

If we regress y_{t-1} on x_{t-1}, then the resulting coefficient matrix is b_{t-1}. This vector of coefficients can be used to generate forecasts of y_t, the value of the dependent variable in time t. This forecast is $x'_t b_{t-1}$, where x'_t is the row vector of observations on the regression in period t. The recursive residual, then is defined as follows:

$$w_t = \frac{y_t - x'_t b_{t-1}}{\sqrt{1 + x'_t (X'_{t-1} X_{t-1})^{-1} x_t}}$$

Here, the numerator is the forecasting error while the denominator is the standard error of the forecast error.

The residuals are then computed for all feasible t that the data permit. If the underlying model is such that its residuals have zero mean and a finite variance, then the recursive residuals will be independently and normally distributed with zero mean and constant variance (= the variance of the residuals of the original equation). See the discussion of this and the other tests about to be described in Hall, Johnston and Lilien (1990).

The CUSUM test plots the cumulative sum of recursive residuals against two lines that represent a confidence interval (at the 5 per cent level) around the residuals; should the plot lie outside these lines, then one can claim instability for those observations at (at least) the 5 per cent level. The formula for the CUSUM plot for a model without AR terms is:

$$W_p = \frac{1}{\sigma} \sum_{i=k+1}^{p} v_i \qquad p = k+1, k+2, \ldots n$$

Here, σ is the standard error of the regression, and the v_i are the residuals from the original regression. The formula for the straight lines establishing the 5 per cent confidence interval around this plot (of W_p) is:

$$W = \pm \left[0.948\sqrt{n-k} + 1.896 \frac{(p-k)}{\sqrt{n-k}} \right]$$

A second test involving the variables used in this study is the CUSUM-Square test, which works with the cumulative sum of squared residuals. The formula for this model is:

$$WW_p = \frac{\sum_{i=k+1}^{p} v_i^2}{\sum_{i=k+1}^{n} v_i^2} \qquad p = k+1, k+2, \ldots n$$

Again, one plots two lines for an arbitrary confidence interval which is, in this case, 5 per cent. The line in this case is:

$$WW = \pm a_0 + \frac{p-k}{n-k} \qquad p = k+1, k+2, \ldots, n$$

See Harvey (1981) for further explanation.

A more familiar test to some users is the Chow (1960) analysis of variance test for structural instability. This test also gives us a method for probing for the breaking point (if such is established) by searching over all possible splits for the highest F-value produced by the test. The test essentially looks for equality of coefficients between two periods, conditional on having the two variances equal. Specifically, for any two subperiods it tests the null hypothesis that the difference between the residual sum of squares from the pooled period and the sum of the residual sum of squares from the two separate periods (adjusted for degrees of freedom) is zero. A 'large' F-statistic would mean that one should reject the hypothesis that the two subperiods are the same.

Data Appendix

Bank deposits

Most of the series used for bank deposits were drawn from Mitchell (1992); these were for Belgium, Denmark, Germany, Norway, Spain and the United Kingdom. The deposits for Austria came from Komlos (1983), those for Italy from Fratianni and Spinelli (1984) and those for Sweden from Jonung (1975).

Consumer prices

Cost of living (consumer price) indices were obtained from the following sources. The data for Austria-Hungary were provided by Komlos (see 1990). For Belgium, Germany, Sweden and the United Kingdom they are drawn from Mitchell (1992). For France they are from Levy-Leboyer/Bourguignon (1990), for Italy from Fratianni and Spinelli (1984), for the Netherlands from van Stuijvenberg and de Vrijer (1982), and for the United States they appear in Wilson (1993). The Norwegian consumer price level was provided by Backus, as used in Backus and Kehoe (1992); the original source of these data was Michael Bordo. The Danish numbers are the result of combining a series from Maddison (1982) and Hansen (1974). Finally, the Portuguese data are drawn from Nunes, Mata and Valerio (1989); all but the 1913 observation are from a single series of the 'cost of living'.

Exports and imports

Both imports and exports are provided in nominal form in Mitchell (1978) for most of the series used in this study. These are for Austria-Hungary, Belgium, Denmark, France, Germany, Italy, the Netherlands, Norway, Spain, Sweden and the United Kingdom. The Portuguese figures come from Nunes, Mata and Valerio (1989). The US figures are from United States Department of Commerce (1975).

Industrial production indices

The industrial production indices for several of the countries studied come from Mitchell (1978, 1992); these are for Germany, Italy, Sweden and the

United Kingdom. An industrial production index for Austria-Hungary was constructed from data provided in Komlos (1983). The French index comes from Toutain (1987), while the Spanish index appears in Carreras (1987). The US index comes from Miron and Romer (1990).

Interest rates

The long-term rates are as follows: Belgium, 2 1/2% Rentes (Homer, 1977); France, long rate on Paris (Levy-Leboyer/Bourguignon (1990); Germany, long rate (Homer, 1977); Italy, long rate (Fratianni and Spinelli (1984); Netherlands, 2 1/2% Perpetual Governments (Homer, 1977); Norway, long rate (Bordo and Jonung worksheets, 1987); Sweden, long rate (Bordo and Jonung worksheets, 1987); United Kingdom, Consol (Capie and Webber, 1985); and United States, corporate bond rate (Friedman and Schwartz, 1982).

The short-term rates are as follows. The French rate is a short-term rate for Paris, from Levy-Leboyer/Bourguignon (1990); the German rate is an open market discount rate from Homer (1977), as is the Netherlands' rate; the rate for the United Kingdom is 'on call' money, taken from Capie and Webber (1985); and the United States rate is that on commercial paper, as calculated by Friedman and Schwartz (1982).

Investment

The data on investment for Denmark, Germany, Norway and the United Kingdom come from Mitchell (1978). For France, they come from Levy-Leboyer/Bourguignon (1990); for Italy from ISTAT (1957); and for Sweden from Krantz and Nilsson (1975). Note that the French figures are nominal rather than real.

Money

The monetary data employed here are measures of broad money. For Austria-Hungary they come from Komlos (1987). For Denmark, they were provided by Backus, as given in the worksheets of Bordo and Jonung (1987). Saint Marc (1983) is the source of the French data; the German data are from Sprenger (1982); and the Italian data come from Fratianni and Spinelli (1984). J. T. Klovland kindly provided the Norwegian data, as used in his 1983 paper; the Spanish money supply was taken from Acena (1990); Jonung (1975) is the source of the Swedish money stock data; The UK money stock data were drawn from Capie and Webber (1985); and the US data come from Friedman and Schwartz (1982).

National product

Real gross national product for Austria-Hungary comes from Komlos (1987). For Belgium and Denmark the measure is gross domestic product, and are drawn from Maddison (1991) and Hansen (1974) respectively. For France, the measure of gross domestic product comes from Toutain (1987). Italian gross national product comes from Fratianni and Spinelli (1984); the original source of these data is ISTAT (1957). German and Norwegian real gross domestic product data come from Mitchell (1978); Portuguese gross domestic product comes from Nunes *et al.* (1989); Spanish gross national product estimates were derived from Molinas and Prados de la Escosura (1989); the Swedish series used is that for real domestic product as it appears in Krantz and Nilsson (1975). For the United Kingdom, we used the gross national product series in Mitchell (1978); this series was derived from Feinstein (1972). For the United States, we used the GNP estimates of Balke and Gordon (1989). The Netherlands national income comes from van Stuijenberg and de Vrijer (1982).

Population

A number of annual population estimates were taken from Maddison (1982, 1991); these were for Austria-Hungary, Belgium and Italy; Population for Denmark comes from Hansen (1974); French population is taken from Toutain (1987); German population comes from Hoffman (1965); the population data for the Netherlands are from van Stuijvenberg and de Vrijer (1982); Norwegian population estimates come from Mitchell (1992); Portugal's population is drawn from Nunes, Mata and Valerio (1989); the Swedish population was derived from estimates of per capita real domestic product in Krantz and Nilsson (1975); for the United Kingdom and Spain, we obtained the data in Mitchell (1992); and Friedman and Schwartz (1982) was the source of the population data for the United States.

Price deflators

For Denmark, the GDP deflator was taken from Hansen (1974); For France, the GDP deflator came from Toutain (1987). For Germany we used the NNP deflator from Mitchell (1978); while for Italy, the GNP deflator came from Fratianni and Spinelli (1984). For Norway, the GDP deflator came from Mitchell (1978); for Portugal, the GDP deflator came from Nunes, Mata and

Valerio (1989); and for Sweden, the RDP deflator was derived from Krantz and Nilsson (1975). For the United Kingdom, the GDP deflator used was from Solomou and Weale (1991); while for the United States, we used the GNP deflator of Balke and Gordon (1989).

Wholesale prices

The wholesale price data employed here come from the following sources. For Austria-Hungary, Belgium, France, Germany, Spain, Sweden, Switzerland and the United Kingdom, they are from Mitchell (1978). For Italy, they are from Fratianni and Spinelli (1984); and for the Netherlands they are from van Stuijvenberg and de Vrijer (1982). For the United States we spliced (at 1890) the wholesale price indices given in the *Historical Statistics of the United States*.

Bibliography

Abramovitz, M. (1986) 'Catching Up, Forging Ahead, and Falling Behind', *Journal of Economic History,* June.
Acena, P. M. (1990) 'The Spanish Money Supply, 1874–1935', *Journal of European Economic History,* Spring.
Akaike, H. (1970) 'Statistical Predictor Identification', *Annals of the Institute of Statistical Mathematics,* vol 22.
Aldcroft, D. H. and P. Fearon (1972) *British Economic Fluctuations, 1790–1939* (London: Macmillan).
Anes, R. (1974) 'El Banco de Espana (1874–1914): un banco nacional', in P. Schwartz and G. Tortella (ed), *La Banca Espanola en la Restauracion* (Madrid: Servicio de Estudios del Banco de Espana).
Ashworth, W. (1987) *A Short History of the International Economy since 1850,* 4th edn (London: Longman).
Backus, D. K. and P. J. Kehoe (1992) 'International Evidence on the Historical Properties of Business Cycles', *American Economic Review,* September.
Bagehot, W. (1873) *Lombard Street* (New York: Scribner, Armstrong).
Balke, N. S. and R. J. Gordon (1989) 'The Estimation of Prewar Gross National Product: Methodology and New Evidence', *Journal of Political Economy,* January.
Barnett, W. A., D. Fisher and A. Serletis (1992) 'Consumer Theory and the Demand for Money', *Journal of Economic Literature,* December.
Barro, R. J. (1979) 'Money and the Price Level under the Gold Standard', *Economic Journal,* March.
Barro, R. J. and X. Sala-i-Martin (1992) 'Convergence', *Journal of Political Economy,* April.
Berend, I. and G. Ranki (1974) *Economic Development in East–Central Europe in the 19th & 20th Centuries* (New York: Columbia University Press).
Berry, B. J. L. and F. E. Horton (1970) *Geographic Perspectives on Urban Systems* (Englewood Cliffs, NJ: Prentice-Hall).
Bloomfield, A. I. (1959) *Monetary Policy under the International Gold Standard, 1880–1914* (New York: Federal Reserve Bank of New York).
Borchardt, K. (1976) 'The Industrial Revolution in Germany, 1700–1914', in C. Cipolla (ed.), *The Emergence of Industrial Societies* (New York: Barnes and Noble).
Bordo, M. D. (1986) 'Explorations in Monetary History: A Survey of the Literature', National Bureau of Economic Research, Working Paper No. 1821, January.
Bordo, M. D. and L. Jonung (1987) *The Long-run Behavior of the Velocity of Circulation: The International Evidence* (Cambridge, Mass:. Harvard University Press).
Bordo, M. D. and A. J. Schwartz (1981) 'Money and Prices in the Nineteenth Century: An Old Debate Rejoined', *Journal of Economic History,* March.

Bordo, M. D. and A. J. Schwartz (1994) 'The Specie Standard as a Contingent Rule: Some Evidence for Core and Peripheral Countries, 1880–1990', National Bureau of Economic Research, Working Paper No. 4860.

Boserup, E. (1965) *Conditions of Agricultural Growth* (London: George Allen & Unwin).

Boserup, E. (1981) *Population and Technological Change* (Chicago: University of Chicago Press).

Brillembourg, A. and M. Khan (1979) 'The Relationship between Money, Income, and Prices: Has Money Mattered Historically?' *Journal of Money, Credit and Banking*, August.

Cafagna, L. (1976) 'The Industrial Revolution in Italy, 1830–1914', in C. Cipolla (ed.), *The Emergence of Industrial Societies* (New York: Barnes and Noble).

Cagan, P. (1965) *Determinants and Effects of Changes in the Money Stock, 1875–1960* (New York: Columbia University Press).

Cairncross, A. K. (1953) *Home and Foreign Investments, 1870–1913* (Cambridge University Press).

Calliari, S., F. Spinelli and G. Verga (1984) 'Money Demand in Italy: A Few More Results', *Manchester School*, June.

Cameron, R. E. (1961) *France and the Economic Development of Europe, 1800–1914* (Chicago: Rand McNally).

Cameron, R. E. (1967a) 'England' in R. Cameron (ed.), *Banking in the Early Stages of Industrialization* (New York: Oxford University Press).

Cameron, R. E. (1967b) 'France' in R. Cameron (ed.), *Banking in the Early Stages of Industrialization* (New York: Oxford University Press).

Cameron, R. E. (1967) 'Belgium' in R. Cameron (ed.), *Banking in the Early Stages of Industrialization* (New York: Oxford University Press).

Cameron, R. E. (1972) *Banking and Economic Development: Some Lessons of History* (New York: Oxford University Press).

Canzoneri, M. B. and C. A. Rogers (1990) 'Is the European Community an Optimal Currency Area? Optimal Taxation Versus the Cost of Multiple Currencies', *American Economic Review*, June.

Capie, F. H. (1992) 'British Economic Fluctuations in the Nineteenth Century: Is There a Role for Money?' in S. N. Broadberry and N. F. R. Crafts (eds), *Britain in the International Economy* (Cambridge University Press).

Capie, F. H. and T. C. Mills (1991) 'Money and Business Cycles in the U.S. and U.K., 1870–1913', *Manchester School* (V. 59, Supplement).

Capie, F. H. and G. Rodrik-Bali (1985) 'The Money Adjustment Process in the United Kingdom, 1870–1914,: *Economica*, February.

Capie, F. H. and A. Webber (1985) *A Monetary History of the United Kingdom*, vol. I (London: Allen & Unwin).

Capie, F. H. and G. E. Wood (1994) 'Money in the Economy, 1870–1939', in R. Floud and D. McCloskey (eds), *The Economic History of Britain since 1700*, 2nd edn. (Cambridge University Press).

Capie, F. H., T. C. Mills, and G. E. Wood (1991) 'Money, Interest Rates and the Great Depression: Britain from 1870 to 1913', in J. Foreman-Peck (ed.), *New Perspectives on the Late Vitorian Economy* (Cambridge University Press).

Caron, F. (1979) *An Economic History of Modern France* (New York: Columbia University Press).

Carreras, A. (1987) 'An Annual Index of Spanish Industrial Output', in N. Sanchez-Albornoz (ed.), *The Economic Modernization of Spain, 1830–1930* (New York: New York University Press).
Chandler, A. (1994) *Scale and Scope: The Dynamics of Industrial Capitalism* (Cambridge, Mass.: Harvard University Press).
Chow, G. C. (1960) 'Tests of Equality Between Sets of Coefficients in Two Linear Regressions', *Econometrica*, July.
Church, R. A. (1975) *The Great Victorian Boom, 1850–1873* (London: Macmillan).
Clark, T. A. (1984) 'Violations of the Gold Points, 1890–1908', *Journal of Political Economy*, October.
Clough, S. B. (1964) *The Economic History of Modern Italy* (New York: Columbia University Press).
Cohen, J. S. (1967) 'Financing Industrialization in Italy, 1894–1914: The Partial Transformantion of a Late-Comer', *Journal of Economic History*, September.
Cohen, J. S. (1972) 'Italy, 1861–1914', in R. Cameron (ed.), *Banking and Economic Development: Some Lessons of History* (New York: Oxford University Press).
Collins, M. (1983) 'Long-Term Growth of the English Banking Sector and Money Stock, 1844–80', *Economic History Review*, August.
Collins, M. (1989) 'The Banking Crisis of 1878', *Economic History Review*, November.
Coppock, D. J. (1972) 'The Causes of Business Fluctuations', in D. H. Aldcroft and P. Fearon (eds), *British Economic Fluctuations, 1790–1939* (London: Macmillan).
Cottrell, P. L. (1991) 'Great Britain', in R. E. Cameron and V. I. Bovykin (eds), *International Banking, 1870–1914* (New York: Oxford University Press).
Crafts, N. F. R. (1977) 'Industrial Revolution in Britain and France: Some Thoughts on the Question "Why was England First?"' *Economic History Review*, August.
Crafts, N. F. R. (1985) *British Economic Growth During the Industrial Revolution* (New York: Oxford University Press).
Crafts, N. F. R., S. J. Leybourne and T. C. Mills (1989) 'Trends and Cycles in British Industrial Production, 1700–1913', *Journal of the Royal Statistical Society (A)* (Part I).
Craig, L. A. and D. Fisher (1992) 'Integration of the European Business Cycle, 1871–1910', *Explorations in Economic History*, April.
Craig, L. A., D. Fisher, and T. A. Spencer (1995) 'Inflation and Money Growth under the International Gold Standard, 1850–1913', *Journal of Macroeconomics*, Spring.
Dickey, D. A. and R. J. Rossana (1990) 'Cointegrated Time Series: A Guide to Estimation and Hypothesis Testing', mimeo, North Carolina State University, Raleigh, North Carolina.
Dickey, D. A., D. W. Jansen and D. L. Thornton (1991) 'A Primer on Cointegration with an Application to Money and Income', *Review*, Federal Reserve Bank of St. Louis, March/April.
Dowd, K. (1989) 'The Evolution of Central Banking in England, 1821–1890', mimeo, University of Nottingham.
Dutton, J. (1984) 'The Bank of England and the Rules of the Game under the International Gold Standard: New Evidence', in M. D. Bordo and A. J. Schwartz (eds), *A Retrospective on the Classical Gold Standard, 1821–1931* (Chicago: University of Chicago Press).

Dwyer, G. (1983) 'Money, Income, and Prices in the United Kingdom, 1870–1913', mimeo, Emory University Altanta, Georgia.

Easton, S. T. (1984) 'Real Output and the Gold Standard Years, 1830–1913', in Michael D. Bordo and Anna J. Schwartz (eds), *A Retrospective on the Classical Gold Standard, 1821–1931* (Chicago: University of Chicago Press).

Edison, H. J. (1987) 'Purchasing Power Parity in the Long Run: A Test of the Dollar/Pound Exchange Rate', *Journal of Money, Credit, and Banking,* August.

Egge, A. (1983) 'Transformation of Bank Structures in the Industrial Period: The Case of Norway, 1830–1914'. *Journal of European Economic History,* Fall.

Eichengreen, B. (1983) 'The Causes of British Business Cycles, 1833–1913', *Journal of European Economic History,* Spring.

Engle, R. F. and C. W. J. Granger (1987) 'Co-Integration and Error Correction: Representation, Estimation, and Testing', *Econometrica,* March.

Feinstein, C. H. (1972) *National Income Expenditure and Output of the United Kingdom, 1855–1965* (Cambridge University Press).

Feinstein, C. H. (1981) 'Capital Accumulation and the Industrial Revolution', in R. Floud and D. N. McCloskey (eds), *The Economic History of Britain Since 1700,* vol. 1 (Cambridge University Press).

Feinstein, C. H. (1988) 'National Statistics, 1760–1920', in C. H. Feinstein and S. Pollard (eds), *Studies in Capital Formation in the United Kingdom, 1750–1920* (Oxford: Clarendon Press).

Fenoaltea, S. (1988) 'International Resource Flows and Construction Movements in the Atlantic Economy: The Kuznets Cycle in Italy, 1861–1913', *Journal of Economic History,* September.

Fisher, D. (1989) *Money Demand and Monetary Policy* (London: Harvester Wheatsheaf).

Fisher, D. (1992) *The Industrial Revolution, A Macroeconomic Interpretation* (London: Macmillan).

Fisher, D. and W. N. Thurman (1989) 'Sweden's Financial Sophistication in the Nineteenth Century: An Appraisal', *Journal of Economic History,* September.

Floud, R., K. Wachter and A. Gregory (1990) *Height, Health, and History: Nutritional Status in the United Kingdom, 1750–1980* (Cambridge University Press).

Ford, A. G. (1981) 'The Trade Cycle in Britain, 1860–1914', in R. C. Floud and D. N. McCloskey (eds), *The Economic History of Britain since 1700,* vol. 2 (Cambridge University Press).

Fratianni, M. and F. Spinelli (1984) 'Italy in the Gold Standard Period, 1861–1914', in M. D. Bordo and A. J. Schwartz (eds), *A Retrospective on the Classical Gold Standard* (Chicago: University of Chicago Press).

Frederico, G. and G. Toniolo (1991) 'Italy', in R. Sylla and G. Toniolo (eds), *Patterns of European Industrialization: The Nineteenth Century* (London: Routledge).

Friedman, D. (1977) 'A Theory of the Size and Shape of Nations', *Journal of Political Economy,* February.

Friedman, M. (1956) 'The Quantity Theory of Money, A Restatement', in M. Friedman (ed.), *Studies in the Quantity Theory of Money* (Chicago: University of Chicago Press).

Friedman, M. (1990) 'Bimetallism Revisited', *Journal of Economic Perspectives,* Fall.

Bibliography

Friedman, M. and A. J. Schwartz (1982) *Monetary Trends in the United States and the United Kingdom, 1867–1975* (Chicago: University of Chicago Press).
Gerschenkron, A. (1962) *Economic Backwardness in Historical Perspective* (Cambridge, Mass.: Harvard University Press).
Gerschenkron, A. (1970) *Europe in a Russian Mirror, Four Lectures in Economic History* (Cambridge University Press).
Goldsmith, R. (1969) *Financial Structure and Development* (New Haven, Conn.: Yale University Press).
Good, D. (1974) 'Stagnation and "Take-off" in Austria, 1873–1913', *Economic History Review* (Feb.).
Good, D. (1978) 'The Great Depression and Austrian Growth After 1873', *Economic History Review* (May).
Goodhart, C. A. E. (1972) *The Business of Banking, 1891–1914* (Aldershot: Gower).
Goodhart, C. A. E. (1984) 'Comment', in Michael D. Bordo and Anna J. Schwartz (eds), *A Retrospective on the Classical Gold Standard, 1821–1931* (Chicago: University of Chicago Press).
Goodwin, B. K. and T. J. Grennes (1994) 'Real Interest Rate Equalization and the Integration of International Financial Markets', *Journal of International Money and Finance* (Feb.).
Graham, M. K. (1925) *An Essay on Gold* (Dallas: Hargreaves Printing Co.).
Hall, A. (1994) 'Testing for a Unit Root in Time Series with Pretest Data Based Model Selection', *Journal of Business and Economic Statistics* (Oct.).
Hall, R. E., J. Johnston and D. M. Lilien (1990) *Micro–TSP User's Manual* (Irvine, Calife.: Quantitative Micro Software).
Hansen, S. A. (1974) *Okonomisk Vaekst i Danmark* (Bind II), no. 6 (Copenhagen: University of Copenhagen, Institute for Economic History).
Hansen, S. A. (1982) 'The Transformation of Bank Structures in the Industrial Period: The Case of Denmark', *Journal of European Economic History*, Winter.
Harvey, A. C. (1981) *The Econometric Analysis of Time Series* (London: Phillip Allen).
Hatton, T. J. (1992) 'Price Determination under the Gold Standard: Britain, 1880–1913', in S. N. Broadberry and N. F. R. Crafts (eds), *Britain in the International Economy* (Cambridge University Press).
Hatton, T. J. and J. G. Williamson (1992) 'What Drove the Mass Migrations from Europe in the Late Nineteenth Century?' NBER Working Papers, Historical Paper No. 43.
Hawtrey, R. G. (1931) *The Gold Standard in Theory and Practice* (London: Longmans, Green and Co.).
Heckscher, E. F. (1935) *Mercantilism* (London: G. Allen).
Heckscher, E. F. (1963) *An Economic History of Sweden* (Cambridge, Mass.: Harvard University Press).
Henderson, W. O. (1961) *The Industrial Revolution on the Continent* (London: Frank Cass).
Henderson, W. O. (1975) *The Rise of German Industrial Power, 1834–1914* (Berkeley, Calif.: University of California Press).
Hendry, D. F. (1979) 'Predictive Failure and Econometric Modelling in Macro-Economics: The Transactions Demand for Money', in P. Ormerud (ed.), *Econometric Modelling* (London: Heinemann).

Hendry, D. F and N. R. Ericsson (1991) 'An Econometric Analysis of U.K. Money Demand in *Monetary Trends in the United States and the United Kingdom* by Milton Friedman and Anna J. Schwartz', *American Economic Review*, May.

Hinderliter, R. H. and H. Rockoff (1976) 'Banking under the Gold Standard: An analysis of Liquidity Management in the Leading Financial Centers', *Journal of Economic History*, June.

Hoffmann, W. G. (1965) *Das Wachstum der Deutschen Wirtschaft seit der Mitte des 19 Jahrhunderts* (Berlin: Springer-Verlag).

Homer, S. (1977), *The History of Interest Rates* (New Brunswick, NJ: Rutgers University Press).

Huck, P. F. (1992) 'Infant Mortality and the Standard of Living During the Industrial Revolution', Unpublished Ph.D. dissertation, Northwestern University Evanston, Illinois.

Huffman, W. E. and J. R. Lothian (1980) 'Money in the United Kingdom, 1833–80', *Journal of Money, Credit, and Banking*, May.

Huffman, W. E. and J. R. Lothian (1984) 'The Gold Standard and the Transmission of Business Cycles, 1833–1932, in M. D. Bordo and A. J. Schwartz (eds), *A Retrospective on the Classical Gold Standard* (Chicago: University of Chicago Press).

Hughes, J. R. T. (1983) *American Economic History* (Glenview, ILL.: Scott, Foresman and Co.).

Hughes, J. R. T. (1986) *The Vital Few: The Entrepreneur and American Economic Progress* (New York: Oxford University Press).

Hutchinson, W. (1992) 'Regional Specialization and Growth: The U.S., 1870–1910', mimeo, Miami University.

ISTAT (1957) *Indagine Statistica Sullo Sviluppo del Reddito Nazionale dell'Italia del 1861 al 1956*, Annali de Statistica Serie 8, vol. 9 (Rome: Instituto Poligrafica di Stato).

Johansen, H. C. (1991) 'Banking and Finance in the Danish Economy', in R. Cameron and V. I. Bovykin (eds), *International Banking, 1870–1914* (New York: Oxford University Press).

Johnston, J. (1984) *Econometric Methods*, 3rd edn (New York: McGraw-Hill).

Jonung, L. (1975) *Studies in the Monetary History of Sweden*, Ph.D. dissertation, University of California (Los Angeles).

Jonung, L. (1976) 'Sources of Growth in the Swedish Money Stock, 1871–1913', *Scandinavian Journal of Economics*, vol. 78.

Jonung, L. (1978) 'The Long-Run Demand for Money – A Wicksellian Approach', *Scandinavian Journal of Economics*, No. 2.

Jonung, L. (1984) 'Swedish Experience under the Classical Gold Standard, 1873–1914', in M. D. Bordo and A. J. Schwartz (eds), *A Retrospective on the Classical Gold Standard, 1821–1931* (Chicago: University of Chicago Press).

Jorberg, L. (1961) *The Growth and Fluctuations of Swedish Industry, 1869–1912* (Stockholm: Almqvist and Wiksel).

Jorberg, L. (1975) 'Structural Change and Economic Growth in Nineteenth Century Sweden', in S. Kolbik (ed.), *Sweden's Development from Poverty to Affluence, 1750–1970* (Bloomington, Minn.: University of Minnesota Press).

Kelley, A. C. (1988) 'Economic Consequences of Population Change in the Third World', *Journal of Economic Literature*, December.

Kennedy, P. (1987) *The Rise and Fall of the Great Powers: Economic Change and Military Conflict from 1500 to 2000* (New York: Random House).
Kenwood, A. G. and A. L. Lougheed (1983) *The Growth of the International Economy, 1820–1980* (London: George Allen & Unwin).
Kindleberger, C. P. (1982) 'Sweden in 1850 as an "Impoverished Sophisticate": A Comment', *Journal of Economic History*, December.
Kindleberger, C. P. (1989) *Manias, Panics, and Crashes: A History of Financial Crises*, Revised ed (New York: Basic Books).
Kindleberger, C. P. (1993) *A Financial History of Western Europe*, 2nd ed (New York: Oxford University Press).
Kitchen, M. (1978) *The Political Economy of Germany, 1815–1914* (London: Croom Helm).
Klovland, J. T. (1983) 'The Demand for Money in Secular Perspective: The Case of Norway, 1867–1980', *European Economic Review*, July.
Klovland, J. T. (1987) 'The Demand for Money in the United Kingdom, 1875–1913', *Oxford Bulletin of Economics and Statistics*, August.
Komlos, J. (1981) 'Economic Growth and Industrialization in Hungary, 1830–1913', *Journal of European Economic History*, Spring.
Komlos, J. (1983) *The Habsburg Monarchy as a Customs Union* (Princeton, NJ: Princeton University Press).
Komlos, J. (1987, 1990) 'Financial Innovation and the Demand for Money in Austria-Hungary, 1867–1913', *Journal of European Economic History*, Spring; and reprinted in J. Komlos (ed.), *Economic Development in the Habsburg Monarchy and in the Successor States* (New York: Columbia University Press).
Krantz, O. and C. Nilsson (1975) *Swedish National Product, 1861–1970* (Lund: CWK Gleerup).
Kuznets, S. (1966) *Modern Economic Growth: Rate, Structure and Spread* (New Haven, Conn.: Yale University Press).
Landes, D. S. (1994) 'What Room for Accident in History?: Explaining Big Changes by Small Events; *Economic History Review*, November.
Levy-Leboyer, M. and F. Bourguignon (1990) *The French Economy in the Nineteenth Century* (Cambridge University Press).
Lewis, W. A. (1978) *Growth and Fluctuations, 1870–1913* (London: George Allen & Unwin).
Lindert, P. and J. G. Williamson (1985) 'English Workers' Living Standards during the Industrial Revolution: A New Look', in J. Mokyr (ed.), *The Economics of the Industrial Revolution* (Totowa, NJ: Rowman and Littlefield).
Lundström, R. (1991) 'Sweden', in R. Cameron and V. I. Bovykin (eds), *International Banking, 1870–1914* (New York: Oxford University Press).
Luzzato, G. (1963) *L'economia Italiana dal 1861 al 1914* (Milan: Banca Commerciale Italiana).
Machlup, F. (1977) *A History of Thought on Economic Integration* (New York: Columbia University Press).
Maddison, A. (1982) *Phases of Capitalist Development* (Oxford University Press).
Maddison, A. (1991) *Dynamic Forces in Capitalist Development* (Oxford University Press).
Mantoux, P. (1961) *The Industrial Revolution in the Eighteenth Century* (Chicago: University of Chicago Press).

Marczewski, J. (1988) 'Economic Fluctuations in France, 1815–1938', *Journal of European Economic History*, Fall.
Marx, K. (1906–1909) *Capital*, E. Untermann (trans.) and F. Engels (ed.) (Chicago: Charles Kerr).
Martín-Aceña, P. (1994) 'Spain during the Classical Gold Standard' in M. D. Bordo and F. Capie (eds), *Monetary Regimes in Transition* (Cambridge University Press).
Mathias, P. (1973) 'Capital, Credit, and Enterprise in the Industrial Revolution', *Journal of European Economic History*, Fall.
Mathias, P. (1983) *The First Industrial Nation*, 2nd ed (London: Methuen).
Matthews, R. C. O. (1959) *The Trade Cycle* (Cambridge University Press).
McCloskey, D. N. (1985) 'The Loss Function has been Mislaid: The Use and Abuse of Significance Tests', *American Economic Review*, May.
McCloskey, D. N. (1990) 'Ancients and Moderns', *Social Science History*, Fall.
McCloskey, D. N. and J. R. Zecher (1981) 'How the Gold Standard Worked, 1880–1913', in Donald N. McCloskey (ed.), *Enterprise and Trade in Victorian Britain* (London: George Allen & Unwin).
McCloskey, D. N. and J. R. Zecher (1984) 'The Success of Purchasing Power Parity: Historical Evidence and Its Implications for Macroeconomics' in M. D. Bordo and A. J. Schwartz (eds), *A Retrospective on the Classical Gold Standard, 1821–1931* (Chicago: University of Chicago Press).
McGouldrick, P. (1984) 'Operations of the German Central Bank and the Rules of the Game, 1879–1913', in M. D. Bordo and A. J. Schwartz (eds.), *A Retrospective on the Classical Gold Standard, 1821–1931* (Chicago: University of Chicago Press).
Meade, J. E. (1955) *The Theory of Customs Unions* (Amsterdam: North-Holland).
Meltzer, A. H. and S. Robinson (1989) 'Stability under the Gold Standard in Practice' in M. D. Bordo (ed.), *Money, History, and International Finance* (Chicago: University of Chicago Press).
Mills, T. C. and G. E. Wood (1978) 'Money–Income Relationships and the Exchange Rate Regime', *Review*, Federal Reserve Bank of St. Louis, August.
Mills, T. C. and G. E. Wood (1982) 'Econometric Evaluation of Alternative Money Stock Series, 1880–1913, *Journal of Money, Credit, and Banking*, May.
Miron, J. A. and C. D. Romer (1990) 'A New Monthly Index of Industrial Production, 1884–1940', *Journal of Economic History*, June.
Mitchell, B. R. (1978) *European Historical Statistics, 1750–1970* (New York: Columbia University Press).
Mitchell, B. R. (1992) *International Historical Statistics: Europe, 1750–1988* (New York: Columbia University Press).
Mokyr, J. (1976) *Industrialization in the Low Countries, 1795–1850* (New Haven, Conn.: Yale University Press).
Mokyr, J. (1990) *The Lever of Riches: Technological Creativity and Economic Progress* (New York: Oxford University Press).
Mokyr, J. (1993) 'Editor's Introduction', in J. Mokyr (ed.), *The British Industrial Revolution* (Boulder, Col.: Westview Press).
Molinas, C. and L. Prados de la Escosura (1989) 'Was Spain Different? Spanish Historical Backwardness Revisited', *Explorations in Economic History*, October.
Morgenstern, O. (1959) *International Financial Transactions and Business Cycles* (Princeton, NJ: Princeton University Press).

Morris, C. T. and I. Adelman (1988) *Comparative Patterns of Economic Development, 1850–1914* (Baltimore, Md: Johns Hopkins University Press).

Muhleman, M. L. (1896) *Monetary Systems of the World* (New York: Charles H. Nicoll).

Mundell, R. A. (1961) 'A Theory of Optimum Currency Areas', *American Economic Review*, September.

Neuberger, H. and H. H. Stokes (1974) 'German Banks and German Growth: An Empirical View', *Journal of Economic History*, September.

North, D. C. (1981) *Structure and Change in Economic History* (New York: W. W. Norton).

Nunes, A., E. Mata and N. Valerio (1989) 'Portuguese Economic Growth, 1833–1985', *Journal of European Economic History*, Fall.

Nygren, I. (1983) 'Transformation of Bank Structures in the Industrial Period, The Case of Sweden 1820–1913', *Journal of European Economic History*, Spring.

O'Brien, P. and C. Keyder (1978) *Economic Growth in Britain and France, 1780–1914: Two Paths to the 20th Century* (London: George Allen & Unwin).

Officer, Lawrence H. (1986) 'The Efficiency of the Dollar–Sterling Gold Standard, 1890–1908', *Journal of Political Economy*, October.

Oliver, J. W. (1956) *History of American Technology* (New York: Ronald).

O'Rourke, K. A. (1994) 'The Economic Impact of the Famine in the Short and Long Run', *American Economic Review*, May.

Overturf, S. F. (1986) *The Economic Principles of European Integration* (New York: Praeger).

Parker, W. N. (1991a) 'Europe in an American Mirror: Reflections on Industrialization and Ideology', in R. Sylla and G. Toniolo (eds), *Patterns of European Industrialization: The Nineteenth Century* (London: Routledge).

Parker, W. N. (1991b) *Europe, America, and the Wider World*, vol. 2 (New York: Cambridge University Press).

Phelps, E. (1965) *Golden Rules of Economic Growth* (New York: Norton).

Pierenkemper, T. (1987) 'The Standard of Living and Employment in Germany, 1850–1980: An Overview', *Journal of European Economic History*, Spring.

Pippenger, J. (1984) 'Bank of England Operations, 1893–1913', in M. D. Bordo and A. J. Schwartz (eds), *A Retrospective on the Classical Gold Standard, 1821–1931* (Chicago: University of Chicago Press).

Pollard, S. (1964) 'Fixed Capital in the Industrial Revolution', *Journal of Economic History*, September.

Price, R. (1981) *An Economic History of Modern France, 1730–1914* (London: Macmillan).

Redish, A. (1990) 'The Evolution of the Gold Standard in England', *Journal of Economic History*, December.

Redish, A. (1994) 'The Latin Monetary Union and the Emergence of the International Gold Standard', in M. D. Bordo and F. Capie (eds), *Monetary Regimes in Transition* (Cambridge University Press).

Rosenberg, N. and L. E. Birdsall, Jr. (1985) *How the West Grew Rich* (New York: Harper Collins)

Rostow, W. W. (1948) *The British Economy of the 19th Century* (Oxford University Press).

Rudolph, R. L. (1972) 'Austria, 1800–1914', in R. Cameron (ed.), *Banking and Economic Development: Some Lessons of History* (New York: Oxford University Press).

Roehl, R. (1976) 'French Industrialization: A Reconsideration', *Explorations in Economic History*, (July).
Saint Marc, M. (1983) *Histoire Monétaire de la France, 1800–1908* (Paris: Presses Universitaires de France).
Sandberg, L. G. (1978) 'Banking and Economic Growth in Sweden before World War I', *Journal of Economic History*, September.
Sandberg, L. G. (1979) 'The Case of the Impoverished Sophisticate: Human Capital and Swedish Economic Growth before World War I', *Journal of Economic History*, March.
Saul, S. B. (1985) *The Myth of the Great Depression, 1873–1896* (London: Macmillan).
Scott, F. D. (1965) 'Sweden's Constructive Opposition to Emigration', *Journal of Modern History*, September.
Sheffrin, S. M. (1988) 'Have Economic Fluctuations been Dampened? A Look at Evidence Outside the United States', *Journal of Monetary Economics*, March.
Simon, J. (1981) *The Ultimate Resource* (Princeton, NJ: Princeton University Press).
Smith, A. (1776) *An Inquiry into the Nature and Causes of the Wealth of Nations*, in E. Cannan (ed.) 1904 edition, reprinted 1976 (Chicago: University of Chicago Press).
Soderberg, J. (1982) 'Causes of Poverty in Sweden in the Nineteenth Century', *Journal of European Economic History*, Spring.
Solomou, S. (1987) *Phases of Economic Growth, 1850–1973* (Cambridge University Press).
Solomou, S. and M. Weale (1991) 'Balanced Estimates of UK GDP, 1870–1913', *Explorations in Economic History*, January.
Sommariva, A. and G. Tullio (1987) *German Macroeconomic History, 1880–1979* (London: Macmillan).
Sommariva, A. and G. Tullio (1988) 'International Gold Flows in Gold Standard Germany: A Test of the Monetary Approach to the Balance of Payments, 1880–1911', *Journal of Money, Credit, and Banking*, February.
Spinelli, F. (1980) 'The Demand for Money in the Italian Economy: 1867–1965', *Journal of Monetary Economics*, January.
Sprenger, B. (1982) 'Geldmengenanderungen in Deutschland in Zeitalter der Industrialisierung (1835 bis 1913)', *Kolner Vortrage und Abhandlungen zur Sozial- und Wirtschaftsgeschichte* (Heft 36).
Stuijvenberg, J. van and J. de Vrijer (1982) 'Prices, Population and National Income in the Netherlands, 1620–1978', *Journal of European Economic History*, Winter
Sylla, R. and G. Toniolo (1991) 'Introduction', in R. Sylla and G. Toniolo (eds), *Patterns of European Industrialization: The Nineteenth Century* (London: Routledge).
Thomas, B. (1954) *Migration and Economic Growth* (Cambridge University Press).
Tilly, R. H. (1967) 'Germany, 1815–1870', in R. Cameron (ed.), *Banking in the Early Stages of Industrialization* (New York: Oxford University Press).
Tilly, R. H. (1986) 'German Banking, 1850–1914: Development Assistance for the Strong', *Journal of European Economic History*, Spring.
Tilly, R. H. (1991a) 'International Aspects of the Development of German Banking', in R. Cameron and V. I. Bovykin (eds), *International Banking, 1870–1914* (New York: Oxford University Press).

Tilly, R. H. (1991b) 'Germany', in R. Sylla and G. Toniolo (eds), *Patterns of European Industrialization: The Nineteenth Century* (London: Routledge).
Toniolo, G. (1990) *An Economic History of Liberal Italy, 1850–1918* (London: Routledge).
Tortella, G. (1972) 'Spain, 1829–1874', in R. Cameron (ed.), *Banking and Economic Development: Some Lessons of History* (New York: Oxford University Press).
Tortella, G. (1977) *Banking, Railroads, and Industry in Spain, 1829–1874* (New York: Arno Press).
Toutain, J.-C. (1987) 'Le Produit Interieur Brut de la France de 1789 a 1982', *Économies et Sociétés*, no. 15.
Trebilcock, C. (1981) *The Industrialization of the Continental Powers, 1780–1914* (London: Longman).
Turner, P. (1991) 'The U.K. Demand for Money, Commercial Bills and Quasi-Money Assets, 1871–1913', in J. Foreman-Peck (ed.), *New Perspectives on the Late Victorian Economy* (Cambridge University Press).
United States Department of Commerce (1975) *Historical Statistics of the United States: Colonial Times to 1970* (Washington, DC: Government Printing Office).
United States Mint (various years) *Report of the Director of the (US) Mint* (Washington, DC: Government Printing Office).
Van der Wee, H. and M. Goosens (1991) 'Belgium', in R. Cameron and V. I. Bovykin (eds.), *International Banking, 1870–1914* (New York: Oxford University Press).
Vicens Vives, J. (1969) *An Economic History of Spain* (Princeton, NJ: Princeton Univerisity Press).
Viner, J. (1950) *The Customs Union Issue* (New York: Carnegie Endowment for International Peace).
Weber, A. (1899) *Growth of Cities in the Nineteenth Century* (New York: Macmillan).
Williamson, J. G. (1985) *Did British Capitalism Breed Inequality?* (London: George Allen & Unwin).
Williamson, J. G. (1992) 'The Evolution of Global Labor Markets in the First and Second World Since 1830: Background Evidence and Hypotheses', NBER Working Papers, Historical Paper No. 36.
Wilson, J. (1993) 'Estimates of Consumer Prices for the U.S.: 1850–1914', mimeo, North Carolina State University, Raleigh, North Carolina.
Wood, G. E. (1984) 'Comment', in M. D. Bordo and A. J. Schwartz (eds), *A Retrospective on the Classical Gold Standard, 1821–1931* (Chicago: University of Chicago Press).
Zamagni, V. (1993) *The Economic History of Italy, 1860–1990* (Oxford: Clarendon Press).
Ziegler, D. (1992) 'The Banking Crisis of 1878: Some Remarks', *Economic History Review*, February.

Index

Abramovitz, M., 9, 287, 307
Acena, P. M., 304, 307
Adelman, I., 192, 315
Agricultural revolution, 23
Agriculture, 163
   migration, 51–3
   growth, 54–6
   see also Agricultural revolution; Business cycles
Akaike, H., 158, 300, 307
Aldcroft, D. H., 239, 307, 309
Anes, R., 92, 307
Arbitrage, 147–8, 154, 292
ARIMA models, 157–8, 298–9
Ashworth, W., 202, 294, 307
Austria-Hungary
   banking, 84–6, 283, 303
   business cycles, 226–9, 269, 279–80
   central banking, 81, 84, 110–11, 117
   data, 303–6
   demand for money, 166, 169, 172–4, 183
   economic growth, 43–6, 67, 194, 227–9, 269
   financial crises, 110
   foreign trade, 194–7, 200–1, 233, 276–7, 303
   industrial production, 230–1, 275, 304
   industrialization, 54–6, 58–60
   inflation, 67, 135–7, 139, 141, 150–1, 153–4, 157–8
   money growth, 67, 135–7, 139, 141, 150, 152
   money stock, 141, 144, 304
   political development, 32–3, 110, 173
   population, 305
   population growth, 49–50, 52–3
   price levels, 141, 144–5, 155, 303, 306
   real income, 226–9, 305
Austrian National Bank, *see* Austria-Hungary (central banking)
Autoregressive (AR) process, 298–9

Backus, D. K., 118, 290, 303, 307
Backwardness, 10, 16
Bagehot, W., 74, 102, 307
Balke, N. S., 71, 305, 307
Banca d'Italia, *see* Italy (central banking)
Bank Charter Act (1844), 101, 103–4
Bank of England, *see* United Kingdom (central banking)
Bank of France, *see* France (central banking)
Bank of the Netherlands, *see* Netherlands (central banking)
Bank of Portugal, *see* Portugal, central banking
Bank of Spain, *see* Spain (central banking)
Banking, 65–6, 192, 281–3
   mixed, 66, 77, 80–2, 84–5
   theories, 75–6
   statistics, 303
   see also industrialization; *and under individual countries* (banking)
Barnett, W. A., 292, 307
Barro, R. J., 8–9, 100, 119–20, 186, 290, 307
Belgium
   banking, 73, 82–3, 87, 283, 303
   business cycles, 226–9, 269–70, 279–80
   central banking, 107–9, 117
   data, 303–6
   economic growth, 43–6, 194, 227–9, 269
   financial crises, 109
   foreign trade, 194–7, 200–1, 233, 303
   industrialization, 56–9
   inflation, 135–7, 139, 141, 144, 150–1, 153, 157–8
   interest rates, 210–11, 215–18, 304
   political development, 22–3
   population, 305
   population growth, 49–50, 52–3

Index

price level, 141, 144–5, 155, 303, 306
real income, 226–9, 305
Berend, I., 287, 307
Berry, B. J. L., 33, 307
Bimetallism, 105–6, 109–10
Birdsall, L. E., 191, 315
Bloomfield, A. I., 88, 100, 107–10, 112–13, 116–17, 290, 307
Borchardt, K., 253, 307
Bordo, M. D., 69, 94, 163, 284, 287, 303–4, 307–12, 314–15
Boserup, E., 48, 308
Bourguignon, F., 106, 249, 303–4, 313
Bovykin, V. I., 309, 312–13, 316–17
Breusch-Godfrey test, 292–3
Brillembourg, A., 94, 308
Broadberry, S. N., 308, 311
Business cycles, 12–13, 222–71, 284
  agriculturally based, 247–50, 252–4, 255, 257–8, 262–3
  cointegration tests, 12–13
  financial causes, 224, 238, 240, 248–9, 253–4, 259–61
  indicators, 222, 226–34, 235–7, 241, 245–8, 251–2, 255, 258–9, 263–4, 269
  long waves, 238–9
  real causes, 224–5, 238–40, 247–9, 254–61, 263–6, 280–1
  see also Financial crises; Great depression; Integration (business cycles); individual countries (business cycles)

Cafagna, L., 259, 308
Cagan, P., 121, 308
Cairncross, A. K., 308
Calliari, S., 176, 308
Cameron, R. E., 76, 79, 82–3, 245, 290, 308–9, 312–13, 315–17
Cannan, E., 316
Canzoneri, M. B., 6, 308
Capie, F. H., 162, 180, 237–40, 294, 304, 308, 314–15
Capital exports, 202–3
Capital markets, 202–21;
  see also Integration (capital markets)
Caron, F., 249, 308
Carreras, A., 304, 309

Catching up, see Convergence
Causality (Granger), 14–16, 66, 93–7, 126–9, 140, 149, 299–300
  cyclical, 224–5
  foreign trade, 199–202
  inflation, 150–1, 153
  interest rates, 217–19
  investment, 207–8
  monetary bases, 126–9
  money growth, 150, 152
  real income, 225
Central banks, 99–129, 192
  discount policy, 104, 107, 109
  lender of last resort, 99–100, 102–4, 106, 108, 110–12, 114
  note issue, 101, 104–10, 112–15
  stabilization policies, 103–4, 109
  moral suasion, 108
  summary, 117
  see also individual countries (central banking)
Chandler, A., 77, 309
Chow, G. C., 175, 177, 301, 309
Chow test, 301–2
Church, R. A., 239, 309
Cipolla, C., 307
Clark, T. A. 290, 309
Clough, S. B., 257, 259–61, 294–5, 309
Coefficient of variation, 45, 288
Cohen, J. S., 90, 114, 289, 309
Cointegration, 12–14, 16, 140, 142, 297
  cyclical, 225
  foreign trade, 198–9
  interest rates, 215–17
  investment, 205, 207, 232
  monetary base, 99, 125–6
  money stocks, 142–4, 225
  price levels, 143–6, 292
  real income, 225
Collins, M., 102, 309
Commercial revolution, 23
Comparative advantage, 5–6, 8, 42
Convergence, 8–10, 287
  see also Integration
Coppock, D. J., 225, 309
Cottrell, P. L., 77, 309
Crafts, N. F. R., 40, 239, 287, 308–9, 311
Craig, L. A., 12–13, 225, 294, 309

320 *Index*

Crédit Mobilier, 78–9, 83–4, 89, 105, 192, 248
Crowding out, 21, 35
Currency areas, 6
Customs unions, 4, 6–7, 29, 46
CUSUM tests, 165, 167–8, 301

Democracy (and growth), 17–18, 20–1, 27
Denmark
  banking, 73–4, 87–8, 283, 303
  business cycles, 224, 226–9, 269
  central banking, 87, 112, 117
  data, 303–305
  demand for money, 166–9, 172, 174, 183
  economic growth, 43–6, 67, 194, 204, 227–9, 269
  financial sophistication, 70–2, 87, 96–7
  foreign trade, 194–7, 200–1, 233, 276–7, 303
  inflation, 67, 135–7, 139, 141, 151, 153
  investment, 204–5, 297, 232, 304
  money growth, 67, 135–7, 139, 141, 150, 152
  money stock, 141, 144, 304
  political development, 31–2
  population, 305
  population growth, 48–53
  price level, 141, 144–5, 155, 303, 305
  real income, 305, 226–9
Dickey, D. A., 297–8, 309
Dickey–Fuller test, 95, 124, 140, 204, 213, 291, 296–7
Dominant technologies, 10
Dowd, K., 100, 104, 289, 309
Dutton, J., 102, 309
Dwyer, G., 94, 310

Easton, S. T., 224, 310
Edison, H. J., 290, 310
Egge, A., 88–9, 112–13, 290, 310
Eichengreen, B., 94, 240, 310
Engels, F., 314
Engle, R. F., 296, 310
Equation of exchange, 68, 93
Ericsson, N. R., 292, 312

European economy, 10, 42, 132
Exports, 193–202, 303
  cointegration, 199
  correlations, 196, 198
  cyclical patterns, 225
  Granger causality, 200–2
  growth rates, 193–4
  see also individual countries (foreign trade)

F-test, 165
Fearon, P., 239, 307, 309
Feinstein, C. H., 40, 241, 305, 310
Fenoaltea, S., 261, 310
Financial crises, *see individual countries* (business cycles)
Financial sophistication, 14–15, 65–6, 68–72, 182–3
  index, 65, 69–72, 93, 95–6, 281, 288
  see also Money demand (income elasticity)
Fisher, D., 12–13, 15, 94, 156, 174–6, 178, 225, 292, 294, 307, 310
Fisher effect, 175, 208, 215, 290
Floud, R., 40, 310
Ford, A. G., 225, 227, 240, 310
Foreign trade
  cyclical patterns, 225, 230, 233–4
  growth, 191, 193–4, 276–7
  see also individual countries (foreign trade); Exports; Imports
Foreman-Peck, J., 308, 317
France
  agricultural production, 247–50
  banking, 73, 78–80, 105–6
  business cycles, 105–6, 226–9, 244–50, 268, 279–80
  central banking, 25, 78–80, 81, 104–7, 117
  cyclical indicators, 246–7
  data, 303–6
  demand for money, 166–70, 172, 174, 183
  economic growth, 43–6, 67, 194, 204, 227–9, 244–7
  financial crises, 105, 248–9
  financial sophistication, 70–1, 79, 96
  foreign trade, 194–7, 200–1, 233, 246–7, 276–7, 303

gold standard, 105
industrial production, 230–1, 246–8, 275, 304
industrialization, 54–6, 58–9
inflation, 67, 135–7, 139, 141, 150–1, 153–4, 157
interest rates, 210–12, 214–19, 304
investment, 204–7, 232, 246–7, 304
money growth, 67, 135–7, 139, 141, 150, 152, 154
money stock, 141, 144, 304
overseas lending, 203
political development, 23–6
population, 305
population growth, 48–50, 52–3
price level, 141, 144–5, 155, 303, 305–6
real income, 226–9, 305
Fratianni, M., 94, 97, 114, 123, 303–6, 310
Frederico, G., 89, 310
Friedman, D., 4, 310
Friedman, M., 68–70, 106, 162–4, 179–83, 209, 217, 223, 227, 237–8, 292, 304–5, 310–12

Germany
  banking, 28, 72–3, 80–2, 85, 107, 283, 303
  business cycles, 107–8, 224, 226–9, 250–7, 268, 279–80
  central banking, 107–9, 117
  cyclical indicators, 251–2, 254–5
  data, 303–6
  demand for money, 166–70, 172, 175–6, 183–5
  economic growth, 43–6, 67, 194, 204, 227–9, 244–5, 250–2, 255, 274
  employment, 254–5
  financial crises, 108, 253–4
  financial sophistication, 70–2, 81–2, 96–7
  foreign trade, 194–7, 200–1, 233, 251–2, 276–7, 303
  industrial production, 230–1, 251–2, 275–6, 303
  industrialization, 54–6, 58–61
  inflation, 67, 135–7, 139, 141, 150–1, 153, 157
  interest rates, 209–12, 214–19, 304
  investment, 204–7, 232, 251–2, 271, 304
  monetary base, 122–4
  money growth, 67, 135–7, 139, 141, 150, 152
  money stock, 141, 144, 304
  overseas lending, 203, 271
  political development, 27–30, 272
  population, 305
  population growth, 48–50, 52–3
  price level, 141, 144–5, 155, 303, 305–6
  real income, 226–9, 305
  unemployment, 254–5
Gerschenkron, A., 10–11, 18–19, 61, 76, 261, 287, 311
Global economy, 11–12, 51
gold
  production, 120–2, 126–8, 142
  see also Gold standard
Goldsmith, R., 73, 311
Gold standard, 13, 45, 66–8, 74–5, 90, 99, 102, 111, 114, 116, 121, 124–9, 130–2, 138, 140, 142–3, 152, 154, 156, 158–60, 163–4, 171–4, 179, 192, 195–6, 198, 208, 216–17, 224, 283–6
  rules of the game, 100, 107, 114, 125, 142, 149
  specie-flow mechanism, 118–21, 124–5, 131, 142, 147–8, 223
  theory, 118–21
  see also Law of one price; Purchasing power parity; Monetary approach to balance of payments
Good, D., 287, 289, 311
Goodhart, C. A. E., 102, 311
Goodwin, B. K., 12, 311
Goosens, M., 82–3, 290, 317
Gordon, R. J., 71, 305, 307
Graham, M. K., 311
Granger, C. W. J., 15, 296, 309
Granger causality, see Causality (Granger)
Great depression (1870s), 239, 245, 253, 259–61
Great Exhibition, 41
Gregory, A., 310

Grennes, T., 12, 311
Growth, 39–61, 274–8
  cyclical interaction, 227–9
  effects, 40–2
  modern, 39–40
  theories, 11, 19, 39–42, 48
  see also individual countries (economic growth, population growth)

Hall, A., 297, 311
Hall, R. E., 301, 311
Hanseatic League, 28
Hansen, S. A., 87, 112, 290, 303, 305, 311
Harvey, A. C., 301, 311
Hatton, T. J., 52, 132, 154, 291–2, 311
Hawtrey, R. G., 110, 311
Heckscher, E. F., 7–8, 11, 72, 264–5, 267, 311
Henderson, W. O., 248–9, 252–3, 311
Hendry, D. F., 180, 292, 311–12
High-powered money, *see* Monetary base
Hinderliter, R. H., 102, 106, 312
Hoffmann, W. G., 250, 288, 294, 312
Homer, S., 304, 312
Horton, F. E., 53, 307
Huck, P. F., 41, 312
Huffman, W. E., 179–80, 224, 240, 312
Hughes, J. R. T., 39, 75, 312
Hutchinson, W., 8–9, 312

Imports, 193–202, 303
  cointegration, 199
  correlations, 197–8
  Granger causality, 201–2
  growth rates, 193–4
  phase coincidence, 233–4
  see also individual countries (foreign trade)
Income, *see individual countries* (real income, economic growth); Monetary neutrality
Indicators, *see* business cycles; *individual countries* (indicators)
Industrial production, 229–31, 275–6, 303–4
  cointegration, 230
  Granger causality, 230
  phase coincidence, 230–1
  unit roots, 230
  see also individual countries (industrial production)
Industrial revolution, 21, 25–7, 29–30, 39–41
Industrialization, 53–61, 76–92, 163
Inflation rates, 13, 65–8, 131–59
  correlation, 133–4, 136–9
  expectations, 190, 209
  Granger causality, 149–54
  standard deviations, 139
  see also Money demand
Integration, 3–16, 50–3, 57–61, 272–86
  capital markets, 163, 189–90, 202–21, 271, 277–8
  cyclical, 223–34, 267–71, 278–81
  economic, 3, 5–16, 190–3
  financial, 5–6, 10–11, 65–74, 108, 111, 128–9, 185–6, 189–90, 202, 208–21, 281–6
  political, 4–7, 17–38, 191–3, 272
  product markets, 189–90, 195–202, 270–1, 273, 276–7
  social, 7
  technology effect, 9–10, 270, 273
  territorial, 4–5, 7
  see also Convergence; Migration
Interest rates, 12, 147, 304
  cointegration, 12, 215–17
  correlation, 209–12
  differential, 164
  Granger causality, 217–19
  nominal, 208–19
  proxy yield, 163–4
  real, 12, 208–19
  unit roots, 213, 215–17
  see also Money demand
Investment, 203–8, 304
  cointegration, 205, 207
  correlation, 205–6
  cyclical pattern, 225, 231–2
  Granger causality, 207–8
  phase coincidence, 231–2
ISTAT, 262, 304–5, 312
Italy
  banking, 33, 73, 89–90, 283, 303

Index

business cycles, 224, 226–9, 257–63, 268, 279–80
central banking, 90, 113–14, 117
cyclical indicators, 258–9
data, 303–306
demand for money, 166, 169–70, 172, 176–7, 183–5
economic growth, 43–6, 67, 194, 204, 227–9, 258–9, 274
financial crises, 114, 259–61
financial sophistication, 70–2, 90, 96–7
foreign trade, 194–7, 200–1, 233–4, 258–9, 277, 303
industrialization, 54–6, 58–9
industrial production, 231, 258–9, 275, 303
inflation, 67, 135–7, 139, 141, 150–1, 153, 157–8
interest rates, 210–13, 215–18, 304
investment, 204–7, 232, 258–9, 271, 304
monetary base, 122–4
monetary neutrality, 94
money growth, 67, 135–7, 139, 141, 150, 152
money stock, 141, 144, 304
political development, 33–5, 89, 113, 272
population, 305
population growth, 48–53
price level, 141, 144–5, 155, 303, 305–6
real income, 226–9, 305

Jansen, D. W., 297–8, 309
Johansen, H. C., 88, 312
Johnston, J., 293, 301, 311–12
Jonung, L., 69, 149, 163, 178, 290, 292, 303–4, 307
Jorberg, L., 265, 312

Kehoe, P. J., 118, 290, 303, 307
Kelley, A. C., 48, 312
Kennedy, P., 35, 313
Kenwood, A. G., 219, 271, 313
Keyder, C., 287, 315
Khan, M., 94, 308

Kindleberger, C. P., 72, 76, 86, 100, 103, 106, 111, 117, 313
Kitchen, M., 252–4, 294, 313
Klovland, J. T., 177–8, 180, 304, 313
Kolbik, S., 312
Komlos, J., 46, 85, 173–4, 287, 289, 303–5, 313
Krantz, O., 266, 304–5, 313
Kuznets, S., 18, 39, 42, 53–4, 261, 313

Landes, D. S., 287, 313
Latin Monetary Union, 105, 109, 113, 115, 289–90
Law of one price, 13, 130–2, 147, 154–6
see also Gold standard (specie-flow mechanism)
Lender of last resort, see Central banking
Levy-Leboyer, M., 106, 249, 303–4, 313
Leybourne, S. J., 239, 309
Lilien, D. M., 301, 311
Lewis, W. A., 313
Lindert, P., 40, 313
Lothian, J. R., 179–80, 224, 240, 312
Lougheed, A. L., 219, 271, 313
Lundström, R., 87, 313
Luzzatto, G., 260, 313

Machlup, F., 3, 7, 287, 313
Maddison, A., 44, 288, 303, 305, 313
Malthus, T. R., 48
Mantoux, P., 39, 313
Manufacturing, see Industrialization
Marczewski, J., 105, 249, 314
Marx, K., 10, 40, 76, 314
Martín-Aceña, P., 116, 314
Mata, E., 303, 305, 315
Mathias, P., 56, 76, 189, 314
Matthews, R. C. O., 225, 314
McCloskey, D. N., 13, 16, 147–8, 159, 310, 314
McGouldrick, P., 107, 314
Meade, J. E., 4, 6, 314
Mean lags, price levels, 154–6
Mean reversion, 156–8, 297–8
Meltzer, A. H., 156–7, 314
Mercantilism, 7–8, 24, 42
Migration, 41, 50–53

Mills, T. C., 94, 180, 237–40, 294, 308–9, 314
Miron, J. A., 54, 304, 314
Mitchell, B. R., 54, 56, 59, 234, 271, 281, 303–6, 314
Mokyr, J., 8, 23, 48, 287, 313–14
Molinas, C., 36, 288, 305, 314
Monetary approach to balance of payments, 13, 127–8, 131, 146–9, 223, 290
Monetary base, 99–100, 107, 114, 121–8, 149
  cointegration, 125–6
  correlations, 122–4
  defined, 121
  Granger causality, 126–9
  unit roots, 124–5
Monetary policy, *see* Central banks; *individual countries* (central banks)
Money
  neutrality, 15, 66, 93–7, 223–4, 240
  stocks, 304
  cointegration, 144–8
  supply, 119
Money demand, 114, 119–20, 123, 131, 147–8, 160–86, 283
  econometrics, 161–5
  income elasticity, 15, 69, 148, 161–2, 182–5
  inflation rates, 164
  interest rates, 161–4
  partial adjustment, 161–2
  stability, 163–5, 167–71, 184–6
Money growth, 13, 67–8, 93, 131–59
  correlations, 133–4, 136–8
  Granger causality, 149–54
  standard deviations, 139
Moral suasion, *see* Central banks
Morgenstern, O., 314
Morris, C. T., 192, 315
Moving average process, 298–9
Muhleman, M. L., 44, 80, 83, 87, 92, 105, 109–10, 112, 114, 116–17, 315
Mundell, R. A., 6, 315

Nationalbank, *see* Denmark (central banking)
National Bank of Belgium, *see* Belgium (central banking)

Netherlands
  banking, 26–7, 73, 83–4, 109
  business cycles, 269–70
  central banking, 83, 109–10, 117
  data, 303–6
  economic growth, 43–6, 194, 269
  foreign trade, 194–7, 200–1, 233, 276–7, 303
  industrialization, 56, 58
  inflation, 135–7, 139, 141, 150–1, 153, 157
  interest rates, 209–11, 213–18, 304
  political development, 22–3, 26–7
  population, 305
  population growth, 48–50, 52–3
  price level, 141, 144–5, 155, 303, 306
  real income, 226, 305
Neuberger, H., 81, 315
Nilsson, C., 266, 304–5, 313
Non-stationarity, *see* Stationarity; Unit roots
Norges Bank, *see* Norway (central banking)
North, D. C., 4, 21, 24, 315
Norway
  banking, 73–4, 87–9, 113, 283, 303
  business cycles, 224, 226–9, 269
  central banking, 88, 112–13, 117
  data, 303–6
  demand for money, 166–70, 172, 183
  economic growth, 43–6, 67, 194, 204, 227–9, 269
  financial sophistication, 70–1, 87, 96
  foreign trade, 194–7, 200–1, 233, 303
  industrialization, 56, 58
  inflation, 67, 135–7, 139, 151, 153
  interest rates, 210–11, 215–18, 304
  investment, 204–7, 232, 304
  monetary base, 122–4
  money growth, 67, 135–7, 139, 150, 152
  money stock, 141, 144, 304
  political development, 31–2
  population, 305
  population growth, 49–50, 52–3
  price level, 141, 145, 303, 305
  real income, 226–9, 305
Nunes, A., 288, 303, 305, 315
Nygren, I., 86, 315

Index

O'Brien, P., 287, 315
Officer, L. H., 290, 315
Oliver, J. W., 40, 315
Open market operations, 109
Optimum currency area, *see* Currency areas
Original accumulation, 10
O'Rourke, K. A., 288, 315
Overturf, S. F., 5, 315

Parker, W. N., 18, 40, 315
Phelps, E., 49, 288, 315
Pierenkemper, T., 254, 315
Pippenger, J., 102, 315
Pollard, S., 76, 310, 315
Population, 305
  growth, 47–53
  see also Migration
Portugal
  banking, 92
  business cycles, 226–9, 269–70
  central banking, 116–17
  economic growth, 43–6, 194, 227–9, 269, 274
  foreign trade, 194–8, 200–1, 233–4, 276–7, 303
  inflation, 135, 137, 139, 141, 151, 153
  political development, 37
  population, 305
  population growth, 49–50, 52–3
  price level, 141, 303, 305
  real income, 226–9, 305
Prados de la Escosura, L., 36, 288, 305, 314
Price, R., 245, 248, 315
Price level, 303, 305–6
  adjustment, 154–6
  cointegration, 13, 144–6
  correlation, 148
  integration, 130
  see also Inflation rates; Law of one price; Purchasing power parity; *individual countries* (inflation, price level)
Property rights, 21, 36
Proto-industry, 23, 27
Proxy yield, *see* Interest rates
Purchasing power parity, 45–6, 68, 120, 288

Quantity theory of money, 67–8, 93–7, 147

Ranki, G., 287, 307
Recursive residuals test, 165, 173, 300–2
Redish, A., 290, 315
Reference cycles, 237–8, 265
Reichsbank, *see* Germany (central banking)
Riksbank, *see* Sweden (central banking)
Robinson, S., 156–7, 314
Rockoff, H., 102, 106, 312
Rodik-Bali, G., 180, 308
Roehl, R., 287, 316
Rogers, C. A., 6, 308
Romer, C. D., 54, 304, 314
Rosenberg, N., 191, 315
Rossana, R. J., 309
Rostow, W. W., 237–8, 240, 315
Rudolph, R. L., 84–5, 111, 289, 315
Rules of the game, *see* Gold standard

Saint Marc, M., 171, 175, 293, 304, 316
Sala-i-Martin, X., 8–9, 307
Sanchez-Albornoz, N., 309
Sandberg, L. G., 14, 72, 86, 288, 316
Saul, S. B., 239, 316
Scandinavian Monetary Union, 111, 177
Schwartz, A. J., 69–70, 162–4, 179–83, 209, 217, 223, 227, 237–8, 284, 292, 304–5, 307–12, 314–15, 317
Schwartz, P., 307
Scott, F. D., 316
Serletis, A., 292, 307
Sheffrin, S. M., 185, 263, 316
Significance
  economic, 13–14
  statistical, 13–14
Simon, J., 48, 316
Smith, A., 42, 316
Soderberg, J., 316
Solomou, S., 71, 239, 305, 316
Sommariva, A., 107, 290, 316
Spain
  agricultural sector, 36
  balance of payments, 35
  banking, 73–4, 91–2, 283, 303
  central banking, 91–2, 115–17

Spain *cont.*
  data, 303–6
  economic growth, 35–6, 43–6, 91, 194, 227–9
  foreign trade, 194–8, 200–1, 233–4, 303
  industrial production, 230–1, 275, 304
  industrialization, 54, 56, 58–9
  inflation, 67, 135–7, 139, 141, 150, 153, 157
  money growth, 67, 135–7, 139, 141, 150, 152
  money stock, 141, 144, 304
  political development, 35, 115–16
  population, 305
  population growth, 48–53
  price level, 141, 155–6, 306
  real income, 305

Specie-flow mechanism, *see* Gold standard
Spencer, T. A., 13, 309
Spinelli, F., 94, 97, 114, 123, 176, 303–6, 308–9, 316
Sprenger, B., 304, 316
Stagflation, 105
Standard of living, 40–1, 49, 287
Stationarity, 12, 95, 124–7, 138, 296
  see also Unit roots
Stokes, H. H., 81, 315
Sweden
  banking, 73, 86–7, 283, 303
  business cycles, 224, 226–9, 263–8, 279–80
  central banking, 87, 111–12, 117, 149
  cyclical indicators, 263–4
  data, 303–6
  demand for money, 166, 169–70, 172, 178–9, 183–5
  economic growth, 31, 43–6, 67, 194, 204, 227–9, 263–4, 274
  financial sophistication, 14–15, 70–2, 86, 96
  foreign trade, 194–7, 200–1, 233, 263–6, 276–7, 303
  industrial production, 230–1, 263–4, 275–6, 303
  industrialization, 54–6, 58–9
  inflation, 67, 135–7, 139, 141, 150–1, 153, 157

  interest rates, 209–11, 215–18, 304
  investment, 204–5, 207, 232, 263–4, 271, 304
  monetary base, 122–4, 127
  monetary neutrality, 94–6
  money growth, 67, 135–7, 139, 141, 150, 152
  money stock, 141, 144, 304
  political development, 30–1
  population, 305
  population growth, 49–53
  price level, 141, 144–5, 155, 303, 305–6
  real income, 226–9, 305
Switzerland
  inflation, 135, 139, 141, 150, 153, 157
  price level, 141, 144, 155, 306
Sylla, R., 287, 310, 315–17
Stuijvenberg, J. van, 303, 305–6, 316

Tariffs, 8, 198
Technological change, 41–2, 48, 53, 55–7, 59–61
Technology transfer, 8, 208
Thomas, B., 316
Thornton, D. L., 297–8, 309
Thurman, W. N., 15, 94, 178, 309
Tilly, R., 76, 80–1, 108, 290, 316–17
Toniolo, G., 89, 259–61, 287, 310, 315–17
Tortella, G., 91, 115, 307, 317
Toutain, J.-C., 244, 304–5, 317
Trebilcock, C., 53, 86, 92, 106, 287, 289, 317
Tullio, G., 107, 290, 316
Turner, P., 293, 317

Unit roots, 95, 296–7
  exports, 194–5
  imports, 194–5
  industrial production, 230
  interest rates, 213, 215
  investment, 204–5, 232
  money stocks, 140–2
  price levels, 140–2
  real income, 226
United Kingdom
  banking, 71, 73–7, 79, 282–3, 303
  business cycles, 223–4, 226–9,

234–44, 268, 279–80
central banking, 21, 74–5, 101–4, 106–7, 117
cyclical indicators, 235–6
data, 303–6
demand for money, 166–7, 169, 172, 179–81, 183
economic growth, 43–6, 67, 194, 204, 227–9, 241, 274
financial crises, 101–3, 242–3
financial sophistication, 65, 68–72, 96
foreign trade, 193–7, 200–1, 233, 235–6, 276–7, 303
gold standard, 101–2
industrial production, 230–1, 275–6, 304
industrialization, 54–60
inflation, 67–8, 135–7, 139, 141, 150–1, 153, 157
interest rates, 210–19, 304
investment, 204–7, 232, 235–6, 271, 304
monetary base, 122–4
monetary neutrality, 94, 96
money growth, 67, 135, 137, 139, 141, 150, 152
money stock, 75, 141, 144, 304
overseas lending, 202–3, 271
political development, 19–22
population, 305
population growth, 49–53
price level, 141, 144–5, 155, 303, 305–6
reference cycles, 237
real income, 226–9, 235–6, 305
unemployment, 235–6, 241
United States
 business cycles, 223–4, 226–9, 242–3
 data, 303–6
 demand for money, 166, 169, 172, 181–5
 economic growth, 43–6, 67, 194, 227–9
 financial crises, 242–3
 financial sophistication, 69–71, 96
 foreign trade, 194–7, 200–1, 233–4, 303
 industrial production, 230–1, 251–2, 304
 industrialization, 54, 56, 58
 inflation, 67, 135–7, 139, 141, 150–1, 153–4, 157
 interest rates, 209–11, 213, 215–19, 304
 monetary base, 122–4
 monetary neutrality, 94, 96
 money growth, 67, 135–7, 139, 141, 150, 152
 money stock, 141, 144, 304
 overseas lending, 203
 population, 305
 population growth, 48–53
 price level, 141, 144–5, 155–6, 303, 305–6
 real income, 226–9, 305
United States Department of Commerce, 303, 317
United States Mint, 291
Urbanization, 52–3, 163

Valerio, N., 303, 305, 315
Van der Wee, H., 82–3, 290, 317
Veblen, T., 9
Velocity, 65, 68–72, 119, 134, 288, 292
 see also Financial sophistication (index)
Verga, G., 176, 308
Vicens Vives, J., 115, 317
Viner, J., 4–5, 317
Vrijer, J. de, 303, 305–6, 316

Wachter, K., 310
Webber, A., 180, 304, 308
Weber, A., 53, 317
Weale, M., 71, 305, 316
Williamson, J. G., 40, 52, 287, 311, 313, 317
Wilson, J., 303, 317
Wood, G. E., 94, 112, 180, 239, 308, 314, 317

Zamagni, V., 260, 317
Zecher, J. R., 13, 147–8, 159, 314
Ziegler, D., 102–3, 317